"MY
NAME
IS
NOT
TOM"

"MY NAME IS NOT TOM"

THE LIFE
OF THE
REVEREND
JOSIAH
HENSON

SUSAN COOKE
SODERBERG

Georgetown University Press / Washington, DC

The publisher is not responsible for third-party websites or their content. URL links were active at time of publication.

Library of Congress Cataloging-in-Publication Data

Names: Soderberg, Susan Cooke, 1944- author.
Title: "My name is not Tom" : the life of the Reverend Josiah Henson / Susan Cooke Soderberg.
Description: Washington, D.C. : Georgetown University Press, [2025] | Includes bibliographical references and index.
Identifiers: LCCN 2024012537 (print) | LCCN 2024012538 (ebook) | ISBN 9781647125363 (hardcover) | ISBN 9781647125370 (ebook)
Subjects: LCSH: Henson, Josiah, 1789-1883. | Enslaved persons—United States—Biography. | African Americans—Biography. | Fugitive slaves—United States—Biography. | Black people—Canada—Biography. | Clergy—Canada—Biography. | LCGFT: Biographies.
Classification: LCC E444.H526 S64 2025 (print) | LCC E444.H526 (ebook) | DDC 973/.04960730092 [B]—dc23/eng/20240409
LC record available at https://lccn.loc.gov/2024012537
LC ebook record available at https://lccn.loc.gov/2024012538

∞ This paper meets the requirements of ANSI/NISO Z39.48-1992 (Permanence of Paper).

EU GPSR Authorized Representative
LOGOS EUROPE, 9 rue Nicolas Poussin, 17000, LA ROCHELLE, France
Email: Contact@logoseurope.eu

26 25   9 8 7 6 5 4 3 2 First printing

Printed in the United States of America

Cover design by TG Design
Interior design by Paul Hotvedt

Cover image (Sketch of the Niagara River) from The New York Public Library, https://digital collections.nypl.org/items/510d47da-f150-a3d9-e040-e00a18064a99

Dedicated to:
Charlotte Henson,
the long-suffering, loyal and dedicated
wife of Josiah Henson and mother of their eight children

Contents

Acknowledgments

As I traveled through several states and into Canada following the trail of Josiah Henson, I was helped in my research by many people. I thank them for mining the files, scanning the documents and images, telling me the stories, and pointing the way. I have many to thank.

In Maryland, Sarah Hedlund, librarian at the Montgomery History Library, and Katharine Rogers, collection manager of Peerless Rockville, gave me invaluable aid on locating sources of local history. Christopher Haley, research director for the legacy of slavery in Maryland, helped locate records involving Henson's owners. Katie Dragan, curator of education and public programs for Heritage Frederick, dragged out the huge portrait of Francis Newman from storage so I could take a picture of it. The staff of the Southern Maryland Studies Center at College of Southern Maryland were most attentive and helpful. At the Maryland Historical Trust, Mary Kate Mansius gave much time and care to scanning photos of properties needed in the book.

My research in Kentucky took me to the Owensboro Museum of Science and History, where the director, Kathy Olson, brought out from the museum's collection an authentic "pass" written for "Si" by Amos Riley, and to the Daviess County Public Library, where Christie Clary and Savanna Warren were most diligent in finding original documents of all kinds for me to read and copy. In Ohio I was given a special tour of Cleveland's National Underground Railroad Freedom Center by the then-director, Spencer Crew.

I never got to meet her in person, but Danielle Pucci of the Boston Public Library helped me locate and have digitized the rare 1879 autobiography of Josiah Henson (the one missing six pages where Josiah is describing his visit with Queen Victoria).

In Canada I had a talk with Steven Cook, the director of the then-titled "Uncle Tom's Cabin Historic Site" in Dresden, Ontario, who told me the history of the creation of the museum and the collection. In the nearby village of Buxton I was pleasantly surprised to meet Bryan and Sharon Prince, who informed me about the evolution of the Elgin Settlement there and how it was the only successful planned settlement of formerly enslaved people in Canada. Sharon gave an enlightening tour of the prominent buildings in the settlement. I really appreciate their taking the time to pay special attention to my inquiry.

A person who must have particular recognition is my friend and fellow historian Tony (Anthony) Cohen, who first gave me the idea to write this biography and gave me the encouragement I needed through my years of research.

A very special thank-you goes out to my readers, historian and editor Eileen McGuckian of Rockville, Maryland, and Chinese historian and editor Linda Cooke Johnson of Williamsburg, Virginia (who also happens to be my sister).

Finally, I could not have accomplished the research and writing of this book without the help of my husband, Bill Soderberg, who accompanied me on the many research trips and was my third reader. Bill is a professor of philosophy, retired, and a former teacher of English composition, so he was a very meticulous editor as well as adviser on logic and reasoning.

Preface

My journey to discover "the Real Josiah Henson" began in 2006 when I was asked to prepare the nomination for the "Uncle Tom's Cabin" Historic Site in Montgomery County, Maryland, to the US National Park Service's National Underground Railroad Network to Freedom program, which maintains the official register of Underground Railroad sites. This site was the farm where Josiah Henson had been enslaved from boyhood to adulthood, now the Josiah Henson Museum and Park.

As I delved into Henson's autobiographies, I began to have more questions than answers. I knew that these memoirs did not tell the whole story. How did he become the representation of Uncle Tom when, from his own story of his life, he was not like the fictional character? The many biographies of Henson at that time were mere copies of the information in the autobiographies, with little or no outside research, and so did not give any additional information.

Because I was under a time constraint from my employer, I wrote the nomination with the scant primary sources I was able to find in a short time, and it was accepted. But I knew that Josiah Henson was an extraordinary man in his own right and should not have the association with "Uncle Tom" that had been placed on him. I felt that more in-depth research into the life of this man could lead to a better understanding of the lives of enslaved people, the relationships between the enslaved and their enslavers, the trials of escape from bondage, and the challenges of a new life in freedom. Slavery is a terrible practice in whatever form it takes and is a stain on the history of our nation that has repercussions that affect our society today. If we want to heal the wounds left by this shameful part of our shared past, we cannot ignore it or conceal it. This just makes the wound fester. We need to have meaningful conversations about the past using factual historical evidence as our basis in order to understand it and to come to terms with it.

To contribute to this conversation, I decided to conduct the intensive research needed and write a more definitive biography of Josiah Henson, an ordinary man who rose from enslavement to the heights of fame. To make him an even better subject for investigating the past, Josiah left behind the story of his life, told in 1849, without embellishments or exaggerations. This first autobiography of the man formed a good starting point for research. I began in earnest on this project after I retired three years later.

For the next twelve years whenever my busy life allowed, I followed in the footsteps of Josiah Henson, conducting research along the way at libraries, museums, and historical societies in the places where he had lived and visited and supplementing these investigations with online research. Visiting the places where Josiah Henson had lived and traveled, even though much had changed over the years, gave me insight into the outside influences on his life and actions. Intensive research—locating primary sources never before included in the stories of his life, learning about people he knew and associations he made, and discovering what other people in his lifetime thought of him—uncovered aspects of the man never explored in previous biographies.

This research has taken many years but has revealed a man much different from the one depicted in his later autobiographies: Josiah Henson was not "Uncle Tom" of Stowe's novel but nevertheless was a man of high moral character and Christian convictions who was able to adapt to untenable situations and overcome challenging obstacles, keep his faith and his love of his fellow man through it all, and reach unimagined heights.

In this biography I have tried to use Henson's autobiographies only as guides, taking from them information that I was able to authenticate and indicating by quotes and attributions what I was not able to authenticate. When anyone looks at their life in retrospect, memories are often warped by the lens through which it is being viewed. In his first autobiography Henson attempted to present his life as best he could recall it but did leave out some incidents that he recalled later. His lens was even more distorted in his later autobiographies after he and his publishers discovered that people were seeing him as the physical embodiment of a fictional hero. For this reason, I use the 1849 autobiography for most of my references to Henson's life up until that date. Because Henson dictated rather than wrote all the autobiographies, I also try not to quote from any of the dialogues written into the texts of the later autobiographies, as it is impossible to distinguish the difference between actual words that Josiah may have remembered from literary enhancements by his ghostwriters.

By placing Henson in his environments and investigating his interactions with other people, I have also discovered how complicated and varied was the relationship between the enslaved and the enslaver, between the free man and the abolitionist, between the formerly enslaved and each other, and between the formerly enslaved and the Canadian and British populace.

The result is an accurate representation, to the best of my ability, of a complex man who was able to rise from enslavement to a position of great respect and honor. Josiah Henson's legacy should not be that he was a model for a somewhat conflated fictional character but instead that he himself should be a model and inspiration for others.

Introduction

THE TITLE FOR THIS BOOK CAME FROM A SPEECH MADE BY JOSIAH HENSON IN HIS later years while addressing an audience in Glasgow, Scotland. He began his speech by saying, "Now allow me to say that my name is not Tom, and never was Tom, and that I do not want to have any other name inserted in the newspapers for me than my own. My name is Josiah Henson, always was, and always will be."[1]

It was important to Josiah to identify himself in that way because he had just finished a speaking tour of one hundred places in and around London in six months where he was advertised as and introduced as "The Real Uncle Tom" at every engagement.[2] This tour was arranged by the publisher of Josiah's fourth autobiography (1876). To take advantage of Henson being mentioned by Harriet Beecher Stowe as one of the models for Uncle Tom in her immensely popular novel, the publisher promoted him as "The Real Uncle Tom." To emphasize this association, the book was titled *Uncle Tom's Story of His Life: An Autobiography of the Rev. Josiah Henson (Mrs. Harriet Beecher Stowe's "Uncle Tom")*. With profit on his mind, the publisher had convinced Josiah to sign over the copyright of the book to him, then planned the book tour to give himself venues to sell the book. Henson never made any royalty from the sale of this book but was allowed to accept donations from the audience at the events.

At the end of this exhausting tour, Josiah and his wife, Nancy, escaped to Scotland at the invitation of a friend. There, away from the eyes of the publisher and tired of having to play the fictional slave instead of himself, Josiah tried to direct the audience away from the "Uncle Tom" label. A man of many accomplishments and a talented orator, he wanted to be appreciated for his own story and his own accomplishments. Like the fictional Uncle Tom, Josiah had suffered enslavement, was a pious Christian, and had lived in Kentucky and traveled down the Ohio and Mississippi Rivers to New Orleans. But unlike Uncle Tom, Josiah Henson had not been sold in New Orleans and had not been beaten to death by his master. The fictional character had never escaped to Canada with his wife and four children, returned to Kentucky twice to bring others to freedom in Canada, become a revered minister, helped found a school for fellow freedom seekers, dictated an autobiography, purchased his freedom from his Maryland owner, become celebrated in the antislavery circles of New England, or traveled to England as did Josiah Henson.

Before he was ever associated with the title character of the famous book, Josiah Henson was well known in Canada, New England, and Great Britain as an influential Christian minister and a great orator and entrepreneur. He had many wealthy and influential supporters in New England, such as Frederick Douglass and US congressmen Samuel Eliot and Abbott Lawrence of Massachusetts. In Canada, Henson was supported by Sir John Beverley Robinson, chief justice on the Court of Queen's Bench in Canada; Sir Allen McNab, Canadian Tory politician; and Essex County representative Col. John Prince. In England, Henson was supported by the likes of Lord Henry Brougham and financier Samuel Gurney of London. Henson was even granted an audience with the archbishop of Canterbury, John Bird Sumner, while on his first trip to London.

Many biographies of Josiah Henson have been written over the years, all of them referring to him in either the title or the text as "the real Uncle Tom." *"My Name Is Not Tom": The Life of the Reverend Josiah Henson* seeks to dispel that myth through research and investigation beyond Henson's autobiographies: exploring the environments, people, and history surrounding him; seeking out newspaper articles, letters, and contemporaneous descriptions of the man and of events he experienced; and studying slave narratives of people he was or may have been close to.

Harriet Beecher Stowe and the "Uncle Tom" Connection

Josiah Henson's connection to "Uncle Tom" began after Harriet Beecher Stowe published *A Key to Uncle Tom's Cabin* in 1853. As her novel *Uncle Tom's Cabin; or, Life among the Lowly* spread across the country like wildfire, people began to question whether slavery was as cruel and demeaning as depicted and if masters were as unfeeling. Stowe felt that she needed to defend her research and bring her real-life sources to the public eye. The full title of her 259-page two-column treatise is *A Key to Uncle Tom's Cabin; Presenting the Original Facts and Documents upon Which the Story Is Founded, Together with Corroborative Statements Verifying the Truth of the Work*. In this volume on page 7 in the description of the influences on her creation of the character Uncle Tom, she states, in referring to Josiah Henson, "It would be well for the most cultivated of us to ask, whether our ten talents in the way of religious knowledge have enabled us to bring forth as much fruit to the glory of God, to withstand temptation as patiently, to return good for evil as disinterestedly, as this poor, ignorant slave." She also inserts some quotes from Henson's 1849 autobiography, all connected to his unquestioning devotion to Christ and the word of God. Under the same heading, before mentioning Henson, Stowe described several other people and stories that helped her to shape the complex fictional character of Uncle Tom.[3]

After the publishing of the novel, Stowe claimed that the first inspiration for Uncle Tom was a Kentucky slave who would visit his wife, a free woman in the employ of her family in Cincinnati, Ohio (a free state), who refused to be disloyal to his master by escaping to freedom in Ohio.[4] Another possible inspiration is a fugitive slave she hid in her home in Brunswick, Maine, in late December 1850, later identified as John Andrew Jackson.[5] On several occasions Stowe visited her brother Henry Ward Beecher in the early 1840s in Indianapolis, where she interviewed a former slave by the name of Thomas Magruder, who was familiarly known as "Uncle Tom" and lived in a cabin in that city that was known locally as "Uncle Tom's Cabin."[6]

According to Stowe, she did not even come across Henson's autobiography until near the end of her serialized novel when she was trying to find a model for an enslaved person who had enough Christian piety and courage to sacrifice his own life for others, that is, to become a martyr. Even though she was still living in Brunswick, Maine, at the time, she spent the month of February 1852 at her husband's professor rooms at the theological seminary in Andover, Massachusetts, for the uninterrupted quiet she needed to finish the novel. Andover is a short train ride from Boston, where her brother lived not far from the Abolitionist Reading Room. It is in this reading room that Stowe said she found Josiah Henson's autobiography.[7] Henson was in England at that time.

Harriet Beecher Stowe publicly denied that Josiah Henson was the sole model for Uncle Tom on several occasions. In a published response to an inquiry in a newspaper in 1877 she states, "No one person is described as in biography [for Uncle Tom]. Traits and incidents of various people are combined. The life of Rev. J. Henson furnished many of these, but not all. He was not Uncle Tom, neither was any other one person."[8] She again denies that Henson is the sole model in the summer of 1882 in another letter published in many newspapers that ended with "After I had begun the story I got, at the Anti-slavery Rooms in Boston, the autobiography of Josiah Henson, and introduced some of its more striking incidents into my story. The good people of England gave my simple, good friend Josiah enthusiastic welcome as Uncle Tom of the story, though he was very much alive and well, and likely to long live, and the Uncle Tom of the story was buried in a martyr's grave."[9] At the end of the novel Tom is beaten to death for not revealing the hiding place of the two women escapees.[10] Fortunately, Henson did not die like Tom but was saved by fortuitous circumstances.

Several other writers and bloggers have indicated several incidents in *Uncle Tom's Cabin* that could have come from Henson's life, but most of these can be attributed to other slave narratives or could have come from Henson's autobiographies published after *Uncle Tom's Cabin*. There are only two things that are comparable between the fictional Uncle Tom and the real Josiah Henson, and both are near the end of the novel, as Stowe claimed.

The first is when a sister in bondage entices Tom to kill his sleeping master with an axe, but he refuses, saying, "No! good never comes from wickedness."[11] This relates to an incident in Henson's life where he tells of being tempted to kill his enslavers with an axe on the boat traveling to New Orleans where he is to be sold, but his Christian beliefs hold him back.[12]

The second is when Simon Legree is threatening to kill Tom unless he tells where the women are hiding. Tom refuses to lie, saying, "I hain't got nothing to tell, Mas'r," and then after being struck and asked again replied, "I know, Mas'r, but I can't tell anything."[13] Josiah similarly refused to lie when he returned to Kentucky with his freedom paper and was told by his wife that his owner said he owed more money for his freedom. He related, "I . . . told my wife I had not seen it [the manumission paper] since I was in Louisville. It might be in my bag, and perhaps it was lost; but at all events I did not wish to see it again at present; and if she should find it, and put it in some place which I did not know." He subsequently told the enslaver that he had last seen the paper when he was in Louisville and that it was not now in his bag and he could not find it.[14]

For readers who are interested in discovering more about the novel, Stowe explains in depth her inspiration for writing the novel in the introduction to a new edition to *Uncle Tom's Cabin* published in 1878 and republished in *Old South Leaflets*, including many letters to Mrs. Stowe from notable people.[15]

So, both Josiah Henson himself and the author of the novel, Harriet Beecher Stowe, denied that he was the main model for Uncle Tom, but did the two ever actually meet? And if a meeting did take place, was it before or after Stowe completed the novel? There are actually two times when Stowe and Henson were in the same place at the same time.

The first was in Boston in the spring of 1850. Henson claimed in his 1879 autobiography, referring to a conversation he had with Stowe in Massachusetts in 1850, that "I called on her at her home, not long before coming to England, and we talked a long time."[16] This could not have been at her home, since she did not live in Massachusetts until 1854, but it could have occurred at that time in Boston.

Stowe was visiting her brother Rev. Edward Beecher and his wife, Isabell, for about a week in early May 1850 to purchase furniture for her future home in Brunswick, Maine.[17] She was probably pressed for time, as she had her five children with her and was busy shopping, but may have attended church and antislavery functions while there.

Josiah Henson was in Boston in April of that year transferring and selling the lumber from the British-American Institute of Science and Industry's sawmill. The second loan agreement between Henson and his Boston benefactors is dated April 12, 1850.[18] He most likely stayed with Rev. Jonathan Bridge as was his custom when in Boston.[19] Rev. Jonathan Bridge was a part of the same antislavery circles as Rev. Edward Beecher, so they most likely knew each other. Henson usually stayed in Boston for several weeks visiting friends and attending meetings.

This meeting between Stowe and Henson is also reported in an article by Stowe's son, Charles Edward Stowe, written many years after his mother's death, stating that she met "Rev. Joshua [sic] Henson" in Boston in 1850.[20] Stowe never acknowledged this meeting, but even if she did meet him, she may not have recalled the meeting, especially if it was at an antislavery gathering or with other people around. The idea of writing a novel about an enslaved man would not occur to her until the following year.

The second time was in 1858. After he learned of his connection to the main character in the popular novel *Uncle Tom's Cabin,* Henson had an idea that he might use his new notoriety to publish a new autobiography and use the proceeds to purchase his brother John's freedom. His second autobiography had been published in England in 1851, but he never saw proceeds from that edition. Henson sought out the author, Harriet Beecher Stowe, in April 1858 at her home in Andover, Massachusetts, and she kindly wrote a short introduction to his third autobiography. She probably also wrote him an introductory letter to her publisher, John Jewett, as Henson's memoir was published that same year by the same publisher. This introduction made no reference to "Uncle Tom." Nevertheless, advertisements for the sale by Jewett of the 1858 autobiography *Truth Stranger Than Fiction: Father Henson's Story of His Own Life*, touted Henson as "H.B. Stowe's Uncle Tom."[21]

The Autobiographies

There are five autobiographies that can be attributed to Josiah Henson. Others are reprints with minor and sometimes unauthorized alterations. Besides the basic story of Henson's life, these books can reveal much about their publishers due to how they were created with embellishments and unauthorized changes and how they were promoted and reprinted, with no profit going to Henson himself from any reprints. Since Josiah Henson had learned to read print late in his life but was unable to write, his autobiographies were based on interviews with him but were actually written by others.

The first and second autobiographies are the most authentic because they are in Josiah's words, with no embellishments by the publishers. The first, published by Samuel Eliot in 1849, was taken down verbatim from Henson, read back to him, changed according to his dictates, and published with these changes.[22] The second, published in 1851 by his friend in London, Rev. Thomas Binney, adds to the first Henson's description of his returns to Kentucky to rescue others from enslavement. It also has an account in the appendix of the British-American Institute, the industrial school Henson was raising funds to support.

The third, published in 1858 by John Jewett, contributes some additional information about Henson's life since 1851 but is highly embellished by the publisher. From this publishing Josiah received a flat fee, which he used to purchase his brother's freedom along with a small number of books to sell himself. Jewett enjoyed the entire profit from the retail sales of the remaining books.

There is an almost twenty-year hiatus before the next autobiography, which was published in 1876 by John Lobb in London, England, the planner of the one hundred–stop book tour. This book copies the 1858 material and adds information, provided by Henson, on the past twenty years of his life. Lobb, as did Jewett in the 1858 autobiography, abundantly embellishes the book, uses the introduction by Stowe, and titles the book *Uncle Tom's Story of His Life*. This is the first reference to Uncle Tom in any of Henson's previous stories of his life. Lobb convinced Henson to grant him the copyright for this book, robbing him of any royalties.

In 1879 after returning from England, Josiah Henson has friends in Boston publish a new autobiography, his fifth, in order to recoup the revenue he lost by signing over the copyright of his fourth memoir to Lobb. This one adds his audience with Queen Victoria and with President Rutherford B. Hayes as well as Josiah's visit to his old home where he had been enslaved in Maryland. Titled *"Truth Is Stranger Than Fiction": An Autobiography of the Rev. Josiah Henson,* followed by "Harriet Beecher Stowe's 'Uncle Tom'" in parentheses in the title. This autobiography also is the first illustrated edition and has a description of the first time Henson learned that he was associated with that fictional character. The fact that this edition is now extremely rare may be due to the fact that Lobb traveled to Canada to publish his own version in 1881 and may have tried to disappear Henson's versions, relying on his copyright of the 1876 edition.

The publishers of Henson's third (1858, Jewett) and fourth (1876, Lobb) autobiographies embellished the books with descriptions and words meant to make them more attractive to readers in order to increase sales. They added new information as Henson's life progressed, but the books were also extremely inflated with stylized Victorian prose, classical and biblical metaphors, similes, elaborate descriptions, and questionable dialogues. Josiah Henson, reading mainly only the Bible after he learned to read late in life, had no knowledge of popular literature and writing styles. The autobiographies, including the first, also contain some inaccuracies, such as the muddling of dates and sequences of events, and leave out many important facts of Henson's life.

As said by historian John Blassingame, "Generally, whenever a fugitive became famous enough to justify an expanded version of his life, the editors were more often concerned with enhancing his stature than with the facts." Blassingame goes on to say that Henson's autobiographies published after the original "raised Henson to the level of a heroic, mythological figure" so that the later editions "almost seem to be fictionalized versions of Eliot's 1849 account."[23]

More than two dozen biographies of Josiah Henson have been published, from the first in 1878 (Henry Bleby) to the most recent in 2019 (Jamie Ferguson Kuhns). Without exception, each author appears to have accepted everything in Henson's autobiographies uncritically with very little or no outside research. Some even have large sections copied directly from the autobiographies, the copyright having run out long ago.

Neither Henson's autobiographies nor the biographies tell the complete or at times the completely accurate story of the remarkable life of this extraordinary man, a hero in his own right and far from any past or present image of "Uncle Tom." The goal of this book is to reveal the true life story of Josiah Henson without the constant comparison to the fictional Uncle Tom. Using primary source material and firsthand observation, this book examines his true character and his strengths and weaknesses, his courage as well as his good heart and moral uprightness, and his personality and prejudices. This book discusses how he was molded by his circumstances, guided by his Christian principles, and influenced by the people around him; how he fits into the tapestry of American and Canadian history; and how his life and works have made a lasting imprint on that history.

1849 Autobiography: *The Life of Josiah Henson, Formerly a Slave, Now an Inhabitant of Canada, as Narrated by Himself* (Boston, Arthur D. Phelps, 71 pages)

Henson dictated the story of his life to Samuel Eliot, who had it published in Boston in 1849. This book was different from the slave narratives of the time, published by abolitionists to bring the true stories of enslavement to the American public while at the same time raising money for the cause of emancipation.[24] With a few exceptions, these narratives were oral histories transcribed by mainly amateur writers. Because the purpose of these publications was to evoke emotional response from the readers and raise awareness of the evils of slavery, sometimes the cruel aspects of punishments inflicted on enslaved people were described in detail, as was the agony of the separation of families. Unlike others of its genre, Henson's autobiography has only two descriptions of cruel punishment. One was a recollection by Henson that as a child he saw his father, owned by a different person than himself, coming home bloodied. The second was Henson's own beating that left him maimed for life, also done by a person other than his owner. This also differs in its depiction of the complex relationship between Henson and his owner and the freedoms and responsibilities Henson acquired while still enslaved.

Another difference is that unlike most other transcribers of slave narratives, Samuel Eliot, although antislavery, was not an active abolitionist, was an experienced writer, and was highly educated. Eliot, from a distinguished Boston family, was a graduate of Harvard College and Harvard Divinity School, was mayor of Boston for three terms, and served in influential political offices.[25] The author of several articles for scholarly journals, he had just completed a massive two-volume history of Rome when he took on the project of writing Henson's life story. Eliot was a man of high integrity who had no other objective than to present an accurate account. As he says in the prologue, "A portion of the story was told, which, when written, was read back to him, that any errors of statement might be corrected. The substance of it, therefore, the facts, the reflections, and very often the words, are his: and little more than the structure of the sentences belongs to another."[26] Verification of this statement can be found in the original manuscript in Eliot's handwriting, with scratch-outs and rewrites, held at the Boston Public Library.[27] This is "the author's fair copy," and all the others are variations. The original book is seventy-one pages long and is not divided into chapters or sections.

1851 Autobiography: *The Life of Josiah Henson, Formerly a Slave, as Narrated by Himself, with a Preface by T. Binney, London*

This edition was published in London in 1851. The most important addition to the 1849 book is the relating of Josiah Henson's two returns to Kentucky to rescue others from bondage. Henson had probably been afraid to tell of these exploits in an American edition because they would have been considered criminal. Other additions in this volume are a final page asking for funds, a preface by Thomas Binney, an elaborate appendix consisting of various stories of escaped slaves, and a description of the British-American Institute.[28] With these additions and no elaborations by the publisher, this is the most authentic autobiography of Henson.

1858 Autobiography: *Truth Stranger Than Fiction: Father Henson's Story of His Own Life*, with an introduction by Mrs. H. B. Stowe (John P. Jewett and Company, Boston, 212 pages)

This third of Henson's autobiographies was published by John Jewett, the same man who had earlier published *Uncle Tom's Cabin* in 1852 and *The Key to Uncle Tom's Cabin* in 1853. It has a preface written by Harriet Beecher Stowe, signed "Andover, Mass. April 5, 1858." In this preface Stowe compared Henson not to Uncle Tom but instead to Simon the Cyrenean who carried the cross for Jesus.[29] It is quite possible that Henson acquired this introduction from Stowe himself as he attended several meetings in and around Boston in the spring of 1858 when Stowe was living in Andover, just twenty-four miles from Boston.[30] Josiah said that he traveled with a friend to meet the famous author at her home, as he said in his 1876 autobiography, but mistook the date as being before 1851 when it must have actually been 1858.[31] It is also possible that when he visited her she gave him a letter of introduction to her publisher, Jewett.[32]

In an interview published in 1883 in the magazine *The Manhattan*, John Jewett spoke of Henson and the autobiography he published in 1858. Jewett apparently was unaware of the existence of the 1849 publication of Henson's autobiography (or the 1851 British edition), as he says that "the first edition of 'Father Henson's Life' did not appear until 1858." Jewett claimed that Henson presented him with manuscripts where half of his life story had been written by a "Unitarian clergyman of Springfield, Massachusetts, [Rev. Francis Tiffany],[33] and a quarter written by the Rev. Gilbert Haven,"[34] adding that "I [Jewett] wrote about one-quarter of the book myself." Jewett said, "It was not an easy job, for it required not a little patience to make a connected story out of Father Henson's jumbled and incoherent talk."[35]

A comparison of the texts of the 1849 book and the 1858 book shows that Henson added a few new recollections to his original story of 1849. Among these are the recollection that his owner "gave me his own Christian name, Josiah, and with that he also gave me my last name, Henson, after an uncle of his, who was an officer in the Revolutionary War"; the recounting of his two trips back to Kentucky to rescue enslaved people and lead them to freedom in Canada; the giving of full names to people only referred to by initials in the first edition; and the adding of more details about the British-American Institute and its lumber and sawmill operations.

The last forty pages examined the additional nine years of his life between the 1849 publication and the new one. This section includes his first trip to England, which he made to display walnut boards from the mill at the British-American Institute in Canada at the 1851 World's Fair in London. It also includes his brief return to Canada in the summer of 1851 to defend himself successfully against accusations of misuse of funds; his subsequent return to England, where he stayed for almost a year; and the death of his first wife in the fall of 1852.

Interspersed throughout the new edition are more details about Henson's emotional reactions and explanations of his past behavior as well as more in-depth descriptions of his enslavers, all made to "dress up," embellish, and expand the original words. It is evident from the usage of complex words and figures from classical mythology and literature popular in the Victorian era and references to world events of the time that these additions were made by the editor/publisher.

One of the literary techniques used by the publishers was to invent dialogues between protagonists to make the text more interesting. There are very few dialogues or quotes in the 1849 edition, as it is difficult for anyone to remember exact words spoken twenty to forty years earlier. This 1858 edition has quite a number of "conversations," many of which seem incongruous when compared to the known discourses by and interviews with Henson. For example, the word "nigger" never once appeared in the 1849 version or in any of the extant speeches by Henson but was found eighteen times in the 1858 Jewett version of the autobiography, always in the quoted words of a white person or in reference to being said by whites, as in this addition to the description of the punishment of Josiah's father, who had beaten off an overseer who was trying to rape his mother:

> The man who did not feel rage enough at hearing of "a nigger" striking a
> white to be ready to burn him alive, was only fit to be lynched out of the
> neighborhood. A blow at one white man is a blow at all; is the muttering
> and upheaving of volcanic fires, which underlie and threaten to burst forth
> and utterly consume the whole social fabric. Terror is the fiercest nurse
> of cruelty. And when, in this our day, you find tender English women and
> Christian English divines fiercely urging that India should be made one pool
> of Sepoy blood, pause a moment before you lightly refuse to believe in the
> existence of such ferocious passions in the breasts of tyrannical and cowardly
> slave-drivers.[36]

An example of the Victorian language and imagery added by the publisher can be found in Henson's excuse for stealing his owner's produce to feed his fellow slaves:

> No white knight, rescuing white fair ones from cruel oppression, ever felt
> the throbbing of a chivalrous heart more intensely than I, a black knight,
> did, in running down a chicken in an out-of-the way place to hide till dark,

and then carry to some poor overworked black fair one, to whom it was at once food, luxury, and medicine. This too was all the chivalry of which my circumstances and condition in life admitted. I love the sentiment in its splendid environment of castles, and tilts, and gallantry; but having fallen on other times, I love it also in the homely guise of Sambo as Paladin.[37]

This 1858 autobiography became the core of the future autobiographies, copied word for word and then added to with Henson's later years of experiences as described by his next publisher, John Lobb in England.

1876 Autobiography: *Uncle Tom's Story of His Life: An Autobiography of Rev. Josiah Henson (Mrs. Harriet Beecher Stowe's "Uncle Tom"), from 1789 to 1876* (edited by John Lobb, London, England 1876, including the original preface by Harriet Beecher Stowe, and "Introductory Notes" by George Sturge, and S. Morley, Esq., MP., 209 pages plus index and appendices)

Josiah Henson traveled to England with his second wife, Nancy, in July 1876 to raise money to pay off a large debt. There he soon met publisher John Lobb, who arranged most of a speaking tour during which Henson gave talks at more than ninety locations in England before the farewell reception at the end of the year, attended by almost six thousand people.[38] Lobb was a publisher of religious tracts and was also a great promoter, never one to miss an opportunity. He gathered more information from Henson and published this much-embellished fourth autobiography.[39]

The entire 1858 autobiography, unchanged, is used as the basis for this book. It has the original preface Harriet Beecher Stowe wrote for the 1858 edition but omits from the preface the date (April 5, 1858) and the last paragraph that relates that Josiah "prepared this edition of his works for the purpose of redeeming from slavery a beloved brother."[40] These changes were made so that the reader would assume Stowe wrote the preface for this particular edition, thus giving it more stature.

Besides the introductory notes by prominent British abolitionists George Sturge and Samuel Morley, the new material in this edition includes a few things that Josiah remembered that had not been in the previous editions, including his being beaten as a child for having a spelling book, his involvement in helping to put down the Canadian Rebellion of 1837, and experiences since the previous edition such as purchasing his brother's freedom, more information on the British-American Institute and the lawsuit against the institute, his dismantling of the sawmill, his being accused of recruiting for the US Army in the American Civil War, the failure of the gristmill, some details about his children, and a description of his third trip to England. These things are not added in chronological order, and they conflate unrelated incidents.

One of the most outrageous inventions in this edition is the entirety of chapter 25, in which Henson claims that Harriet Beecher Stowe created the characters in *Uncle*

Tom's Cabin from real people in his own life story that he related to her when he visited her at her home in Andover, Massachusetts, in 1850.[41] As previously explained, this was not possible, as Stowe did not live in Andover until the summer of 1852, and she publicly disclosed that she did not discover Josiah Henson's story until she was almost finished writing the book and that the character of Uncle Tom was made up of many traits from many people.[42] Even though the incidents Henson described may have occurred in his life, extensive research has been unable to verify the existence of the people he associated with those incidents who have similar names to characters in the fictional *Uncle Tom's Cabin*. The descriptions are also in conflict with Stowe's own revelation of the origins of her characters in *The Key to Uncle Tom's Cabin*.

The final chapter is almost entirely devoted to a description of the analysis of Josiah's character through the study of the bumps on his head by phrenologist Professor Lorenzo Fowler. According to the book, this analysis was published in Lobb's *Christian Age* before it was published in the book. Because of the popularity of this article, the magazine had to add additional printings to the eighty thousand copies already circulating.[43] Of particular interest in the 1876 autobiography is the disclosure that Henson signed over the copyright of that edition to John Lobb.[44] In 1877 and 1878 Lobb reprinted the 1876 edition.

Lobb went on to write and publish a partly fictionalized biography based on the autobiographies, the "Young People's" edition in 1877, *Uncle Tom's Story of His Life*, which is illustrated and in the frontispiece has an engraving from a photograph of Henson and Lobb together. This book begins with "Uncle Tom's Address to the Young People of Great Britain," which is purportedly a talk he gave to the King Edward Industrial School and Girl's Refuge and includes Josiah's signature at the end. However, compared to the text of several speeches that were transcribed word for word by reporters, this is not a speech by Henson. Josiah Henson received no compensation for any of these British editions published by Lobb.

1879 Autobiography: *"Truth Is Stranger Than Fiction": An Autobiography of the Rev. Josiah Henson (Mrs. Harriet Beecher Stowe's "Uncle Tom")* (Boston: B. B. Russell & Co., 1879), with the original (1858) preface by Harriet Beecher Stowe and the addition of introductory notes by Wendell Phillips and John G. Whittier and an appendix "On the Exodus" by Gilbert Haven (336 pages)

This rare American printing, the fifth and last autobiography by Henson, is unique for several reasons. The book has a chapter that is found in no other edition and is the first printing of Josiah Henson's autobiography with illustrations. Included in the book are introductory notes by two distinguished Americans, the poet John Greenleaf Whittier and the distinguished Boston abolitionist Wendell Phillips, and there is an article in the appendix by Josiah's friend and possible coauthor of his 1858 autobiography, Rev. Gilbert Haven.[45] Both Whittier and Phillips were members of the

Garrisonian American Anti-Slavery Society, which dissolved in 1870. As expressed by Mr. Whittier, this 1879 edition was printed to raise funds to erect a meetinghouse near Henson's home in Canada, and, as expressed by its publisher, the cost of the printing of the book was a donation to that cause.[46]

The text of this edition is identical to the 1876 British edition, with the following changes. In chapter 31 of this edition, "My Third and Last Visit to England," Henson omits the paragraph that appeared in the 1876 edition relating that he turned over the copyright to John Lobb. In fact, Lobb is not mentioned once in this 1879 edition.

Chapter 32, "My Visit to Windsor Castle," which cannot be found in any other edition, is an entirely different account of Henson's meeting with Queen Victoria than Lobb's account in the 1881 and subsequent reprints and in newspapers based on Lobb's press releases. Henson describes that while on a speaking tour in Scotland he received a telegram from the queen inviting him to an audience. He and his wife, accompanied by his Scotland host, Reverend Boardman, traveled back to London for the visit with the queen. Henson's description of the people, the conversations, the details of the luncheon, and later presentation to the queen were quite different from that of Lobb and did not include Lobb.

The new material in this volume, in the final chapter, includes a description of Henson's visit with US president Rutherford B. Hayes and of Henson's return to his old home in Maryland, where he is recognized by his former mistress.

The Purloined 1881 Autobiography: *An Autobiography of the Rev. Josiah Henson ("Uncle Tom") from 1789 to 1881* (edited by John Lobb, London, Ontario, Canada, 1881, 227 pages plus index and appendices)

After discovering that friends of Josiah Henson had published a new autobiography in Boston, John Lobb, feeling that his London copyright had been violated, traveled to Canada. It is not known whether he bought up copies of the 1879 autobiography and destroyed them, but today that edition is very rare. One copy discovered in the Boston Public Library had the six pages describing Henson's audience with Queen Victoria torn out. This is the description that did not mention Lobb and was supplanted in Lobb's 1881 edition by his own description of that audience in which he, of course, plays a prominent part.

Lobb then had a new edition of Henson's autobiography published in London, Ontario, in 1881. This Canadian edition by Lobb includes "Introductory Notes by George Sturge, S. Morley, Esq., MP" that were in the 1876 edition but deceitfully adds the "Notes" by the Americans Wendell Phillips and John G. Whittier that were in the Boston 1879 edition while omitting the "Publisher's Notes." Lobb also adds to this edition Henson's description of his trip to visit President Hayes and to his old home in Maryland from the 1879 Boston edition, and a "Conclusion" by Lobb. In the appendix there is the addition of a transcript of the beginning of one of Henson's talks and the continuation of the list of places where Henson gave talks after the 1876 edition was published. The most glaring change in this edition is the omission of Henson's description of his introduction to Queen Victoria that left out Lobb and the substitution of Lobb's own version of the meeting with the queen in which Lobb himself plays a prominent part. There is a statement at the bottom of the frontispiece: "Only Authorized Edition and Copyright."

A final reprint, published posthumously, was authored in 1890 by Lobb in London that includes Henson's death and funeral in 1883 but omits some of the end material of the 1881 publication. There have been some pirated copies of all the editions and some translations into other languages with no significant changes to the text.

Contemporary Descriptions of Josiah Henson

There are several descriptions of Josiah Henson by people who knew him that give insight into his personality as well as his appearance.

The first quote is from his enslaver in Kentucky, Amos Riley Jr., which shows Henson's strength as well as his sauciness:

> He was a large, well-built man, who would tip the beam at 175 or so, and was remarkably powerful, especially in the arms and shoulders. Many is the time I have worked with him in the wheat field. I was about 20 years old at the time and pretty stout myself, but when I tried to keep up with Si with a cradle, I invariably got left behind. By reason of his great strength he was able to use a cradle with a blade about a foot longer than mine. He would start out with this and by cutting an enormously wide swath, walk away from me in a way that I despised. "Come 'long boss;" he used to shout back at me, "nevah do fo' you to git lef' behin'!"[47]

In 1849 Rev. Ephraim Peabody, in his review of Henson's 1849 autobiography, said he was "simple, straightforward, and to-the-point." Peabody, who knew Josiah well, praises him as being "large-hearted, large-minded, tolerant, calm, benevolent and wise."[48]

The most definitive physical description of Josiah Henson is provided by Henry Bleby, a missionary to Jamaica from the British Methodist Conference who met Henson in July 1858 at a gathering of Methodist ministers in Boston. In Victorian prose, Bleby described Henson as being viewed as a gentleman and an equal by men of high station. Henson, Bleby wrote, was

> manifestly regarded by those who sat near him as "a man and a brother." He exhibited a person of the middle size, firm and well knit; his skin was of the true African jet; and clothed in a new glossy suit of clerical broad cloth, he was all over black, except the spotless cravat and a set of pearly white teeth,

that might have been made of the finest ivory Africa can produce, so brightly did they glitter, when some flash of oratory in the debate, or some sally of Father Taylor's sparkling wit, caused the broad African features to expand into a smile, or provoked a hearty laugh. And this was very often the case. Again and again, as I sat and looked upon him, did laughter spread itself over all the lines of his countenance, and tell of a rollicking, fun-loving spirit, that could not often, or for long together, be clouded with gloom. . . . [On being introduced to him Bleby observed,] On looking at him more closely as he stood before me, holding a glossy white beaver hat in one hand, while he extended to me the other in friendly salutation, I observed that both his arms were crippled, so that he could by no means use them freely.[49]

Another person, John Jewett, publisher of Henson's 1858 autobiography, noted the man's disability, remarking on the fact that he could not put a hat on his head the usual way: "He had to lay the hat on a table and, by a wriggling motion, insert his head into it."[50]

In addition to the descriptions, two etched portraits from drawings and three photographs have survived.[51] Unfortunately, due to the constraints of photography at the time, Henson is not smiling in any of them, and according to descriptions, he had a wonderful smile.

Some who knew Henson, however, had a more negative view of him. John Jewett, publisher of Henson's 1858 autobiography, said, "He had not the mental capacity to dictate a continuous narrative."[52] On the other hand, Martin Delany, well-known African American writer, said, "Father Josiah Henson makes use of as good language as any one in a thousand Americans."[53] Mary Ann Shadd, a free African American who moved to Canada and became editor of the newspaper *The Provincial Freeman*, accused him of "false representations" and of "great injury done to the coloured people."[54] Conversely, a number of gentlemen from Ontario attested that Henson "has ever borne the highest character in this community, and is worthy of the confidence of the public."[55] And in England, George Sturge, Esq., said of Henson that "his Christian simplicity, and the absence of all bitter feeling towards those who have oppressed him, will have commended him to all who have made his acquaintance."[56]

Modern historians who are very familiar with Josiah Henson's life beyond his autobiographies give unique slants on his character. Sister Mary Ellen Doyle describes Henson as a "shrewd, self-glorifying, witty or pompous, but always fascinating man."[57] Robin Winks sees him as a natural leader, "imaginative and independent in his approach to immediate problems . . . but prone to seek out quick approbation rather than long-range solutions." Winks also sees Henson as vain, proud, possessive, and manipulative and at one point called him a "rascal."[58]

After extensive in-depth research and physically following in his footsteps, this author sees Josiah Henson as a righteous and devout Christian, an honest, truthful, and hardworking man who was devoted to his family and to his fellow refugees in

Canada. He had a gift of oratory that he used to help his comrades in need as well as to support his family and purchase his freedom. He was brave and clever with a talent for invention and taking advantage of opportunities. His sense of humor and enthusiasm never let him despair over failures. His most egregious faults were his tendency to exaggerate, which was part of his storytelling talent, and his pride, which got him into trouble on more than one occasion. But all in all, Josiah Henson was a remarkable person and one to be emulated.

1

Born Enslaved

I<small>N</small> S<small>OUTHERN</small> M<small>ARYLAND</small> <small>DURING THE CLOSING YEARS OF THE EIGHTEENTH CENTURY,</small> two very different men met to strike a bargain: a poor country doctor, whose ancestors had emigrated from Scotland generations before, and a wealthy newcomer of the English gentry. The doctor, who owned no land, agreed to lease a woman he owned to the gentleman landowner, and she gave birth to a son while working on his farm. Never in their remotest imaginings could these two men have foreseen that their names would be engraved in history only because of the fame of this little African American boy enslaved by one and born on the property of the other.

The boy's name was Josiah Henson, and later in life after he was free, he became a well-known leader and preacher in Canada, New England, and England. He was also active in the Underground Railroad, leading several enslaved people to freedom. He would dictate the story of his life to a writer who had it published. His autobiography was, by chance, read by Harriet Beecher Stowe, who used part of his story in a novel called *Uncle Tom's Cabin* that became the most famous book in the nineteenth-century English-speaking world. This connection, when it became known, catapulted Josiah into celebrity, and he went on to dictate more autobiographies that revealed much more of his life and the names of his enslavers. Many thousands of copies of his autobiographies were printed and reprinted, some even translated into other languages, and sold around the world. Henson was a hero in his own right, and his fascinating story of escape from enslavement and rise to positions of leadership and authority might never have been widely known without this association.

When Henson began telling the story of his life he was already past fifty years of that life. It is typical for autobiographies to begin with the earliest memories, so he was trying to bring to mind recollections of his childhood. As with most people, those memories tend to be fleeting and vague, pictorial more than linguistic and focused on the shocking rather than the mundane. But those early years are important formative years, the years in which character is molded, personality is developed, and principles are instilled that often influence the rest of one's life.

Although Henson was born enslaved, he was unaware of his situation during his early years.[1] He was more affected by his senses of the land, the climate, and the people who touched his life. Most influential were the people he was close to, his mother and family, his playmates, and, in his case, his enslaver.

The place where Josiah Henson was born, Southern Maryland, has a unique environment and a long history that influenced in many ways the people who lived there. The land itself is a triangular peninsula, with the brackish water of the Chesapeake Bay on the east and the clear flow of the Potomac River on the west. This flat coastal plain is intersected by a dozen rivers and creeks with more than a hundred small tributaries. The ebb and flow of these tidal waters create many marshlands around the shorelines. Because of all this water, the climate is almost tropical, with hot and sultry summers and short, mild winters. Most of the people who grew up on this watery environment over the centuries up to the present learned how to swim, fish, and handle a boat at a young age, so it is not improbable that Henson also acquired these skills here, as demonstrated by several incidents later in his life.

The land was inhabited by Native Americans, Creoles, Europeans, Africans, and mixtures of all. The Indigenous people had been there for hundreds of years before the others came. They were peaceful people of the Algonquin language group who lived in towns, where they farmed, fished, and hunted. They had a great respect for the land that gave them abundant food and means for shelter before the first invaders from Europe arrived on March 25, 1634, aboard the *Ark* and the *Dove*. These two ships brought about 130 people from England who had come to establish a haven for those who practiced Catholicism, forbidden at that time in that country.[2] Even though it was already occupied, the newcomers considered this their own land to do with as they pleased and hopefully return a profit. The original inhabitants welcomed the strangers at first, thinking they might provide protection from the warlike Susquehannocks menacing from the north.

As the newcomers populated the land and established farms and towns, they kept the names of the waterways such as Yaocomico, Piscataway, Mattawoman, Patapsco, Anacostank, Chesapeake, and Potomac, but they gave Christian religious and English aristocratic names to the towns and counties that they formed—such as St. Mary's, Prince George's, Charles, and Calvert—putting their personal stamp on their new property. They also gave the natives measles, smallpox, and syphilis, so a majority of the native people had disappeared by the end of the seventeenth century, succumbing to disease or killed in battle with the Europeans.

From the beginning, the settlers did not lack for food. The waters of the rivers teemed with fish, and there was an abundance of wildlife for hunting. The soil was fertile for growing a variety of crops for food, but the English people found difficulty adapting to the warm, humid climate. The many marshes bred mosquitoes that spread malaria, leaving survivors weak and susceptible to other diseases. In the first fifty years of the colony the mortality rate among the immigrants was very high, and the life span shortened so that only about 6 percent of fathers lived to see their children grow to adulthood.[3] Disease and harsh living conditions continued to plague the European residents well into the nineteenth century. Henson's enslaver as well as his father both died young.

Slavery was not a part of this Maryland colony in the beginning. Some of the immigrants were indentured servants, and some of these were of mixed race. These first people of color, called Creoles, were partly European and partly African and were usually Christian, well versed in trading, sea commerce, and laws and languages of different countries. Most of them had traveled to many lands and spoke several languages. Some owned land or were craftsmen. In these early days they worked alongside Europeans and had equal treatment under the law.[4] One of these extraordinary worldly wise people, Mathias de Sousa, arrived with the first settlers and went on, after completing his indenture, to become a ship captain, own land, vote, and serve in the colonial legislature.[5] Others with African heritage also achieved freedom from indenture in the 1600s, including John Baptiste and Thomas Hagleton.[6]

The colony was founded on religious freedom, so there were immigrants from countries other than England such as the Netherlands, Ireland, Scotland, and Portugal.[7] This intermingling of races and cultures gave the early settlers an all-inclusive attitude toward their community. This would change later as the colonizer, England, became more intolerant of religions other than Anglican and entered into war with other countries.

As the land was cleared, towns were built, and more settlers arrived, the colonists began to grow a crop for export to bring profit for themselves and their country. This crop would be tobacco, which had already become popular in England from export by the Virginia colony. Because tobacco required intense year-round cultivation, it needed more workers than other crops. Thus began the importation of Africans, a cheap source of labor that, unlike the indentured servants, worked their whole lives and, in this chattel form of slavery, made more enslaved persons through procreation because their children were also in bondage from birth.

When the population of enslaved grew to outnumber the Europeans and Creoles, a "slave society" was created. According to historian Ira Berlin, in such a society "slavery stood at the center of economic production, and the master-slave relationship provided the model for all social relations."[8] Farms became plantations, farmers became planters, and slaveholders became the ruling class, controlling the government and making the laws.[9] Many of these laws were designed to limit the freedoms of enslaved people and make them unconditionally subservient to their enslavers.

Since enslaved persons were distinguished by the color of their skin and many of the Creoles usually had darker skin than the Europeans, some Creoles were forced by these new laws to move westward or take to a seagoing life, as did Mathias de Sousa. Some did, however, stay and intermarried with the natives or with whites. As their second and third generations became whiter and whiter, they blended in with the landowning population, some even becoming part of the ruling class and slaveholders themselves.[10]

Slavery in Southern Maryland came in a variety of forms and changed over time and place. The one consistency was the subjugation of one group of people by another. In an attempt to justify the holding of human beings in slavery for life, the enslavers made the claim that what they called the "African race" was inferior to the white race and incapable of self-governing, rational thinking, and self-control. They therefore needed to be looked after and guided. This was the paternalistic justification that became the mainstay of the slave society. The master was often a harsh father. In order to maintain control, he was the absolute ruler of the enslaved person's life, demanding complete obedience. Punishment for breaking the rules was swift and harsh, most often by the lash but sometimes involving even harsher measures such as prolonged torture and maiming. Although slave owners were allowed by law to take the life of a person they owned, this rarely happened because slaves were considered valuable property for not only their labor but also their ability to procreate and produce more slaves.

Josiah Henson was born into this slave society, but by the time he came into the world in the late eighteenth century, the culture was in the flux of change again. Maryland, along with the other states that had recently been colonies of England, had been changed by the American Revolution. The slave societies of the South, which had controlled the culture and laws for many generations, began to see small fissures erupt from the pressure of freedom for the enslaved. All the states north of the Mason-Dixon Line, which formed the northern boundary of Maryland, passed laws freeing the enslaved people within their boundaries, making this line the permanent division between North and South: "free states" and "slave states."[11] The Northern states became a refuge for the enslaved people in the South seeking freedom, and in those states a movement grew of people—abolitionists—who thought of slavery as an abomination and sought to eradicate it in the South as had been done in the North.[12]

Agriculture was changing as well. In Maryland many plantations moved from tobacco to growing wheat and corn because tobacco had depleted the soil of nutrients and was no longer needed to pay rent to the English Crown. People were moving west to find new land and fortunes. The enslaved population continued to increase, but since the new crops were not as labor-intensive as the cultivation of tobacco, slave owners often sold their surplus human property, sometimes separating families. "The Chesapeake became the net exporter of slaves."[13] Families of enslaved people were also torn apart as slaveholders took their chattel with them when they left the area, since husbands and wives often lived on separate plantations.

For those left at home, life on the plantation was changing. Instead of focusing on one product such as a factory, the plantations now diversified and became little villages, with enslaved people performing a variety of tasks they had not done before. The enslaved population was no longer composed of mostly field hands and instead was trained in animal husbandry, mechanics, crafts, and horticulture. Those trained in crafts such as blacksmithing, carpentry, fine sewing, or weaving had extra value, as they could generate more income for the slaveholder when rented out to non–slave owners. This could never happen on a single-crop plantation, as all work was concentrated on making a profit from that one product.

People trained in crafts benefited greatly because if their labor was not needed at the plantation they could live at another farm or in town and have a bit of freedom, even though still enslaved. They might also be able to earn a little money working at their trade after the obligation to their slaveholders had been paid. Some even saved up enough to purchase their freedom. Since this privilege was granted to very few, parents tried to negotiate with the master to have their children trained in a craft to have this advantage.[14]

But as some enslaved people gained more freedom within the plantation, new laws clamped down on movement outside their homes. As more people escaped bondage by fleeing to the North, often helped by abolitionists, slave owners searched for new means of control, some by making punishment more severe for running away, others by giving the enslaved reason to stay. "Term slavery" became a way for slave owners to rid themselves of their human property who were past their prime working years and at the same time gave to the enslaved person the beckoning hope of freedom. Term slavery involved legal contracts freeing enslaved persons at a certain age. Although these contracts were registered at the courthouse, they were flexible and could be used by the owners to exert punishment by adding years of bondage or to reward by subtracting years.[15]

Another change came to the slave community beginning in the mid-1700s. The Great Awakening religious fervor, which originated in New England, had slowly spread south, and as it did, it began to affect the Black enslaved people as well as the white inhabitants in the latter half of the eighteenth century. Christianity, before mainly used as a tool of slave owners to reinforce their control over enslaved people, now reached out to those in bondage, promising to believers freedom in the afterlife and all the bounties of heaven. Formerly mainly adhering to their beliefs from their homeland, the newer generations of African Americans now turned to Christianity and held on to this new religion as a drowning man grasps a rope.[16] Josiah Henson's mother was described by him in his autobiography as having "deep piety and devotional feeling and habits."[17] Seeing his mother praying and listening to her supplications had a deep effect on the child that would last throughout his life.

Josiah Henson maintained that he was born in Charles County, Maryland, not far from Port Tobacco.[18] This was an area steeped in history and prehistory. Charles County, the third county jurisdiction formed in colonial Maryland in 1658, was named for Charles Calvert, son of the lord proprietor of the colony. The governor at the time was Josias Fendall, an ancestor of Josiah Henson's owner.[19] In 1790 Charles County had 10,085 Black enslaved people, about the same number as white inhabitants.[20] Port Tobacco was the seat of local government and was at the time a busy port and urban center of Southern Maryland. The town lay on the Port Tobacco River, which

Figure 1.1. La Grange, home of Francis Newman, owner of Josiah Henson's father. Maryland Historic Trust.

flows south into the Potomac River. In 1608 when Captain John Smith sailed up the Potomac River, he noted a navigable creek flowing from the north where there was a large village of natives called "Patopacos." This name easily slid into "Port Tobacco" when the English later settled their own town there as a tobacco trading center.[21] Still a busy commercial center when Josiah was a boy, the town practically disappeared after the river silted up in the mid-nineteenth century, and the bustling port was no more. There is only a small village at the site today.

The owners of Josiah Henson's parents point the way to discovering where he was born and his earliest experiences (figure 1.1). The wealthy newcomer of the English gentry upon whose farm Henson said he was born was Francis Newman (figure 1.2), who had arrived in Southern Maryland in 1796.[22] He was a man with a very colorful past. Born in England in 1759 into a wealthy landed family and well educated, he was a bit of a renegade. When his wife was unable to give him a son, he ran off to France with his neighbor's wife and married her there in a Catholic church, disregarding their Anglican marriages. He immigrated with his new wife and their two children to America in 1795, fleeing scandal and land disputes. Francis Newman was naturalized as a citizen of the United States on May 7, 1796. In August of that year his wife, Lydia, died and was buried in Baltimore.[23]

Francis Newman must have brought a great deal of money with him, as he was introduced into the upper crust of society and immediately began purchasing property to build his "New World empire." Newman's land holdings in Charles County began with the purchase of Hogg Range, 21 acres, in June 1796, and that was followed in

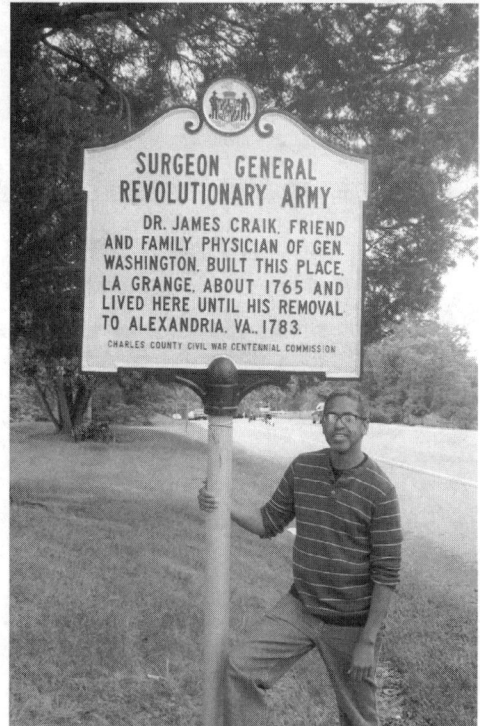

Figure 1.2. La Grange historic marker with historian and author Tony Cohen. Photo by author.

the same year by a purchase from Alexander Hamilton of 194 acres (Moore's Ditch and Luckett's Benefit).[24] As will be established later, Josiah Henson was born in 1796 and so could have been born on one of these two properties. However, at that time Newman could have been renting and living at La Grange, the large estate near Port Tobacco that he purchased in 1798. The owner, Dr. Craik, had been living in Alexandria, Virginia, for at least ten years by that time, and his son, William Craik, was living in Georgetown, so the house at La Grange was vacant.[25] Newman most likely knew either or both men, as he moved in the same circles. Newman also acquired many enslaved people to work on his growing property, as the 1800 census shows him owning twenty-six slaves.[26]

In 1798 Francis Newman married Elizabeth Hannah Friers, from a prestigious Rhode Island family, and brought her to La Grange to begin a new family. Apparently, Newman's self-promotion knew no bounds, as he had his portrait painted by his wife's cousin, Charles Bird King, in the uniform of a colonel even though Newman had resigned his commission in the Maryland militia after serving for only a few months (figure 1.3). When War with England commenced in 1811, he would have forfeited his property in England if he had continued to serve.[27]

Francis Newman was a wealthy and ambitious man. His past life showed that he believed he was above the law and was authoritarian. His marriage into a prominent family, his land dealings, and his correspondence with high officials in the government demonstrate that he cultivated relationships with people of importance so he

Figure 1.3. Francis Newman in an infantry colonel's uniform. By Charles Bird King, 1811. Heritage Frederick (MD).

could make his place in the upper crust of the society of this new country. To do this, he needed to make friends with not only the rich and powerful but also the old established families.

Josias Hanson McPherson, the poor country doctor who leased Josiah Henson's mother to Newman, probably was unaware of the man's past in England and his need to exert control over his workers in order to be accepted into the ruling class of the slave society. McPherson did not own land, but he was descended from a long line of prominent men on both his mother's side and his father's side that reached back to the early days of the colony. The fact that McPherson was raised as a gentleman and had a good education may have influenced the way he treated the enslaved people he owned. His mother, Benedicta Hanson McPherson, was the daughter of Maj. Samuel Hanson and a cousin of John Hanson, first president of the US Congress.[28] Benedicta's brother, Samuel Hanson, served in the American Revolutionary War. Benedicta gave three of her five children "Hanson" as a middle name. Her mother was Mary Fendall, and Benedicta could trace her lineage back to Josias Fendall, an early governor of colonial Maryland.[29]

The McPhersons were also a prominent family in Southern Maryland. Josias McPherson's great-grandfather Alexander McPherson had emigrated from Scotland between 1706 and 1717 and had acquired many properties.[30] Some of the estates in Charles County owned in the 1790s by Josias's uncles included Pomfret, Brierwood, and Dalready, all near Port Tobacco. Henry McPherson, Josias McPherson's father, was a child when his father died and only inherited one horse, the above estates going to his three older brothers.[31] In his forty-two years of life, Henry McPherson was not able to acquire any land or slaves, so he probably lived and raised his family on one these estates owned by a brother. This most likely would have been Dalready, since Henry's mother, Barbara Acton McPherson, was given life tenancy on that estate, and Henry was still a young boy under her care.[32] It is probable that Henry also raised his own family there since his mother did not die until 1797, after both Henry and his wife had died, and she left small legacies to Henry's children, including Josias.[33]

When Henry McPherson died intestate on November 6, 1774, he did leave over £500 and a crop of tobacco to his widow. The probate record shows that his creditors included Dr. James Craik and Dr. Gustavus Brown, who are also listed in wills and probate records of other family members, indicating that they were friends of the McPhersons and Fendalls.[34]

Henry McPherson's widow, Benedicta Hanson McPherson, may have stayed on at the house where they had been living with Henry's mother. When she died in 1790 her estate consisted of eight enslaved people, a crop of tobacco, and some household goods. Her children were Alexander, Samuel Hanson, Josias Hanson, Henry, and Ann Hanson. She also had two grandchildren listed in her will: Henry Thomas McPherson (son of Josias) and Ann McPherson (daughter of Henry). Josias was bequeathed "a negro boy," Romeo, and one thousand pounds of tobacco.[35] Romeo would remain with Josias for the rest of his life.

Josias McPherson married Elizabeth Beall Hanson (b. 1771) in 1788. She was the daughter of Samuel Hanson (the younger), brother of Benedicta Hanson McPherson, making her Josias's first cousin.[36] They had three children: Henry Thomas (b. February 2, 1789), Elizabeth Hanson (b. August 25, 1791), and Mary Ann (b. December 16, 1795).[37]

Josiah Henson was owned by Dr. McPherson and was born on the farm of Francis Newman, but when did that momentous event occur? Henson's autobiographies all begin with "I was born June 15, 1789, in Charles County, Maryland, on a farm belonging to Mr. Francis Newman," but he must have been mistaken about either his age or the farm, because the records demonstrate that Francis Newman did not enter this country until 1795 and did not acquire land in Southern Maryland until 1796. The date Henson gave for his birth is also contradicted by the death inventory of his owner, Josias H. McPherson, conducted in April 1805, which states Henson's age as nine and his brother John's age as twelve.[38] Since their mother, Celia, was also listed in the inventory, it is most likely she who gave the ages of her sons. The brother, John Henson, was later listed in the death inventory of his next owner, Adam Robb, in May 1847, as age fifty-five.[39] This corroborates the age listed in the Josias McPherson inventory and establishes John's birth year at 1792 and puts Josiah's birth year at 1796. This same 1847 inventory lists Romeo, first enslaved by Josias McPherson, as being sixty-five years of age, which means that when he was given to Josias in his mother's will in 1790 he was only eight years old.[40]

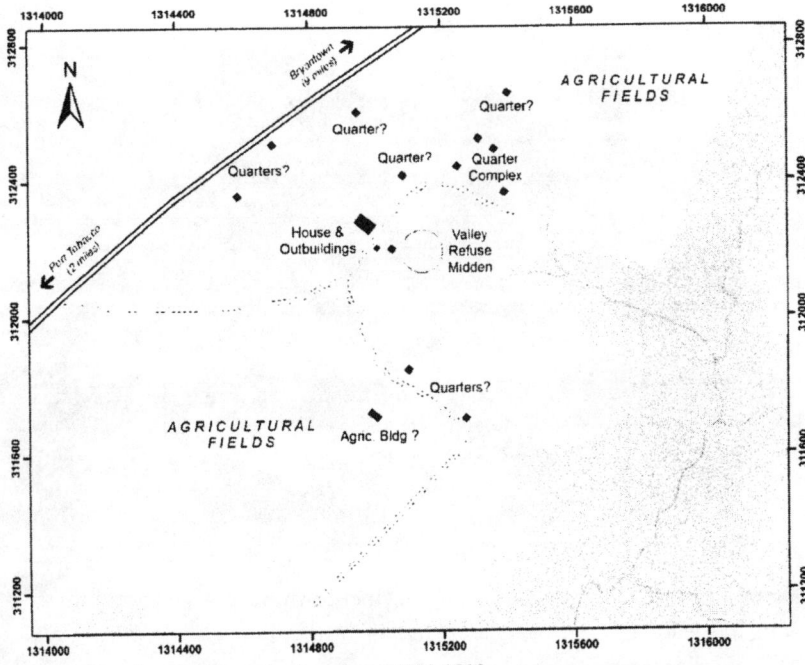

Figure 1.4. Hypothesized plantation layout for La Grange ca. 1800–1810 showing the possible locations of slave cabins and outbuildings. From Rebecca J. Webster, Alex J. Flick, Julia A. King, and Scott Strickland, *In Search of Josiah Henson's Birthplace: Archaeological Investigations a La Grange Near Port Tobacco, Maryland* (St. Mary's City: St. Mary's College of Maryland, 2017).

It was very unusual for persons born into slavery to know the exact date of their birth, as noted by many historians and even commented on by Frederick Douglass in his autobiography: "I never met with a slave in that part of the country who could tell me with any certainty how old he was. Few at that time knew anything of the months of the year or of the days of the months."[41] The reason why Josiah Henson stated that he was born on June 15, 1789, is unknown, but in interviews later in his life he sometimes used other dates.[42]

There is another possible link between Josias McPherson and Francis Newman that gives more evidence that Josiah Henson was born on La Grange (figure 1.4). Josiah remembered his owner as "Dr. McPherson," and evidence that he was a doctor is indicated by his death inventory, which listed more than fifty medical books and many instruments of that trade.[43] Since he also served as a county clerk on many transactions, he evidently was well educated and had good handwriting. He may have received his medical training under Dr. Gustavus Brown of Rose Hill, who had advertised to tutor medical students in his home in 1789 (figures 1.5 and 1.6).[44] Dr. Brown was notably a friend of the family, as he was listed as a witness in several of Josias McPherson's relatives' wills. Dr. Brown was also a good friend and colleague of his neighbor Dr. Craik of La Grange and most likely of the estate's new owner, Francis Newman.

Figure 1.5. Rose Hill, home of Dr. Gustavus Brown, with his doctor's office wing in the foreground. Maryland Historic Trust.

Newman was father to two children whose mother, Lydia, had died: a boy aged nine and a girl aged four in 1796. Being well educated himself and putting a high value on education, Newman most likely hired a tutor. It was common at that time, with no public schools, for a tutor to take in other area students of similar ages to provide companionship and competition. So, it is possible that Josias McPherson may have sent his son, Thomas, about the same age as Newman's son, Jean Francois, to be schooled with him while he was studying medicine with Dr. Brown at Rose Hill, which is within walking distance of La Grange, where his slaves were living. McPherson had money to invest in furthering his education from his 1790 inheritance, and there were several dwellings on the La Grange property outside of the "Quarter Complex, as well as living quarters for students above the office wing of Rose Hill" (figure 1.5).[45]

The crucial agreement by McPherson to lease Josiah Henson's mother to Newman resulted in an incident that Josiah recalled that greatly affected both the future of the young Josiah Henson and the relationship between the two white men. "The only incident I can remember which occurred while my mother continued on Mr. Newman's farm, was the appearance one day of my father with his head bloody and his back lacerated."[46] This traumatic scene left a lasting imprint on the mind of the young child. He said that he only learned later in life that his father had been whipped and had an ear cut off for hitting the white overseer who was assaulting his wife, Josiah's mother. This was a common punishment at that time and place for a slave who assaulted a white man. Maintaining "order and obedience" was of highest importance to the slave owner. Josiah would have been about six years old in 1802 and so could have a distinct memory of his father's beating and mutilation.

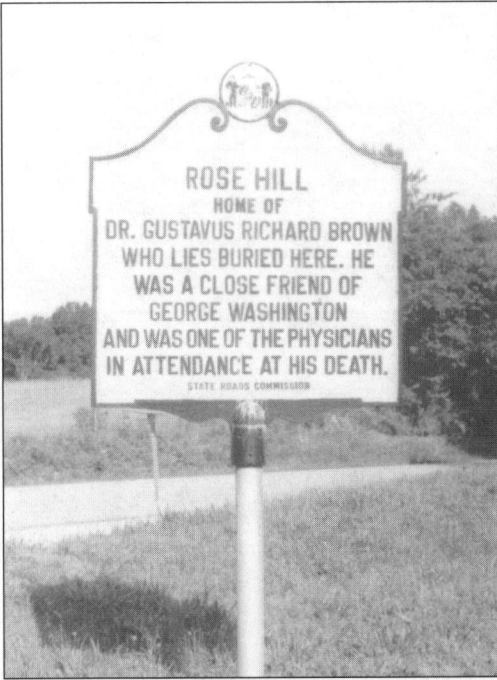

Figure 1.6. Rose Hill historic Marker.
Photo by author.

In his first memoir Josiah Henson recalled that his father was sent with Francis Newman's son to Alabama.[47] Subsequent memoirs leave out Newman's son and just say that Henson's father was sent to Alabama, never to be heard of again. However, it is possible that his father did end up in Louisiana, not Alabama. Newman's oldest son, Jean Francois, born in France, enlisted in the army in 1803 at age seventeen and was sent to New Orleans in Louisiana, newly acquired by the United States. He quickly rose to the rank of captain of artillery and remained in Louisiana after leaving the army.[48] Commissioned officers were allowed to have a servant, so it is possible that Josiah Henson's father did go with him, but there is no clear evidence that is what happened to him.

Josiah Henson's owner, Josias McPherson, moved from Charles County to Montgomery County, Maryland (future Rockville), in the spring of 1797, soon after the sudden death of his brother Samuel at age twenty-six (figure 1.7).[49] This is probably what precipitated his leasing Josiah's mother to Newman. As evidence of his residency in that town, McPherson was an official witness to a sale of an enslaved person to Adam Robb in Rockville in 1797.[50] He was also a witness at a Maryland House of Delegates hearing in November 1799 regarding the constitutionality of the recent election in Montgomery County.[51] In the 1800 census Josias McPherson was listed as living in Montgomery County with no family and no slaves. He was enumerated in the census only five names above Dr. James Anderson and just three names below Adam Robb, who owned a tavern and an inn across the street from the doctor near the courthouse.[52] These juxtapositions might indicate that McPherson was staying at Robb's Tavern and could have been apprenticed to Dr. Anderson for his medical training. According to tax assessment records, "Doctor Josias McPherson" was living

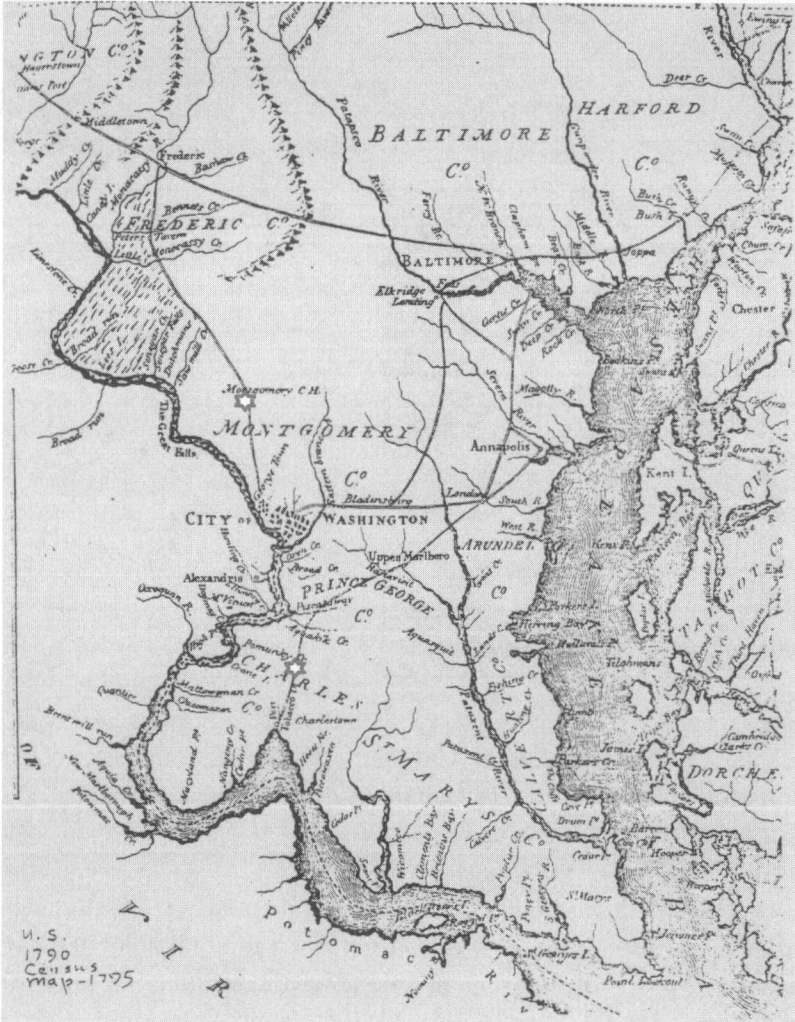

Figure 1.7. 1790 map of Charles County and Montgomery County, Maryland, showing the location of where Josiah was born near Port Tobacco and where he grew to adulthood in Rockville. Section of larger map of the state of Maryland by Dennis Griffith, originally published in 1795 by J. Vallance, Philadelphia, Library of Congress, https://lccn.loc.gov/76695380.

in the town in 1798, accompanied by his slave Romeo, but by 1802 had moved all of his five slaves to Rockville with him."[53] His wife and children probably remained in Charles County, living with a relative until he was established and had a home for them. This would corroborate the possible date of 1801–1802 that he removed Josiah's mother and family from the farm of Francis Newman after the beating and maiming of her husband.

In 1801 and again in 1802 Josias McPherson was listed as one of three commissioners appointed by the Maryland General Assembly to survey the land for Rockville,

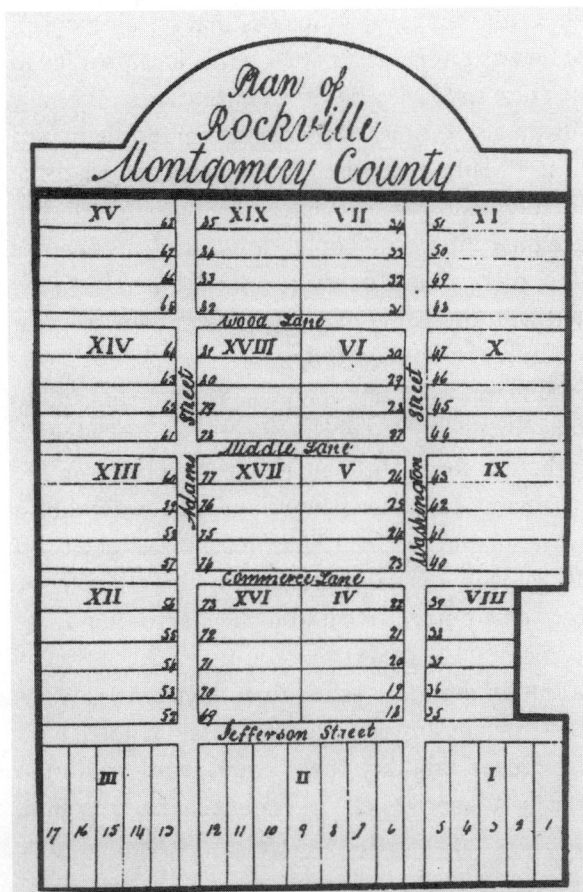

Figure 1.8. Map of Rockville in 1803. Robb's Tavern was located on lot 6. Montgomery History (MD).

formerly known as Williamsburg, as it was the county seat (figure 1.8). The survey was completed, and the plat was recorded in 1803.[54] Also in 1803 Josias was called "Justice of the Peace" in a newspaper notice about a found horse.[55]

Since Josiah Henson was born in 1796, Josias McPherson must have owned his mother, brother, and sister before then, but no sales record has been found in Maryland. However, in April 1795 a Josias H. McPherson is in the records of Edge-field County, South Carolina, as witness to several bonds there.[56] No other Josias H. McPherson could be found in the state during, before, or after this transaction. It is not known why he might have been in South Carolina at that time, but it is quite possible that he purchased Josiah's mother and siblings there.

Josiah Henson was marked as exceptional in the enslaved community from birth just by having a first and last name. As he says in his second autobiography, "As the first negro-child ever born to him, I was his especial pet. He gave me his own Christian name, Josiah, and with that he also gave me my last name, Henson, after an uncle of his, who was an officer in the Revolutionary war."[57]

Since pronunciations become distorted with different dialects and entrenched by usage, his owner's name, Josias, became Josiah, and the uncle's name, Samuel

Hanson, became Henson.[58] But the significant element here is that Josiah Henson was named after his owner and that he was given a last name, symbols of prestige in both the enslaved and enslavers' societies. As slavery became entrenched in the New World, the naming of enslaved individuals became a way of demeaning them and exerting control. Historian Ira Berlin explains that "their very names reflected the contempt in which their owners held them. Most answered to some European diminutive—Jack or Sukie.... To emphasize their inferiority, some were tagged with names such as Bossey, Jumper, and Postilion, more akin to barnyard animals then [sic] men and women. Others were designated with the name of some ancient deity or great personage like Hercules or Cato as a kind of cosmic jest."[59]

To be given both a first and last name was unusual for an enslaved person, and to be named for the master was a great honor, giving that enslaved person a special place in the slave community. In the slaveholder society little meaning was placed on the name of an enslaved person because a name could be changed and often was when a slave changed owners, which sometimes happened frequently. Josiah was called "Si" by his later enslavers.[60] But to Josiah Henson, his name alone gave him self-esteem, sometimes giving him an overarching self-confidence that would lead him later in life to accomplish great things.

Henson described his master as "far kinder to his slaves than the planters generally were, never suffering them to be struck by any one. He was a man of good, kind impulses, liberal, jovial, hearty. No degree of arbitrary power could ever lead him to cruelty."[61] Since Henson was his master's "special pet," he was likely close to him, helping him with odd jobs and running errands, perhaps even being groomed to be a valet. It was most likely during these few years in Rockville, between the ages of six and nine, that Henson learned his numbers. This sort of treatment by a caring master would contrast greatly with Henson's later cruel and unfeeling masters but, coming as it did in his formative years, laid the foundation for his intellect and temperament as well as his feeling of equality with and trust of whites.

All this positive experience of Henson's early years ended abruptly when Josias McPherson died suddenly sometime between November 1804 and February 1805.[62] According to Henson, his master drowned in a small creek after falling from his horse on returning from a party late at night. Henson's innocent happy world would be suddenly turned upside down, leaving him bewildered and alone.

2

Growing Up Enslaved

On February 2, 1805, Elizabeth McPherson, her father, and two of her brothers entered into administrative bond for the estate of her deceased husband, Josias H. McPherson, at the Charles County Courthouse.[1] Since he had not made a will, his estate had to be inventoried and sold and creditors paid before his wife and children could inherit. The inventory of his property, recorded on April 9, 1805, did not include any land but did include one horse and saddle, household and clothing items, medical instruments, and more than sixty medical books. The human property included "one negro man named Romeo age 23, one negro woman named Delia age 17, one negro woman Celia age 50 (infirm), one negro boy named John age 12, and one negro boy named Sye age 9 (infirm)."[2] "Sye" was the shortened name for Josiah. This nickname was used throughout his life as an enslaved person. His worth was $30, which was $10 less than the horse (figure 2.1).

On April 10, 1805, Elizabeth McPherson and her brother Josias Hanson petitioned the Charles County Court that the deceased's estate would have to be sold in order to satisfy creditors. The court ordered them to "make sale of the whole of the Personal Property of said deceased" and to give "three weeks notice of said sale by advertisements set up at the Courthouse, Poor House, and other public places in the County."[3] Because the estate did not include land and there was little personal property, the sale did not need to be advertised in the newspapers and, in the interest of a quick and efficient sale, was probably held at the place where the property was housed or at the courthouse in nearby Port Tobacco. If Josias McPherson's slaves had been living with him in Rockville, they would have been returned to his wife's household in Charles County upon his death. Josiah Henson said that after the sale he was taken about forty miles to Rockville, which would have been about the right distance from Port Tobacco on the roads of that time.

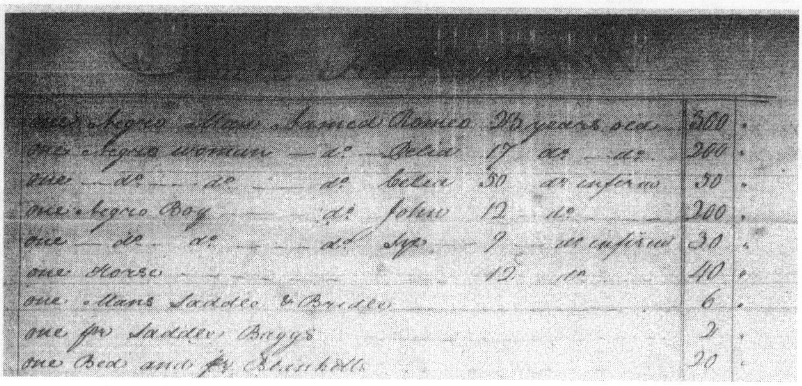

one Negro Man named Romeo 26 years old	300
one Negro woman — do — Delia 17 do — do	200
one — do — do — do Celia 30 do infirm	30
one Negro Boy — do John 12 do	200
one — do — do — do Sye 9 — do infirm	30
one Horse — — 12 do	40
one Mans Saddle & Bridle	6
one pr Saddle Baggs	2
one Bed and fy Blankets	20

Figure 2.1. Portion of the death inventory of Josias McPherson showing Josiah Henson ("Si") and his mother Celia and brother John. Maryland State Archives.

Josiah Henson's description of the auction and of his mother pleading with her new master to also purchase her youngest son and of being beaten and kicked away by him was a scene too often played in the South[4] The tearing apart of families and especially the wrenching of a child from the arms of his mother was an appallingly callous action that disheartened many parents and often turned the little one's hearts to stone or laid the internal fire for future rages.[5] The separation of families happened much more often than white Southerners of the time wanted outsiders to know. According to historian Michael Tadman, the slave trade "destroyed about one in five marriages, and wrecked an even higher proportion of parent-child relationships" of Blacks in the slave-exporting regions, of which Maryland was a part.[6] Slave auctions were usually held at taverns, markets, slave trader's headquarters, or a designated place near the center of a town.

Josiah's statement in his autobiographies that "my brothers and sisters were bid off one by one" contradicts the official death inventory of Josias McPherson, which listed only Josias, one brother John, one possible sister Delia, their mother Celia, and the unrelated Romeo. Josiah, who was very ill at the time of the auction, may have been remembering his enslaved playmates when he talked in his autobiographies about having five brothers and sisters.[7] Because McPherson owned no land, he would have been living on someone else's farm where there would have been other enslaved children. Josiah never, in any of his memoirs, states the names of any of these individuals, his closest family, although he did name one of his daughters Celia and created his second autobiography to raise the funds to purchase his brother John's freedom. The purchaser of Josiah's mother was Isaac Riley. Josiah, John, and Romeo were bought by Adam Robb.[8]

In his new home in Montgomery County the little boy, "Sye," found himself in a new world among strangers. He did not mention in his memoir that his brother John and friend Romeo were with him but said about Robb that "he took me to his home, about forty miles distant, and put me into his negro quarters with about forty others, of all ages, colors, and conditions, all strangers to me. Of course nobody cared for me. The slaves were brutalized by this degradation, and had no sympathy for me. I soon fell sick, and lay for some days almost dead on the ground. Sometimes a slave would give me a piece of corn bread or a bit of herring."[9] Josiah may have been separated from John and Romeo, as Adam Robb owned more than one property. Because Josiah was so very ill, Robb allowed Isaac Riley, who owned Josiah's mother, to take him. Riley agreed to pay Robb with a horse-shoeing if the boy lived.[10] This might explain why this sale does not appear in the county records.

Adam Robb, an emigrant from Scotland, owned seven slaves and a tavern in Rockville near the courthouse in 1800. By 1810 Robb owned thirty-four slaves at his farm on the outskirts of Rockville.[11] At his death in 1847 he owned a substantial amount of land and thirty-one slaves. Among those listed in his death inventory were John Henson, age fifty-five, and Romeo, age sixty-five. John Henson, Josiah's brother, went to Robb's granddaughter Margaret Beall in the division of property.[12] It is evident that Adam Robb and Josias McPherson, Josiah's former owner, knew each other: McPherson signed as witness to a sale of a slave to Robb in 1797.[13] Also, they are listed only three names apart from each other in the 1800 census in Rockville, and they were both Scotsmen. McPherson may have been staying in Robb's Tavern, a commodious brick building in the center of town that had opened in 1799 and was a popular stage-coach stop.[14] It was also a place where public auctions, including those of slaves, were held.[15]

The new region in which Josiah Henson found himself, although not very far from his original Southern Maryland home, was very different in climate, crops, and culture. It was in the Piedmont area as opposed to the Atlantic Coastal Plain. The climate was less sultry, the land less marshy and more rocky, with some rolling hills and fast-running streams. Most farms in Montgomery County at the turn of the nineteenth century were under fifty acres, and much of the land was still covered by forests. The farmers had organized in order to find ways to bring the soil back into cultivation after being depleted of nutrients from years of planting tobacco. The Sandy Spring Farmer's Society, formed in 1799, and the County Board of Agriculture helped the farmers learn to rotate crops, plant nutrient-rich clover, and fertilize with gypsum and manure. Farmers began using these methods to grow wheat, rye, flax, and corn, and more land was being cleared for tilling.[16] Water-powered gristmills were popping up all over the county to process these crops into flour and meal, and new roads were built to bring these products to markets. Most farms were diversified, growing a variety of crops and raising animals for market.

Montgomery County had been formed out of the larger Frederick County in 1776. Plantations and farms in this area were smaller than in Southern Maryland, and the enslaved population made up only one-third of the total population rather than the half in Charles County.[17] In 1790, only thirty-six planters in the county owned twenty or more slaves, and only two owned more than fifty; 80 percent of the enslavers owned fewer than ten slaves, with one-third of those owning only one or two.[18] As the county moved into the nineteenth century it shifted further away from a slave society and toward a more diversified society of small farmers, millers, and providers of services such as taverns and inns, blacksmiths, wheelwrights, and produce sellers along the well-traveled roads. Representatives of the people came from these occupations as well as from the "old school" of planters. In addition, the county had a large settlement of non-slaveholding Quakers in the eastern area, many of whom were quite influential in the society and government.

The port cities of Maryland, Baltimore and Annapolis, continued to do a brisk business in the importation and sales of people until the importation of slaves from outside the United States was banned in 1808.[19] Even though the selling of people still occurred after the ban, it was within the United States. In Montgomery County the commerce in humans was mainly from estate sales, not as a business with holding pens and auction blocks. Individual slaves were sometimes sold to slave traders, but this was usually done discretely or outside of the county.

The only major town in Montgomery County when it was formed was the bustling port of Georgetown, which was ceded to the new capital city of Washington, District of Columbia, in 1791. The road from Georgetown to the older town of Frederick, now Route 355, was already well established as part of "the way west" when it was made a turnpike in 1805.[20] About midway between these two towns, this main thoroughfare was crossed by two other roads, one leading east to Annapolis via Bladensburg and the other (Route 28) eventually leading to Baltimore. To the west, roads led to major crossings of the Potomac River into Virginia.

As often happens at major crossroads such as this, places of service were soon accommodating travelers passing through. Lawrence Owen built the first tavern in the 1750s, soon followed by Charles Hungerford's tavern in 1769, which became famous later as the meeting place of the area's revolutionaries who drafted the Hungerford Resolves in 1774.

When the General Assembly of the provisional government formed Montgomery County in 1776, it appointed a commission to purchase land for a county seat. The commissioners chose this crossroads, which then became known as Montgomery Court House. Taking advantage of this selection, speculator William Prather Williams bought a large amount of land near the courthouse, divided it into streets and lots, and called his development Williamsburgh. As noted previously, Josiah's former owner, Josias McPherson, was one of the appointed surveyors for this new town, which became officially Rockville in 1803.[21] It was near the courthouse that Adam Robb established his tavern, where McPherson may have lived.

As the county seat, Rockville—and all of the area along the busy road to Georgetown—benefited greatly from the cosmopolitan atmosphere of the port city. Being on the stage line on a busy road, taverns and hotels grew up around the courthouse hub. Several churches of different denominations appeared in the town, and wealthier residents built substantial brick homes, which gave the town a more affluent and permanent look.[22] But when Josias McPherson was there at the turn of the nineteenth

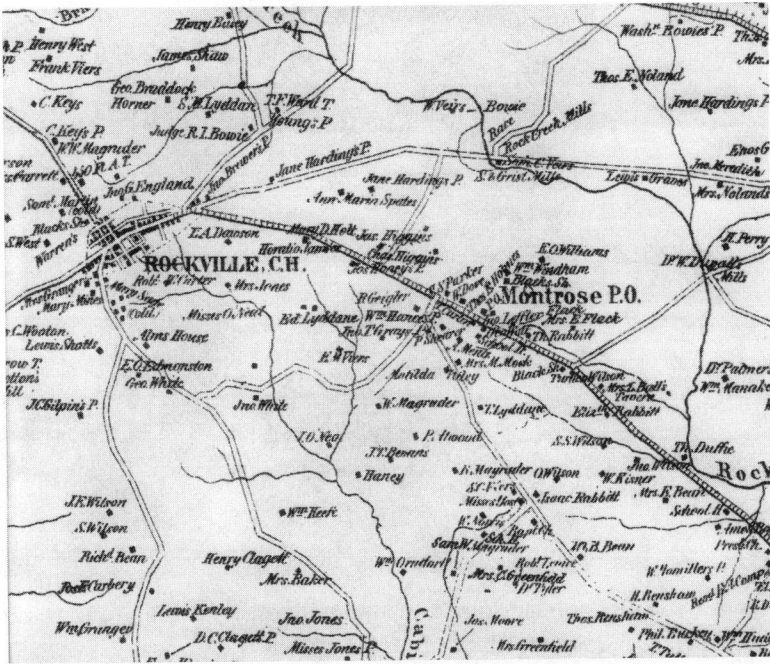

Figure 2.2. Section of 1869 Martinet and Bond map showing Rockville and environs map. "Matilda Riley" house on Old Georgetown Road is in the center. Matilda was Isaac Riley's wife. Montgomery History (MD).

century, the town had only about two hundred residents, and everyone, due to close proximity, knew one another.

So, Josiah's new home had a healthier climate than his previous abode. His new location consisted of diversified small farms rather than large plantations and had fewer enslaved people and a thriving, growing town nearby. There were more people generally and a greater variety of people than in the country environment where he had spent his formative years. This new world also provided much more stimulation and opportunities for expanding his knowledge during his adolescent years. In all, he was much better off than he would have been if he had remained in Southern Maryland. His new owner, Isaac Riley, although crueler and much less refined than his first owner, Josias McPherson, would extend Josiah's experiences by way of his community and family relations.

Isaac Riley's farm lay about three and a half miles south of Rockville on the west side of the Georgetown Road.[23] It was here on this busy thoroughfare, just south of a major town, that Josiah would grow up enslaved. When Riley acquired Josiah Henson in 1805, the farm was owned by his older brother George Riley, who purchased the 520 acres in 1797.[24] Isaac may have been living on that farm in 1805 when he acquired Josiah Henson and his mother. By 1809 Isaac was paying taxes on that property, so he probably had an informal gradual payment arrangement with his brother for the land (figure 2.2).

Figure 2.3. House of Isaac Riley, third owner of Josiah Henson, 1919, North Bethesda, MD. Kiplinger Library, DC History Center.

George Riley married Sarah Willson in 1793, and they lived on the farm that she had inherited called Two Brothers in the northern part of the county.[25] When Sarah died in 1810 without children, George married Mary Richards, and they had three daughters before he died in 1815. Isaac was executor and manager of the estate of his late brother. George's widow, Mary, married Arnold T. Winsor in 1818, and Winsor would cause Isaac Riley some major trouble over the estate.

Isaac Riley's house, which has been preserved, was built between 1800 and 1815 (figure 2.3).[26] When it was built it was a simple frame house of one and a half stories, with four rooms on the first floor and two upstairs. Although small, it is distinguishable as the "Big House," as the master's house was called, by being on high ground and constructed of clapboard rather than logs and having six rooms and two chimneys. The log kitchen with a large fireplace was attached to the house on the gable end but with no interior access when it was described for insurance coverage in 1856.[27]

In keeping with other log cabins in that time and place, the kitchen would have had a dirt floor, as described in Henson's autobiographies. The age-dating of one of the logs of the kitchen shows that this log was from a tree cut down in 1850, indicating that the log building was constructed after Josiah Henson left this farm.[28] The kitchen that he described in his autobiographies would have been near the house and similar to this one but probably burned down, as was common for log kitchens at the time (figure 2.4).[29] That is why they were separated from the main house.

Josiah's new owner, Isaac Riley, was born in 1774, the eighth of twelve children. Two of his older brothers, James and Amos, moved to Kentucky, as did at least one of his sisters and, later, the three daughters of his brother George. In 1800 Isaac owned

Figure 2.4. House of Isaac Riley today. Josiah Henson Museum and Park, North Bethesda, MD. Photo by author.

only two slaves, but by 1820 he was paying taxes on twelve.[30] Isaac served as a private in the Maryland Extra Militia under Capt. Thomas Gettings in the War of 1812, which was essentially the home guard.[31] It is not known whether he saw any action.

Isaac Riley may have been farming this section of his brother George's land from the time George purchased it, as George was living on the Two Brothers farm on the other side of Rockville. Existing records on the acreage of the farm are confusing, so it is difficult to say just how large it was at any specific time. This could be because part of it was still technically part of George Riley's estate, which was in limbo for many years, and part of it belonged to Isaac. The size of the property was also reduced from the original 520 acres in the years after George's death as parcels were ceded back to his estate to settle debts. The farm was still partially wooded and not dependent on a single crop, producing a harvest variety that included wheat, oats, barley, potatoes, corn, tobacco, and apples as well as sheep and pigs.[32] The sheep were kept in fenced pastures, but the pigs often ran wild in the woods.

Josiah Henson describes the living situation of the enslaved people on the farm:

We lodged in log huts, and on the bare ground. Wooden floors were an unknown luxury. In a single room were huddled, like cattle, ten or a dozen persons, men, women and children. All ideas of refinement and decency were, of course, out of the question. There were neither bedsteads, nor furniture of any description. Our beds were collections of straw and old rags, thrown down in the corners and boxed in with boards; a single blanket the only covering. Our favorite way of sleeping, however, was on a plank, our heads raised on an old jacket and our feet toasting before the smouldering fire. The wind whistled and the rain and snow blew in through the cracks, and the damp earth soaked in the moisture till the floor was miry as a pig-sty. Such were our houses. In these wretched hovels were we penned at night, and fed by day; here were the children born and the sick—neglected.[33]

Henson also said that they were able to grow a few vegetables that each might raise for himself and his family on the little piece of ground assigned to him for the purpose, called a truck patch, which was usually near a family unit cabin (figure 2.5). In another part of his memoir Josiah indicated that he was living in a separate cabin with his own family by the 1820s.[34] His description of sleeping on a plank indicates that he was residing in communal housing at some point. From these various descriptions we can see that his living situation improved slightly as Riley's fortunes altered and after Josiah had a family.

Often referred to as "quarters," housing for enslaved people varied in Montgomery County depending on the number of slaves, the work assigned, and the prosperity, frugality, or cruelty of the master. There were essentially three types: the loft quarter in the attic of the main house, the kitchen, the barn, or an outbuilding; the single-unit dwelling housing one family or extended family; and the multiunit dwelling housing many people in barracks or dormitory style. The multiunits were usually built in twos, one for males and one for females and children. They were usually found on the larger plantations, of which there were few in the county. The predominant construction of the single-unit quarter was of log and had a chimney with a fireplace and one room with a ladder to a loft. Sometimes these were constructed as double units or duplexes with a central chimney. They were usually built on the ground with no flooring and had only one window or no windows. But into the mid-nineteenth century as slaves were trained as carpenters and constructed their own housing, many were built with foundations, floors, windows, and interior partitioning.[35]

When Isaac Riley purchased Josiah's mother in 1805 he was a bachelor, so she probably worked as a cook and housekeeper. If he owned or rented a house at that time, she and her son, Josiah, were most likely housed in the attic of the house or the loft of the kitchen. Later when Isaac had more slaves working on the farm, they would have been housed separately but nearby. The twelve slaves on his farm would not have been conducive to the expense of building barracks-style quarters but instead would have been housed in individual log cabins constructed as the labor force grew.

Josiah's description of his work and how it changed as he grew older and became healthier was fairly typical for a small plantation. "My earliest employments were, to carry buckets of water to the men at work, and to hold a horse-plough, used for weeding between the rows of corn. As I grew older and taller, I was entrusted with the care of master's saddle-horse. Then a hoe was put into my hands, and I was soon required to do the day's work of a man; and it was not long before I could do it, at least as well as my associates in misery."[36] On such a diversified plantation where the workers had to learn a variety of tasks, he might also have become skilled at planting and harvesting a variety of crops; slaughtering pigs and curing meat; mending tools, wagons, and harnesses; cutting down trees; constructing fencing; splitting wood; and carpentry. All of this learning would serve him well later in life in many ways.

Josiah's description of the clothing also corresponds with other accounts of the time. "Our dress was of tow-cloth; for the children nothing but a shirt; for the older

Figure 2.5. Slave cabin at Sotterley Plantation, Hollywood, MD. This is a typical one-room and loft cabin for housing enslaved people in Maryland. Habs/Haer building survey, Library of Congress.

ones a pair of pantaloons or a gown in addition, according to the sex. Besides these, in the winter a round jacket or overcoat, a wool hat once in two or three years, for the males, and a pair of coarse shoes once a year."[37] However, many planters clothed their slaves much more poorly, giving them new clothing only when the old fell off their bodies. Wealthy and indulgent masters often gave their slaves, especially the house slaves, cast-off clothing of their own and a second set of good clothing for church. Josiah's description, then, indicates that Riley was a middling sort of master, neither very harsh nor very generous.

As Josiah regained his health, his strength grew with his body. He had happy memories from his childhood of winning competitions of strength and agility, enjoying dancing at celebrations and being admired for his performance, and good food and fun at Christmas.[38]

Unlike the authors of other slave narratives published around the same time, Josiah never accused any of his masters of severely beating him or any of the other people enslaved with him. The only exception is the memory brought up, not until his fourth publication in 1876, of being beaten with a cane by Riley upon discovering he had a spelling book and was trying to learn to read. This beating left a scar on his head for the rest of his life but was the result of sudden rage, not a planned public whipping. The lack of reports of serious beatings does not reflect the leniency of Riley but does indicate the general attitude toward the punishment of slaves in Montgomery County at this time. The cruel punishments of the eighteenth century, such as public whippings of as many as one hundred lashes and the cutting off of an ear for hitting a white man, although still enforced in the southern areas of the state where the Black population outnumbered the white, had largely become dormant in the central and northwestern part of the state. New, more lenient laws took their place. For instance, the state limited the number of lashes to ten and required slave owners to provide adequate food, clothing, shelter, and rest.[39] Because freedom lay just across the northern border of the state, slave owners in Maryland realized that they could gain more loyalty and more work from their slaves by giving rewards and withholding privileges rather than using cruel punishments. Owners could be prosecuted or suffer a loss of good standing in the community if they became known as cruel masters. In Montgomery County the prominence of Quakers in some high offices influenced this attitude. This is not to say that masters didn't abuse their slaves in private or find ways to hide their cruelty. Besides, the ultimate cruelty of separation from family lay just around the corner with the next slave trader.

Josiah attributed much of his attitude toward life and liberty as an adult to his conversion to Christianity as a teenager. He wrote several times in his memoir about the piety and frequent prayers of his mother but did not think much about religion until he heard an itinerant preacher speak at Newport Mill in 1813 when Josiah was eighteen. Even though he spoke of his mother as being very pious, Josiah said in his autobiographies that he had never set foot in a church or heard a sermon before this instance. He said that the preacher he listened to was John McKenny, a baker from Georgetown. This is undoubtedly true even though no sign of that name can be found in the 1810 or 1820 Washington, DC, census records or city directories of the time. A John McKenny is listed in the 1820 census in Frederick, Maryland, just thirty miles to the north of Rockville. Itinerant preachers were frowned upon by the legitimate circuit riders and congregations, who considered them a threat, and thus these preachers moved frequently. Since Josiah said he listened to the sermon outside the door of the mill, he never met the preacher at that time. Josiah may have found out his name from someone else attending the gathering and was reacquainted with the baker/preacher years later in Georgetown when Josiah was Riley's marketman.

The young Josiah Henson was quite taken by the words of the preacher and especially by the quoted verse from the Bible: "But we see Jesus, who was made a little lower than the angels for the suffering of death, crowned with glory and honour; that he by the grace of God should taste death for every man" (Hebrews 2:9, King James version). Josiah remembered these words, or a version of them, for the rest of his life because he saw that these words of salvation were for the enslaved as well as for the free and gave him hope for salvation after death. He was so affected by this that he knelt down in the woods on the way home and prayed to God and vowed to dedicate his life to Christianity and the sharing of the gospel:

> At all events, I date my conversion, and my awakening to a new life—a consciousness of power and a destiny superior to anything I had before conceived of—from this day, so memorable to me. I used every means and opportunity of inquiry into religious matters; and so deep was my conviction of their superior importance to everything else, so clear my perception of my

own faults, and so undoubting my observation of the darkness and sin that surrounded me, that I could not help talking much on these subjects with those about me; and it was not long before I began to pray with them, and exhort them, and to impart to the poor slaves those little glimmerings of light from another world, which had reached my own eye.[40]

This faith stayed with him for the rest of his life, keeping him afloat in times of adversity and giving him guidance in times of uncertainty. One thing, however, differed from most Christian teachings today: white preachers were admonished by the slaveholders to emphasize certain parts of the Bible that advised servants and slaves to know their place, to obey their masters and be good servants.[41] From these sermons, Josiah believed that since he was born enslaved God had put him in that position to test him, and so it was his duty to forgive those who abused him and be the best slave he could be. This was the "unwritten contract" of the master-slave relationship.[42] This agreement of "I'll do this for you if you do this for me" did not mean that a slave could not trick or manipulate his master or that a master could not trick a slave if it was for mutual benefit and did no real harm. It was also a sham contract, because the people involved did not have equal power.

This kind of relationship could not exist if an enslaver wanted only total control and total obedience from his slaves or was sadistic and cruel by nature whereby enslaved people lived in fear and hatred of the master. But even under these conditions they were not always under total domination by the slave owner. The enslaved people knew their masters' need for order over chaos, their need not to lose face in front of their neighbors, and, most importantly, their need for profit. Slavery and capitalism were intricately intertwined from the beginning of our nation.[43] Through unified actions such as work slowdowns, breakage of tools, stealing of livestock for food, negligence of livestock, and general sabotage, they were often able to negotiate for such things as better living conditions, more food, shorter hours, Sundays off, and private vegetable gardens.[44] Individuals, especially house slaves, personal servants, and cooks, had special relationships with the master or mistress and were often treated to special favors such as cast-off clothing, better food, days off, and passes to travel to run errands, go to markets, or visit other plantations.[45] A master might convince a slave that he perceived had the respect of the others to be his spy and his envoy. This slave might then use the confidence that the master had in him to feed him misinformation. The relationship between master and slave was a never-ending dance of guise and manipulation, pretense and deception.

These are just the sort of master/slave games that transpired soon after Josiah's conversion to Christianity. By close observation he was able to disclose to his master the thievery of the white overseer and was put in the overseer's place to supervise the labor of the enslaved people and to manage the farmwork. This was not unusual on a farm or small plantation if a trusted slave had the respect and leadership of the others. It saved the cost of paying an overseer.

But Josiah was not one to wield a whip over his fellows in bondage. Instead, he convinced them that it was in all of their best interest to make the farm prosperous. He showed that he cared for his fellow slaves by doing such things as stealing and butchering the master's chickens and pigs to provide meat for them, letting the pregnant women off from heavy labor, and allowing his fellows secret privileges. Thus, he gained their confidence and got them to work harder and more efficiently than they had under the cruel overseer.[46] Josiah convinced them that they should take pride in the produce since they had created it. This pride enhanced their self-respect by giving them a basis to believe that they were not inferior to the white race as they had been taught.[47]

In this way Josiah gained the master's trust by increasing the profits of the plantation.[48] Josiah also gained the trust of his companions in bondage through his compassion and ability to manipulate the master, thus raising his status to the highest within the enslaved community.[49] Josiah justified his own deceptive behavior by convincing himself that since he had the management of the slaves, it was in the best interest of the plantation to keep them healthy, well fed, and happy so they could be more productive, a mutual benefit for the master and the people he enslaved.[50]

> And sometimes, when I have seen them starved, and miserable, and unable to help themselves, I have helped them to some of the comforts which they were denied by him who owned them, and which my companions had not the wit or the daring to procure. Meat was not a part of our regular food; but my master had plenty of sheep and pigs, and sometimes I have picked out the best one I could find in the flock, or the drove, carried it a mile or two into the woods, slaughtered it, cut it up, and distributed it among the poor creatures, to whom it was at once food, luxury, and medicine. Was this wrong? I can only say that, at this distance of time, my conscience does not reproach me for it, and that then I esteemed it among the best of my deeds.[51]

Producing a profit from the plantation was the major objective of the slaveholder, and keeping his slaves healthy so they could procreate and content enough so they would not run away or misbehave was a part of this.[52] An overseer who could accomplish this was most highly valued, and one who did not have to be paid would indeed be a treasure. Such an enslaved plantation manager or overseer expected certain privileges in return for his beneficial work.[53]

And so, an unwritten agreement evolved between master and slave, an agreement based on trust and, at least on Josiah Henson's part, a Christian faith that put a great deal of emphasis on loyalty and keeping promises. For Isaac Riley it meant that he had a reliable leader of his enslaved workers who made his farm more profitable. As long as this was the case, Riley could overlook a few indiscretions, but he also knew that in the end he had the ultimate power and could resort to selling his human property, which he attempted to do years later.

3
Maimed and Adapting

As Josiah Henson continued to gain the trust of his owner, Isaac Riley, he was given the privilege of being the personal servant and bodyguard of Riley when he went to large gatherings and to taverns. Josiah's charge was to protect Riley from assault and see that he got home safely when he was inebriated. On one of these occasions Riley got into a fight with Brice Letton, overseer for his brother George, which turned into a serious brawl.[1] When it looked as if Riley was getting the worst of it with too many opponents, Josiah, at his call, rushed in to extricate him. In the process he accidently shoved Letton with his elbow. This would turn out to be a very bad move.

Brice Letton had ties to the Riley family that Josiah may not have known but that would affect his life. The Rileys and Lettons were related by marriage. George Riley, Isaac's elder brother, married Brice Letton's niece Mary Richards in 1810, and they had three daughters. This tie between the families continued later when some members of both families moved to Kentucky, where one of George and Mary's daughters, Tabitha Riley, married one of Brice Letton's sons, Ninian Letton, in 1835, and another daughter, Mary, married John Letton, a nephew of Brice Letton.[2] The Letton family had a 405-acre plantation, Oatry, southeast of Rockville, not too far from where Isaac Riley lived. Both Brice Letton and Isaac Riley served in the Maryland Militia home guard during the War of 1812 and may have known each other in the service. Letton was a captain, and Riley was a private.[3] It is not known what the argument in the tavern was about, but Josiah said he was about nineteen or twenty years old at the time, which puts the date at about 1815.[4] After George died on May 9, 1815, his estate was in limbo, and Isaac was executor of his brother's will, which included Letton's niece, so the dispute could possibly have had to do with Riley's handling of the estate.

About a week after the tavern brawl when Josiah was returning on horseback from running an errand for his master, Letton was waiting for him with three slaves to flog him for his alleged offense. They forced him to dismount and chased his horse away. But Josiah, being a young man in the prime of his strength, fought them and successfully caused one to run off with his injuries, leaving only three opponents. According to Josiah, it was Letton who, exasperated at not being able to tie him up for a flogging, picked up a fence rail and attacked him, breaking his arm and causing him to fall to the ground. Letton then struck him repeatedly with the rail, breaking his shoulder blades as well as his arm and several ribs. They finally left him bleeding and semiconscious.

When the horse returned home without Josiah a search was made, and he was brought home. Riley filed a complaint at the courthouse, but Letton swore that Josiah had set upon him first, so there was nothing to be done since a Black man could not bear witness against a white man in court at that time. Letton's purpose in the beating may have been more directed toward Riley than Henson, depriving him of his farm manager and body guard, and, of course, reducing the value of his property. Henson's injuries were serious:

> Besides my broken arm and the wounds on my head, I could feel and
> hear the pieces of my shoulder-blades grate against each other with every
> breath. No physician or surgeon was called to dress my wounds, and I never
> knew one to be called to a slave upon R.'s estate, on any occasion whatever,
> and have no knowledge of such a thing being done on any estate in the
> neighborhood. I was attended, if it may be called attendance, by my master's
> sister, who had some reputation in such affairs; and she splintered [*sic*] my
> arm, and bound up my back as well as she knew how, and nature did the rest.
> It was five months before I could work at all.[5]

Josiah did not say where he was going when he was attacked but did say that he took a shortcut across a different property separated by fencing and gates. If Isaac Riley was living in the house at the south end of his brother George's property at that time, then Josiah might have been heading north across this property if he was heading to Rockville. George had been living at the time of his death on the estate of his deceased wife's inheritance, Two Brothers, north of Rockville, with his second wife, Mary Richards, so it would make sense that he had a caretaker for this land on the south side of the city who might very well have been Brice Letton (figure 3.1). By taking Riley's most prized slave out of commission, using the injury inflicted on him during the brawl as an excuse, Letton was most likely sending a warning to Riley to not cheat his niece and her daughters out of their inheritance.

The severe beating inflicted on Josiah changed his life forever. The shattered bones of his arm and shoulder blades were not set correctly and knitted together in an uneven fashion so that he was never again able to raise his hands as high as his head.[6] This deformity required that Josiah figure out new ways of doing things, even simple mundane things in life that most never give a second thought. He could not even wash his face properly or shave or brush his hair. He had to find new tolerable

☞ Take Notice.

I do hereby forewarn all persons from Tresspassing on my enclosures, either by riding or driving through my fields, and pulling down my fences, as I am determined to put the law in force against all such as disregard this notice. Masters will do well by giving their servents caution of this notice, as they will be surely dealt with on the spot, if caught riding through my fields.

Brice Letton.

April 17.   18w1f.

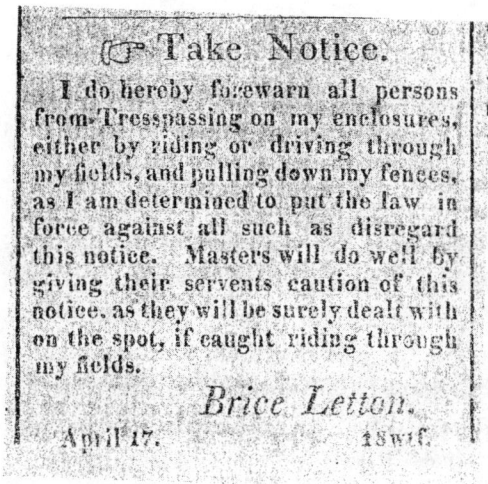

Figure 3.1. Newspaper ad placed by Brice Letton forbidding trespassing on his property. *Rockville True American* 3, no. 19, Wednesday, April 24, 1822 (also April 3, 1822, and may have been in earlier newspapers). Montgomery History (MD).

ways of sleeping, and the everyday process of eating and drinking required the learn-ing of new skills: simple actions such as bringing a fork to his mouth and sliding in the cut of meat, manipulating a spoonful of soup sideways until it reached his lips, and keeping a mug of water half full so that it would not spill until he could tilt it into his mouth. Dressing himself would have also been a new learning experience. Putting on trousers was the easy part, but to don a shirt, vest, and jacket he would need to advance his arms first in one direction and then in the other direction to compel them to enter the sleeves. Many years later it was observed by the publisher of his second autobiography that in order to put on a hat Josiah needed to lay it on the edge of a table and then maneuver his head under it.[7]

The idleness of the five months of recuperation from his injuries caused by the beating would have forced him to look inward, to search his soul for the strength to carry on and to use his mind for ways that he could survive in the future as a "maimed and mutilated" man.[8]

As Henson indicated, never again would he be able to "run faster and farther, wrestle longer, and jump higher, than anybody" around. His pride and ambition "to be first in the field, whether we were hoeing, mowing, or reaping; to surpass those of my own age, or indeed any age, in athletic exercises; and to obtain, if possible, the favorable regard of the petty despot who ruled over us," was gone, stolen by Letton with his vengeful beating.[9] Henson needed to find new ways to gain the respect of his fellow slaves and the confidence of his enslaver.

Josiah's mental anguish must have been almost as great as his physical suffering. He was no longer the person he once was. That strong, agile, fun-loving man was gone forever. And why? Why was this done to him? Why did he have to suffer so? His good Christian mother surely would have tried to quell this fire with admonitions to forgive rather than lash out. His own Christian faith was most likely what sustained him and comforted him as he worked through his physical agony and mental turmoil. Whether he was actually able to forgive his tormentors, his actions and activities after his injury indicate that he at least resigned himself to his condition and the futility of resistance. A period of sadness and hopelessness must have followed, but Josiah was smart, resilient, and adaptive.[10]

Henson knew that Riley had sued Letton over the incident and had lost and thus was unable to recoup any money for the loss of labor of his slave.[11] Riley also knew that Henson could never again work in the fields. Raising a hoe or an axe was beyond him. When he tried to use a plow, he injured his shoulder blades again.[12] It was common knowledge among the enslaved community that a "worthless" slave was usually sold. The worst fear of any enslaved person was to be sold away from his family. Josiah's love for his mother must have deepened as she nursed him back to health: feeding him by hand, changing his bandages, and seeing to his every need as if he were her baby again, her youngest and dearest. Josiah must find a way to stay on the farm, to stay with his mother. To do this he could not dwell on what he had lost; instead, he needed to examine his strengths. He no longer had his youthful strength, but he still had his good mind. He could not read or write, but he knew his numbers, and he was good at solving problems. He was no longer capable of being his master's bodyguard, but he still had his master's trust.

As Josiah sat idly waiting for his body to heal, he watched the life of the plantation pass by. He saw the field hands march off at dawn and return at dusk, no longer under his supervision. He watched the cook go to the Big House to prepare the morning fare, and he saw the young ones drawing water, feeding the chickens, and weeding the garden. The plantation worked like a well-oiled machine, with every person playing their part. The slave owner sat at the helm directing and manipulating as he saw fit to make sure that the machine worked to bring him profit. Josiah knew that in his time as overseer he had gained Riley's confidence by proving that he was trustworthy, loyal, and smart but most of all by making the farm more profitable. Josiah had become, in the eyes of Riley, indispensable.

Josiah had also, beyond all expectations of any servant, become the confidant of his master. Riley, constrained by the unwritten rules of enslavers to not speak to the enslaved except about work, saw Josiah as his agent, dispensing his orders and carrying out his will.[13] As time went on, Riley depended increasingly on Josiah and gained a respect for his skills and his intelligence, seeing him as his right-hand man and sounding board.[14]

At the same time Josiah's fellow laborers looked to him as a leader, even in his youth, who worked them hard but made sure that they reaped some personal benefit from their labor. They looked up to him also as a religious and moral leader, guiding them through the conflicting path of being both a slave and a man or a woman, thus retaining their individuality, their unique personhood.

So, Josiah knew that he had to prove to Riley that he could still play this part. Josiah could still have a role in keeping the machine running in good order. His best assets were his knowledge of farm management and his ability to do math. He never knew how or when he learned mathematics; perhaps it was in his very early years when he

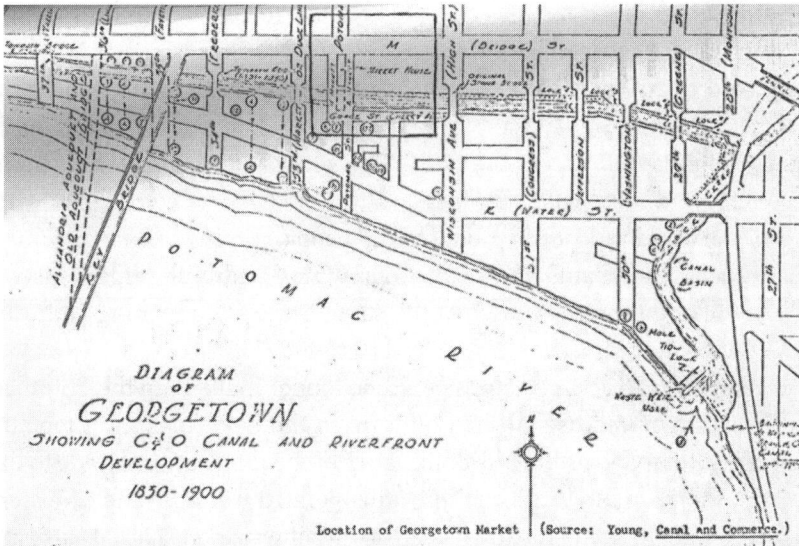

Figure 3.2. 1850–1900 map of Georgetown with the market in a square, upper center. This was after Henson had left for Kentucky. The C & O Canal took part of the original market property. Young, "Canal and Commerce," Martin Luther King Library, Washington, DC

had been the favorite of his first owner, Dr. McPherson, and possibly helping him to count pills and mix formulas. Nevertheless, as Josiah himself noted, he was very good at calculations.[15] Even if he couldn't work in the fields, he could still supervise the loading of a wagon with produce and take it to market. If he could not be the best at hoeing, mowing, and reaping, he could prove himself to be the best peddler, showing that he could still bring in a profit. So, besides managing the farm, Josiah became Isaac Riley's trusted marketman.[16]

Public markets were essential in large cities so that urban dwellers could have access to fresh food from the surrounding farms. A well-regulated market benefited the city, as the people were assured of good food and good value, and also benefited the sellers, as they were assured a central place to sell their goods and be confident of fair dealing. There were two main markets in the area at the time: the Center Market and the Georgetown Market (figure 3.2). In order to maximize return, Henson might sell at one on one day and at another on an alternate day.[17]

The older one (by two years) was the Georgetown Market. Located at the last deep anchorage on the Potomac River before the falls, Georgetown had existed as a port town since 1745, when the Maryland General Assembly established a tobacco warehouse there. A town was laid out in 1752.[18] At that time it was part of Frederick County but became part of Montgomery County when it was formed from Frederick County in 1776. When the District of Columbia was created in 1792, Maryland ceded part of its land, including Georgetown, to the new capital city. The well-established Georgetown retained its identity and self-governance until after the American Civil War. At that time, the names of the streets of Georgetown were changed to conform with the street pattern of the District of Columbia.

During colonial times Georgetown was the place where farmers brought their tobacco to be collected and shipped to England and also the place where they would purchase goods to take home to the farm. The wharfs were lined with warehouses, and the streets were lined with merchants. It was a center of commerce, with ships from all over the world unloading products and people coming from many miles away to purchase them. Merchants and bankers grew rich and built large houses on the high ground surrounding the port.[19] At the same time, a burgeoning community of free Blacks established churches on the lower ground.[20]

Unfortunately, by 1800 large ships could no longer make it up the Potomac River as far as Georgetown because silt had built up in the river, making it too shallow.[21] Georgetown was forced to give up its dominance of the international trade to the ports downstream. A ferry to the Virginia shore still operated from the end of Water Street (Wisconsin Avenue), helping the town keep its thriving market. The city also attracted people from outside because of its reputation for intellect as the site of Georgetown University (founded in 1789) and as the home of the elite and noteworthy, a reputation it still retains.

A market lot was reserved in the original plan for the town (figure 3.3). It was first used as a butchers' market and then for a debtors' jail. A wood frame market building was not constructed until 1795. When the city purchased the property in 1803, the owner, Adam King, stipulated in the deed that the site was "for the use of the market aforesaid, and for no other use, interest, or purpose whatsoever."[22]

According to local chroniclers, "The sprawling building with stalls selling meat, fruit, vegetables and all sorts of other goods and household items, quickly became the busiest place in the city to shop and socialize."[23] The interior of the building was reserved for butchers and fishmongers, the elite of the merchants. Sides of beef and hogs and dead birds and rabbits hung on the stalls. Butchering was done on site, and gutters carrying the blood and cleaning waters ran through the building and down the hill to the river. Around the outside of the building vendors would set up temporary stalls to sell produce and hand-crafted items. Farther downhill there were enclosures for live animals for sale.

The large doors on the sides of the building were usually open, but the stench of dead carcasses and fish and manure must have been overwhelming inside and outside. The outside was muddy in the rainy times and dusty in the dry times, and there were flies everywhere at all times except in the coldest winter months.

There were slave auctions at the market. The dark and airless holding pens for the slaves waiting to be sold still exist in the basement of the building built in 1865 on the foundations of the old one.[24] This Market Building is at 3276 M Street, between East and West Market Streets. The market lot surrounding the building was larger in Henson's time, reaching almost to the river, but a large portion was taken in 1830 for the construction of the C & O Canal.[25]

Figure 3.3. 1865 Georgetown Market building. Habs/Haer building survey, Library of Congress.

Josiah was probably selling Riley's produce at the market from about 1816 through 1824, so it is not implausible that he knew Yarrow Marmout, a free Black man and a well-known wise elder who owned his own house in Georgetown, had shares in the local bank, and lent money to friends. Yarrow was born in Africa and was enslaved until he was about sixty years old, when he was set free in exchange for making bricks for his owner. Yarrow made nets and baskets to sell and was known to have "conducted trade, hacking from a small cart," and he lived until 1823.[26] The fact that he was well known and respected in both the white and Black communities is shown by the fact that two artists, Charles Willson Peale and James Alexander Simpson, painted portraits of Yarrow Marmout.[27] Henson's interest in religion may have brought him into contact with Yarrow, who was known for being a very religious man himself although of the Islamic faith. This would have broadened Josiah's knowledge of the free Black community and of differing religious practices.

According to a historian for the National Park Service, "It was also the period when it was considered fashionable to be seen at the market. It was always the source of the latest gossip. Coaches and fours brought ladies dressed in their most fashionable finery through the cobblestone streets to the market on market days, which were on Tuesdays, Thursdays and Saturdays."[28] No doubt they carried perfumed handkerchief's to blot out the smells emanating from the market. Politicians and orators took advantage of the large crowds to put forth their opinions on the latest issues.

The Center Market was established by George Washington, who in 1797 designated that it be in the very center (as its name indicates) of the new capital city on

Pennsylvania Avenue between 7th and 8th Streets (where the National Archives is today), comprising two acres.[29] The market building was not constructed on the site until December 1801. With this huge market came regulations to ensure good quality and make sure that customers were not purchasing for resale, sellers did not cheat customers, and sellers did not conspire to set high prices. Government-appointed clerks walked the market making sure that the rules were observed and settling disputes, and some of the revenue collected from stall rental went to the poor. With a population of more than thirty-three thousand by 1820, Washington had a lot of mouths to feed. A traveler from England, Henry Bradshaw, remarked in 1818 that African Americans, both free and enslaved, were the chief sellers in the Center Market. In the markets could be found an assortment and intermingling of humanity: the farmer and the foreigner, the privileged and the poor, the slave and the free.

Besides being his workplace, the markets also became Josiah's school. Having learned to be a careful observer from his months of forced inactivity due to his injuries, he watched all of the goings-on of the market. He saw how people interacted in this environment, so very different from that of the farm. He realized that he was a part of a different hierarchy, one based not on race or servitude but instead on skill and character and the quality of the products being sold. Butchers, for instance, ruled the market and always occupied the center because their products were the most highly valued by the customers. Butchers always wore white shirts and aprons and also wore top hats to demonstrate their higher place in the social order.[30] Here, where he was treated differently and given a measure of independence, Josiah could imagine what it would be like to be free.

Josiah said that he paid close attention to his gentlemen customers, observing how they spoke and the words they used, and imitated them.[31] By delivering produce to their houses, he learned how the well-to-do lived.[32] He observed how they dressed and how they carried themselves, their manners and customs. Through careful observation and patient practice, he learned how to talk, dress, and carry himself like a gentleman, a very singular feat for an enslaved person who had been taught from childhood to be subservient. The civility of the marketplace also contrasted with the crude manners of his master, and learning the manners and speech of gentlemen gave Josiah a way of compensating for being enslaved. By walking and talking and having the manners of a gentleman, he could feel in his own mind superior even if still enslaved.[33]

Several people who met Josiah commented on how he dressed well. Two eyewitness reports described him as wearing a white beaver hat, a very expensive item.[34] It is evident that he knew how to speak excellent English because he gave talks to both Americans in Massachusetts and English gentry, presented acceptable sermons before his fellow ministers of the faith, and was introduced to English lords and ladies. When he had an audience with the archbishop of Canterbury on his visit to England in 1851–1852, his excellency inquired what university Josiah had attended, to which he answered "the University of adversity." According to Josiah, the archbishop, John

Bird Summer, then said, "'But is it possible that you are not a scholar?' 'I am not,' said I. 'But I should never have suspected that you were not a liberally educated man. I have heard many negroes talk, but have never seen one that could use such language as you. Will you tell me, Sir, how you learned our language?' I then explained to him, as well as I could, my early life; that it had always been my custom to observe good speakers, and to imitate only those who seemed to speak most correctly."[35]

By listening to conversations between lawyers, Josiah learned a bit about law, knowledge he would use in the future to protect his own and others' rights. He also observed in the market how men make contracts with a handshake, agreeing to perform mutual acts such as loans, trades, and tasks and pledging their word of honor. He knew that a person who broke this agreement was considered untrustworthy and shunned, sometimes even leading to a duel. He listened to the orators and heard how they interspersed their speech with humor and made their words more interesting through gestures and changes in the pitch and inflections of their voice.

Just as important were the lessons in the art of salesmanship. Josiah noted how the sellers enticed people to buy their products. Various aspects of his future life, as portrayed in his autobiographies, demonstrate that he was a very good salesman of his goods and of his ideas. As he competed with other vendors in the market and bargained and dickered with customers, he learned that the art of salesmanship lies not in the promotion of your product but rather in convincing the customer that he wants your product and that he wants it from you. You do this by first gaining his trust. A good salesman is clean and conservatively well-dressed. He smiles and compliments the customers and asks them about themselves and tries to discover something about their likes and dislikes and their cultural preferences before ever mentioning a product he is selling. He tries to find something, even a little thing such as liking the taste of cantaloupe or being from the same area, that they have in common. Evoking sympathy was always a good start to achieve this trust, and Josiah achieved this merely through his appearance or demonstration of his physical limitations. He realized that building a good relationship with the customer is almost as important as getting a good price, as it will pay off in the future. The fact that Josiah knew many of his regular customers by name and that they referred to him familiarly as "Si, or Siah," demonstrates that he knew how to gain this trust.[36] As to his maimed body, he found that far from being a disadvantage, his disability gave him an edge by way of sympathy and compassion that other sellers could not readily achieve.

All of these lessons helped to form the character of the man. They were lessons Josiah would carry with him, and they served him well in his later life. One thing that did not change for Josiah was his religious fervor. He continued to teach his fellows in bondage about Christianity and to attend local camp meetings. Some white churches had for many years allowed Black people to attend services but only from the balcony; and they could accept communion only after the whites. The first African American church to be established in Montgomery County was Sharp Street United Methodist Episcopal Church in Sandy Spring in 1822.[37] It attracted parishioners from many miles around the town but was ten miles from Rockville, a far distance for walking, and few Black people, free or enslaved, owned or had access to a horse.

The alternative were camp meetings, which allowed much more intermingling of the races because they were usually held outside or in a barn. Amid the Second Great Awakening of religious fervor in the early nineteenth century, itinerant preachers went from town to town and gave long emotional sermons preaching that people could make direct connection with God without the intermediary of a minister. This idea was particularly attractive to Black people, whose only formal minister had been a white man.

Some Black Christians took to preaching themselves and formed their own clandestine congregations.[38] Maryland had passed laws against large gatherings of slaves, but the leaders in Montgomery County turned a blind eye to these religious meetings, seeing them as either harmless, as encouraging good behavior, or perhaps inevitable.[39] These meetings became popular among both slaves and free Blacks, preferring their own kind of preaching and hymn singing to that of the established churches. In going to these services, the enslaved person found just a little bit of freedom and escape from the ever-watchful eye of the master.

It was at one of these religious meetings in 1817 that Josiah at age twenty-two met Charlotte Stevenson, the woman with whom he would share many adventures and who would bear him ten children.[40] Because they were both very religious people, they must have insisted on an official marriage ceremony, but, unfortunately, they could not live together, as Charlotte was owned by a different person. Their first child, Thomas, was born soon after their marriage. It is possible that he was named after Henry Thomas (the son of Henson's first owner, Josias McPherson), with whom Josiah had spent his happy formative years.[41]

In 1818 Josiah's owner, Isaac Riley, married Matilda Middleton. He was forty-four years old, and she was eighteen.[42] She was from a long-established and well-to-do family of Southern Maryland. Her mother had died when she was seven, and when her father, Samuel Middleton, died in 1817, he left a fairly large estate consisting of a farm and eleven slaves that were divided between Matilda, her sister, and three brothers. Earlier in 1817 the siblings had also inherited property from their grandfather on their mother's side.[43] Josiah said she "had some little property, and more thrift. Her economy was remarkable, and was certainly no addition to the comfort of the establishment."[44]

Since both of Matilda's parents had passed away, Riley was appointed guardian of Matilda's young brother Francis, or Frank, who moved in with the newlyweds. Young Frank found his sister strict and very sparing with meals.[45] As a growing and curious teenager, Frank quickly found a friend in Josiah and came to his cabin often to seek comfort from his overbearing sister and get extra food.[46]

The farm prospered under the management of Josiah and the efficiency of Matilda. Josiah had his own cabin, and Riley increased his number of slaves from two in 1810 to twelve in 1820.[47] Somehow during this period Josiah got Isaac Riley to purchase his wife, Charlotte. This may have been due to the fact that she was "renown for her cooking," but it may be no coincidence that Josiah and Charlotte's second child, born in 1819, was named Isaac.[48] Also, it was common knowledge among slaveholders that a male slave who was together with his family was more dependable and less likely to run away. According to scholar John Blassingame, "The simple threat of being separated from his family was generally sufficient to subdue the most rebellious 'married' slave."[49] And, of course, there was the profit motive, as the children of the enslaved mother were the property of the owner of the mother. Thus, as Josiah's family grew, so did Riley's fortunes.

Josiah's preaching, his provision of good food, and his ability to manipulate the master made him a respected and trusted leader to his fellow slaves. Because Josiah was known to be wise, they felt that they could come to him for advice and direction. Because of his religious convictions, they knew that he would keep their secrets. Because he cared for them, they knew that he would give judicious remedies to their conflicts. He became their spiritual leader, their counselor, and their mediator.[50]

Josiah did not have a high opinion of his owner, Isaac Riley, seeing him as coarse, blasphemous, and inclined to drink too much and fight too easily. Nevertheless, Josiah was loyal to Riley:

For many years I was his factotum, and supplied him with all his means for all his purposes, whether they were good or bad. I had no reason to think highly of his moral character; but it was my duty to be faithful to him in the position in which he placed me; and I can boldly declare, before God and man, that I was so. I forgave him the causeless blows and injuries he had inflicted on me in childhood and youth, and was proud of the favor he now showed me, and of the character and reputation I had earned by strenuous and persevering efforts.[51]

Both men had growing families and seemed content with their working relationship and the prospering farm that they managed together. Even though Josiah was enslaved, he had achieved a high status as an enslaved person. He even had a glimmer of hope to purchase his freedom in the future with some money he had gained on the side, most likely from tips and services provided at the markets, and was building up for that purpose. But dark clouds were gathering, and an unforeseen event was coming that would change both of their lives forever.

4
Journey to Kentucky

THE YEAR 1825 BROUGHT A MOMENTOUS CHANGE TO JOSIAH HENSON'S LIFE, AND A burdensome task unfortunately brought trouble he could not have foreseen. His leadership skills would be severely tested, and certain decisions he made would haunt him for the rest of his life. It all began when Henson's owner, Isaac Riley, came to his cabin one cold night in February in great anxiety pleading with him to promise to do something for him or all would be lost. Riley refused to tell Josiah what he wanted him to do, only demanding his promise to do it, because he knew that Josiah placed great importance on his own word of honor.[1] At the markets in the city Josiah had seen men pledging their word of honor with a handshake to repay a debt or complete a task, and he had most likely seen what could happen to a man who did not keep his word. In any case, his faith alone would have compelled him to keep a promise.

After Josiah agreed to perform the unknown task, Riley revealed that he wanted him to take most of the slaves he owned to the plantation of his brother, Amos Riley, in Kentucky. Speed and secrecy were critical, for if they did not depart soon, they were in danger of being sold at auction to satisfy a debt, Josiah and family included. Riley said that as soon as his affairs were settled, he and his wife and children were planning to move to Kentucky. Riley pleaded with Josiah through the night and became very emotional, appealing to his good nature.[2] Josiah took the threat of sale seriously, because the worst fear of any enslaved person was to be separated from his family. He must have looked at his wife, Charlotte, and their two little boys, Thomas and Isaac, and imagined never seeing them again.

Isaac Riley's legal problems probably had to do with his deceased brother's estate. When George Riley, Isaac's elder brother, purchased the land that became Isaac's farm in 1797, he and his brother may have had an unwritten agreement allowing Isaac to clear and farm the land while paying his brother for the land over time. Isaac built or improved a house on the land probably about 1806 after he received some inheritance and two slaves from his father's will and was paying taxes on it by 1809.[3] But when George died on May 9, 1815, the only will that was recorded in the courthouse left his slaves, individually named, to his wife, Mary, and their children and appointed Isaac as administrator.[4] The farm where George had lived since 1793, Two Brothers, just north of Rockville, which had originally belonged to his first wife, Sarah, now deceased, went to his widow Mary as dower. In 1818 Mary married Arnold Thomas Winsor, who assumed guardianship of her three young daughters.[5] This left any un-written agreement between George and his brother Isaac in limbo, as often happens when a person dies unexpectedly at a young age, having neglected to make certain agreements legalized.

On January 22, 1825, almost ten years after George Riley's death, Arnold Winsor filed a suit against Isaac Riley claiming he had mismanaged the estate of George Riley and that much of the land, including the farm on which Isaac resided, actually belonged to George's widow, Mary, and her children. Consequently, in the fall of 1825 Winsor had a public sale of more than 650 acres, livestock, and "one Negro man (Ste-phen) and one negro girl (Rose)." Three hundred sixty-five acres of this land was from property on which Riley was living, and the rest was from the Two Brothers farm.[6]

Isaac filed a countersuit, but the dispute went on for twenty years in the courts, long after Mary's three daughters had married and moved to Kentucky, withdrawing any claims to property of their father. In the end Isaac Riley either retained or pur-chased back the land and the house, which went to his wife when he died in 1850.[7]

But on that night in February, Isaac Riley was very afraid of losing his land and his slaves and was desperate enough to devise a plan for Josiah to take the slaves to Isaac's brother Amos's plantation seven hundred miles away in Kentucky. There was no guarantee that they all would reach that destination. On such a long journey, some might die or be injured or succumb to the temptation of freedom when passing by Ohio, but Riley was willing to take that chance. He could explain the sudden disap-pearance of his slaves by saying that they had all escaped together or been stolen, as had happened to others.[8]

Josiah argued that he had never traveled beyond Washington and knew nothing of the land or how to get to Kentucky, but Riley assured him that he would give him detailed instructions, provisions, and some money for a horse and wagon, accommo-dations, and food along the way. He also promised that none of the people under Josi-ah's care were ever to be sold. The final argument that convinced Josiah to undertake the task was an appeal to his pride and his loyalty. "My pride was aroused in view of the importance of my responsibility, and heart and soul I became identified with my master's project of running off his negroes."[9]

So, Josiah agreed to the proposition. According to Josiah there were eighteen en-slaved people under his care, in addition to himself and his wife and two children, bringing the total to twenty-two. But according to census and tax records in Maryland and Kentucky, the total number of enslaved people in the party was twelve, including Henson and his wife and two children.[10] Henson's mother, Celia, now seventy years old, would not be coming with them.[11] The last time that mother and son had been separated, when he was nine years old, he fell so ill that he could not work and was returned to his mother's loving care. Imagine the tearful parting of mother and son and grandchildren as they said goodbye, not knowing if they would ever see each other again. And in fact, Celia would die before Josiah returned briefly to Maryland almost four years later.[12]

Because the enslaved people were told that they were sure to be sold if they did not go and trusted Josiah as a good and intelligent leader, they packed up their meager belongings and followed him. It also helped that they had no idea how long and arduous a journey it was going to be. A single horse cannot pull a very large wagon; there was just enough space for provisions and maybe two or three people. So, the travelers except for Josiah's wife, who may have been pregnant, and the youngest children would have walked alongside the entire distance to the Ohio River, where they would then travel by boat.[13] Because of the circuitous route taken by the party, the distance traveled by foot in fact turned out to be about 500 miles (with an additional 663 miles by river). This is almost twice the distance of a more direct route. The trip took two and a half months, from early February to mid-April, and covered many more miles than a direct route because, in Josiah's words, "Under these circumstances no difficulty arose from want of submission to my authority, and none of any sort, except that which I necessarily encountered from my ignorance of the country, and my inexperience in such business."[14]

According to Josiah, they "went through Alexandria, Culpepper [Culpeper], Fauquier, Harper's Ferry, Cumberland, over the mountains on the National Turnpike, to Wheeling." In looking at this route on the maps of the time, one can see how he may have gotten lost a few times. The fact that Josiah could not read may not have been a disadvantage on the long journey, since there were no road signs in those days. He knew how to tell north from south and east from west and could understand a map showing rivers, mountains, towns, and roads without knowing the words. He also had an excellent memory and could remember long, detailed directions.[15]

They left in the middle of the night,[16] and they went south, perhaps because most people looking for them, thinking they were escaping to Pennsylvania, would assume they headed north. Following the route described by Josiah, they went down the Georgetown Road (Route 355 today), then southeast across Washington City, a route Josiah would have been familiar with from his days selling his owner's produce at the Center Market, to cross over the Potomac River on the Long Bridge (the 14th Street bridge today) to Alexandria. Long Bridge had a toll that would have amounted to $2.56¼.[17] They could also have taken Chain Bridge, upriver from Georgetown, that had a similar toll or the ferry from Georgetown, costing a bit less. The advantage of the ferry may have been that Josiah, from his many years at the market, probably knew the ferryman and could bribe him or exact a promise of secrecy from him.

From Alexandria they headed west on the Old Post Road to Culpeper. Post roads were laid out and maintained by the federal government and were well established by

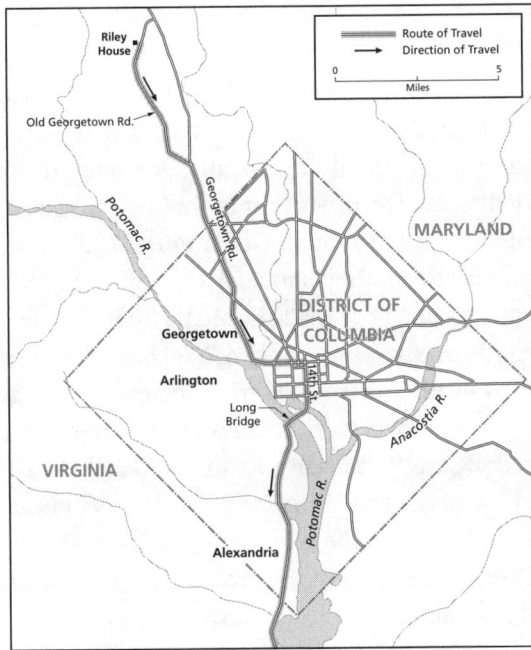

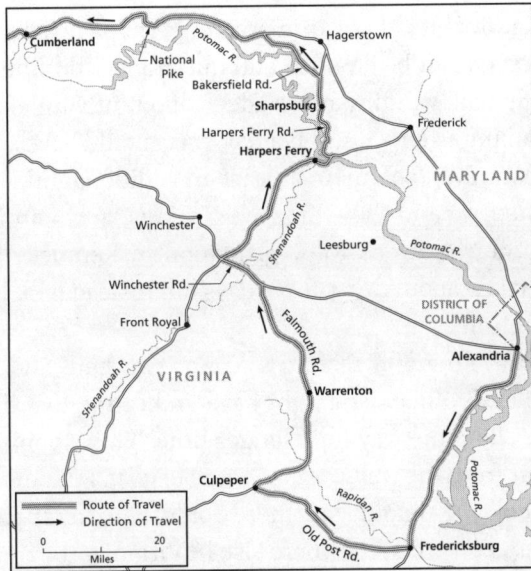

Figure 4.1. Map of the route taken by Josiah Henson and his charges from Rockville, Maryland, to Owensboro, Kentucky, in 1825.

1825, providing easy access between cities and large towns.[18] At Culpeper they turned north to Warrenton in Fauquier County, where they caught the Falmouth Road leading to the Winchester Road heading northwest. When they reached the Winchester Road they had traveled about 130 miles, but at this point, according to Josiah's enumeration, they deviated from the most traveled route. If their destination had been the well-traveled National Road, they should have continued fifteen miles west on the Winchester Road, a major post road that led across the Blue Ridge Mountains and across the Shenandoah River by bridge to Winchester, and from there taken the "Great Road" (Route 11) north for forty-two miles to arrive at Hagerstown, Maryland, and the National Road westward to Cumberland and then on to the Ohio River.[19] Instead, they detoured off the Winchester Road and traveled east along the winding Shenandoah River to Harpers Ferry, Virginia (now West Virginia).

In addition, on the next leg of the trip the path they took from Harpers Ferry to Cumberland was again on small, winding roads through mountains, whereas the most direct and least strenuous route from Harpers Ferry to Cumberland would have been to travel directly north twenty-eight miles to Hagerstown and then about seventy miles west on the National Road to Cumberland. Perhaps Josiah was avoiding major roads to stay hidden and not be stopped and questioned, but the detour to Harpers Ferry and the use of small, winding roads added about fifty miles to their trip. Figuring an average of walking twenty miles per day, this should have added two and a half days to their trip. Instead, it took them at least an additional fifteen days, until about April 1, to reach Wheeling and the Ohio River.[20] Thus, a trip on foot and boat from Rockville, Maryland, to the Amos Riley plantation in Kentucky by the most direct route ought to have taken about thirty-three days but instead took Josiah and his party more than twice that time.

Even with slow traveling and resting a day or two here and there, the journey took much longer than it otherwise might have, indicating that the party must have stopped somewhere along the way for a longer time. This stopping place must have been along the detour from the well-traveled route to go to Harpers Ferry. Josiah never explained why he took the detour, but there could be several possible reasons for holding up at Harpers Ferry or somewhere else in Virginia. It may have been because of bad weather, equipment repair, to wait for the ice to thaw on the rivers, or to keep concealed for a longer time before reentering Maryland. The delay may also have been due to illness of one or more members of the party, it being midwinter. It is possible that Charlotte may have had a miscarriage or lost an infant, since she had no children born between 1819 and 1827, and Josiah said many years later that she gave birth to ten children, having only eight who lived to adulthood.[21]

It may be a mere coincidence, but the detour that Josiah took from the Winchester Road to Harpers Ferry led them near the plantation of Leonard Davis, brother-in-law of Isaac Riley's brother George. In 1786 Leonard and his wife, Mary Willson; their five children; and an undetermined number of slaves had moved to the plantation in Berkley County, Virginia (now West Virginia), owned by Mary's father, Joseph Willson.

Davis had apparently acquired the property from his father-in-law by selling him his tavern in Rockville and some slaves. This transaction involved some kind of "secret trust." When Joseph Willson died four years later, seventeen of his slaves went to his daughter Ann Worthington and sixteen to his daughter Sarah, who would marry George Riley in 1793. There was some contention about who owned which slaves, and since the secret trust was never recorded, there is no way of knowing precisely. By 1825 both Leonard and Mary Davis had died, and the Berkley County property was owned by Leonard Davis Jr., who had married a stepdaughter of Ann Willson Worthington, sister-in-law of George Riley.[22] If Josiah might have been delivering enslaved people from the contested Davis/Worthington/Riley estates that Isaac Riley may have "borrowed" or was keeping to be delivered to Leonard Davis, we will never know. But it would explain Josiah saying that he left Rockville with eighteen slaves besides himself and family but delivered only twelve to Amos Riley in Kentucky.

When they reached Cumberland, they still had 140 miles to travel over six mountains to reach Wheeling and the Ohio River. The National Road, completed only seven years earlier, was wide and paved and carried much traffic including stages, mail wagons, big commercial wagons, and families in smaller wagons and carriages.[23] Many inns and taverns had sprung up along the way to accommodate travelers. Sometimes the white drivers of coffles of slaves, bringing them to an auction or to another owner, stopped at these hostels.[24] Josiah never considered himself a slave driver even though he kept company with such men and enjoyed their privileges. To those who called him a "driver," he was proud to note that the enslaved people in his charge had come of their own free will and were not chained together to keep them from running off:

> At the places where we stopped for the night, we often met negro-drivers with their droves, who were almost uniformly kept chained to prevent them from running away. The inquiry was often propounded to me by the drivers, "Whose niggers are those?" On being informed, the next inquiry usually was, "Where are they going?" "To Kentucky." "Who drives them?" "Well, I have charge of them," was my reply. "What a smart nigger!" was the usual exclamation, with an oath. "Will your master sell you? Come in and stop with us." In this way I was often invited to pass the evening with them in the bar-room; their negroes, in the meantime, lying chained in the pen, while mine were scattered around at liberty.[25]

When they reached Wheeling and the Ohio River, Josiah had been instructed to sell the horse and wagon and use the money to purchase a boat to carry everyone down the river to Kentucky and the Riley plantation. The sale of one horse and wagon provided enough money for a boat that Josiah termed a "yawl," which was propelled by oars.[26] It was apparently big enough to hold all twelve people and let them sleep, but it must have been open since a covered boat or a boat with a cabin, such as a river keelboat, was much too expensive and was controlled by a rudder and sweeps, not oars.

There were many types of floating vehicles available along the upper reaches of the Ohio River to sell to travelers. Since the flow of the river carried the craft west, almost anything that could float would do, from a raft to a forty-foot flatboat to a ninety-foot barge, and they all went by a variety of names.[27]

Called "La Belle Riviere" (Beautiful River) by the first French explorers, the Ohio River reaches from the Allegheny Mountains in the East one thousand miles to flow into the grand Mississippi River in the Midwest. The broad waterway was the main route west for both pioneers and commerce in the nineteenth century.[28] It was early April when Henson's group embarked in their little boat, so the river may well have been flowing high and fast with snowmelt from its northern tributaries. The distance on the river from Wheeling to Yellow Banks (now Owensboro), Kentucky, where Amos Riley's land lay, is 661 miles and, with the high water, would have taken them about ten days to travel.[29] This stretch of the river is deep, the only obstacles being other vessels that were mostly traveling at the same speed, drifting with the flow of the water. The only times that the oars were likely to be used were to navigate through the rapids of Louisville and to maneuver the boat to a landing to tie up for the night. Being in a small boat on a big, fast-flowing river must have been terrifying at first for people who were not used to water travel and probably did not know how to swim, but they likely soon became accustomed to the speed at which the landscape passed by and the gentle rocking of the craft.

Because it was small, the boat could be tied up at practically any wharf. But problems arose when they docked on the Ohio side of the river. Ohio was a free state; slavery was not allowed there. When they tied up for the night or for provisions, people came to them and encouraged them to step off the boat to freedom. It was a tantalizing temptation. What a glorious prospect to be free, to not have to answer to anyone, obey a master, or be beaten. People offered to help them and guide them. After more than two months of hard travel, just days from their destination, Josiah was faced with mutiny: a challenge to his authority, a threat that he might not succeed with his assignment. Of course, Josiah himself had always wanted to be free but by earning the money to purchase himself from his owner. He thought of escaping as dishonest. In his own words, "I had a sentiment of honor on the subject. The duties of the slave to his master as appointed over him in the Lord, I had ever heard urged by ministers and religious men. It seemed like outright stealing. And now I felt the devil was getting the upper hand of me."[30]

And so, he ordered his men to shove off from the dock and continue downstream to Amos Riley's plantation. Josiah admitted that his own conceit had something to do with his decision. "I had promised my master to take his property to Kentucky, and deposit it with his brother Amos. Pride, too, came in to confirm me. I had undertaken a great thing; my vanity had been flattered all along the road by hearing myself praised; I thought it would be a feather in my cap to carry it through thoroughly; and had often painted the scene in my imagination of the final surrender of my charge to master Amos, and the immense admiration and respect with which he would regard me."[31]

This was the first chink in Josiah's armor of self-righteousness, of his belief that his master's trust made him an equal with his master. It was the beginning of the realization that a Black man could never be seen as an equal by a white person who owned him. Josiah came to sorely regret this decision on the Ohio River later in his life.

Kentucky had sufficient settlers to become a state in 1792, but much of it was still a frontier wilderness in 1814 when Amos Riley moved to the area on the Ohio River about a hundred miles west of Louisville, where he purchased one thousand acres along Blackford Creek.[32] The soil in this region was very fertile, and the land was being populated so quickly that by the following year a new county was formed in this section from the larger Ohio County. The new county was named for a local War of 1812 hero, Col. Joseph Hamilton Daveiss, but a clerk misspelled the name, reversing the "e" and "i," and it became Daviess County.[33] The nearest town to the Riley plantation, about ten miles west, was Yellow Banks, a steamboat landing on the Ohio River named for the color of the soil along the river at that spot. The name was changed in 1817 to Owensborough (now Owensboro) after Col. Abraham Owen, another War of 1812 hero.[34] But it was still referred to as Yellow Banks by locals for many years.

Upstream just above the falls of the Ohio River lay the fast-growing city of Louisville, Kentucky, a commercial port that benefited from the falls because all the flatboats and steamboats arriving from upriver had to unload above the falls and reload cargo and passengers below the falls (figure 4.2). The small boat that carried Josiah and his charges could have been able to navigate around the rocks of the falls without much trouble. It was only the larger vessels that had to stop.

A vast majority of the settlers in Kentucky came from Virginia and Maryland. Like both of these states, Kentucky was a slave state and a slave society. The number of slaves in Kentucky grew from 11,830 in 1790 to 40,343 in 1800. By the time Josiah arrived in 1825, the enslaved population had grown to more than 140,000, comprising one-quarter of the entire population.[35] The land, originally a part of Virginia, had been laid out in the old colonial system of metes and bounds. When the new territory was created in 1779, all the new settlers, who had been granted property by Virginia, had to resurvey their property lines with the new American metes and bounds. Sometimes the new boundary lines did not coincide with earlier delineations, which triggered many lawsuits. Land speculators (and lawyers) thrived as new lands opened up.

For example, Thomas Lincoln, Abraham Lincoln's father, had purchased three hundred acres in Kentucky near Hodgen's Mill on Nolin's Creek, about sixty miles south of Louisville, in 1808. Abraham was born there on February 12, 1809. But the land was contested, and Lincoln had to move his family to another farm near Knob Creek in 1811. That land was also contested, so in 1816 Thomas and Nancy Lincoln moved with their children Abraham and Sarah across the Ohio River to Indiana Territory, where the land grants were all new and the land surveys fresh.[36]

Many of the laws in Kentucky governing the lives of enslaved people were similar to the slave laws in other Southern states, but two in particular had specific relevance to the little group of travelers from Maryland. The 1814 Importation Statute

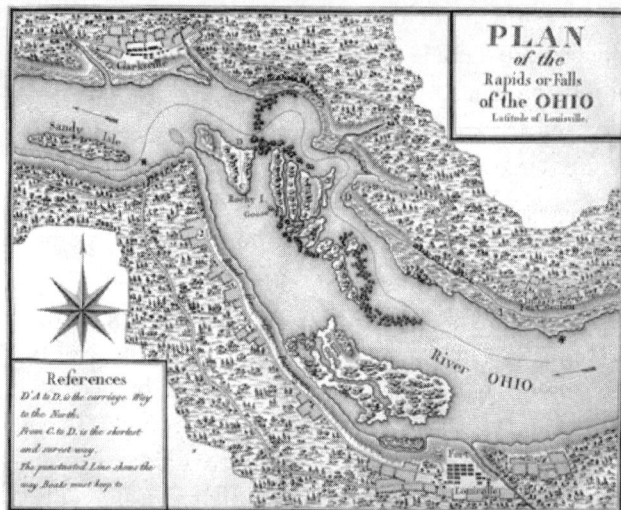

Figure 4.2. Map of the rapids of the Ohio River. Georges-Henri-Victor Callot, *A Journey in North America,* "Map of the Ohio River Rapid, 1826," Atlas, University of Pittsburgh, Darlington Digital Library.

prohibited the importation of enslaved Blacks by any migrant who did not intend to settle in Kentucky; and the 1815 Slave Trade Statute prohibited the introduction of Blacks into Kentucky for the purpose of selling them.[37] These laws may indicate that Isaac Riley might never have had any intention of moving to Kentucky as he told Josiah but instead removed his slaves to his brother's plantation in Kentucky so they could be sold after they had lived in the state long enough to be established as Amos Riley's property.[38] If the slaves traveled to Kentucky on their own, they could not be considered to have been imported by a migrant and so would still be legal even if Isaac Riley did not move to Kentucky. After living there for three years the enslaved people would have been residents and so not coming into the state for the purpose of sale. Since Amos paid taxes on these slaves while they were living on his plantation, they were considered his property in Kentucky. Isaac Riley told Josiah that he was intending to follow and establish residence in Kentucky but later said that his wife refused to go there. But he also could have been sending the slaves to Kentucky to avoid them being confiscated in Maryland to pay off his debts, as he told Josiah.

This new place was very different from where Josiah had lived in Maryland on a small farm near a busy county seat and next to a well-traveled road. Here in northern Kentucky the commerce was mainly by river. The roads were few, the terrain was hilly and rocky, the farmhouses were far apart, and the nearest town was almost ten miles away. Several additional farms had been added to Amos Riley's original one thousand acres, presenting a wide range of scattered holdings. When Josiah and his charges arrived in the spring of 1825, Amos Riley's twenty-one slaves were clearing trees, plowing, and planting on the cleared ground.[39] The main crops of this part of Kentucky at this time were corn and tobacco. The soon-to-be famous Kentucky bourbon was produced from the corn. Just to the south of the Riley property Yelverton Overly had built a house and a blacksmith shop at a crossroads that would soon become the village of Yelvington.[40] The steamboat landing named "Iceland," a mile below the ferry

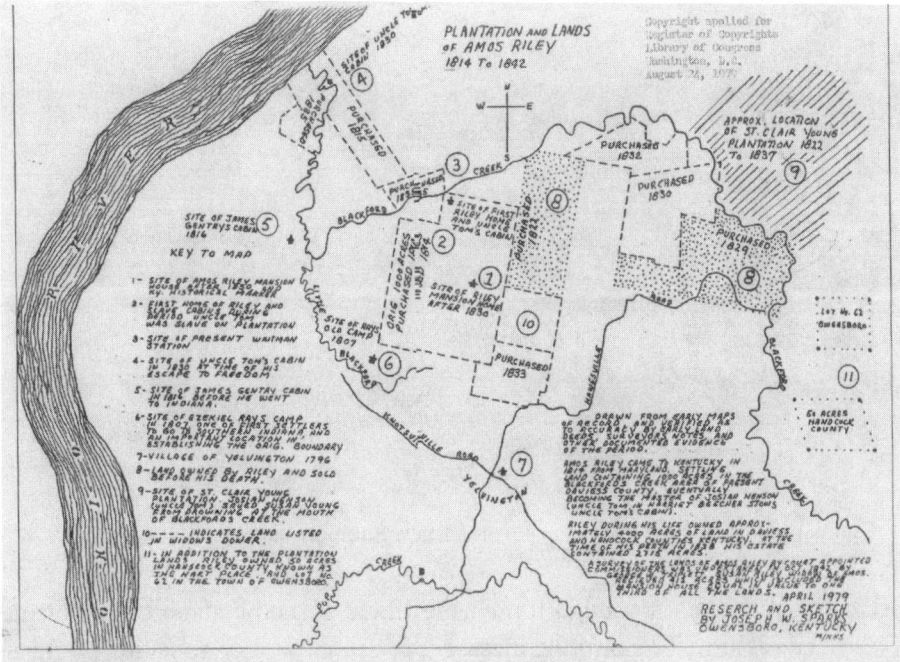

Figure 4.3. Map of Amos Riley's land holdings. Joseph W. Sparks, 1979, Kentucky Historical Society.

across the Ohio River to Rockport, Indiana, lay about five miles by road from the Riley place. Another ferry across the river, established later, lay just north of Riley's house at the mouth of Blackford Creek.[41]

Amos Riley had first moved to Jefferson County, Kentucky, around 1800, probably with his older brother, James.[42] There Amos met and married in 1803 Susannah (Susan) Phillips. By the time they moved to Daviess County, Kentucky, in 1814 they had five children. Four more were born after the move. Two of their sons, Amos Jr. and Camden, would both become prominent citizens of Owensboro, Amos Jr. a judge and Camden a lawyer elected to the Kentucky State Senate. Amos Riley was one of the wealthiest men and largest landowners in the county when he died about 1837, leaving a large amount of property to his wife and nine children (figure 4.3).[43]

In 1825 when Josiah's group arrived at Amos Riley's home, they were immediately put to work matching their abilities and training. According to Josiah, he was given general management of the farms "in consequence of the recommendation for ability and honesty which I brought with me from Maryland."[44] An original pass for "my man Si" by Amos Riley dated August 1827 can be seen in the Owensboro Museum at Yelvington that allowed him "safe and unhindered passage to and from Yellow Banks and my place to attend to the affairs of the plantation" (figure 4.4).[45] This was probably not the first pass given to Josiah, but it indicates a great privilege to be granted to an enslaved person. It meant that the owner had a steadfast trust in that person and

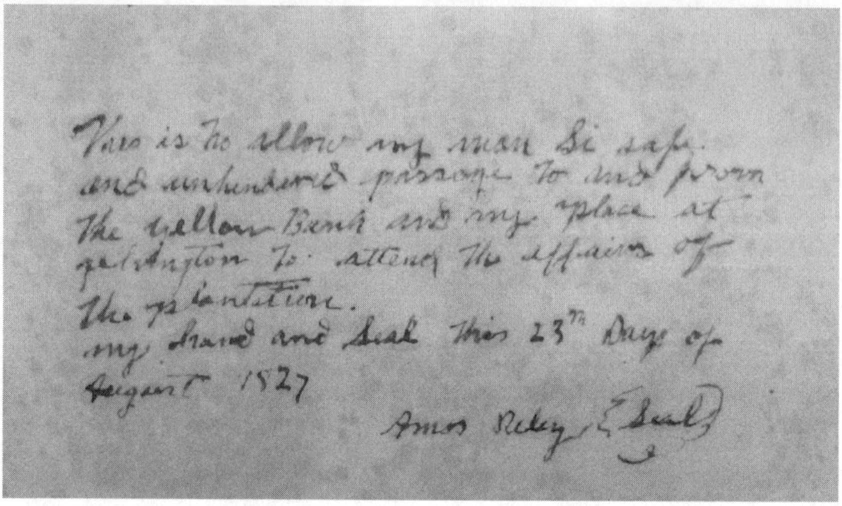

Figure 4.4. Pass for "Si" written by Amos Riley. Photo by author.

respected his intelligence enough to manage affairs of the plantation. The business may have been as simple as carrying messages or as complicated as selling produce or making purchases. Both required the trust of not only the master but also the people with whom he was conducting business.

Josiah's general pass also allowed him to attend religious camp meetings, which he said were more numerous than in Maryland. At these meetings his Christian faith was renewed and invigorated. These were probably sponsored by the Methodist Episcopal Church, which was very strong in Cincinnati and sent missionaries into the South to preach at open camp meetings in order to attract adherents and establish churches there.

The Methodist Episcopal (ME) Church was originally formed in England by John Wesley in 1739 and came to America in the 1760s. In the beginning the ME Church, like Wesley himself, was against slavery and admitted African American members, both enslaved and free, into the fold. It grew rapidly in the free states and in Maryland, where the General Conference was located in Baltimore. In 1800 the General Conference approved the ordination of "our African brethren" as deacons if they had approval from two-thirds of the male members of the congregation. According to historian of the church Rev. Lewis Marshall Hagood, "This action . . . gave the colored people to understand, that though in bondage to earthly task-masters, they were fellow-heirs of the inheritance of the saints, heirs of God, and joint heirs with Jesus Christ, the righteous."[46] The ME Church attracted many Black members, both enslaved and free, but even in the Northern churches, the African American members and ordained minsters were looked down on and segregated from the white ministers and congregations. Because of this prejudice, Rev. Richard Allen founded the African Methodist Episcopal church in Philadelphia in 1816.[47] From the early 1800s the ME

Church in America began to loosen its antislavery stance in order to attract more Southerners into its fold.

Josiah may not have been able to read or write, but he certainly could preach.[48] He carefully observed the preachers at the camp meetings and realized that certain words and phrases and manners of delivery could arouse excitement in the audience. A visiting Congregational minister from Massachusetts, Nehemiah Adams, who had attended a number of Methodist camp meeting in the South, remarked on the emotional prayers and supplications of the slaves, who seemed to be overtaken by the Spirit.[49] Just like studying those who were successful at the Georgetown and Washington markets and practicing their ways had made him into a good speaker and salesman, now the same method afforded Josiah the opportunity to become skillful at preaching. "No great amount of theological knowledge is requisite for the purpose. If it had been, it is manifest enough that preaching never could have been my vocation; but I am persuaded that, speaking from the fulness of a heart deeply impressed with its own sinfulness and imperfection, and with the mercy of God, in Christ Jesus, my humble ministrations have not been entirely useless to those who have had less opportunity than myself to reflect upon these all important subjects."[50] And so, Josiah was ordained a deacon in the ME Church and allowed to preach to the people. With this, he felt that he had found his true calling and that he was able to redeem himself by helping others discover Christian religion.[51]

But Josiah's burden of guilt was now to be increased. In the spring of 1828, just three years from the date that he had been coerced into delivering Isaac Riley's slaves to his brother in Kentucky where he would soon be living, after being told that they would surely be sold if he did not undertake the task, Josiah found that Riley was not moving to Kentucky and that the slaves he thought he had brought to safety were now to be sold, excepting himself and his family. His grief at seeing the families he knew so well separated and the people he had become so close to during their long sojourn callously auctioned off was inconsolable. The perfidy of Isaac Riley revealed to Josiah that as long as he was enslaved he would always be considered a commodity rather than a human being and that he could never trust the word of a slave owner. This brought out in him "the bitterest feeling of hatred of the system and those who sustain it."[52] Josiah thus resolved to concentrate all of his efforts to free himself and his family from these pitiless chains.

5
The Cost of Freedom

A$_\text{T THIS POINT IN HIS LIFE}$ J$_\text{OSIAH}$ H$_\text{ENSON WAS CONSTRAINED FROM ESCAPING, WHICH}$ —by his Christian convictions and his sense of honor—he thought of as stealing himself and his family from his owner.[1] He resolved to somehow earn the money to purchase his freedom and then earn more to purchase his family. An idea of how this might be done was suggested by a Methodist circuit preacher whom he met several times. This minister assured Josiah that he would provide him with a letter of introduction to another minister in Cincinnati who could arrange for him to earn money by preaching. If Josiah could only manage to acquire a pass from Amos Riley to allow him to return to Maryland, he could be free to travel across the river to the Ohio city to earn money from his preaching and then go on to Maryland to meet with Isaac Riley.[2]

Josiah never revealed the name of either pastor, but a history of Methodism in Kentucky compiled for the church identifies Samuel Julian as the circuit rider for Yellow Banks in 1828.[3] Later in 1839, Reverend Julian was living in Piqua, Ohio, just north of Dayton, which had a station on the Underground Railroad.[4] Methodist bishops began to take action against slavery as early as 1780 by advising members to set their slaves free and by 1816 forbidding slave owners from holding office in the church, although these rules were eased later as the church moved South. According to Wilbur Siebert, author of *The Underground Railroad from Slavery to Freedom* (1898), "Among the Wesleyan Methodist Connection and of the older society of the North there were a number of zealous underground operators."[5]

Josiah's description of his method of obtaining this pass is a good example of how an interplay between enslaver and enslaved worked. A slaveholder allowed only his most trusted slave to give him a shave, and Josiah was a trusted slave. One morning in mid-September 1828 after the fall harvest was in and his management of the farms was not needed for a while, Josiah broached the question while he was shaving Amos

Riley. Josiah's shrewd command of the situation demonstrates how an enslaved person can sometimes manipulate his owner. "I opened the subject one Sunday morning while shaving Mr. Amos, and adroitly managed, by bringing the shaving brush close into his mouth whenever he was disposed to interrupt me, to 'get a good say' first. Of course, I made no allusion to my plan of buying myself; but urged my request on the sole ground of a desire to see my old master." Unsuspecting of his true motive, Amos Riley told him that he had earned such a privilege and gave him a pass to travel freely between Kentucky and Maryland. Josiah embarked immediately for Cincinnati in the fall of 1828.[6]

When Josiah reached Cincinnati he was able to make contact with the Methodist preacher he had met in Kentucky, who introduced him to others and arranged for him to speak at several locations. Methodists, among others at that time, were especially moved by a preacher when they observed a "divine presence" in an oration, as if they felt the presence of the Lord in the speaker.[7] Apparently, this is the impression given by Josiah Henson. "I made my appeal with that eloquence which spontaneously breaks forth from a breast all alive and fanned into a glow by an inspiring project. Contact with those who were free themselves, and a proud sense of exultation in taking my destiny into my own hands, gave me the sacred "gift of tongues." I was pleading an issue of life and death, of heaven and hell, and such as heard me felt this in their hearts."[8] He was able in the first week of preaching in Cincinnati to raise a considerable amount of money toward his self-purchase.

Josiah then accompanied his new friend to the Ohio Annual Conference of the Methodist Episcopal Church in Chillicothe. This meeting was extremely important to the Methodist Church. Since 1821 there had been a reform movement within the church to make governing more accessible to laity. This was a threat to the hierarchical structure of the church and the power of governing bishops. The conflict within the church had come to a head at the Baltimore General Conference in fall of 1827 when a number of ministers were expelled from the church for challenging the authority of the bishops. Afterward those expelled appealed to other conferences, and the annual conference held at Chillicothe was crucial for the church in the Midwest.[9] This conflict eventually led to a split in the church. One of the suggestions of the reformers was to allow laymen to be given the right to preach for the church. Whether Henson was brought to the conference to demonstrate the ability and persuasive appeal of lay preachers is unknown, but it was a successful venture for him because after preaching there he had enough money to purchase a good suit of clothes and a horse for his long journey.

Josiah's words describing his feelings as he set out from Cincinnati for Maryland to purchase his freedom, with good prospects for achieving this end, express the heart of many oppressed by the cruel institution of slavery. He had never before set foot in a free state, nor had he been surrounded by so many people so opposed to the wretched institution of slavery.

Everywhere I met with kindness. The contrast between the respect with which I was treated and the ordinary abuse, or at best insolent familiarity, of plantation life, gratified me in the extreme, as it must any one who has within him one spark of personal dignity as a man. The sweet enjoyment of sympathy, moreover, and the hearty "God speed you, brother!" which accompanied every dollar I received, were to my long starved heart a celestial repast, and angels' food. Liberty was a glorious hope in my mind; not as an escape from toil, for I rejoiced in toil when my heart was in it, but as the avenue to a sense of self-respect, to ennobling occupation, and to association with superior minds. Still, dear as was the thought of liberty, I still clung to my determination to gain it in one way only—by purchase. The cup of my affliction was not yet full enough to lead me to disregard all terms with my master.[10]

The respect he received from people in the North began to show him, by contrast, how what he had thought was respect by Southerners was really condescension in disguise.

Josiah arrived at Isaac Riley's farm in Maryland at Christmas. Of the three-month journey from Cincinnati to Maryland, Henson only says that he "travelled leisurely from town to town, preaching as I went, and, wherever circumstances were favorable, soliciting aid in my great object. I succeeded so well, that when I arrived at Montgomery county, I was master of two hundred and seventy-five dollars, besides my horse and my clothes."[11] This account leaves much to speculation, but it is not too difficult to imagine that even though he had a pass, he must have stayed on the northern side of the Ohio River for safety. He most likely kept to the main roads connecting the larger towns, following suggestions of his Methodist and Quaker friends and sometimes being accommodated by them along the way, with one person suggesting another to contact in the direction he was traveling. These contacts would come in handy later in his life when he would be escaping to Canada and even later when leading other people to freedom.

Isaac Riley admonished Henson for taking so long, as the five hundred–mile journey by horse should have taken less than a month. Riley was surprised and disturbed to see that his slave owned a horse and was so finely dressed. Riley, wanting to impress upon Josiah that no matter how fancy he was still a slave, ordered him to sleep with the other slaves in the loft above the kitchen and took his pass away for safe keeping until he decided to send him back to Kentucky.

Josiah, however, had other intentions. He no longer saw himself as the obedient, subservient slave, bowing to his master's every command. His taste of freedom had hardened his resolve to achieve that state permanently. But he still wanted to achieve that freedom legally. In another example of cleverness, Josiah waited until Isaac Riley was out of the house and asked Riley's wife, Matilda, for the pass, as he had seen her put it into the desk after Riley had taken it from him. He told her that he wanted to visit her brother, Frank, who had become his friend when he was living with them as a boy. She gave him the pass, telling him to come right back, which he had no intention of doing.[12]

Josiah found Francis (Frank) Middleton, now a lawyer living in Washington, DC, who agreed to help Josiah. Frank met with Isaac Riley and tried to convince him that with a pass and a horse, Henson could easily escape but preferred to purchase his freedom. While waiting for Riley to make a decision, Josiah stayed with his friend in the city. While he was waiting, he thought that he might earn some donations by preaching, as he had done throughout Ohio and Pennsylvania. But he found out that the laws were different in the Southern states. When he asked the mayor of Alexandria, Virginia, permission to preach in that city, he was immediately arrested and, under the law, would have to pay a fine of $25 and receive thirty-nine lashes at the public whipping post. Josiah sent word to his benefactor, who intervened for him, but Josiah had to sell his watch to pay the fine. On leaving, he saw that a supportive crowd had gathered around the city jail, so he gave them a sermon despite the law and then hurried back to the District of Columbia.[13]

After a couple of months Riley agreed to accept the offer of purchase and set the price for Josiah at $450, which was considered a suitable price for a man of his age and ability. Of this amount, Josiah was able to supply $350 with his earned money and the sale of his horse. The remaining $100 was in a promissory note.[14] Josiah Henson's manumission was recorded in the Montgomery County Courthouse records on March 9, 1829 (figure 5.1). This record is signed by Isaac Riley and witnessed by Robert W. Middleton (uncle of Francis Middleton).[15]

Josiah was given an official document of manumission to carry on his person. This document has remained with his descendants. The following duplicates the wording in the recorded document:

State of Maryland Montgomery County. I do hereby certify that Josiah Henson, the bearer hereof, a black man, about 30 years of age, very black complexion, five feet and a half inches high, straight and well formed, both arms are stiff, occasioned by some injury in the elbow joints, has rather a broad nose, and is a tolerable likely fellow—that the said Josiah Henson is a freeman and was manumitted and set free by Isaac Riley, of the County aforesaid by Deed of Manumission duly executed and recorded in my Office on the ninth day of March, In the year of Our Lord One Thousand Eight Hundred and Twenty Nine.

   In testimony whereof I have hereunto subscribed my name and affixed the public seal of said County Court Office on the ninth day of March, In the year of Our Lord One Thousand Eight Hundred and Twenty-Nine.

   Brice Selby, Clerk of Court of Montgomery county Court[16]

Josiah now intended to return to Kentucky to be with his family. He could then earn money he needed to purchase the freedom of his wife and children by preaching

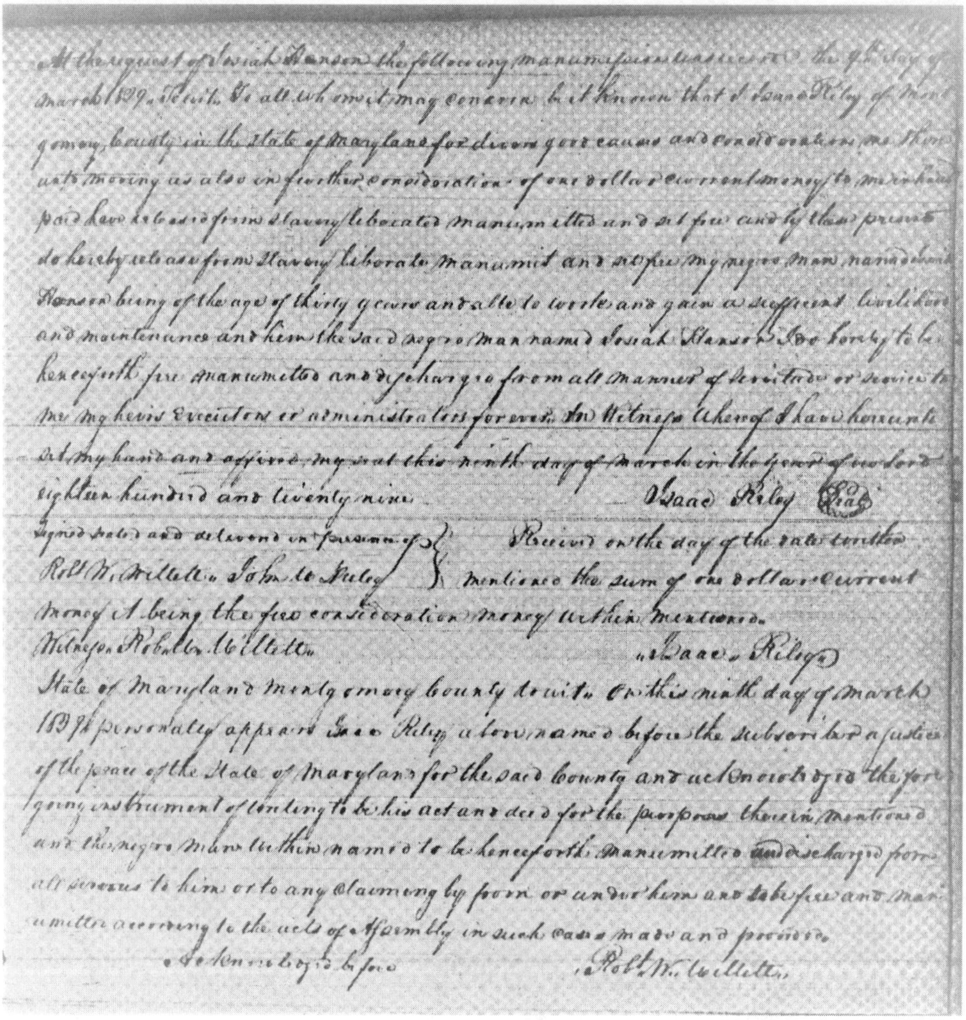
At the request of Josiah Henson the following manumission was recorded the 9th day of
March 1829. To wit. To all whom it may concern be it known that I Isaac Riley of Mont
gomery County in the State of Maryland for divers good causes and considerations me there
unto moving as also in further consideration of one dollar current money to me in hand
paid have released from slavery liberated manumitted and set free and by these presents
do hereby release from slavery liberate manumit and set free my negro man named Josiah
Henson being of the age of thirty years and able to work and gain a sufficient livelihood
and maintenance and him the said negro man named Josiah Henson I do hereby to be
henceforth free manumitted and discharged from all manner of servitude or service to
me my heirs executors or administrators forever. In Witness whereof I have hereunto
set my hand and affixed my seal this ninth day of March in the year of our Lord
eighteen hundred and twenty nine — Isaac Riley (Seal)
Signed sealed and delivered in presence of — Robt W. Willett, John W. Riley
Received on the day of the date written mentioned the sum of one dollar current
money it being the full consideration money within mentioned.
Witness Robt W. Willett — Isaac Riley
State of Maryland Montgomery County to wit. On this ninth day of March
1829 personally appeared Isaac Riley above named before the subscriber a justice
of the peace of the State of Maryland for the said County and acknowledged the fore
going instrument of writing to be his act and deed for the purposes therein mentioned
and the negro man within named to be henceforth manumitted and discharged from
all services to him or to any claiming by from or under him and to be free and man
umitted according to the acts of Assembly in such cases made and provided.
Acknowledged before — Robt W. Willett

Figure 5.1. Josiah Henson manumission. Maryland State Archives, Land Records, Montgomery County.

in Ohio. Before he left Maryland, Josiah said that Isaac Riley told him the manumission paper could be stolen from him, but if he enclosed it in an envelope addressed to Amos Riley in Kentucky and closed it with a wax seal, this made it an official document, protected by law from anyone except the addressee to open. Josiah thought that was a very kind offer from his former owner and watched as his precious freedom paper was enclosed within two envelopes and sealed with three seals.[17]

Josiah set off by foot to Wheeling on March 10, 1829. As he passed through Maryland and Virginia, he was arrested several times but was always released by the magistrate when shown his pass from Amos Riley allowing him free passage between Kentucky and Maryland.[18] Josiah boarded a boat in Wheeling, Virginia, that took him to Louisville, Kentucky. Because of the falls below Louisville, he had to wait to find another boat that would drop him off at the Iceland Landing, five miles from the Riley house. When he finally reached his cabin to reunite with Charlotte and the children it was late at night, but they all woke up to give him a warm welcome and rejoice in his freedom.

However, in the morning Josiah discovered that he was not as free in Kentucky as he thought he was in Maryland. Charlotte told him that she had heard that he needed to pay an additional $1,000 to complete the deal. Josiah was shocked and asked her to repeat what she had said and tell him how she had heard about it. She revealed to him that the information came from letters that Amos Riley had received from his brother weeks ago, which had been read to her to let her know that her husband was on his way home. Josiah now saw how he had been tricked. He could not read, but he knew his numbers, and he knew perfectly well that the promissory note he had placed his mark on was for $100. He also knew how easily that figure could be changed to $1,000 by the addition of one simple zero. He was now far from Rockville, Maryland, from the notary who had witnessed the note and from his friend Frank Middleton. Josiah had no white friends nearby who could help him. He was in an unfriendly land under the total domination of the enslavers. In despair, he knew of no way out of this situation, so he decided to bide his time, trust in God, and play the willing servant until he could contact his friends across the river.

One thing Josiah could do was to not hand over his freedom paper in the sealed envelope to Amos Riley. Instead, Josiah told his wife where to find it in his bags and advised her to hide it and not tell him where she had hidden it. When he reported to the Big House the next day and was asked by Amos for the envelope addressed to him, Josiah said that "the last time I had seen it was at Louisville, and that now it was not in my bag, and I did not know what had become of it."[19] In this way he would not be guilty of lying.

Refusing to give in to despair and trusting in God to show him a way out of his dilemma, Josiah plunged into work. One of the tasks at the end of summer was harvesting wheat by cutting and laying the cuttings in long rows by using a cradle scythe. This was an implement that Josiah could handle well because it did not require raising arms above waist level, the task being accomplished with a twisting motion of the body and arms in unison. Amos Riley's son, Amos Jr., described Josiah's proficiency in an interview many years later:

He was a large, well-built man, who would tip the beam at 175 or so, and was remarkably powerful, especially in the arms and shoulders. Many is the time I have worked with him in the wheat field. I was about 20 years old at the time and pretty stout myself, but when I tried to keep up with Si with a cradle, I invariably got left behind. By reason of his great strength he was able to use a cradle with a blade about a foot longer than mine. He would start out with this and by cutting an enormously wide swath, walk away from me in a way that I despised. "Come 'long boss"; he used to shout back at me, "'nevah do fo' you to git lef' behin'!"[20]

Josiah recounted that several times during the next year he was told by Amos that Isaac had asked for his payment in a letter to his brother, to which Josiah replied each time that he had no money. Perhaps the Rileys assumed that he could earn money by preaching as he had before, and perhaps he had, but he was not going to give it to swindlers. Even though Josiah had returned to working on the plantation, Amos Riley considered him a risk because his knowledge of travel and connections in Ohio meant that he might escape, taking his wife and children with him. Besides, he was an "uppity negro," a major offense and often a reason for selling a slave south.[21]

In the spring of 1830, about a year after his return from Maryland, Josiah was told by Amos Riley that he was to accompany his son, Amos Jr., on his first flatboat trip to New Orleans to sell products from the plantation. This trip was a common rite of passage for young men from the area, and Amos Jr. was nearing his twentieth year, the right age for the initiation.[22] This was no easy assignment. Many a young man had been lost to the treacherous waters of the Ohio and Mississippi Rivers, to thieves waiting at the ports along the way, and to the gambling dens of New Orleans. Travel through the lawless territories and to the largest international port city in the South was indeed dangerous. This is presumably why Amos was sending the trustworthy servant Josiah to protect his son. Josiah was known to be both intelligent and strong, a worthy bodyguard.

Josiah had a different view of the assignment. He had seen many enslaved people, both friends and strangers, put on boats heading downriver, never to be heard of again. He had heard many tales of the major slave markets in New Orleans and how slave dealers from all over the country gathered there to get the highest prices for their merchandise. He knew that he had been a trouble to the Rileys and that if they could not get their money from him, they would try to procure it by selling him. He also knew that as soon as he revealed his freedom paper it would be taken from him. He could take his paper and flee to the North, but he did not want to leave his wife and children. The only thing that he could do was to obey the order and pray to God for his deliverance. He did have Charlotte retrieve the manumission paper and put it into a piece of cloth that was fitted to his body and sewn securely so that it would always be with him under his clothing. This might save him if an attempt was made to put him up on the auction block.

Josiah boarded the flatboat with the young Amos Jr. and found aboard three white men—the captain and two hired boatmen—who would disembark when they reached New Orleans. The flatboat itself would be sold at the end of the journey, as these boats were designed to only float downriver and had no way to return against the strong current. Josiah relates that the cargo consisted of "beef cattle, pigs, poultry, corn, whiskey, and other articles from the farm and from some of the neighboring estates."[23] There were several ports on the Mississippi where the products could be sold, bringing a higher price in the wilderness areas than in the immense port of New Orleans, which was already overloaded with products from all over the country and the world.

A flatboat was a long, rectangular wooden boat with a flat bottom. It was guided by a large rudder attached to a long pole in the rear. On either side were detachable oars called "sweeps," thirty- to fifty-foot-long poles that were used for navigating into or away from a landing and were stored lengthwise along the hull when not in use. A covered cabin at one end or in the center provided sleeping quarters for the crew and for storing more valuable items, such as whiskey, and non-rainproof items, such as flour. Sometimes the cabin could occupy the whole length of the vessel; some even had stoves for cooking inside. Flatboats had a wide range of sizes depending on the cargo to be transported. They could be anywhere from 4 × 16 to 20 × 100 feet.[24]

The Rileys' flatboat must have been a large one because of the amount of cargo and the number of crewmen. It most likely had a cabin in the center, with the cattle in the open area at one end and the pigs in the open area on the other end and with a separate enclosure for chickens. Eggs produced along the way would be a nice supplement to the diet of the crew, usually consisting of salt pork and hard biscuits along with fish caught in the river.

An average of three thousand flatboats traveled down the Ohio and Mississippi Rivers every year between 1810 and 1820,[25] and the commerce was probably heavier by 1830, the year Josiah and company were traveling. From where they set off, the trip of about 1,300 miles usually took four to five days on the Ohio River, followed by three to four weeks on the Mississippi River.[26] Since it was June when they arrived in New Orleans,[27] they must have embarked in late April or early May. This was the usual season for boats to set off when the ice melt from upriver made rivers run high and fast. Two years earlier in April 1828, a young man of nineteen by the name of Abraham Lincoln set off in a similar flatboat with his friend Allen Gentry from Gentry's Landing in Rockport, Indiana, across the river from and almost exactly opposite the Iceland Landing in Kentucky from which the Riley flatboat launched (figures 5.2 and 5.3).[28]

Josiah did not comment much in his memoirs about the four- to five-week voyage—the perils of the waters, the sights along the way, the many overnight tie-ups at landings, or incidents that occurred—but a good idea of such a trip can be seen in the detailed description by historian Richard Campanella in *Lincoln in New Orleans: The 1828–1831 Flatboat Voyages and Their Place in History*, which is based on many first-person accounts. The voyage down the Ohio River was probably uneventful and fast. With an experienced captain they could travel at night, a usually dangerous practice, as well as by day and so may not have tied up at any landings for the 264 miles to the Mississippi River. The moon was waxing and would be full on May 8, making travel by night easier.[29] The main hazards along this stretch were islands and sandbars to navigate around and turbulence at the confluence of the Wabash River and then the Tennessee River.

Entrance into the Mississippi River was another matter. Even though the Missouri

Figure 5.2. Plaque on the monument at Lincoln's launching site, Rockport, Indiana. Photo by author.

River to the north had added volume to the Mississippi River, the Ohio River was still usually larger at the point of confluence, so when the Ohio emptied into the Mississippi, the volume of water created unique and extremely dangerous conditions that required an experienced captain and hard work by the crew. A guidebook warned the boatmen: "When the Ohio is the highest, your boat is taken half way across the Mississippi. When the latter is master, you will have to row pretty hard, to reach the [Mississippi] current, the Ohio, in such cases, being backed up for several miles. . . . [W]hirls, or swells or boils . . . are so large and strong that a boat is thrown half around it in passing over them, and sometimes shot so rapidly out of them . . . that it takes strong rowing to get underway again."[30] After entering the Mississippi the voyage would have been relatively smooth, with long hours of idle drifting. Josiah recounted that as the only Black man aboard, he was given three daily shifts instead of the one shift that the others had. He took advantage of this by learning the craftsmanship of handling a flatboat from the captain and how to manage the complexities and temperaments of the river. Josiah became so adept that he could manage the boat by himself.

This proved to be a good thing, because soon after they were on the grand Mississippi, Josiah described how the captain became blind from the glare of the sun on the water and could no longer navigate by sight. From that point on, the experienced captain depended on Josiah to describe the landmarks, the appearance of the water, obstacles ahead, and changing water and weather conditions and to then give verbal directions for navigation. Josiah had demonstrated in the past that he was a quick learner and had a good memory, but the demands of guiding a flatboat and the complexities of the river made navigating very challenging. There were many more

Figure 5.3. Monument marking Lincoln's launching site, Rockport, Indiana. Photo by author.

hazards to contend with than avoiding steamboats and sawyers (trees floating down the river or snagged on the bottom) that he referred to.[31] Every time a major river emptied into the Mississippi, swift and unpredictable eddies and currents made handling the boat difficult. Lower on the big river, man-made levees along the banks and diversion dams caused debris to pile up, creating major obstacles. In the last three hundred miles navigation around these impromptu islands demanded maneuvering the boat first to the east side and then to the west to follow the channel.[32]

Since the crew lacked an experienced captain, they had to tie up at landings overnight, which greatly slowed their progress. A watch had to be kept on board at all times when they were tied up to prevent thieves from stealing their cargo. The landings could have been one of the plantation wharfs or a larger one at a town or city. The large settlements along the Mississippi consisted of two parts: high bluffs where the well-to-do lived near their shops and offices and the riverfront landing area where produce was traded. The latter were rough and dangerous places, as they usually held bars, gambling dens, and brothels for the entertainment of the boatmen.[33]

Memphis was the first major landing downstream from the Ohio River. The crew would have taken turns going ashore to explore this enticing city after long, boring days on the river. Many years later, Amos Riley Jr. recalled that they had a layover there and that "Si, in prowling around the town, got into a trouble with police, out of which he extricated himself by giving leg bail, escaping with no further loss than that of a big white beaver hat of which he was very proud."[34]

There were many other landings along the one thousand miles of the Mississippi below the Ohio for tying up at night, which they had to do for twenty to thirty nights. The cargo on the flatboat might be sold at any of these landings so that by the time they reached New Orleans they could have little or nothing left. It was at one of these stops that Josiah ran into some of the people he had led from Maryland who had then been sold, contrary to Riley's promise. He said that "their haggard and wasted appearance told a piteous story of excessive labor and insufficient food."[35] This sight awakened in him not only a tremendous feeling of guilt for having guided them to this destiny but also a great fear that this was to be his fate as well.

Perhaps the reason that Josiah did not report in his memoirs many details of this momentous trip was that his mind was overwhelmed by "the storm of passions contending within me, and the imminent risk of the shipwreck of my soul, which was impending over me nearly the whole period of the voyage."[36] He saw no way out, and the fear of being sold and the injustice of such an act ate into his mind until it became deranged with fury, while outwardly he remained calm.

As they neared New Orleans and his impending doom, this heightened emotional state, including his rage and resentment, led to the greatest test of his Christian faith. He plotted to kill his white companions as they slept and to escape to the North. But as he raised the axe over the figure of his young enslaver in the innocence of slumber, Josiah suddenly comprehended the reality of the crime he was about to commit and that the sin of murder would hang over him for the rest of his life, even if he were able to get away with the deed. "I was about to lose the fruit of all my efforts at self-improvement, the character I had acquired, and the peace of mind which had never deserted me."[37] He decided to forgive Amos Jr., as he was only following the orders of his father, and Josiah realized that both men were part of a culture and society that had molded their characters, just as it had his own.[38]

New Orleans of 1830 was the third-largest city in the country, the largest in the South, and the largest slave-trading market as well. The busy international port was host to sailing ships of every size and cargo from faraway countries. As they approached the metropolis the river widened, and the boat traffic increased. Smoke and steam from the factories were the first thing that indicated their destination was near, and the flatboat wharf that extended almost a mile upriver from the center of the city was the next indication. The steamboat wharf was at this center, while downriver lay the moorings of seagoing ships. About three to four ships entered the harbor every day, while an average of two to three steamboats docked at the city per day.[39] As for flatboats, there could be as many as 160 tied up at one time in high season, some of them two to three deep as they neared the steamboat landing and marketplace. Near the flatboat wharf were the bars, gambling joints, and brothels as in the cities along the way, only more of them. As they tied up at the wharf, both Josiah and Amos Jr. were unaware of how much they would be amazed and fascinated by the multicultural city they were about to step into, unlike any other they had experienced.

The first difference newcomers noticed about the big city was the topography: at

New Orleans the river and wharfs were above the level of the city instead of below as they were in the upriver cities because here the river was held back by a tall levee. New Orleans was also distinguished by the variety of people from different countries speaking various languages and wearing strange clothing and by the food, an assortment of strange fruits and vegetables from other lands and the distinctive Creole cuisine.[40] Strange music coming from unfamiliar instruments drifted out of the tavern doors. Even the smells were different, some coming from the tropical plants and flowers growing in the open areas and some from the various foods being cooked. The warm air was heavy with moisture, and tangles of gray Spanish moss hung from the trees.

After flatboat owners finished selling whatever they had left and then selling the boat itself to locals for wood, they usually took a steamboat upriver and home. Some stayed on the flatboat right up until it was time to board a steamboat, and some stayed for a few days in a hotel to visit the sights and entertainments of the city. Most people stayed at least a few days. It was a rare man who could resist the enticements of exotic New Orleans.

After they docked, Josiah's fear of being sold was soon to be realized. Amos Riley Jr., after paying the boatmen, attempted to sell Josiah. As Josiah accounted in his memoir, "There was no longer any disguise about the purpose of selling me. Mr. Amos acknowledged that such were his instructions, and he set about fulfilling them. Several planters came to the boat to look at me; and I was sent off on some hasty errand, that they might see how I could run. My points were canvassed as those of a horse would have been; and doubtless some account of my human faculties was thrown into the discussion of the bargain, that my value as a domestic animal might be enhanced."[41] Deceit by slave owners and traders in the selling of their supposed property was not uncommon.[42] And as Solomon Northup discovered, papers were not required in New Orleans.[43]

All of Josiah's hopes for a better life, a life of freedom from enslavement for himself and his family, were about to be dashed. Josiah feared that the end was near. Yet, why didn't he take the opportunity, when Amos was sleeping or away from the boat, to just leave? With his manumission paper, Josiah could have slipped away into the maze of city streets or found work aboard one of the sailing vessels, of which there were always a dozen or more in port. Instead, he stayed on the boat to await his fate. Perhaps he thought he could present his freedom paper at the auction when authorities should be present or hoped he could escape later and make his way back to save his family. It is also plausible that Amos Jr. threatened Josiah with the sale of his family if he attempted to escape. This is one of the unanswered mysteries of Josiah's memoirs.

Fortunately, providence intervened. The next morning young Amos fell terribly ill and worsened as the morning progressed. He had probably contracted yellow fever, which was prevalent in New Orleans at that time.[44] Josiah related that Amos asked him to take the money and arrange passage for him on a steamboat home, so by noon Josiah had both of them aboard a steamboat for Louisville, Kentucky. He was lucky to find one leaving immediately, as steamboats heading to Louisville left New Orleans only one or two times a week. Josiah also recounted that he was able to place his young master in a room reserved for sick passengers and remained with him for the entire trip, which would have been about two weeks. Yellow fever is highly contagious, and the steamboat crew would have been happy to let Josiah stay with the patient and attend to him instead of being relegated to the lower deck area assigned to Blacks. According to Josiah, young Amos almost died and probably would have without his attendance. When they reached the home landing, on about July 10, 1830, the young man had to be taken by litter to the house, and it took him more than a month to recover.[45]

Amos Jr. himself, in an interview in 1884, spoke of his trip to New Orleans but never mentioned his illness. He also denied ever trying to sell Josiah. He claimed that his father had received a letter from Isaac Riley asking that Josiah and his family be sent back to Maryland. This might have provided the providential chance for Henson to escape with his wife and children at this time and also why there were no adver-tisements in the papers for their capture. At the beginning of the interview, Amos Jr. recounted how surprised he was to find in a newspaper article that this former slave had published a book with Amos Jr.'s name and the names of his family members in it. Of course, as a retired judge and a prominent local figure at the time of the in-terview, Amos Jr. had his own image to preserve. So, he needed to discredit Josiah in order to protect his reputation and standing in the community.[46]

After the return from New Orleans, Josiah soon realized that even though he had saved Amos Jr.'s life, the Rileys were still intent on selling him. His treatment as a piece of property and his betrayal by Isaac dissolved any contract he may have thought that he had with his owner. As Josiah expressed, "If Isaac would only have been honest enough to adhere to his own bargain, I would have adhered to mine, and paid him all I had promised. But his attempt to kidnap me again, after having pocketed three-fourths of my market value, absolved me from all obligation, in my opinion, to pay him any more, or to continue in a position which exposed me to his machinations."[47]

Since the contract had been broken by his owner, not by himself, Josiah Henson no longer felt any obligation to the man or his family. Josiah's whole life had been spent faithfully serving this family, and still they treated him like one of their prized bulls—useful for certain tasks but dangerous and expendable—and ignored his ef-forts to free himself by legal means. Josiah's next step became clear.

6

Escape

Now that Josiah Henson was determined to escape from bondage, it was necessary to make a plan. He was certain of two things: he needed to reach Canada to be safe from capture, and he was taking his family with him. He did not know how far away their destination was or how long it might take to get there. He may have spoken with others who had traveled to or from Canada, but even if he had, their means of transportation, routes, and experiences would have varied widely. Slave catchers were especially vigilant at the docks and crossings of the Ohio River, and many freedom seekers had been caught before they could make their way across.[1]

Josiah would be on his own without a pass or a guide, which took a lot of courage. But he knew he had no choice. His eyes had been opened. After his experience in New Orleans, he knew he was soon to be sold. Even though he had purchased his freedom, he knew that piece of paper had little value in Kentucky, and besides, it did not apply to his wife and children, who were kept at the plantation merely as insurance against his leaving. Isaac Riley and his brother had been manipulating him, using him for their own ends, and now that Josiah had served his purpose and was proving to be more trouble than he was worth, they intended to sell him. His only recourse was to free himself and his family from bondage by escaping. He did have some resources he could turn to. He knew people in Cincinnati who would help him. He knew how to travel. He knew the North Star and the lay of the land. As with many other freedom seekers, he had a beacon of hope in front of him and fear threatening from behind.

Although networks of people aiding freedom seekers were being set up in the Northeast by 1830, the helpers were still very fragmented in the Midwest. The term "Underground Railroad" had not even been invented, since there were no city connecting railroads in the United States until the mid-1830s.[2] Quaker Levi Coffin, one of the first people to set up networks of helpers in the Midwest from his home in Indiana and who was instrumental in establishing the Underground Railroad networks centered in Cincinnati, did not move to that city until 1847.[3] When Coffin had arrived in Newport, Indiana, from North Carolina in 1826, he found few even among fellow Quakers who were willing to aid fugitive slaves.[4] Many followers of that faith had been led to be against the abolitionist movement since it was in defiance of the law. Others, however, following their core belief that people should live their lives in accordance with their faith, helped those freedom seekers who personally asked for their aid.[5]

Most of those who had helped the freedom seekers in the past had been from African American settlements, and there was no network to aid in directing them North, only good-hearted people willing to risk arrest by giving fugitives food and rest.[6]

Josiah knew he could rely on the contacts he had made on his earlier trip to Cincinnati to give him and his family aid and direction. So, reaching Cincinnati was his first goal. On his previous trip to that city, however, he had traveled freely with a pass and so had most likely taken the quickest route: by steam packet up the Ohio River.[7] This time he would be traveling in secret and with his family, walking at night and hiding during the day, skirting towns and farms, and carrying all their supplies on their backs. Never having traveled this route before, Josiah did not know how long it would take them to reach Cincinnati; he just knew they would need to go as fast as they could to elude pursuers. Being unfamiliar with the region on this route, he had no idea whether people were friendly to freedom seekers or might turn them in.

The most difficult task of all, however, would be for Josiah to convince his wife to accompany him and to bring the children. In 1830 Charlotte had her own private cabin, which must have given her much comfort and allowed her a bit of freedom and a place to raise vegetables for the family.[8] We do not know what her tasks were, but since the cabin was distant from the master's house, she may not have had much supervision. Perhaps she did piecework that could have been collected weekly such as laundry, sewing, spinning, and weaving. Since, as indicated below, she had access to cloth, needles, and thread, at least part of her work may have been sewing. She refused to escape with Josiah at first, fearing for the safety of her children. Her anxiety may also have been accentuated by her recollection of the arduous journey from Maryland over the mountains in the winter five years earlier. That trek must have been quite an ordeal for her, traveling over miles in the winter with two small children. She finally relented after Josiah stated that he would go without her and take their three older children with him.[9]

As to the children, the two oldest, Tom and Isaac, ages about thirteen and eleven, could walk the long route, but the two youngest, Jane and Josiah, were only three and two years old and would have to be carried at least part of the way.[10] He would need to devise a way to carry them, since unlike the previous journey of the family when they had a horse and wagon, this time they would need to walk the entire distance. In order for him to be able to carry them and still have his hands free, Charlotte created a large knapsack to go over Josiah's shoulders with room for one child in the front and one in the back. She made knapsacks for herself and the boys to carry supplies. The oldest, Tom, was to carry the food.[11] Josiah told how after his day at work he would practice carrying the little ones, getting his body ready for the long haul and the children ready to adjust to their ride. Most likely Charlotte would be getting ready for the trip by sewing and mending clothes, gathering food, drying meat, and baking bread.

Since Josiah and Charlotte had been on the road before, they knew what they would need and the limits on what they could carry. These items were likely similar to essentials a person today might take on a long hike: blankets for warmth, oilcloth for rain, a small sewing kit, a small first aid kit, a hatchet for cutting wood for a fire, and a fire-starting kit. They also needed to wear all their clothing, dressing for cold weather since they were heading into fall. Josiah revealed in his second autobiography that he also had two pistols and a knife for protection.[12]

All the children were at home except their oldest son, Tom, who was at the Big House, about two miles distant, being trained to be a house servant. Josiah planned to leave with his family on a Saturday night, since the slaves were given Sunday off and they would not be missed for several days. This was the usual timing for planned escapes. The evening of the escape, Josiah reported on his work to Amos Riley and asked that Tom be allowed to come home so that his mother could mend his clothes. As he said good night to his master and left with his son, Josiah was secretly delighted, knowing that this would be not only the last "good night" but also the last time he would see Riley or ever call him master again.[13]

Josiah had talked a friend, a fellow in bondage, into rowing them across the Ohio River, which was about 2,500 feet across above the confluence of Blackford's Creek, their probable departure point. This place would become a ferry landing a few years later. Josiah stated that it was about the middle of September and a moonless night.[14] That would make it about September 17 or 18, 1830.[15] The unnamed boatman stopped in the middle of the river to express his fear that if Josiah were captured and brought back his name might be revealed. After Josiah assured him that he would never tell anyone who had helped them escape, he continued to row them to the opposite shore. He was apparently inspired by their escape, as Josiah said. "He, too, has since followed in my steps; and many a time in a land of freedom have we talked over that dark night on the river."[16] Similarly, another enslaved boatman, Arnold Gragston, who rowed hundreds of people across the Ohio River to Underground Railroad station master John Rankin in Ripley, Ohio, before escaping to freedom himself, recalled, "No, I never got anything from a single one of the people I carried over the river to freedom. I didn't want anything; after I had made a few trips I got to like it, and even though I could have been free any night myself, I figgered I wasn't gettin' along so bad so I would stay on Mr. Tabb's place and help the others get free. I did it for four years."[17]

As the family stood on the bank of the river and heard the slaps of the oars on the water fade into silence, they realized just how alone they were and how long and treacherous was the way before them. Charlotte could not stop trembling with the fear of being discovered.[18] But they had to move fast to put as much distance as they could between themselves and the Riley plantation. The pace soon warmed them, and the rising sun before them gave hope for a new life.

The population along the river at this time was mainly centered in the port towns. Upland from the river, much of the land was still forested. This would have afforded them many places where they could hide from sight to rest during the day. Since Josiah reported that they traveled on the roads, this would have meant the high roads rather than the low road along the river, so they would avoid the larger port towns and having to cross the larger waterways feeding into the river. It was also shorter than the river road, which meandered along the shoreline.

There were a few villages along these high roads at the time of their travel. These were Portersville, Paoli, Salem, New Lexington, and Madison. Paoli was a Quaker settlement with an African American neighborhood called Lick Creek composed of freed slaves the Quakers had brought with them from North Carolina. The people of Lick Creek were reputed to help escaping slaves, but whether Josiah knew this or made contact with them he did not report in his memoir.[19]

Josiah described how they ran out of food two days before they reached Cincinnati, so he had to risk going from door to door in the daytime asking for food. Rebuffed at first, he finally found a kindly farmer's wife who gave him enough food to last the rest of the journey and refused his money.[20] The high road came nearer the Ohio River as it got closer to Cincinnati, so this incident would have been in the vicinity of Madison, Indiana, a large port town. Joshua told how the venison given to them was so salty they became parched with thirst; Josiah had to go into the woods to search for a stream and then had to use his shoe to hold the water to bring to his family, not having brought a container with him.

When the family reached the larger town of Lawrenceburg they were faced with having to cross a major waterway, the Miami River. The only way to cross this wide river was by ferry or skiff.[21] Josiah had some money with him, but paying fare openly to a ferryman would have been a big risk. Perhaps he hired someone upriver to row them across. In the 1840s and 1850s Lawrenceburg was to become a center of Underground Railroad activity, and it was here in 1837 at a Presbyterian church that abolitionist Henry Ward Beecher, Harriet Beecher Stowe's younger brother, undertook his first ministerial assignment.[22] But Josiah did not recount knowing anyone who helped him here in 1830.

Once across this last barrier it was only twenty-five miles to Cincinnati, where, as Josiah said, he "felt comparatively at home."[23] It had taken them two weeks to travel a distance of about two hundred miles, so they averaged about fourteen miles a night.[24] Josiah left his wife and children hidden for safety on the outskirts of the city so he could hasten to the city to locate his friends and make sure they were willing and able to help them.

Cincinnati was a large city in 1830 (figure 6.1). It had grown from about 1,000 residents in 1803 to about 10,000 in 1820, and had doubled to more than 20,000 by 1829. A major port on the Ohio River with a variety of manufacturing, it was known as the Queen City of the West.[25] The people who had befriended Josiah in 1828 were white Methodist ministers, but he also could have been in contact with some who

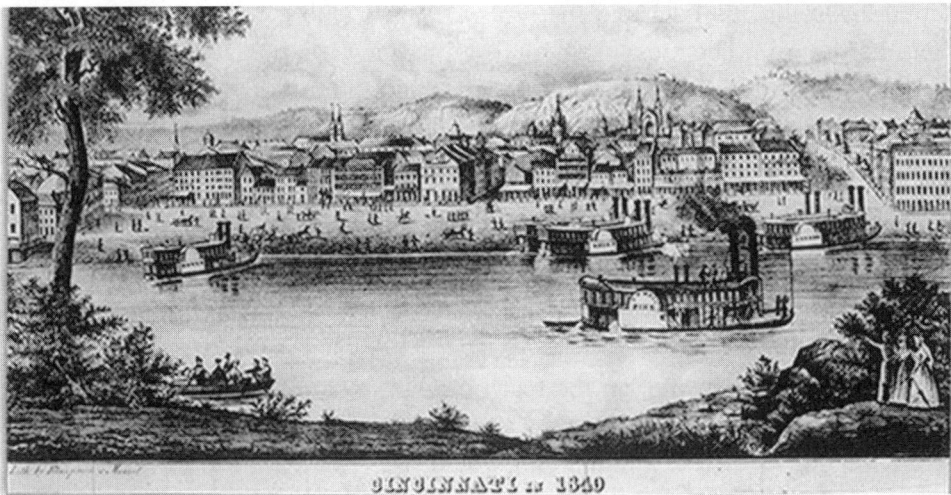

Figure 6.1. Cincinnati waterfront in 1840, from Newfoundland Bitters advertisement in the *Times-Picayune* (New Orleans), April 4, 1869. Peachtree Bottle Company, "I wish someone would find me a Newfoundland Bitters," posted on November 19, 2014, by Ferdinand Meyer V.

were African Americans there, since he previously had referred to being "in contact with those who were free themselves."[26] Because it was a destination for many Blacks from the South, both free and freedom seekers, the Black population of Cincinnati had grown to 2,258 by 1829, making up 10 percent of the population.[27] However, in that year there were attempts by many whites to drive the Blacks out of the city by enforcing the so-called Black Laws of 1804–1807. When this did not work, they changed tactics to intimidation, physical attacks, and finally court action to make Blacks leave the city. Because there was no choice after the court action, local Quakers, other local churches, and national abolition groups raised funds to help with the immigration of the Black residents to the new town of Wilberforce in Canada in August 1829. As many as half of the Black residents of Cincinnati were removed.[28] If Josiah's contacts were African American, he would have been lucky to find them among the remaining residents a year later.

The Black residents who stayed mainly belonged to one of two churches in the city: the Methodist Episcopal Church, a branch of the white church of the same name in which Josiah had contacts, and the African Methodist Episcopal (AME) Church, a separate church from the Methodist Episcopal, formed by Rev. Richard Allen in 1816 in Philadelphia.[29] Both of these churches were very active in Cincinnati and still remain today, the latter as the Allen Temple AME Church.

It did not matter if their rescuers were white or Black, Josiah, Charlotte, and the children were glad to have some good food, a bed, and rest before starting on the next segment of their journey.[30] They stayed with their friends for several days before they were refreshed enough to set off again on their flight to freedom.

The helpers took them about thirty miles from the city in a wagon, giving them supplies and directions to find the old abandoned Hull's Road, which would take them northward.[31] The most likely route, aiming toward the town of Kenton where they were to enter Hull's Road, would have been north-northeast on the current Route 42. This would place them at the town of Lebanon, a place that was not unfamiliar with the passage of fugitive slaves. As reported to Professor Wilbur Siebert, "Mr. R. C. Corwin, of Lebanon, writes: 'My first recollection of the business dates back to about 1820, when I remember seeing fugitives at my father's house, though I dare say it had been going on long before that time. From that time until 1840 there was a gradual increase of the business.'"[32] Here Josiah and his family most likely received supplies and instruction on the route to follow.

From Lebanon, walking on the road as before, according to Josiah, they would have continued along today's Route 42 to Xenia, passing a gristmill and a sawmill where the future town of Mount Holly would rise. Changing to a directly northern route, they then would have traveled on the current Route 68, passing the growing town of Springfield and the small towns of Urbana, West Liberty, and Bellefontaine before reaching the Scioto River and the beginning of Hull's Road, having traveled 105 miles by foot. This would have taken the family eight to ten days.

Hull's Road was formed in the spring of 1812 during the War of 1812. Brig. Gen. William Hull had forged the road through the wilderness to Detroit to attack the British.[33] Axmen felled the trees, and the road was made wide enough for artillery and supply wagons to use. There were camps established about twenty-five miles apart, fortified against Indian attacks.[34] Fort McArthur was built by General Hull's forces on the north side of the Scioto River, and this is where Josiah and his family entered the trail.[35] The modern town of Kenton now lies next to the site of Fort McArthur, the starting point of Hull's Road, now called Hull's Trace or Hull's Trail (figure 6.2).[36]

When the Hensons walked the trail it had been abandoned for eighteen years, and no settlements had been built along this section except the small town of Findley, laid out in 1821 on the site of Hull's Fort Findley, twenty-eight miles north of Fort McArthur. It was indeed wilderness, and the forest had nearly engulfed the trail in those years, reclaiming the scar created by the necessities of war. Unused with few inhabitants nearby, it would seem to be perfect for a hidden escape route. As it turned out, however, it made their journey more difficult and slowed them down, having to climb over fallen trees and make their way through thick brush. In addition, Josiah, unaware that it was an abandoned trail through forests, had not brought enough food for his family.[37] Having lived on farms all his life, he was inexperienced with living off what nature provided. It was a very scary place, with nothing to meet the eye but more trees and not any sign of human habitation. On one night they spent in the forest Josiah thought he heard the howling of wolves, which added to their terror.[38] At one point Charlotte collapsed from fatigue and hunger but was revived by Josiah with a little bit of meat he had saved.

With many local trails crossing the overgrown army-forged road, it was inevitable they would stray off course. According to Henson's recollections, they did not see

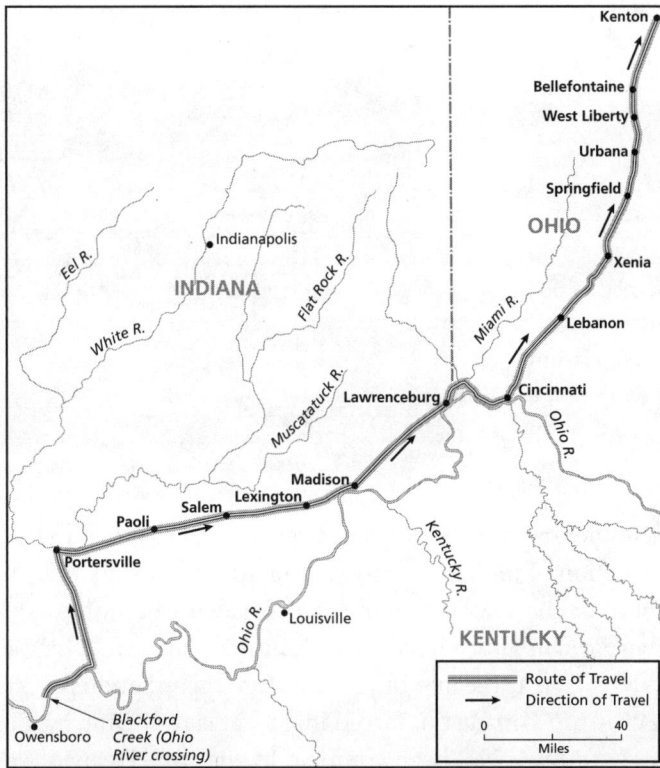

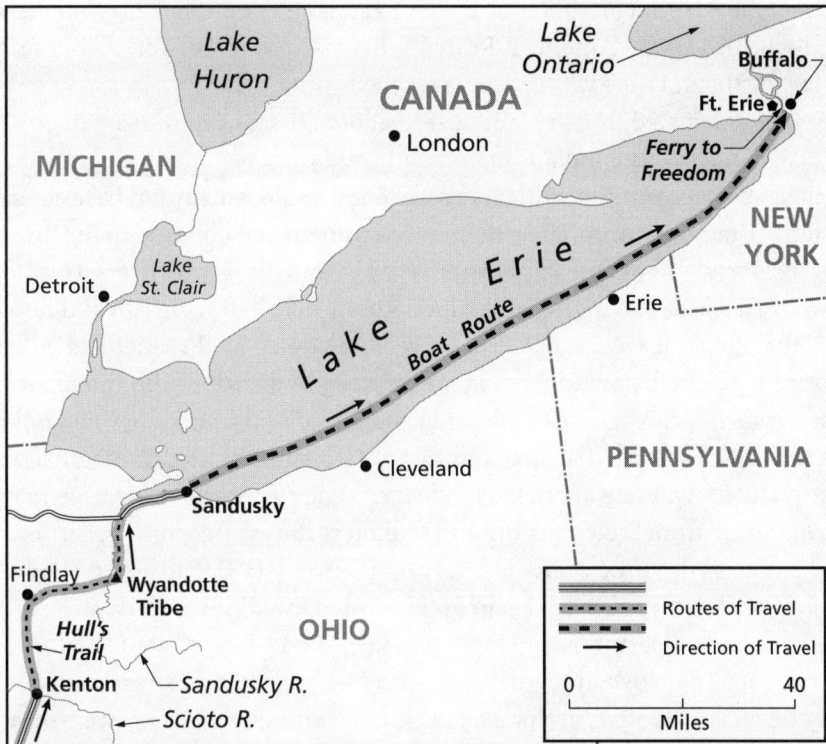

Figure 6.2. Map of the route Josiah Henson and his family took in their escape from enslavement.

Figure 6.3. Hull's Trail Historic Marker #12-23. Erected by Country Connection Club and Ohio Historical Society Located near Dunkirk, Ohio, Hardin County, at the intersection of Ohio Route 701 and County Rd. 135. Photo by author.

HISTORIC MARKER

HULL'S TRAIL

Hull's Trail was a rough passageway through Ohio to the Canadian border, used by General William Hull's army during the War of 1812 on its way to attack the English at Detroit. Woodsmen cleared the trail to permit the Ohio Army Militia with its artillery and baggage to travel through the unbroken wilderness. The route through Hardin County has been marked by stone columns from the old county courthouse.

COUNTRY CONNECTION CLUB
AND
1994   THE OHIO HISTORICAL SOCIETY   12-33

anyone on or near the trail until happening upon a small group of Indigenous people. Because of the location of the Indian reservation, this means that they must have left the trail just south of the town of Findley and headed in a northeasterly direction. Traveling the two days on Hull's Road as he indicated, this would have brought them near a Wyandotte village at the site of present-day Upper Sandusky. The Wyandotte Indians, originally from Canada but forced into what is now Ohio by the Indian Wars in the seventeenth century, had been confined by the 1817 Treaty of Fort Miegs to a reservation of twelve square miles at Upper Sandusky, Ohio. They had fought on the side of the British in the American Revolutionary War and the War of 1812 and continued to be a threat to the white settlers on their former land.[39]

When the exhausted, hungry, and lost freedom seekers ran into a party of Wyandottes, Josiah said that the Indians ran off with loud whoops. They were probably startled by the sudden encounter with strangers. They would usually not have considered Josiah and his family a threat since there was a woman and children in the group and they were Black, so they came back to help the lost and hungry travelers. Overcoming their own fears, never having contact with native people before, Josiah and his family followed them to their village, where they were welcomed by the chief and given food and a place to sleep for the night. The description by Josiah of the Indians coming up shyly to touch the skin of the children leads one to believe that they had not much contact with Black people. He also said that they communicated through signs, not being acquainted with one another's language.[40] The members of the tribe may have been made aware from their scouting and trading parties of freedom seekers escaping enslavement passing through the territory on their way to Canada, so the tribe most likely thought of them as comrades in opposition to the white settlers.

The Wyandotte reservation in Upper Sandusky had been reduced to such a small area that it could not sustain the tribe, so they had to sometimes reach outside their arbitrary invisible boundary to forage and hunt. Consequently, they were very careful not to have contact with any people from the outside world, which made them

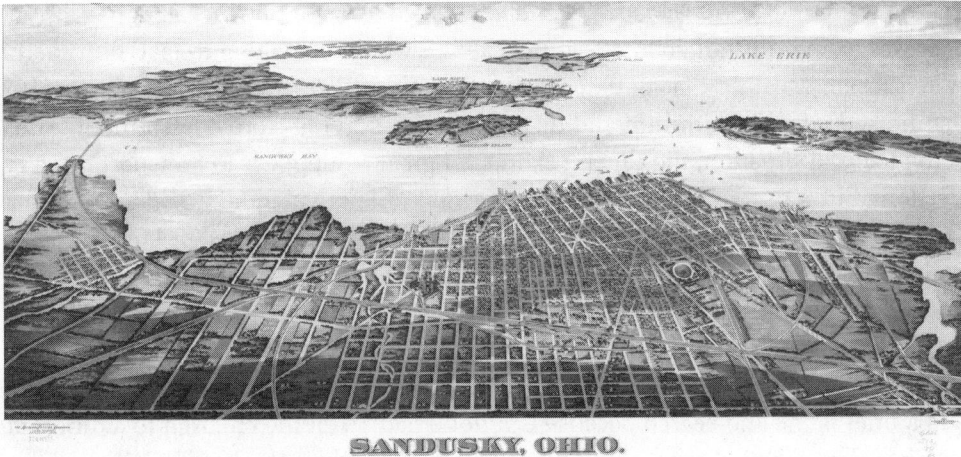

Figure 6.4. Bird's-eye map of Sandusky, Ohio, ca. 1898, by the Alvord-Peters Company. Wikimedia Commons, https://commons.wikimedia.org/w/index.php?curid=17030089.

extremely isolated. These last Native Americans in Ohio were removed to Oklahoma in 1843, leaving behind only the names of some waterways and landmarks.

The next morning the family was directed by their Wyandotte hosts to the port of Sandusky on Lake Erie, where they might find transport to Canada. Some of the tribe traveled with them to the turn-off from the trail onto the road leading to Sandusky. After fording the Sandusky River that ran across the road, wide and shallow at that point, the Henson family spent one last night in the woods before coming upon the treeless plain southwest of the town. When they could see the buildings of the town, Josiah told his family to hide in the bushes while he went down to see if he could find someone to help them get across the lake to Canada.

The little bay at the south end of Lake Erie provided a good place for harboring boats of all sizes, protected from the sometimes wild weather of the lake. It had been a trading place for the Indians, the French traders, and the English. Americans took over the site after the War of 1812 and quickly built a town that was incorporated by the state of Ohio in 1824. The name "Sandusky" is derived from the Wyandotte word *saundustee*, meaning "water."[41] The bustling city of Sandusky became busier after the Erie Canal was completed from Albany to Buffalo, New York, in 1825, with many cargo and passenger ships sailing back and forth between the two ports (figure 6.4).

As Josiah approached the western edge of town, he saw a schooner being loaded with sacks of grain. Soon he was called to come and help load the boat, which had to be ready to sail as soon as possible to catch the prevailing wind. The captain, a Scotsman, offered to pay him good money for his labor but, when he saw that Josiah was crippled, doubted whether he could do the job. After Josiah flung a sack of corn over his back and demonstrated that he could work as well as any man there, the captain hired him.[42]

In conversation with the African American laboring next to him, Josiah related that he wanted to go to Canada. The fellow, called "Doctor" by the captain, said the boat was sailing to Buffalo and that the captain would be willing to take him there. When Josiah was told that Buffalo was just across a river from Canada, he revealed that he had a family with him and that they were escaping from enslavement. After being told the situation, the captain expressed great willingness to transport them to freedom, but for safety they would have to wait until dark, and he would then send a skiff out to pick them up on the east side of town.[43] Later a hotbed of Underground Railroad activity, Sandusky in 1830 was a dangerous place, with many slave catchers on the lookout for fugitives on their way to Canada.[44]

The captain, sacrificing his schedule, laid anchor near shore and sent out the skiff. Some of the boatmen accompanied Josiah to bring back his wife and children. There was a brief panic and search because Charlotte had taken the children to a different location after nightfall for a better hiding place and, when she heard Josiah calling, was afraid it was a trap because of the men with him. But they were all aboard the schooner in good time and reached Buffalo the next evening.

Because of its location on a narrow section of the Niagara River, with Canada lying on the other side, Buffalo was a destination for many freedom seekers even before the Underground Railroad had a station there.[45] Today there is a historic marker in Broderick Park on the waterfront marking the "Underground Railroad River Crossing." This is where the ferry going across the river was located at Black Rock port. The next day, October 28, 1830, they would arrive at their destination after a harrowing forty days on the road to freedom.[46]

After spending the night aboard the vessel, the freedom-seeking family was directed to a ferryman named Green to take them across the Niagara River to Canada. Josiah recalled in 1849 that "the friendly captain, whose name I have gratefully remembered as Captain Burnham, put us on board the ferry-boat to Waterloo, paid the passage money, and gave me a dollar at parting. He was a Scotchman, and had done enough to win my enduring gratitude, to prove himself a kind and generous man, and to give me a pleasant association with his dialect and his country."[47]

In his first autobiography, Josiah remembered the captain's name as Burnham but omitted that name in later autobiographies. Later in life Josiah said that he could not remember the name but was sure that he was a Scotsman. There is no Burnham in Don J. Wood's inventory of shipping personnel in Sandusky, but there is a George D. Bannan, a name common on the Isle of Man, just outside of Scotland.[48] According to Josiah in his 1858 autobiography, the captain said, "You will be a good fellow, won't you?" to which Josiah answered, "Yes, I'll use my freedom well. I'll give my soul to God."[49] This pledge Josiah would keep.

7
Freedom in Canada

Once they set foot in Canada, Josiah Henson and his family were transformed from fugitives to refugees. Freedom was sweet, and Josiah, as many before and after him, kissed the earth of the free land. Josiah was no longer subject to a white man's bidding and no longer living in fear of the lash and the auction block and was at liberty to go wherever he wanted, whenever he wanted, and pursue his own goals. On the other hand, he now needed to provide food, shelter, and clothing for himself and his family. Being very resourceful and multitalented, Josiah had confidence that he could do this, but the challenges would be many, as Canada was a new country with a climate, a culture, a society, and laws different from his previous home (figure 7.1).

Josiah, along with the others fleeing from bondage in the United States, thought of British North America, now known as Canada, as the promised land of freedom, but even though it had been a thing of the past for a generation, slavery had a long history and many residual effects in this land.[1] Slavery had come to the northern part of North America (Canada) a little later than it did in the southern part and took a different form and trajectory. The first European conquerors in the territory we now know as Canada came from France in the early 1600s. Some of the French settlers had enslaved Native Americans, called "panis," but these were few.[2] The first influx of slaves from Africa into the north country did not occur until the mid-1700s.[3] The French usually used slaves only as domestic servants, valued Negroes above panis, were opposed to harsh punishment, rarely separated families, and insisted that they all be baptized in the Catholic Church. When the English took over the land in 1763, they brought their own stricter British law that changed the relationships between slave owners and slaves, but this did not have a great overall effect on the lives of enslaved people, since the customs of the French-style treatment of slaves was entrenched. The new government divided the mainland country into Upper Canada (now Ontario) for the English-speaking populace and Lower Canada (now mainly Quebec) for the

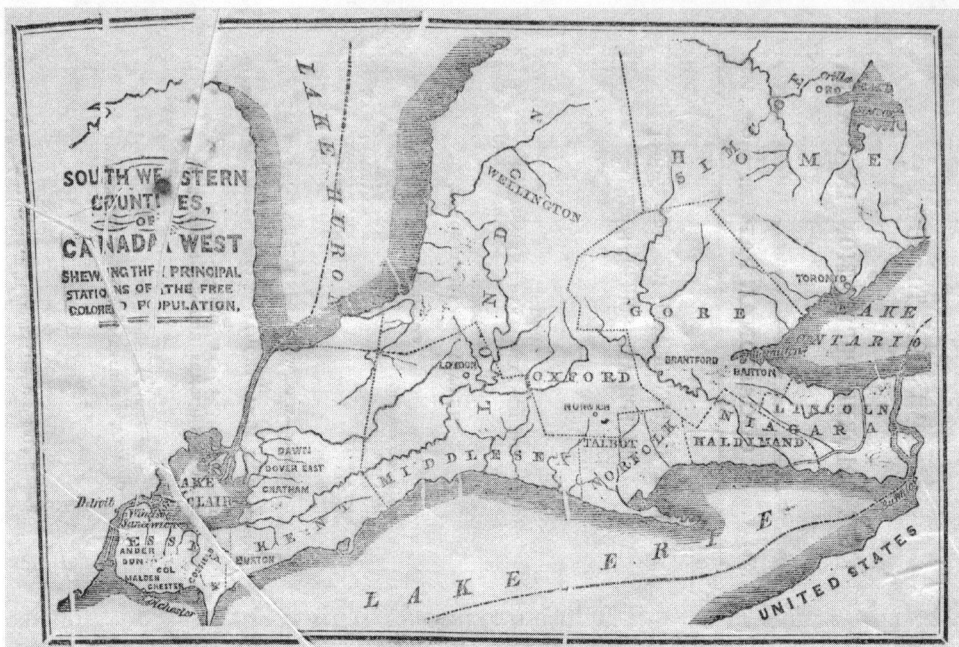

Figure 7.1. *Map of Southwestern Counties of Canada West showing the Principal Stations of the Free Colored Population.* Archives of Canada, Pamphlet 1855 #41.

French speakers.[4] The population of both whites and Blacks was greatly increased in the 1770s by British Loyalists fleeing from the American Revolution, bringing their slaves with them.

Slavery in Canada was different than in the Southern United States, not so much because the French and British were kinder but because the climate and the land were not favorable for large agricultural enterprises. The new white settlers soon found that keeping even a moderate number of slaves was not cost-effective even though, in spite of dire warnings, the people of African descent did not "die like flies" in the cold climate. As the number of slaves increased, what to do with the excess and costly human property became a big problem. The enslaved people resisted being sent to Africa, as they did not see that continent as their home after generations in North America. Some were shipped to the Deep South of the United States for sale, but more were apprenticed in a trade and then rented out or simply manumitted. When the number of free Blacks rose above the number of those enslaved, the color of one's skin no longer marked a person as enslaved.[5]

Slavery had essentially ended in Upper Canada in 1793 when, spurred by Lieutenant Governor John Graves Simcoe, a bill was passed by both houses of the Upper Canada legislature to ban the importation of slaves and to free, at age twenty-five, all children of current slaves born after the bill was passed and to declare any children of these children to be free. This effectively ended slavery in the province by the 1820s.[6] News of this spread quickly throughout the slave states of the United States, making Canada a mecca for freedom seekers. Nevertheless, Southern American slaveholders continued, usually unsuccessfully, to pursue their human property into Canada until they were finally thwarted in 1819 by the ruling of Upper Canada attorney general John Beverley Robinson that once the formerly enslaved people reached Canada, they were free. This was backed later by British chargé d'affaires Gibbs Antrobus who, in answer to a letter from US secretary of state John Quincy Adams, replied, "The Negroes have by their own residence in Canada, become free . . . and should [there be] any attempt to infringe upon this right of freedom, these Negroes would have it in their power to compel the interference of the courts of law for their protection."[7]

To conclude the matter, Great Britain abolished slavery in all its territories by an act of Parliament on August 28, 1833, to take effect on August 1, 1834. Even though they were not usually accepted as equals and were segregated in most places where they lived, free Blacks in Canada had full rights of citizenship, including the vote, and could make a living and raise their children as they pleased.[8]

Previous to Josiah and his family, many others had already sought refuge in Canada, finding the Northern states in the United States not safe enough from conniving and persistent slave catchers. And many more followed. Between 1830 and 1860 an estimated twenty thousand Blacks from the United States found new homes in Canada, with the bulk arriving after the passage of the 1850 Fugitive Slave Act in the United States.[9] The first refugees were usually destitute and, having no funds to travel farther, settled near the borders where they had entered: Fort Erie and St. Catharines in the east, across from Buffalo; and Windsor, Amherstburg, and Colchester in the west, across from Detroit.

Josiah was no different and, being eager to begin his new life as a free man, immediately began searching for work near their landing at Fort Erie after first finding lodging for Charlotte and the children. After asking several people in the town, he was directed to Mr. Hibbard, who had a large farm six or seven miles away with several tenancies on it.[10] This farm was most likely somewhere between Fort Erie and St. Catharines, as at that time many farms occupied the fertile land of the twenty-five miles that separated the two port towns. Mr. Hibbard hired Josiah and allowed him the use of a vacant tenant house on the farm. Josiah first had to chase out the hogs occupying the first floor and clean it thoroughly before bringing his wife and children from their lodging to their new home. Charlotte was happy to have a frame house with a wood floor rather than the dirt floor of the log cabins they had occupied before. Josiah brought in straw for their bedding, shored up by logs into the corners, which made a nice three-foot-deep mattress.[11]

Charlotte and the children, worn down by their long journey and not used to the colder climate or perhaps from the residue of the hogs, all became very ill. Josiah found food and fuel in abundance on the farm, and his family was able to survive their first winter in Canada. Charlotte and Mrs. Hibbard became friends. This made Charlotte feel welcomed and helped to heal her spirit. Josiah rented their house and small plot of land by sharing his crop with the owner of the farm and also worked for wages. At the end of three years Josiah owned some pigs, a cow, and a horse.[12]

During this time the Henson family attended a nearby church. This may have been the Bethel Chapel, an African Methodist Episcopal (AME) church (later Salem Chapel, British Methodist Episcopal) in St. Catharines (figure 7.2). Founded in 1820 by African Americans escaping enslavement in the Southern states, this church was a meeting place for refugees from slavery and a hub of Underground Railroad activity. It was the church attended by Harriet Tubman when she lived in St. Catharines from 1851 to 1858.[13] Josiah happened to run into an old friend from Maryland there who asked him why, with his talents in preaching the word of God, he was not preaching here.[14] Since this church was not officially received into the AME Conference until 1837, it had no regular minister, only traveling circuit preachers, as did most churches in the sparsely populated area. After his friend spread the word about Josiah's talent in the field, Josiah was often called on to preach not just to Blacks but also to whites. Even though he could not read and had no seminary training, he always felt that preaching was his calling. "Religion is not so much knowledge, as wisdom," Josiah wrote, "and observation upon what passes without, and reflection upon what passes within a man's heart, will give him a larger growth in grace than is imagined by the devoted adherents of creeds, or the confident followers of Christ, who call him Lord, Lord, but do not the things which he says."[15]

Another benefit of living free in Canada was that Josiah's children could have an education. His employer, Mr. Hibbard, paid for Tom and Isaac to attend the local school.[16] Tom became quite a proficient reader, and Josiah called on him to read him sections of the Bible, especially on a Sunday morning, so that he could memorize a verse for his sermon. One Sunday Tom was instructed to open the Bible "anywhere" and read what appeared in order to give his father material and inspiration for the sermon he was to give in the church that day. The Bible opened on King David's Psalm 103: "Bless the Lord, O my soul." This twenty-two-verse psalm is one of the best known of the psalms and is a regular part of Jewish and Christian liturgies. Josiah was so moved that he was brought to tears as his son read, recalling all of the "dangers and afflictions from which the Lord had delivered" him throughout his life. As Josiah said, "the words 'Bless the Lord, O my soul,' with which the Psalm begins and ends, were all I needed, or could use, to express the fulness of my thankful heart."[17]

Seeing how much the words affected his father, Tom asked him to tell him more about King David. Josiah was forced to admit to his son that he did not know because he could not read. He explained to his son that as a slave, he had not been allowed to learn to read, and now he was too old and had no time to spare from his work or money to pay a tutor. Tom then offered to instruct his father at night after all the work was done. This offer, kind as it was, created a dilemma in Josiah's mind. To be taught by his son was at the same time a challenge to his authority and a wound to his self-esteem. But to know how to read was a goal that he had wished for since his childhood. At an early age he had been beaten by his enslaver for having a spelling book in his possession.[18]

Figure 7.2. Salem Church, St. Catharines, Ontario, Canada. Photo by Renée Ater, "NY State Network to Freedom: Harriet Tubman in St. Catharines, Ontario," October 31, 2019, https://www.reneeater.com /on-monuments-blog/2019/10/31/ny-state-network-to-freedom-harriet -tubman-in-st-catharines-ontario.

Rather than answer Tom immediately, Josiah went into the woods to pray for an answer to his dilemma. So intense was the turmoil in his mind that he missed both his appointment to give a sermon at church and also missed his dinner.[19] How could he face his growing congregation if they knew that he could not read and was taking lessons from his own son? But if he knew how to read, he could see the word of God in the holy book himself. He could gain much knowledge and give even better sermons. He would have more respect from his congregation and his fellow ministers. In the end, he decided to go ahead with the plan suggested by his son.

The path to literacy turned out to be more difficult than either of them had anticipated. They could not afford an oil lamp or candles, so they had to read by the light of a burning pine knot. Tom, being a young lad, was impatient with his father, and Josiah, even though he pledged himself to the task, was resentful of being directed and scolded for his mistakes by a twelve-year-old. Eventually Josiah was able to read, as he reported, "a little."[20] However, he never mentioned ever learning how to write. Although evidence shows that he could sign his name, no other certified samples of his writing have been found.[21]

This new knowledge and ability that Josiah gained not only opened a new world to him but also made him think about the poor people still in bondage and not allowed the opportunity for this kind of enlightenment. He wished that he could do something to help them.[22] This aspiration was put to the test when he was personally asked to travel back to Kentucky to bring an enslaved family to freedom in Canada.

The request was made by James Lightfoot after hearing Josiah preach at a large meeting at Fort Erie, entreating the congregation to fulfill their obligation to help others to find freedom now that they, with the help of God, had achieved it.[23] Unless it was an outdoor gathering, this sermon was probably delivered at St. Paul's Anglican Church, built in 1824 and the only church in Fort Erie at the time.[24]

James Lightfoot was so moved by Henson's sermon that he was afflicted with guilt at leaving his family behind in bondage while he was enjoying a good life in freedom. During his five years in Canada, he had acquired some property and was fairly well-to-do and so was able to finance Josiah's journey.[25] Josiah agreed to the task and left in 1832 after the fall harvest was in and his family was well stocked for the winter, since he did not know when he would return.[26] James Lightfoot's family lived near Maysville, Kentucky, 440 miles from Fort Erie. Josiah was traveling by foot, so it would have taken two to three weeks to arrive at his destination.[27] Unlike his first journey to Canada, he could now travel faster without his family on the reverse trip. When he reached the Lightfoot family in Kentucky, he showed them a token given to him by James Lightfoot so they would know that he was the emissary of their brother and son. However, Henson's arrival was so sudden and his proposal to guide them to freedom such a challenging idea that they were hesitant about escaping, even though the light of freedom was beckoning. Lightfoot's parents felt that they were too frail to attempt such a journey, and his three sisters all had small children. His four brothers were more interested but needed more time to prepare. They agreed that Josiah should return in a year when they could be ready to travel.[28]

But Josiah's journey back into slave country would not be wasted. An advantage of this trip, just two years after his own escape to freedom, was that the underground network of people helping freedom seekers was now being established. People who had helped him before gave him the names of others, and these new people then gave him directions to other people in the network. Josiah found through his new contacts that there was a group of people about fifty miles south of Maysville in Bourbon County, Kentucky, waiting for someone to guide them to Canada. Walking at night, he reached the meeting place and reported that he found there were about thirty people who had gathered there from various states. After spending a week making plans and preparations, they left on a Saturday night.[29]

A group of thirty dark-skinned people would be difficult to hide even when traveling at night, so either Josiah pretended to be their slave driver or there were actually fewer people. The route Josiah described taking with the fugitives was different from the one he had first traversed with his family. He must have had help moving them through the territory and finding food enough for them on the long journey, so the route had to have been well planned, with helpers at stops along the way, indicating that Josiah now had connections with people involved in a much more established Underground Railroad, some of whom have become well known today.

Josiah reported that it took them three days to reach Cincinnati. Going straight north from Bourbon County for two days, they probably crossed the Ohio River from a landing about ten miles downstream from Maysville, Kentucky, the launching point for many a freedom seeker, and landed a little downstream at Ripley, Ohio.[30] Ripley was a major hub for the secret helpers aiding the fugitives, and Josiah had most likely been directed there. One of the legends about how the Underground Railroad got its name tells of a man who swam across the Ohio River to Ripley while being chased by slave catchers in a boat. The men in the boat saw him emerge from the water and head into the town, but when they questioned people in the town, no one admitted having seen him, and he was nowhere to be found. The pursuers said that it was as if he had disappeared on an "underground railroad."[31]

Ripley had been the home since 1822 of John Rankin, a Presbyterian minister. He found that there were others in the town who had been helping freedom seekers, so he joined with them. In 1829 he moved his family to a house on the top of an escarpment overlooking the town. Here he and his wife and children could watch for any fugitives coming their way and for slave catchers chasing them. A lantern was always hung in the window at night that could be seen from the shore and beckon the travelers to safety. More than two thousand freedom seekers are estimated to have been aided in their flight by the Rankin family.[32] To ferry thirty people across the river must have taken two or three trips, and bringing them through town without raising suspicions would have been a major feat. This could have been accomplished only with the aid of the experienced and well-prepared Rankin family, or there could have been fewer people requiring only one boat. Instead of sending them straight north, as was his custom, Rankin sent them northwest to his comrade Levi Coffin in Newport (now Fountain City), just north of Richmond, Indiana.

From the time that Levi and his wife, Catharine, moved to Newport they had been aiding escaping slaves. Both Quakers, they had been involved in this work in their former home in Tennessee. Their house in Newport became "the converging point of three principal routes from Kentucky,"[33] and the house was also the hub of an underground network of helpers set up by Levi, a network that was not named the Underground Railroad until years later.[34] It was undoubtedly he with whom Josiah connected, even though Coffin said, "The largest number of slaves ever seated at our table at one time numbered seventeen."[35] Perhaps the Coffins just gave them food and sent them on their way, or perhaps Josiah had exaggerated the number, as we will see him do on several other occasions. No one else could have managed such a crowd and sent them on to Toledo where another helper was waiting to take them across the lake to freedom.[36] They most likely landed at Colchester, the nearest main port at the time. This was at the western end of Upper Canada (Ontario) and was still two hundred miles from Josiah's home at the eastern end. The long walk home, however, gave Josiah a chance to explore the land and learn about the farming and settlements along the way, which would be an advantage in his later ventures.

A year later Josiah returned to Kentucky to aid the Lightfoot family in escaping. The journey south to Maysville, most likely on the same route as the previous year, took two weeks. He went through Lancaster, Ohio, where on November 13, 1833, he saw the historic Leonid meteor storm that so frightened people all over North America.[37] When he reached Portsmouth, Ohio, on the Ohio River he was forced to disguise himself because of the presence of slave catchers and people from Kentucky who might recognize him. He inserted leaves in a piece of cloth and wrapped the cloth around his head so that he looked as if he had been wounded in the head and teeth and could not talk above a mumble. This masquerade worked through several confrontations until he could board the steamboat that would take him to Maysville.[38]

There he found five members of the Lightfoot family ready to accompany him to Canada. Even though there were fewer people to transport than the year before, this trip was more fraught with dangers and near calamities than the one the previous year. First, the boat they had borrowed to cross the Ohio River sprang a leak, forcing them to pull onto the northern shore and walk the last ten miles to Cincinnati. Faced with crossing the wide Little Miami River, they were about to give up when, about a mile upstream, they observed a cow walking through the water to the opposite side. Following that cow, they forded the river even though it was freezing, with bits of floating ice in it. The youngest boy collapsed from the cold and had to be carried the rest of the way. The delay caused them to miss the Sunday afternoon stage to Sandusky, so once again they had to walk. The route was familiar to Josiah from his first trip north with his family, but the added burden of the sick and feverish boy, even when carried on a litter, proved to be a laborious task, slowing their progress. They almost left him, at his wishes, in the woods to die, but compassion prohibited them even if it meant being overtaken by slave catchers.[39]

Knowing they were being followed, the weary Lightfoot family had almost given up hope when fortune intervened with the acts of three different strangers met along the way. The first was an encounter with a Quaker driving a wagon of produce to market. Upon learning of the plight of the youngster, he turned his wagon around and led them to his home, where his family welcomed the travelers, fed them, put them up for the night, and agreed to take care of the ailing boy while the others continued their journey.

As the party proceeded on their way toward Sandusky the next morning, well provided with food for their journey by the Quaker family, they met a second stranger, a white man walking on the road. He turned out to be a fugitive as well but from justice rather than bondage. Nevertheless, he was friendly and helpful and turned out to be an asset to the freedom seekers. At the edge of Lake Erie in the early morning they sought food at a tavern. As they were waiting for the food to be prepared, Josiah had a feeling of foreboding and led his charges into the bushes to hide. His instincts were true, and they watched as horsemen rode up to the tavern and asked if anyone had seen the group of escaped slaves. The members of the Lightfoot family recognized the men and were very much afraid of being captured. However, they were saved by their traveling companion, who told the riders that he had seen just such a party heading toward Detroit to the west, and the men rode off in that direction. With much relief but still anxious to get across the lake before the chasers might return, they hurriedly finished their breakfast. The tavern keeper (the third stranger), upon learning of their plight, offered to sail them across the lake in his own skiff, and they were soon in the free land of Upper Canada.

The boy who had been left behind with the Quakers was able to join his family there after two months. Later they discovered that Frank Taylor, owner of the Lightfoot family, who possessed twenty-seven slaves in 1830, decided to free the other members of the family after he recovered from a severe illness.[40] So, the Lightfoot family was soon reunited. It is interesting to note that in the same county in Kentucky where Frank Taylor lived, an African American by the name of John Lightfoot owned slaves.[41]

Josiah claimed to "have been instrumental in delivering one hundred and eighteen human beings out of the cruel and merciless grasp of the slaveholder."[42] He may have accomplished this even though he describes only the two trips in 1832 and 1833, where he led a total of thirty-five (or twenty-one) people to freedom. He does indicate that from 1835 to 1841, "I was glad to help such of my old friends as had the spirit to make the attempt to free themselves; and I made more than one trip, about this time, to Maryland and Kentucky, with the expectation, in which I was not disappointed, that some might be enabled to follow in my footsteps. I knew the route pretty well, and had much greater facilities for travelling than when I came out of that Egypt for the first time."[43] He does not say that he actually led them to Canada, so he may have been giving detailed instructions so that they could set themselves free. His first two autobiographies were published before the American Civil War freed the slaves, at a time when aiding fugitives from slavery was a criminal offense and highly dangerous, especially in the Southern states. Keeping the names of the helpers and even of the escaping slaves a secret was extremely important; thus, Josiah avoided naming his contacts or even giving any clue to where they lived.

When he returned to Upper Canada, Josiah Henson, after having spent three years on the farm of Mr. Hibbard, took up residence on the nearby farm of Mr. Riseley. Here Josiah continued his ministry and his farming. His ultimate aim was to acquire his own plot of land where he did not have to pay rent or answer to a landlord, to be his own boss. He found it difficult to raise enough money for this kind of enterprise himself. In his travels he had heard of and perhaps even visited the cooperative colony of Wilberforce (today Lucan), where Black people of Cincinnati had relocated in 1829. This might have given him the idea of forming a group to purchase the land and share its bounty. He saw in this new country much potential and was inspired by what he called the Canadian's "indestructible character for energy, enterprise, and self-reliance."[44] He saw no reason why the newcomers, even after years of servitude, could not acquire this enterprising spirit. But he saw around him many who had escaped from bondage who were happy just to be free and earning money to support their family, with no ambition to own their own farm.

Soon, however, Josiah was able to find a few men with aspirations like his own. Mr. Riseley, agreeing with Josiah's aims, allowed him to hold meetings with some ten or twelve men at his house.[45] They made an agreement to purchase land to the west

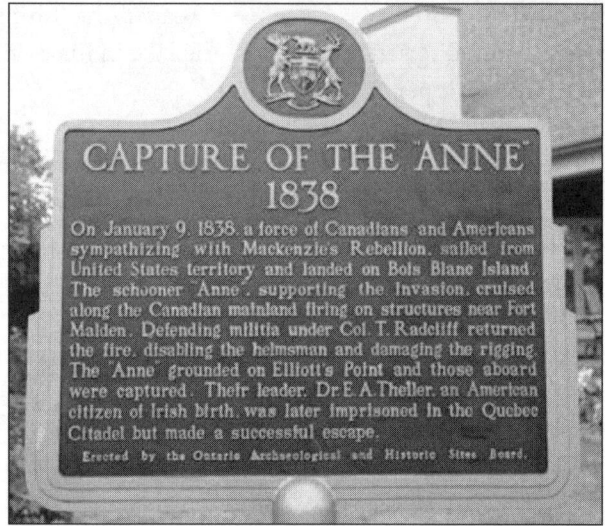

Figure 7.3. Capture of the *Anne* 1838 historic marker. Erected by the Ontario Archaeological and Historic Sites Board. Location: Amherstburg, Ontario, N9V 3B2, Essex County.

and sent Josiah to look for good farmland. He set out in the fall of 1834 to explore the land between Lakes Erie and Huron. He settled on the fertile land to the east of the St. Claire Lake in the far western part of the province. When he reported back to his group, they were impressed but insisted that he go back in the spring to see the country in a different season. This he did and, when exploring close to the shores of Lake Erie, came across some already cleared but empty land that he discovered was owned by the government and had been granted to Mr. McCormick to rent to settlers. Thinking that they could gain an advantage by raising crops immediately on land ready for planting and selling the products, they could then raise even more money to purchase their own land by working cooperatively. This land had probably been cleared by other African Canadian settlers who were cheated out of their land by unscrupulous mortgage lenders after their hard work of cutting down the trees and pulling up the roots.[46]

In 1835 the Hensons and twelve other families moved to this tract near Colchester in Essex County and planted mainly wheat and tobacco. By this time Josiah and Charlotte had six children. Thomas and Isaac were in their teens and able to help on the farm. Celia Jane and Josiah were ages eight and seven, and the two born in Canada were Charlotte Matilda, age three, and baby Elizabeth, about age one. After a year they discovered that Mr. McCormick had not satisfied the conditions for the grant and so should not have charged rent to the settlers. After winning their case in court, Josiah and his friends no longer had to pay rent and could save more money. But they still did not own the land, so after six years they disbanded the cooperative, split the profits, and went their separate ways.[47]

Josiah was so dedicated to his adopted country that he took up arms to protect it while living in this part of the country. A group composed of Canadians and Americans formed in 1836 to foment a rebellion against Upper Canada (now Ontario) to make it an independent and democratic state. The group was never large or powerful enough to pose a serious threat, but damage was caused and people on both sides were killed in several attacks by the rebels. In January 1837 rebels seized the schooner *Anne* and bombarded Fort Malden at Amherstburg (figure 7.3).[48] The Canadians so disabled the schooner with return fire that it ran aground.[49] Josiah said that he served in the armed forces opposing the rebellion at Fort Malden from Christmas 1836 to May 1837 and was among the party that boarded the ship and captured prisoners and arms. "I was appointed a captain to the 2nd Essex Company of Coloured Volunteers. Though I could not shoulder a musket, I could carry a sword."[50] There is no formal record of Josiah Henson serving in the British armed forces in Canada, but perhaps he served as a volunteer and so was not listed on the payroll.[51]

Ever concerned with the welfare and betterment of his fellow refugees from slavery and not wanting them to be taken advantage of, Josiah gave lectures at gatherings about the proper management of farming: how, for instance, it is better to plant more than one crop so that if the value of one goes down you may be able to compensate with the other.[52]

While in Colchester in 1836, Josiah met a missionary, a graduate of Oberlin College by the name of Hiram Wilson, who had been sent to Canada on a mission to create schools for the formerly enslaved refugees.[53] A few years later the two men would form a partnership with just that aim. This new enterprise would set Josiah on a different trajectory that would change his life.

8

A New Dream

JOSIAH HENSON NEVER HAD A FORMAL EDUCATION, BEING DENIED THE OPPORTUNITY by those who had authority over him when he was in bondage. However, he knew the value of a good education, especially after his son taught him to read "a little," and his eyes were opened to a whole new world. He made sure that all his children, including his daughters, went to school.[1] He saw education as the means to lift his fellow refugees out of poverty and improve their condition, as he said at the end of his first autobiography. "We look to the school, and the possession of landed property by individuals, as two great means of the elevation of our oppressed and degraded race to a participation in the blessings, as they have hitherto been permitted to share only the miseries and vices, of civilization."[2]

But most African Canadians did not have access to public schooling. Common schools, as they were known, were provided free to all residents of Canada, but the catch was that the community could choose to have a segregated school, and a majority did.[3] Although most white Canadians were against slavery, they were, at the same time, racists, believing in the inferiority of the African "race." According to historian Amoaba Gooden, this was not due to American influences but came "out of a radicalized global colonial architecture" that was deep-seated in the minds of white Canadians long before the large influx of freedom seekers from the South.[4] Segregation was most pronounced in the large cities, where Blacks were forced to the outskirts.[5] Josiah had been able to find schooling for his children in St. Catharines and Colchester, but as the number of refugees grew, so did the prejudice.

The only solution for the Black refugees was to form communities of their own where schools could be established. The biggest obstacle to achieving this goal was that most of the refugees were poor, having escaped from slavery with no possessions. They needed to find the funding to help them purchase land so they could form their own communities.

Figure 8.1. Hiram Wilson. Nelson Hackett project, University of Arkansas, https://nelsonhackettproject.uark.edu/6-hiram-wilson/.

When Josiah met Hiram Wilson in 1836, he not only found a friend who shared his determination to educate the refugees but was also introduced to the antislavery societies (figure 8.1). Born in New Hampshire in 1803, Wilson was a kind and gentle soul, a dedicated abolitionist, and one of those rare white men of nineteenth-century America who considered Black people his equals. He enrolled in the Lane Theological Seminary in Cincinnati in 1833, the same year as another abolitionist, Theodore Weld. Heading the seminary at the time was Lyman Beecher, father of Harriet Beecher Stowe. In the fall of 1834 after heated debates had disrupted the school and the city, the board of trustees forbade any discussion about slavery or abolition. In opposition to this rule, Weld led a majority of the Lane students to transfer to Oberlin College in Oberlin, Ohio. Weld's group was later referred to as the "Lane Rebels."[6] Wilson was one of them. Oberlin was an abolitionist school that admitted Blacks as equal to whites. Weld came to be involved later in the American Anti-Slavery Society that would aid Wilson in his goals, at least in the beginning.

Hiram Wilson was neither a leader nor an eloquent speaker, but he was devout and dedicated to not only the cause of freeing enslaved people but also educating them after freedom as well so they could make a good living for themselves and their families and become contributing members of society. In 1836 the head of the Theology Department at Oberlin, Charles Grandison Finney, conferred with Theodore Weld, then head of the American Anti-Slavery Society, and decided that the society could finance Wilson in establishing schools for Blacks in Canada. With this funding

Wilson moved to Toronto, where he formed the Canada Mission.[7] By 1839 he had established ten schools but was always short of money, especially after the spring of 1838 when the American Anti-Slavery Society, strapped for funds, stopped supporting the mission.[8]

Wilson knew that now he had to find a different way of financing schools for the refugees. As a young man he had attended the Oneida Institute in upstate New York.[9] Founded in 1827 and based on a European model, the Oneida Institute "sought to unite classical education with agricultural, horticultural, and mechanical labor."[10] In this way the school provided for the physical exercise and training in trades for the students along with a quality education and at the same time produced commodities that could be sold to support the school. It was the first school of its kind in America and also one of the first to admit both white and Black students.

Wilson's dream was to establish that kind of school in Canada for the Black refugees. To make this dream a reality, he needed an African American spokesperson to spread the word among the Blacks and be a spiritual leader, because in the African Canadian communities churches and schools were intertwined.[11] And he also needed a wealthy individual to provide seed money to purchase the needed land and construct the buildings. He found the first in Josiah Henson, who was already well respected in the area and enthusiastic about the idea of a manual labor school, since it coincided with his own ideas for the improvement of his people.[12] The second person was found in a Quaker immigrant from England, James Canning Fuller. Fuller had been an abolitionist in England and continued that work when he moved his family to a farm in Skaneateles, New York, in 1833.[13] In June 1840 Fuller attended the World Anti-Slavery Convention in London, England, as the representative of the New York state Anti-Slavery Society. While in England he used his influence and connections in the country to solicit funds for the proposed school. Meanwhile at home, Wilson and Henson promoted the idea of such an institution and searched for people who might serve as trustees.

Fuller returned from England in the late summer of 1840 with $1,500. A year later, after legally establishing the school, Wilson and Fuller called a meeting in London, Ontario, to create the school organization and plan of action.[14] A board of trustees was formed consisting of three whites and three Blacks. The three whites were James C. Fuller, farmer, New York; John Roaf, Congregational minister, Toronto; and Frederick Stover, farmer, Norwich, Canada. The three Blacks were James C. Brown, merchant and innkeeper, Toronto; Peter Smith, blacksmith, Chatham; and George Johnson, farmer, Dawn.[15]

A committee of three—Henson, Wilson, and one other—was appointed to search for suitable land on which to establish the school. According to Josiah, "after traversing the country for several months, we could find no place more suitable than that upon which I had had my eye for three or four years, for a permanent settlement, in the town of Dawn."[16]

Accordingly, the trustees purchased two hundred acres along the Syndenham River in November 1841 for $800. The indenture for the sale stated that it was "for the sole purpose . . . of Education Mental Moral and Physical of the Coloured inhabitants of Canada not excluding White persons and Indians."[17] From the beginning the school was intended to be self-supporting, with the students devoting a certain part of their time to the farm and mill operations.[18] The new school, named the British-American Institute of Science and Industry (BAI), officially opened its doors on December 12, 1842, with fourteen students. In the first year the school cleared twelve acres of land and built a sixty-student-capacity schoolhouse and a school dormitory.[19] Josiah purchased for his family three hundred adjacent acres with his own money, having gotten a large discount from the seller for paying cash. He sold one hundred acres to the school (thus making the BAI a three-hundred-acre tract).[20]

The area around the BAI has been referred to as the "Dawn Settlement" and the BAI as the "Dawn Institute" locally at the time and in many references even in modern times, leading many to mistakenly assume that there was a planned settlement around the BAI, like Elgin and Wilberforce, and that this settlement supported the BAI. But in fact, the opposite was true. In the words of Hiram Wilson, "The 300 acres of land were purchased and deeded to the Trustees to subserve educational purposes, and no families have settled upon any part of the tract, except as they were employed about the Institute."[21] Some of the people involved with the BAI had farms and homes nearby. People, both Black and white, had settled in the area and established farms and businesses there many years before the BAI was established, but they were not organized in a planned settlement.[22]

The name "Dawn" goes much further back and has a complex history. It never had any legal standing other than the title of a large geopolitical area, the Dawn Township. Originally, this area belonged to the Native Americans and was purchased from the Chippewas by the Canadian government in 1823. Immediately, immigrants began to flood in and clear the land for farming. Some of these immigrants had formerly been enslaved in the United States, and one of the theories about the origin of the name "Dawn" for the region lies with them. Many of the freedom seekers had followed the North Star to find their way there. The North Star is located by its position to the constellations Ursa Major (Big Bear, or the Big Dipper) and Ursa Minor (Little Bear, or the Little Dipper). The settlers named the waterways in their new home Big Bear Creek and Little Bear Creek. Big Bear Creek was later named the Sydenham River. Because it represented a new beginning of life in freedom, they called the area where they settled Dawn.[23]

When Colonel Taylor built a gristmill and a woolen mill on the Sydenham River he adopted the local term, calling his industry Dawn Mills. A mill or a group of mills was the center of activity in a grain-growing area, so stores and services such as a blacksmithing or a wagon repair shop would naturally be established there and form what could be called a small town. A post office was established there, and this is where the BAI and other residents of the area received mail, so Dawn Mills, or just Dawn, became linked with the identity of the BAI.[24]

Another complication in the identification of the location of the BAI came in 1850 when counties were formed. At first, the geographic area of Dawn Township was placed in Lambton County, but when residents around the Sydenham River objected because the seat of that county was too far away, a triangular area, or gore, was separated from Dawn Township and placed in Camden Township in Kent County. After 1850 the official location of the BAI and of Josiah Henson's adjacent farm was the Gore of Camden, Kent County.[25] So, the BAI was not even in the Dawn Township after 1850.

Dawn Mills lay to the east of the BAI property, and the farm of Josiah Henson lay to the west (figure 8.2). North of Henson's farm, a commercial area was growing along the Syndenham River that would become the town of Dresden in 1852. It had been named by a German immigrant who built a sawmill there in the 1820s. In 1856 the post office that had been at Dawn Mills was moved to Dresden. William Whipper, a wealthy African American, was the principal founder of Dresden. He was an abolitionist and created in Dresden a terminus for the Underground Railroad where refugees could receive comfort and direction for the continuation of their lives in freedom. Dresden was also where Josiah Henson preached at the Methodist Episcopal Church on Queen Street.[26]

When Josiah moved his family to Dawn Township in 1842, the family had increased considerably. The oldest, Thomas, was twenty-four years old. Isaac was twenty-three, Celia Jane was fifteen, Josiah was fourteen, Charlotte Matilda was ten, Elizabeth was eight, and there were two new ones: Peter, age six, and Julia Ann, age two. Julia was the last child born to Josiah and Charlotte, putting the total number of children who survived to adulthood at eight (see appendix B in this volume).

Josiah was the spiritual guide and spokesperson of the BAI, preaching at the BAI and camp meetings in the community, ministering to the needs of the people, and, at the same time, managing his farm. But he was often absent from home during the winter months as he traveled around Upper Canada (Canada West) preaching in churches and at gatherings and meeting with individuals and groups, using his considerable powers of persuasion and oration to raise funds for the BAI and attract new students.[27] As he traveled around the country and eventually into New England, he became aware of and inevitably involved with various antislavery societies. He became personally acquainted with many of the people engaged in these societies. These individuals would be crucial to his success in raising funds for the BAI and to his defense against certain false accusations made against him in the early 1850s, so it is important to know more about the societies.

The antislavery societies in America and England and individual abolitionists were to be intricately connected to the fate of the school and to the future of Josiah Henson. Although individuals and local societies opposing slavery had existed for some time,

Figure 8.2. Josiah Henson's house in his later years. Josiah Henson Museum of African Canadian History. 29251 Freedom Road, Dresden, Ontario, N0P 1M0, Canada.

the movement gained a significant boost after a large meeting of African Americans in Philadelphia in 1817 denounced the American Colonization Society as an organization with the objective of removing free Blacks, who had become symbols for those wishing for freedom from enslavement, to other countries. After the 1817 meeting, most of the Black leaders who had formerly supported the colonization movement then formed or joined antislavery societies instead.[28] Whites also formed antislavery societies, and both as well as some integrated societies continued to increase in membership and funding throughout the 1820s and 1830s.

The antislavery movement was complex, and the participants had different motivations and ideas on how to achieve the goal and even disagreements on what that goal actually was. This led to petty arguments, different interpretations of goals, feuds over leadership, and finally a split. One thing the societies had in common was that they wanted to free enslaved people. How and when to do so were matters of heated debate, and once that goal was achieved, most abolitionists were not concerned with helping those they had freed adjust to their new autonomy. According to historians William Pease and Jane Pease, "Few well-known antislavery leaders and no major antislavery organization ever sponsored an organized negro community."[29]

The abolition of slavery in the British Empire by the Slavery Abolition Act of 1833 had many repercussions in the United States, one of which was to goad Northern abolitionists into action. Antislavery newspapers emboldened their rhetoric and increased their circulation, sometimes causing a backlash by proslavery Northerners who wrecked printing presses and intimidated leading abolitionists.[30] Boston news-paperman William Lloyd Garrison and abolitionist leader Theodore Dwight Weld founded a national organization, the American Anti-Slavery Society, in 1833. The goal of the organization was the immediate and uncompensated emancipation of all slaves.[31] This seems like a simply stated objective, but the word "immediate" could be interpreted as "right now by force" or "gradually by non-violent means starting right now."[32] So, the American Anti-Slavery Society was divided from the beginning in the interpretation of the mission and the ways to carry out that mission. Local and state branches and women's auxiliaries soon formed. Whether motivated by religious con-viction or an ideal of equality, the members differed in their ideas of how to achieve freedom for the enslaved: by publishing newspapers, by giving lectures, by way of politics, or through churches or other local organizations and whether to be loud and blunt or gentle and persuasive. They eventually divided into the followers of Garrison, Garrisonians, working for radical and immediate social change and the followers of the wealthy New York merchants Arthur and Lewis Tappan, Tappanites, who believed in a more conservative approach.[33]

Many women were not satisfied with working in "auxiliaries" and demanded more leadership roles in the American Anti-Slavery Society. It was the Garrisonians' in-clusion of women in the committees of the society that impelled the conservative Tappanites to split off and, in the spring of 1840, form a separate organization called the American and Foreign Anti-Slavery Society.[34] One of the Garrisonian women who gained seats on several antislavery committees and boards was Boston socialite Maria Chapman, a good friend of Garrison.[35] She would become a severe critic of Josiah Henson in both New England and England. Female abolitionist leaders on both sides of the ocean were incensed and radicalized after being denied admittance as dele-gates into the World Anti-Slavery Convention in London in June 1840, organized by the English Quaker Joseph Sturge.[36] This led them to include women's rights in the American Anti-Slavery Society platform, which led to more dissension.

The operations of the Underground Railroad may also have brought more dis-pute into the American Anti-Slavery Society. Not a formal part of the society, the Un-derground Railroad was a loosely organized network of abolitionists, many of them women, who personally aided individuals, families, and groups of slaves on the road to freedom. The involvement of some of the members of the antislavery societies in this endeavor was frowned upon by others who claimed that it was more import-ant to work for total emancipation than individual freedoms and thought that the underground activity, being illegal, might endanger the legitimacy of the American Anti-Slavery Society.

This infighting and the lack of positive results caused public support of both the American Anti-Slavery Society and the American and Foreign Anti-Slavery Society to wane in the 1840s. As their funding dwindled, so did their power and influence, and the smaller state and local groups took over the antislavery cause. Also, during this time Black leaders began to break away from the white antislavery societies to form their own groups and initiatives.[37] On the political side, the Liberty Party was formed in 1839 with the sole purpose of ending slavery. The party never achieved success in electing candidates, but it did influence the public mind, as the populace soon accepted the Republican Party with a similar but much more conservative agenda.[38]

The BAI that Wilson and Henson had founded seemed to flourish in the beginning. Five years after the founding, the BAI had one hundred acres of cleared farmland, fifteen wooden buildings, two brick buildings, a barn, and two schoolhouses. The BAI also boasted a water-powered gristmill, a sawmill, and a ropewalk. The value was listed as $11,000. In 1845 there were eighty students enrolled taught by two teachers, one for primary education and one for those aged twelve to twenty-five, but enrollment had begun to decline by 1847.[39] The area around the school continued to grow, and about five hundred residents in nearby farms grew corn, wheat, oats, and tobacco.[40] By 1851 ten of the former students had gone on to become teachers themselves in nearby districts.[41]

In 1856 Benjamin Drew described the BAI in *A North-side View of Slavery*: "The Rev. Hiram Wilson originally conceived the plan of establishing here an Industrial School; and he directed and managed the school for nearly seven years from its commencement in the wilderness. At that time there were no more than fifty colored persons in all, in the vicinity of the tract purchased. Mr. Wilson began the school with fourteen boarding scholars, received the refugees as they arrived, and did what he could for their encouragement."[42]

Hiram Wilson was the respected leader of the BAI. When he founded the school, he dreamed of it being cooperative like Oneida, but it would take years for it to become fully self-supporting, for good teachers to be attracted to give instruction, and for students to graduate and spread the word of the school. In addition, Wilson had a good heart but not the managerial or administrative skills to run the school or raise funding. There was no longer any money coming from the antislavery societies. Lewis Tappan considered Wilson a poor administrator and thus a bad investment, and the Garrisonians were against funding the BAI because they were more interested in funding freedom than in aiding the free and believed that Black communities and schools should be able to support themselves. Wilson went to England in the fall of 1843 to try to raise funds there but apparently did not have much luck.[43]

At the same time, Josiah Henson increased his efforts to raise funds for the BAI at home. He even ventured into the US Northeast. In January and February 1845, he was on a nineteen-stop speaking tour for just such a purpose with Rev. J. C. Aspenwall in Vermont.[44]

Henson's innate sense of humor was demonstrated on a canal boat on the Erie Canal in November 1844, as reported in the *New York Tribune*: "After discussing politics with several upon the deck for a while, he [Henson] resolved to have the sense of the passengers on the Presidential question which he obtained as follows—They were near a bridge and the Steersman as usual cried out, 'A bridge!' No sooner said than Henson cried out, 'All in favor of Birney for the Presidency bow down.' In a moment all bowed to the deck [to avoid being struck by the bridge]. It was a palpable hit—and produced roars of laughter, as it did at the meeting where he related it."[45]

Josiah was not hesitant to knock on the door of a manor house if he had a letter of introduction or sometimes if he was just passing by. In 1846 he paid a call to Henry Wadsworth Longfellow at his home, Craigie House, just west of Boston, as noted by Longfellow in his journal:

> 26th [June 1846] . . . In the evening Mr. Henson, a negro, once a slave, now a preacher, called to get subscription for the school at Dawn, Upper Canada, for the education of blacks. I had a long talk with him, and he gave me an account of his escape from slavery with his family. There was never anything more childlike in his manner. Not one word of abuse. The good-natured ebony face, the swarthy-bearded lip, the white teeth, the whole aspect of the man so striking and withal so wild—it seemed as if some Egyptian statue had come to life and sat speaking in the twilight sonorous English not yet well learned. What pleases me most in any negro is his bonhomie. Moreover, almost every negro has the rheumatism. This man had it. His right arm was crooked and stiff. It had been broken by a savage blow with a stake from a fence.[46]

These efforts by Henson and Wilson did not bring in enough funds for financial support of the BAI, so in 1845 Wilson hired a new secretary of the executive committee of the BAI by the name of Rev. William P. Newman.[47] Newman, an escaped slave, had come to Canada in 1844 after graduating from Oberlin College in Ohio and being ordained as a Baptist minister.[48] The BAI had seventy students at the time but had existed for only two and a half years at this point, and little of the three hundred acres had been cleared for planting. Although the school and the chapel had been built, many of the farm buildings were still under construction, so the school was still very much dependent on donations.

Newman found discrepancies in the books of the BAI and the reports of the agents collecting donations. He called Josiah in from his travels in the east and convened a public meeting in 1846 with the executive board. The board exonerated both Henson and Wilson of wrongdoing. But Josiah and William Newman had a serious argument, resulting in Newman returning to Cincinnati that September. Josiah had made an enemy who would continue to criticize him and the BAI and cause serious problems for both later.[49]

A "Convention of the Colored People of Canada" was called in August 1847 in Drummondville, Canada, to investigate the possible misappropriation of funds coming from England to benefit the colored residents of Canada and the potential for establishing a centralized organization to oversee the distribution of such funds. There were fourteen representatives from Canada and eight from the United States at this convention. Josiah did not take his seat as the delegate from Dawn until the third day of the convention. Perhaps realizing that he was going to be called to task, Josiah moved for the following resolution: "Whereas it is our duty to contend for truth and justice, if any gentleman brings a charge against the character of a man, whether present or absent, and cannot substantiate the fact by good proof, he is chargeable with immorality, and is unworthy of public confidence."[50] This motion was tabled for further consideration but was never voted on.

The convention unanimously resolved "That the Dawn Institution belongs to the People of Colour in Canada generally" and appointed a committee of five to audit the books of the BAI.[51] The convention also resolved that the British American Anti-Slavery Society of Toronto, established a few months earlier, be recognized as the only organized society of its kind in Canada. Josiah Henson was questioned, but after he produced his account book, the convention resolved that it was "satisfied with his conduct."[52] The BAI was a private corporation, not a government body, and so did not "belong to the People of colour generally." So, this committee had no legal authority to audit the BAI books but did so anyway. Neither the people of color in Canada generally or the British American Anti-Slavery Society contributed to the financing or management of the BAI.

Wilson resigned from the executive board of the BAI in December 1847, but it may only have been partially due to pressure from the outside, as his wife was gravely ill at the time, and his friend and supporter James Fuller had died a month before.[53] Two years later Wilson moved his family to St. Catharines, where he and his second wife opened a new school for refugees. William Newman continued to plague him with public criticisms even in his new home.[54] Newman's motivation for trying to thwart every move of Wilson and Henson is unknown and seems from the outside to have been a kind of personal vendetta. The BAI was left without a leader and, with its outside funding dried up, drifted further into debt, which by 1849 was between $4,000 and $5,000.[55]

Meanwhile, Josiah had been pursuing an idea that he thought could save the BAI by giving it a viable self-supporting industry. He envisioned building a new efficient steam-powered sawmill to make use of the abundance of hardwood trees on the property that were currently being burned to make way for crops. Even though there was a considerable amount of forested land in Canada, such forests were dwindling in the eastern United States. He thought that by sawing the wood into boards and shipping them to New England, they could be sold for much more than in Canada and bring a handsome profit to the school. He had begun to pursue his idea before the 1846 and 1847 investigations into the affairs of the BAI. While traveling in New England, he visited many sawmills to ascertain the best equipment needed. He visited the lumberyards to see what the profit margin might be.[56] He then looked for people who might invest in his project. For a depiction of the kind of mill Henson built, see figure 8.3.

Josiah was very sociable, and when he met someone new, he would often get that

INTERIOR OF FRANKLIN MILL.

Figure 8.3. Interior of Franklin Mill, Franklin, Massachusetts, ca. 1850. This is the type of sawmill that Josiah Henson built at the British-American Institute of Science and Industry with the help of his Boston friends. Granger Collections, 244 Fifth Ave., Suite 2110, New York.

person to introduce him to others who might be of help, and so he got to know some very influential and wealthy people. This good business practice is today called networking. He approached his friend Rev. Ephraim Peabody, Unitarian minister and chaplain of King's Chapel in Boston, to get advice on whom he might approach for a loan for such a project. Peabody introduced him to Unitarians Amos Lawrence (figure 8.4a), Henry Bowditch (figure 8.4b), and Samuel A. Eliot (figure 8.4c).

Amos Lawrence along with his brother Abbott had gained vast wealth through the textile industry. Beginning with a single mercantile store, they grew their commercial empire to include cloth factories and a wholesale import-export business in cotton and woolen goods. After retiring from the business, he became well known for his philanthropy.[57] Samuel Eliot was an academic from a wealthy Boston family. As the former mayor of Boston and a senator in the Massachusetts Assembly, he was a powerful political figure.[58] Henry Ingersoll Bowditch was a physician, an active abolitionist, and an influential member of the Boston Vigilance Committee, an organization that assisted people fleeing enslavement.[59]

These men were able to raise $1,625, which they transferred to Josiah in the form

Figure 8.4. Josiah Henson's three benefactors in Boston. From left to right: Amos Lawrence, Henry Ingersall Bowditch, and Samuel Atkins Eliot. Wikimedia Commons; Massachusetts Historical Society, https://www.masshist.org/database/viewer.php?item_id=886; Wikimedia Commons.

of a loan against the trustees of the BAI. Josiah and his sons built the sawmill on BAI property but spent all the money before the mill was operational, so Josiah had to go back to the charitable Unitarians for more. This time they loaned $2,500 but put the funds in a bank account to be drawn upon as needed.[60] This way, they could be sure that the expenditures were fully accountable. Josiah said that he took $1,800 from the account to complete the mill.[61]

Josiah found an experienced miller and began to turn the forest logs into fine black walnut boards. According to Josiah's report in his autobiographies, he transported eighty thousand feet of boards by ship to Oswego, New York, a port on Lake Ontario. At that time the Sydenham River was navigable to the St. Claire River and then into Lake Huron, but to transport his cargo east he could have either loaded the boards on wagons to St. Catharines and loaded on a boat there or taken a shorter route by wagon to Port Alma on Lake Erie to load the boards on a boat and then taken the Welland Canal to Lake Ontario. The second improved Welland Canal, able to carry large boats, was completed in 1845.[62]

Josiah ran into some difficulty transporting the load from there to Boston, but with the help of Amos Lawrence he finally landed his cargo in Boston to be purchased by piano manufacturer Jonas Chickering for $3,600. Josiah reinvested some of the money to finance the next two transports.[63] By the third trip he was to discover that unfortunately, the boards were not selling for as much, the market having been glutted. Obviously, the sawmill could no longer make a profit selling lumber in New England. So, Josiah thought he might try his luck in England, an idea that had support from his Unitarian investors. Josiah had many friends who could provide him with letters of introduction to influential people in England, and he had heard that there was to be a grand world industrial exhibition there in the spring of 1851. If he could exhibit some of his excellent boards there, they might attract some English investors or perhaps partners for his enterprise.

There was another source of revenue that Josiah had found for the BAI. While he was in Boston in 1849, Samuel A. Eliot convinced Josiah that if he might dictate his most fascinating life history to him, Eliot would write it down and publish it in a book. Such autobiographical books had garnered much revenue for the antislavery societies and so might raise some money for the BAI. Josiah was already practiced in relating his story and was ready for fame and fortune, so he agreed. *The Life of Josiah Henson, Formerly a Slave, Now an Inhabitant of Canada, as Narrated by Himself* was published by Arthur D. Phelps of Boston in 1849 at Eliot's expense.[64] In the first page of the book Eliot writes, "The Following memoir was written from the dictation of Josiah Henson. A portion of the story told, which, when written, was read to him, that any errors of statement might be corrected."[65] Since only about five hundred copies were printed, Josiah's autobiography did not bring much money to the BAI. He apparently pedaled the books himself, going door to door or at his orations. Eliot must have deposited one at the Boston Library, along with his original notes taken of Josiah's dictation, and one at the Abolitionist Reading Room in Boston that was later read by Harriet Beecher Stowe, who put some of the incidents from it in her novel, *Uncle Tom's Cabin*. This would bring Josiah fame a few years later and change his life.

The fact that Josiah dictated his life to a friend who then wrote the book indicates that he could not write. The fact that the dictation was then read back to him and corrected by Eliot indicates that he could not read handwriting. Josiah's son may have taught him to read "a little," but that would have been in printed books. Josiah's inability to read script handwriting is evidenced by his bringing his mail, whenever he was in Boston, to Rev. Jonathan D. Bridge, whose son, Wells Bridge, would open and read to Josiah, then write replies for him from his dictation.[66] This is reiterated in Josiah's 1876 autobiography when he thanks Mr. Thomas Church "for so ably assisting in my correspondence."[67] It is also hinted at in various places in his memoirs where he indicates that he gives a missive to another to read aloud.

Rev. Ephraim Peabody wrote a review of several published slave narratives for the July 1849 *Christian Examiner* in which he highly praised the newly published narrative by Josiah Henson, calling it "simple, straightforward, and to the point, as the character which it describes." He praises Henson as being "large-hearted, large-minded, tolerant, calm, benevolent and wise" and his enterprise of improving his fellow Blacks through education, habits of industry, and endeavoring to own the land they cultivate as being comparable to the principles of economy put forth by Adam Smith and John Stuart Mill.[68]

The growing number of fugitives from slavery in the United States increased rapidly after 1840, creating resentment by the white inhabitants of Canada West (Upper Canada). This conflict escalated after the Fugitive Slave Act of September 1850 forced many more fugitives to flee to Canada. In an effort to address this problem, Josiah

Henson and Henry Bibb called a meeting of "People of Colour" in Sandwich, Canada West, on November 11, 1850. A society was formed under the leadership of Henson and Bibb. The main focus of the society was the housing, improvement, temperance, and schooling of the incoming fugitives. One of the major resolutions of this society was to establish a newspaper that would serve to broadcast their concerns and accomplishments and be "the advocate of the coloured people of Canada West." This newspaper was *The Voice of the Fugitive*, Henry Bibb, editor. The first paper was published on January 1, 1851.[69] Henry's wife, Mary Bibb, was a major contributor and editor of the newspaper and often took over complete control of the publication during her husband's frequent absences, making her the first woman newspaper publisher in Canada.[70]

The concern about schools was due to the 1850 Separate School Act, which allowed families of five or more to form a separate common (public) school. Originally enacted to give Catholics the opportunity to establish their own schools, the act was subverted by whites to form a school that did not allow Blacks, forcing Black communities to establish their own schools, embedding segregation in towns and cities across the province.[71]

The BAI was not directly affected by the Separate School Act, since it was a private school and was integrated, but it continued to suffer financial difficulties, so the trustees decided that drastic changes were necessary for the school to survive. In 1850 they separated the sawmill and some forested land from the BAI and put it in Josiah's hands with instructions to use it to pay off the debt within four years. They then turned the BAI and its land over to the American Baptist Free Mission Society under the leadership of Rev. Samuel Davis.[72] Davis was a graduate of Oberlin College, preaching at that time at a church in Detroit.[73] The influential and financially stable American Baptist Free Mission Society, a predominantly white antislavery institution, was brought to Canada by none other than that other graduate of Oberlin College, Rev. William Newman, with the specific intention of taking over the BAI.[74] Henson, on his way to England by then, had no way of preventing this and may not have even known about it.

Confident that he could raise the money to pay the debt by finding partners in England to sell the fine Canadian black walnut boards, Josiah left the sawmill in the hands of experienced miller Peter Smith and proceeded with his plan.[75] Josiah left for Boston with some fine specimens of black walnut boards, confident that his friends there would help him get to England and provide him with letters of introduction to prominent men there.[76] One thing that he had not counted on was the considerable criticism of his good friend Samuel Eliot, at that time a congressman from Massachusetts, because of his vote in favor of the 1850 Fugitive Slave Act. Eliot became a pariah with the Boston abolitionists, and sales of Josiah's book probably suffered by association.[77]

Knowing that the political atmosphere would be very different on the other side of the ocean, Samuel Eliot and others paid for Josiah's and his son Isaac's passage to England.[78] Josiah is also listed as an agent for the newspaper *The Voice of the Fugitive*, giving him more credentials for his trip.[79] Josiah and his son sailed for Liverpool, England, on the steamship Cambria on November 27, 1850, with high hopes, with Josiah unaware of a devil on his tail.[80]

9
England

WHEN JOSIAH HENSON TRAVELED TO ENGLAND EARLY IN 1851, HE WAS ACCOMPANIED by his son Josiah.[1] Because of his inability to raise his arms above his shoulders, Josiah needed someone to help him dress properly, tie his ascot, brush his hair, and attend to his wardrobe. He usually had a member of his family with him on his overseas journeys.[2] His main objective in traveling to England, as stated in his memoirs, was to exhibit prized finished walnut boards from the sawmill of the British-American Institute of Science and Industry (BAI) at the Great World Exhibition in London in order to find an overseas market for the product to help support the school.[3]

Another way to raise money for the school, as had been demonstrated in New England, was to give lectures to audiences who might then donate to the worthy cause. Since slavery in the United Kingdom had been abolished in 1833, many Britons had turned their attention to the problem of slavery in the United States. In England at the time there was also a fascination with exotic people and places. An eloquent and articulate Black man, especially one who had been enslaved in the United States and found freedom in Canada, was a big draw. Philanthropic men of London, already involved in antislavery activities as well as other humanitarian causes, saw Josiah as a means of raising money for needs closer to home as well as Josiah's own objective.

Before traveling to England, Josiah Henson gathered letters of introduction from several prominent people in Canada and the United States. The Canadians included Rev. John Roaf, a respected Unitarian minister in Toronto who had been active in the antislavery movement for many years and was still an active member of the board of trustees of the BAI;[4] Sir John Beverley Robinson, chief justice on the Court of Queen's Bench since 1829;[5] Sir Allen McNab, Canadian Tory politician and businessman;[6] and Col. John Prince, lawyer, soldier, judge, and member of the Canadian legislature representing Essex County.[7]

The Americans included Amos Lawrence, wealthy textile merchant of Boston; Rev. Dr. George Duffield, pastor of the First Presbyterian Church of Detroit, Michigan;[8] Judge Shubael Conant, first president of the Detroit Anti-Slavery Society;[9] Judge Ross Wilkins, a US district judge of eastern Michigan;[10] and Charles Sumner, US senator from Massachusetts and the leading antislavery senator (and future secretary of war).[11]

Letters of introduction were not given to strangers, so the fact that Josiah Henson carried these letters indicates that he knew influential people in Detroit and Boston as well as in Ontario, Canada. With letters of introduction from such distinguished men, it is no wonder that Josiah was welcomed and supported by equally distinguished men in England.[12] These included Rev. Dr. Thomas Binney (figure 9.1), Congregationalist minister of King's Weigh House Chapel, London, as well as an active member of the British and Foreign Anti-Slavery Society (BFASS) and chair of the 1840 World Anti-Slavery Convention;[13] wealthy financier Samuel Gurney, known as the "banker's banker," who was chair of the second World Anti-Slavery Convention in 1843;[14] Lord Henry Brougham, one of the members of the House of Lords who had pushed for the passage of the 1833 Slavery Abolition Act and now retired from politics but still very influential;[15] and Abbott Lawrence, brother of Amos in Boston, who just happened to be the ambassador from the United States to England at the time.[16]

One of the first people Josiah sought out was Rev. Thomas Binney, who was of particular help to him throughout his stay. Reverend Binney said in the introduction to the 1851 British edition of Josiah Henson's autobiography, referring to the letters of introduction, that "one of the documents was from a personal friend, with whose hand-writing I was well acquainted. This gentleman stated, moreover, that he was a trustee of the Institution, on behalf of which Mr. Henson visits England."[17] This could only have been Rev. John Roaf, who had been born and schooled in England before immigrating to Canada in 1837 as an agent for the Congregationalist Colonial Missionary Society to establish churches in Upper Canada.[18] Henson also mentioned that he preached to Binney's congregation on February 12, 1851, at Weigh House Chapel and held the audience's "utmost lively attention" for nearly two hours.[19]

In the months before the World's Fair commenced on May 1, Josiah attended many gatherings with his new associates, and they introduced him to others so that he did a great deal of traveling in and around London speaking at meetings in halls and churches. Being open-minded and gregarious, Josiah was ecumenical and preached in the pulpits of many different denominations. In addition to the Congregational church of Reverend Binney, Josiah spoke in the Baptist congregation of Bloomsbury Chapel of Reverend William; the Evangelical church of Baptist Noel, tenth son of the Earl of Gainsborough; and the Presbyterian church of Rev. Dr. Robert Burns. Outside of London, Josiah spoke at the church of Congregationalist minister Rev. James Sherman in Reading.[20]

Many of these clergymen were members of the BFASS. Despite the similarity in name, this organization was unlike the antislavery societies in the United States.

Figure 9.1. Thomas Binney. Electric Scotland, https://electricscotland.com/bible/homepreacher/week33.htm.

Embedded deeply in British utilitarianism, the BFASS had the goal of ridding the world of slavery and so was more interested in ending the institution than in freeing individuals. Utilitarianism is a philosophy that claims that an action is right if it produces the greatest net benefit. Established in 1838 by the Quaker Joseph Sturge and Lord Henry Brougham, the BFASS was well financed and stable enough to last well into the twentieth century.[21] Josiah was among the speakers at a grand soiree on May 19, 1851, sponsored by the BFASS (figure 9.2). Other speakers that evening included African Americans Rev. Alexander Crummell, an Episcopalian missionary, and Henry Highland Garnet, a Presbyterian minister and prominent abolitionist from New York.[22]

Josiah's and Henry Garnett's paths would cross often in England, as Garnett was also sponsored by the BFASS to give fundraising lectures around the country for the next two years.[23] Garnett's family, which included a recently adopted young woman by the name of Stella Weems who was escaping enslavement, would join him in August 1851. Stella may have brought Josiah news of his brother, as she was the daughter of John and Arabella Weems who had been owned by Adam Robb in Rockville, Maryland. This was the same man who had owned Josiah for a few months when he was nine and had continued to own Josiah's brother John.[24] Robb died in 1847, and his estate was split up in 1849, with John Henson going to one daughter and the Weems family to another daughter, but the enslaved people still lived near enough to each other to stay connected.

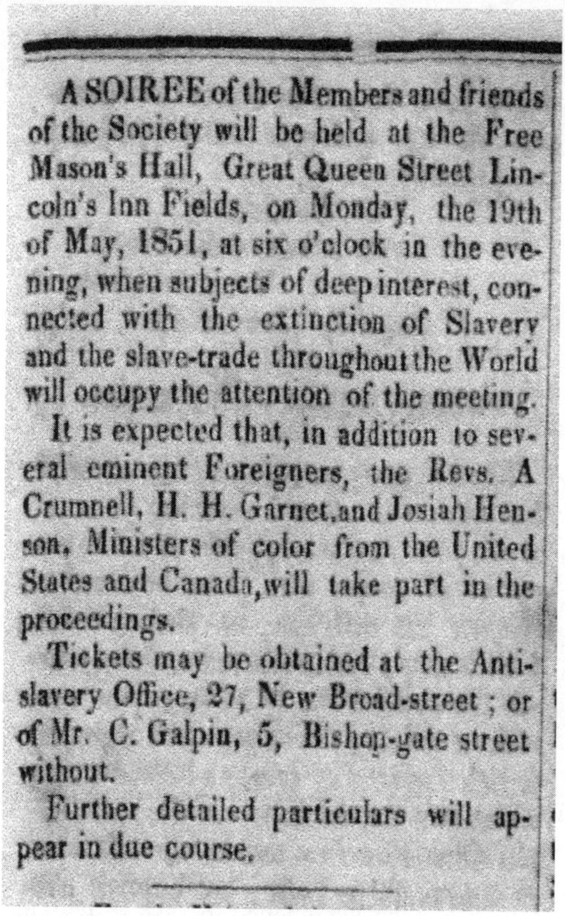

A SOIREE of the Members and friends of the Society will be held at the Free Mason's Hall, Great Queen Street Lincoln's Inn Fields, on Monday, the 19th of May, 1851, at six o'clock in the evening, when subjects of deep interest, connected with the extinction of Slavery and the slave-trade throughout the World will occupy the attention of the meeting.

It is expected that, in addition to several eminent Foreigners, the Revs. A Crumnell, H. H. Garnet, and Josiah Henson, Ministers of color from the United States and Canada, will take part in the proceedings.

Tickets may be obtained at the Anti-slavery Office, 27, New Broad-street ; or of Mr. C. Galpin, 5, Bishop-gate street without.

Further detailed particulars will appear in due course.

Figure 9.2. Account of Josiah Henson and H. H. Garnett giving presentations at a soiree at the Free Mason's Hall, London, on May 19, 1851. *Voice of the Fugitive*, June 4, 1851, 3, col. 1.

Josiah did not mention the Weems family in his memoirs, but surely he must have noticed that some of his former neighbors from Maryland moved into his neighborhood in Canada. William Henry Bradley and his wife, Annie, had escaped enslavement and come to Canada in the fall of 1850 when Josiah was in Boston getting ready to embark for England. In Maryland they had been known as Abraham Young and Annie Maria Talbot Young and had escaped with the aid of abolitionist William Chaplin. Ann was the sister of Arabella Talbot Weems, and they had been enslaved by Adam Robb along with Josiah's brother John. The Bradleys purchased a farm near Josiah's in December 1851 and prospered there. They were soon joined by their niece, Ann Maria Weems. A few years later other former slaves of Robb who had escaped moved to nearby Chatham, and among them were John and Arabella Talbot Weems and Mary Jones with her husband Lewis (owned by a different person).[25] These were all former enslaved people who had escaped from Rockville, Maryland, and were now living near Josiah in Canada. Josiah's brother John may have been enticed to escape with the others, since we know that Josiah had asked Chaplin to help him, but John was not yet ready to go.

In the last weeks of April, Josiah had been engaged in setting up his booth at the Great Exhibition of the Works of Industry of All Nations in Hyde Park, London, which opened on May 1, 1851, and continued to mid-October. This international exhibition, overseen by Prince Albert, was housed in a huge building known as the Crystal Palace, the central part of which was an arched glass structure with a tiered fountain in the center. The building was so tall that it encompassed several large elm trees growing in the park. The exhibition displayed over fifteen thousand objects of art, manufacture, and invention from all parts of the world—from pottery to machinery—more than half of them from countries other than Britain. There were concessions for food and, unique to such exhibitions, private toilets. Queen Victoria visited the exhibition several times, often with her children.[26] The exhibition was the major event of the year in London and attracted local people of all ages and status as well as visitors from many countries, some traveling specifically to view the exhibits.

Josiah ran into a bit of trouble when he registered to set up at the exhibition. Jonas Chickering, the Boston piano manufacturer, had packed and shipped Josiah's four black walnut boards, each seven by four feet, with other items bound for the exhibition. The man in charge of the United States section of the exhibition hall refused to allow Josiah to take his boards to the Canadian section, saying that they arrived on a US ship and therefore were under his control. Josiah thought that if his boards must remain in the US section, he could at least let the visitors know who he was, so he "hired a painter to paint in good large white letters on the tops of my boards: 'THIS IS THE PRODUCT OF THE INDUSTRY OF A FUGITIVE SLAVE FROM THE UNITED STATES, WHOSE RESIDENCE IS DAWN, CANADA.'"[27] The superintendent was so embarrassed by the sign that he allowed Josiah to remove his exhibit to the Canadian section and never even charged him the cargo fee. The humorous conversation between Josiah and the superintendent in front of an audience of English visitors—as depicted in his memoir, where he threatens to leave the boards and sign where they are until the superintendent practically begs for him to take them away—shows how Josiah could turn a potential confrontation into a triviality.[28]

The exhibition was exciting to Josiah at first, but his active mind soon grew bored because the people walking by were so numerous that they became a faceless crowd flowing like a river by his island booth. He does mention that Queen Victoria walked by his exhibit and remarked on it to a companion.[29] After he was back home in Canada, he received the bound *Official Descriptive and Illustrated Catalogue of the Great Exhibition, Great Britain*, with his name in it (figure 9.3). He is listed in the catalog as representing Dawn, Canada, and exhibiting "Black walnut plank and Indian corn in the ear." Sent along with the catalog were a bronze medal and a commemorative picture of the royal family.[30]

A high point in Josiah's visit to England was when financier Samuel Gurney managed to arrange for Josiah an audience with the archbishop of Canterbury, John Bird

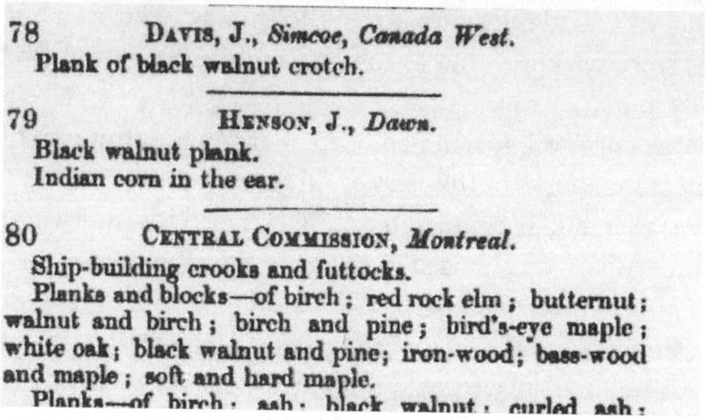

> 78   Davis, J., *Simcoe, Canada West.*
> Plank of black walnut crotch.
>
> ---
>
> 79   Henson, J., *Dawn.*
> Black walnut plank.
> Indian corn in the ear.
>
> ---
>
> 80   Central Commission, *Montreal.*
> Ship-building crooks and futtocks.
> Planks and blocks—of birch ; red rock elm ; butternut;
> walnut and birch ; birch and pine ; bird's-eye maple ;
> white oak; black walnut and pine; iron-wood; bass-wood
> and maple ; soft and hard maple.
> Planks—of birch · ash · black walnut , curled ash ;

Figure 9.3. Josiah Henson's name in the Great Exhibition catalog *Catalogue of the Great Exhibition of the Works of Industry of All Nations, 1851* (London: Spicer Brothers, Wholesale Stationers; W. Clowes and Sons, Printers), 963, No. 79.

Sumner, who had given the opening prayer at the Great Exhibition. They met at his home, Lambeth Palace, in London. According to Josiah, the archbishop was fascinated with Josiah's story and also with his knowledge, educated speech, and gentlemanly manner, finding it difficult to believe he had been raised in slavery, and asked him "at what university did you graduate?" to which Josiah replied "the university of adversity, your grace." The archbishop was so entranced by Josiah that he handed him five golden sovereigns on his departure.[31]

Unfortunately, Josiah was forced to leave England right in the middle of the exhibition and return to Canada due to libelous charges brought against him by some men back home. These charges had appeared in England in the form of newspaper articles and flyers handed out to the public, forcing his supporters and benefactors in London to address the charges.

The dispute began when Rev. William Newman, former secretary of the BAI, moved back to Canada in the fall of 1850 to avoid the Fugitive Slave Act in the United States and settled in Chatham, Ontario, near Dresden and the BAI. Newman had a grudge against Josiah ever since the argument they had five years earlier about the operation of the school had induced him to leave Canada and move back to Ohio. Newman is described by a colleague in *The Voice of the Fugitive* newspaper as "using offensive language, being untruthful," and having "fits of insanity."[32] In a letter to Frederick Douglass in 1850 in protest of the Fugitive Slave Act, Newman revealed a radical disposition and a willingness to resort to violence if necessary.[33] He was also apparently able to hold a grudge for many years, as the sole purpose of his moving back to Canada seemed to be to seek revenge on Josiah.

In March 1851 Newman and his friend Rev. Edward Matthews of the American Baptist Free Mission Society, now in charge of the BAI, called a meeting in Chatham of the "colored citizens of Chatham." The new management of the BAI insinuated that Henson was raising funds in England and the support of the BFASS in order to

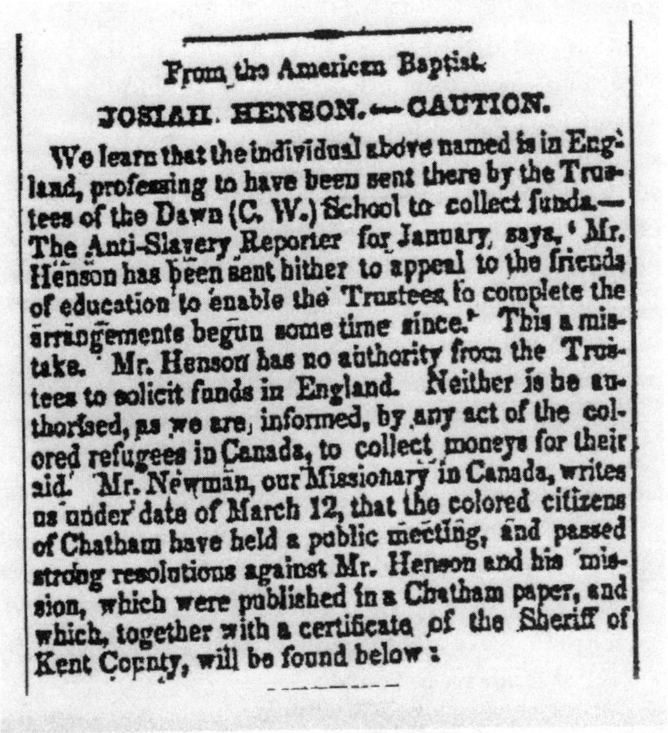

From the American Baptist.

JOSIAH. HENSON.—CAUTION.

We learn that the individual above named is in England, professing to have been sent there by the Trustees of the Dawn (C. W.) School to collect funds.—The Anti-Slavery Reporter for January, says, 'Mr. Henson has been sent hither to appeal to the friends of education to enable the Trustees to complete the arrangements begun some time since.' This a mistake. Mr. Henson has no authority from the Trustees to solicit funds in England. Neither is he authorised, as we are, informed, by any act of the colored refugees in Canada, to collect moneys for their aid. Mr. Newman, our Missionary in Canada, writes us under date of March 12, that the colored citizens of Chatham have held a public meeting, and passed strong resolutions against Mr. Henson and his 'mission, which were published in a Chatham paper, and which, together with a certificate of the Sheriff of Kent County, will be found below :

Figure 9.4. Newspaper notice warning readers that Josiah Henson is not authorized to raise funds for the "Dawn School" in Canada West. *The Liberator* 21, no. 15 (April 11, 1851), 60.

take over the BAI. This meeting issued a public statement, not naming the accusers, claiming that "Mr. Josiah Henson has never colonized or settled a community of Fugitive Slaves in this country, and that he is not the agent of any public Society in Canada, and has no rightful authority to collect funds in the name of the colored people of this Province." This public statement was accompanied by a "certificate" from the local sheriff declaring that he (the sheriff) did not say the things that were reported as being from him in the January *Voice of the Fugitive* in support of Josiah Henson.[34] The statement was reprinted in several newspapers, including William Lloyd Garrison's *The Liberator* (figure 9.4).[35]

One of the resolutions of this meeting was "to inform the benevolent of England, Ireland, and Scotland, that Josiah Henson is a totally unworthy medium through which to transmit their donations for the poor fugitive slaves arriving in Canada." The article was published in a London newspaper and in pamphlets distributed there by Reverend Matthews, who had traveled to London. The fact that both Newman and Matthews, as well as a later critic of Josiah, James Brown, were of African descent is testimony to the continual infighting occurring in Canada among the Blacks, some of whom came from families who had lived in Canada for generations, while others had been free in the United States before immigrating to Canada and still others were fugitives from enslavement.

When members of the BFASS heard these accusations against a man and an institution they had supported, they convened a meeting. First, in order that there could be no further questions or accusations, they set up a committee of three to oversee all the funds, about £1,700 already collected, according to Josiah, and any funds he received in the future. This agency consisted of John Scoble, Rev. John Branch, and Eusebius Smith, with Samuel Gurney Jr. as treasurer.[36] Second, they arranged a hearing with both Henson and Matthews present to discover if there was any truth to the accusations. At this meeting Matthews admitted that not only were there no members from the BAI at the Chatham meeting but also that he had forged the accusatory document himself.[37] Another deciding factor was that American abolitionist Lewis Tappan, when contacted by the committee, said that although he did not think the funds he had donated to the BAI were well managed, he had respect for Reverend Henson himself.[38]

Thus, Josiah was exonerated, but the BFASS knew there was something amiss at the BAI and so decided to send John Scoble with Josiah Henson to Canada to investigate the charges and settle disputes. This was in May 1851, but they were not able to travel until August because of previous commitments. Josiah's son, Isaac Henson, took over as agent for *The Voice of the Fugitive* until at least October 1852.[39] Isaac was attending a theological seminary in London.

The Congregational minister John Scoble was an enthusiastic abolitionist, was one of the founding members of the BFASS, and had served as secretary of that organization since 1842. On a trip to America in 1839 he witnessed the rift in the American antislavery movement between the followers of Garrison and the followers of the Tappan brothers. Scoble became a supporter of the more conservative Tappanites and reported his findings to the BFASS, which supported the more conservative view as well. Even though this was clearly in keeping with the ideology of the BFASS, it made him an enemy in the eyes of the Garrisonians.[40] When the BFASS sent Scoble to Canada, it was not only to clear Josiah Henson's name but also to investigate the affairs of the BAI, which the BFASS had supported since its founding. Scoble saw this as an opportunity to pursue his ambitions in a new venue, since promotion seemed impossible in England because of his low birth.

It is not known whether they traveled together or separately, but since Josiah spoke at the League of Brotherhood, a society chaired by his publisher Charles Gilpin, on July 30, 1851, he must have left for Canada soon after, as both Josiah Henson and John Scoble were in attendance at the North American Convention of Colored Freemen, held in Toronto, Canada, on September 11–12, 1851.[41] At that convention Scoble, in support of Henson, "offered an amendment that Mr. J. C. Brown's name be stricken from the list as vice-president, and some respectable person be appointed in his stead." The motion was upheld by a committee of seven because "the case is undergoing legal investigation."[42]

Scoble stayed for about three months in Canada making inquiries, inspecting the BAI and its books, and questioning everyone involved so he could make a detailed report back to the BFASS. Josiah, after helping Scoble all that he could, returned to London in late September with the help of funding from Amos Lawrence again to finish the last few weeks of the exhibition.[43]

Josiah must have made a positive impression on the British public, because at the end of the exhibition in October 1851, he was convinced by his English friends to stay for a bit longer to raise more funds for his cause and for theirs. One man, Lord Henry Grey, actually offered Josiah a position in India having to do with the cultivation of cotton there, which he turned down. Three men were especially helpful to Josiah in England at this time. He said that he was invited to dine at midday every day by both Samuel Morley and George Hitchcock, but his main benefactor was Rev. Thomas Binney. These benefactors lived within blocks of each other in central London near St. Paul's Church: George Hitchcock on St. Paul's Churchyard, Samuel Morley on Wood Street a few blocks to the north, and Binney's King's Weigh House Chapel just a half mile to the east at Fish Street Hill.[44] Morley was a member of Binney's congregation there. Morley and Hitchcock were both textile wholesalers, Morley in hosiery and Hitchcock in draperies, so they most likely received a recommendation from Amos Lawrence, the Boston textile merchant who was a benefactor of Josiah Henson and living in London at that time. Morley, a supporter of the antislavery movement, was later elected a member of Parliament.

After his return to England, Josiah continued to give lectures at public events and speak at church meetings in and around London for almost a year through August 1852. He was on the roster at the annual meeting of the BFASS on May 17, 1852.[45]

In Josiah's own words, "While in England I was frequently called upon to speak at public meetings of various kinds. I was deeply interested in the Ragged School enterprise, and frequently addressed the schools, and also public meetings held in their behalf. I spent two months of May [May 1851 and May 1852], in that country, and attended many of the great anniversaries, and was called upon to speak at many of them. On several occasions I did what I could to make known the true condition of slaves, in Exeter Hall and other places."[46] Ragged schools were institutions for the poor that were supported by charity because the British government at the time did not offer free schooling. The Ragged School movement began simply by individuals opening schools in various places in England and Scotland and being supported by missionary societies. An official Ragged School Union was formed in 1844, joining them all together, and Lord Shaftesbury, an influential British abolitionist, was the chairman of the organization for thirty-nine years. Many other philanthropic men and women contributed and raised funds for the organization, some of whom were also involved in antislavery meetings.

One of the highlights of Josiah's second visit to England (end of September 1851 to September 4, 1852) was the grand picnic at Pembroke Lodge, the elegant estate of the prime minister, Lord John Russell, in London (figure 9.5). Pembroke was opened for a day to ordinary people, referred to by Josiah in his memoir as "Sabbath School teachers."[47] He was particularly impressed by the deer and birds wandering the grounds

Figure 9.5. Pembroke Lodge, 1885. Old print owned by Peter Damian, released to public domain 2008.

and the lovely scenery. He spoke with many "intelligent men and women" he met as he strolled the park. All the guests were brought inside in the late afternoon, seated at long rows of tables in the large ballroom, and given a resplendent feast. Josiah was asked to give a blessing and sang the common grace:

> Be present at our table lord,
> Be here and everywhere adored,
> These creatures bless,
> And grant that we may feast
> In Paradise with thee.[48]

There were many toasts honoring the host and the queen, some of which were given by Josiah, and several speeches were made. Josiah said it was "one of the pleasantest days of my life."[49]

Throughout August 1852 Josiah was working on a major revision of his autobiography with Thomas Binney. Binney was an author of many essays, books, and hymns, so it is not surprising that he had already published a British edition of Josiah Henson's autobiography in 1851, which is a copy of the 1849 autobiography with the addition of the description of Josiah's Underground Railroad activity. The autobiography also has a closing paragraph by Henson, not to be found in any future editions, in which he thanks the many people who have helped him along his way to self-improvement; a short preface by Binney; and a lengthy appendix consisting of a series of stories and essays by Binney.[50] The book sold more than two thousand copies.

On September 3, Josiah received a letter that upset all of his plans in England. The letter was from his family in Canada announcing that his wife was deathly ill and wanted to see him one last time before the end came.[51] He dropped everything and rushed home as fast as modern transportation could take him.

Josiah's claim of traveling from London, England, to his home in Canada, in just sixteen days (September 4–20) is truly astounding for the time but possible. He could have taken a train from London to Liverpool to possibly embark on the same day, but the fastest steamer in 1851 still took ten days to cross the Atlantic, and most took two weeks, bringing him to Boston around September 16–18.[52] It was possible to travel by rail in one day from Boston, Massachusetts, to Buffalo, New York, at that time.[53] In Buffalo a suspension bridge had been built across the Niagara River that could carry a horse-drawn stage coach.[54] He could then have boarded another train on the Great Western Railway, which was not yet completed to Chatham but would have gotten him part of the way.[55] Josiah himself must have been amazed at the changes in the means and speed of travel in less than two years since he first left his home for England in November 1850.

Josiah made it home before his wife died and was met in front of the house by his four daughters. Charlotte lived a few more weeks after his return and passed away gently after saying her goodbyes to Josiah and their children. Josiah pays her tribute in his memoir. "I can truly and from an overflowing heart say, that she was a sincere and devoted Christian, and a faithful and kind wife to me, even up to the day of her death arranging all our domestic matters in such a manner as to contribute as largely as possible to my comfort and happiness."[56] He also quotes a verse from the hymn "How Sweet the Hour of Closing Day":

> Who would not wish to die like those
> Whom God's own spirit deigns to bless?
> To sink into that soft repose,
> Then wake to perfect happiness?[57]

At the time of her death Charlotte and Josiah had eight living children. Thomas, the eldest, was born about 1818 in Maryland, and Isaac was also born in Maryland about 1819 or 1820.[58] The two born in Kentucky were Celia Jane (a tribute to Josiah's mother) in 1827[59] and Josiah in 1828.[60] In Canada, Charlotte Matilda was born in 1832,[61] Elizabeth in 1834,[62] Peter in 1836,[63] and Julia Ann in 1840.[64] There were also grandchildren by the end of 1852, as Celia Jane had married a man named Christee and had as many as five children by then, and Charlotte Matilda married Everett Charles Richey (Richie) and had given birth to four.[65] The little ones living nearby must have given delight to the ailing grandmother, especially when her husband was absent.

Charlotte Stevenson Henson was between fifty and sixty years old at her death.[66] In his 1849 autobiography Josiah Henson says, "She has borne me twelve children, eight of whom survive."[67] The eight living children listed above are mentioned at the time of Charlotte's death. The seven years between the birth of Isaac about 1820 and the birth of Celia Jane in 1827 might have been the time when two or more babies were lost. It is possible that Charlotte gave birth to one of the babies who died on the trip to Kentucky from Maryland in 1825 when the group had to stop for several weeks in or near Harpers Ferry, Virginia. All the other births are about two years apart except for the last child, Julia, who came into the world four years after her nearest sibling. Charlotte could have been about forty years old at that time. Unfortunately, Isaac was not able to be present at his mother's death, as he was still in England at the time studying to be a Methodist minister.[68]

After his wife's death Josiah seems to have gone into a period of mourning, absenting himself from the affairs of the BAI for several months. While Josiah had been in England, John Scoble had immigrated to Canada with his family and taken over the management of the BAI, and trouble was brewing, with a growing conflict between the old school, represented by Trustee James Brown, and the reorganization, represented by Scoble.

10

Discord at Home

For more than ten years Josiah Henson had dedicated his life to helping establish and support the British-American Institute of Science and Industry (BAI) for the benefit of his fellow escapees from slavery. From the time he had first settled in Canada he felt a calling to help them adapt to freedom and a new country, be educated, and find good employment. He now found his efforts and his methods challenged from within the very community he sought to advance. He also discovered that some people he had thought were allies would turn out to be the opposite.

One of these deceitful allies was the Englishman John Scoble (figure 10.1), who had been secretary of the British and Foreign Anti-Slavery Society (BFASS) in London for many years. The BFASS allowed Scoble to take charge of the money Josiah had raised for the BAI in England in order to invest it in the school but voted against giving continual support to the school.[1] The goal of the BFASS was to work toward ending slavery worldwide, not to finance institutions or settlements of freed slaves. During his previous visit in 1851 Scoble had been approved by the majority of the board of trustees of the BAI to take over its management and had worked to balance the books of the BAI, and he then returned to England.

The colloquial name for the BAI as the "Dawn Institute" continued to be used locally even though there was no town or settlement named Dawn, and at this time the BAI no longer even existed in the Dawn Township because of the redrawing of the government boundaries.[2]

In July 1852 a committee of local residents, in a survey of the schools of Kent County, said that "the Dawn Institute is in a languishing state. Everything seems to be going downhill, so that it is, in fact, unworthy of the name of an Institution." They go on to recommend that the management of the school be taken over by another party.[3] The Congregationalist minister John Scoble, being well educated but of low birth, had no prospects of advancement in England, so he decided to start a new life in Canada.

Figure 10.1. John Scoble from the Anti-Slavery Convention of 1840. Painting by Benjamin Robert Haydon (see gallery image 5.3). National Portrait Gallery, London.

He resigned from the BFASS in September 1852 and moved to Canada with his family later that year to take over management of the BAI.[4]

Scoble had already garnered the disapproval of the Garrisonians by supporting a political adversary of theirs in England, so it is not surprising that this move was highly criticized by the followers of William Lloyd Garrison in both America and Great Britain. As an example, Garrisonian John Estlin wrote to wealthy Maria Weston Chapman about influencing the editor of London's *Morning Advertiser*, James Grant, to publish articles critical of Scoble, saying, "We are getting on capitally in putting Mr. Scoble into 'a fix.' I am sure he is very uncomfortable."[5] Another friend of Mrs. Chapman's, Emma Mitchel, said in a letter to her, "I expect that S. [Scoble] will not be here [London] to patch over his evil deeds and that the tail of the serpent will be fully brought to light, and judgement go forth accordingly. His reception in Canada is not to be envied. It is said that there are those who will 'make it too hot to hold him.'"[6] The Garrisonians saw Scoble as being insincere and racially prejudiced because of, among other things, his suggestion to the painter of the 1840 Anti-Slavery Convention portrait that he not be placed next to a Black attendee.[7] Indeed, the fact that Scoble was already in political hot water in England, putting an end to his political ambitions, may have had something to do with his departure for Canada.

Josiah was also in a bit of hot water himself at home. Besides Edward Matthews and William Newman, another critic of both Henson and Scoble appeared in Dresden in the person of James C. Brown, one of the original trustees of the BAI still holding that office. Brown had first appeared in Canada as the head of the group of refugees who had emigrated from Cincinnati in 1829 to form the Wilberforce settlement just north of London, Ontario.[8]

Brown claimed to have independently led 460 people from Cincinnati to Canada in the fall of 1829 and to have contracted, by himself, for four thousand acres with the Canada Company, which owned large tracts of land.[9] Actually, it was a group formed in Cincinnati in the summer of 1829 that appointed agents Israel Lewis and Thomas Cresap to find the land in Canada and purchase it, and it was they, not Brown, who contracted with the Canada Company. James C. Brown did lead the first group of settlers to the township of Biddulph (now Lucan-Biddulph) in Ontario, where he was elected president of the first management committee. The settlement was named Wilberforce in honor of the British parliamentarian who had led the movement to abolish slavery. Unfortunately, the group had no money with which to purchase the land, so an appeal went out, and a group of Quakers in the Ohio and Indiana Meetings purchased eight hundred acres for the group that would be mortgaged in lots of fifty acres to the immigrants.

The management of the settlement changed two years later, leaving Brown out. He soon left for Toronto, later to move to Chatham, where he became a trustee of the BAI. The Wilberforce settlement remained impoverished. A school was never built. Agents sent out to solicit funding kept most of the money raised, and the chairman of the board of directors finally dissolved the organization and left Canada in 1837. By 1850 there were only fifty-two of the original number of settlers left in the community.[10]

James C. Brown was a supporter of Garrison's ideals (see chapter 8) and became a source of great annoyance to Scoble, who assumed management of the BAI early in 1853, paid off the debts, and began a complete renovation. The American Baptist Free Mission Society, which had been in charge of the BAI for two years, left the institute soon after, taking anything of value from the buildings with them.

By this time Josiah Henson, having paid off his debt and in mourning for his wife, had largely separated himself from the business affairs of the school, as he had confidence in the abilities of his friend John Scoble. Josiah trusted John Scoble because the esteemed BFASS had put its trust in Scoble and in 1851 had cleared Josiah's name of any wrongdoing and set the finances of the BAI on the right track. Josiah had seen how disastrous the previous management had been for the school and had been personally attacked by some of the people involved in that administration. In addition, Scoble had personally defended and supported Henson and discredited James Brown. Josiah assumed that "any enemy of my enemy is a friend of mine." Josiah, being highly respected by the community as their spiritual leader, had great influence with the local residents, so they supported Scoble and his reorganization plan on Josiah's recommendation.

But things did not go so well as expected. Unable to find a suitable tenant, Scoble farmed the BAI property himself, with profits going to the school. Gone was Hiram Wilson's ideal of a self-supporting school, with the students learning agriculture and trades as well as receiving a good education by farming the land themselves and turning the products into salable goods. Scoble tried to reorganize the school and incorporate it to protect individuals from liability but was thwarted in every move by James Brown, who was still a trustee of the BAI and contended that Scoble did not have the authority to assume control of the institute. Brown accused Scoble of making his own profit from the BAI by selling timber and livestock and brought unsuccessful suit against Scoble twice for this reason. Scoble lived apart from the Black community in a large house and did not interact socially with the local community, accentuating the fact that he was an outsider and reinforcing the impression that he had a paternalistic attitude toward Blacks.[11]

As early as November 1851 Scoble had been criticized for his encouragement of the immigration of American Blacks to the West Indies by Garrisonian Parker Pillsbury of Ohio in a letter to the editor of Garrison's newspaper, *The Liberator*. Pillsbury quotes William Wells Brown, a prominent escaped slave and abolitionist in Boston, as saying that Scoble had a "deep-laid scheme to entrap the unsuspecting into the power of men who would place the chain upon the limbs of the emancipated slave"[12] by enticing them to Haiti. In July 1852 John Scoble was vilified in *The Liberator* as being unscrupulous, mean, and selfish because of his political actions in England, and a columnist in the paper warned the people of Canada to beware of his scheming. In spite of these criticisms Josiah continued to support John Scoble, putting his confidence in a man he looked up to, a man who was trusted by and had the confidence of noblemen, clergymen, and men in high office in England.

The year 1853 was momentous for Josiah, bringing new and influential friends and unexpected celebrity in the fifty-seventh year of his life. The publishing in March of *A Key to Uncle Tom's Cabin, Presenting the Original Facts and Documents upon Which the Story Is Based Together with Corroborative Statements Verifying the Truth of the Work*, by Harriet Beecher Stowe, proved that Josiah was indeed one of the models for the main character of the book and gave him local fame that spread to greater realms during the next few years and changed his life forever.

In June of that year Josiah attended and was elected president of the General Convention for the Improvement of the Colored Inhabitants of Canada, held in Amherstburg. This was a continuation of the organization, which had originally been formed in November 1850, when it established *The Voice of the Fugitive* newspaper. The 1853 convention made several resolutions in support of the African Americans in Canada, including statements against begging and the misuse of funds, in support of education, in support of temperance, and in support of immigration to Canada and the West Indies but in opposition to colonization in Africa. The convention called for vigilance committees to oversee the collection and distribution of funds raised in aid of the "coloured" settlers and the formation of a "League of Africo-Americans," as suggested by the General Convention held in Toronto in 1851.[13] The Convention for the Improvement of the Colored Inhabitants of Canada gave thanks to Harriet Beecher Stowe and her famous book as well as to John Scoble and to the antislavery societies.[14]

As it happened, this Convention for the Improvement of the Colored Inhabitants of Canada was also attended by a man named Lewis Clark (*sic*) of Sandwich, Ontario. It is not known whether this is the same Lewis Clarke whom Harriet Beecher Stowe acknowledged was the model for the fictional character George Harris in *Uncle Tom's Cabin,* but in a later autobiography Josiah claimed that he knew Clarke and traveled with him. They may have met at this gathering.[15]

Figure 10.2. Frederick Douglass, by George Kendall Warren, ca. 1879. https://historylink.tours /stop/douglass-truth-branch-of -seattle-public-library/.

In July 1853 Josiah's son Isaac returned from England as an ordained Wesleyan minister, having attended seminary there.[16] It must have warmed Josiah's heart to know that his son was following in his footsteps and had a calling to do holy works. Isaac married and settled near his father.

Josiah continued his support of Scoble and the BAI throughout the contentious years of 1854–1855. In August 1854 Frederick Douglass (figure 10.2) visited Dresden and the BAI at the invitation of Scoble to address the celebration there of the twentieth anniversary of the British emancipation of slaves. Douglass praised both Scoble and Henson in the newspaper *Frederick Douglass' Paper* after his visit. Douglass stayed his first night there in the home of Josiah Henson, whose family greeted him with graciousness even with the lateness of the hour of his arrival. Douglass observed that

Father Henson, though well stricken in years and in labors, advancing towards seventy [Josiah, since he had published that he was born in 1789 instead of 1796, continued to use the former as his birth date], was up, bright as a boy, and gay as a lark, gave us a cheering welcome to his home in the woods. Pointing to lights peering through the thick bramble and trees around in different directions, he said, there lives one son, and there another. I have eight children, and have only to leap upon a stump and give a hoop to be at once surrounded by them.[17]

At the festivities the next day Douglass enjoyed the procession and the introductory speech of Henson and opined that Scoble, in explaining the history of the event and the people involved, was "always fluent, exact, rhetorical, and sometimes truly eloquent." He also observed that Father Henson "was everywhere treated with marked respect and affection—not as the robber of Dawn, but as the honor of Dawn."[18] Douglass showed his support for John Scoble, saying that he was "in every way qualified" to manage the settlement, and criticized James Brown for marring the celebration with unfounded accusations against Scoble.[19]

Josiah continued to be supported by his community, even as attacks by the Garrisonians increased. The followers of William Lloyd Garrison, publisher of the abolitionist newspaper *The Liberator*, took a more radical and action-based view of freeing slaves than the more conservative followers of the Tappan brothers, such as Scoble and Henson, who believed in convincing people of the moral evil of slavery through education and religious conviction. Besides being criticized in *The Liberator*, Scoble and Henson came under increasing attack by a new newspaper in Canada, the *Provincial Freeman*, published and edited by Mary Ann Shadd (figure 10.3), a free Black schoolteacher who emigrated from Pennsylvania. Her parents were Underground Railroad participants, and she had put herself in danger by publicly calling for Blacks to be more active in the abolition movement in a letter published in *Frederick Douglass' Paper*.

Because women were not considered capable of being newspaper editors at that time, Miss Shadd had first Samuel Ringgold, a Black abolitionist, and then William Newman as the named editors of the *Provincial Freeman* when it was published first in Windsor, Canada, in 1853 and then in Toronto in 1854. In the spring of 1855, moving the paper to Chatham, Shadd openly assumed her editorship, partnering with H. Ford Douglass and her brother, Isaac Shadd.[20] William Newman left the area for good in 1859 to be a missionary in Haiti and so was no longer a threat to the good name of Josiah Henson.[21]

Throughout 1854 Shadd was critical of Scoble for what she called his arrogance and paternalistic attitude toward Blacks and of Josiah for what she considered begging but what Josiah considered solicitation of funds for the support of the BAI. She also published letters highly critical of Frederick Douglass after his visit, saying that he was "a foreigner, who knows nothing of our grievances in this matter," and that he only came because he was paid.[22] James Brown, supported by Shadd, continued his malicious attacks on Henson and Scoble, giving a speech in April 1855 calling for an audit of the accounts of the school and a new election, by "the people," of trustees for the BAI, to be held in August.[23] A letter to the editor by James Brown suggesting that

Figure 10.3. Mary Ann Shadd, 1850s. Courtesy of National Archives of Canada, C-029977.

Scoble forcibly took over the BAI aided by Henson was published in the *Provincial Freeman* in May 1855.[24]

Brown held a public rally in Chatham two days before the August meeting to elect new trustees for the BAI. This rally was advertised as a public meeting at which Josiah Henson could defend himself against accusations by James Brown and where Brown could defend himself against accusations made by Henson. According to the *Provincial Freeman,* John Scoble was also in attendance, and the "house was filled to utmost capacity." The report of the meeting by Mary Ann Shadd claimed that Brown won the debate over his adversary by means of his "giant intellect" and the "overwhelming applause frequently given to Mr. Brown." The writer complained that Henson's defense was evasive and overly long. She also criticized Scoble for his conceit and paternalism. The audience hissed when Scoble spoke of his authority over the BAI, the mismanagement that had preceded him, and his altruistic motives in assuming control.[25]

The verbal attacks soon turned violent. The following tumultuous meeting to elect new trustees for the BAI on August 29 was reported by Brown in the *Provincial Freeman* in September 1855. John Scoble and friends, according to Brown's report, had padlocked the BAI's meetinghouse where the group led by Brown was to meet, so they had to gather in the nearby Methodist meetinghouse. Scoble and associates, including Josiah Henson, followed Brown's group there, where the meeting descended into chaos and name-calling, with Scoble calling Brown and friends "Brutes" and Brown calling Scoble a "tyrant and a slave driver," saying that now "the Devil is loose."[26] In spite of this scathing critique, Scoble continued to manage the BAI with a new board of trustees.

A less biased view of the BAI came from Benjamin Drew, a Boston abolitionist who traveled though Canada in the early 1850s interviewing people who had escaped from bondage and describing their settlements. His objectives were to both arouse support for the antislavery movement through personal accounts of enslavement and escape and to promote the concept that Blacks could become self-supporting and good contributing citizens in freedom. His results, with no embellishments or comments, were published as *A North Side View of Slavery, the Refugee: or the Narratives of Fugitive Slaves in Canada, Related by Themselves* by John Jewett company (publisher of *Uncle Tom's Cabin*) in 1856. Even though Josiah Henson was not present at the time of Drew's visit, this book gives a window into Josiah's world from an outside observer, unacquainted with the arguments and controversies swirling around the communities he visited. The book includes descriptions of twelve spontaneous and two planned settlements (Elgin in Buxton and the Refugee's Home Society in Sandwich) of formerly enslaved people in Canada and 125 interviews with residents. He also visited and describes the BAI near Dresden.

In describing the informal settlement at St. Catharines, Drew paid tribute to Hiram Wilson, cofounder of the BAI, as a kind soul who welcomed the new arrivals and instructed them on how to make their way in their new home. Also in St. Catharines, Drew interviewed a person whose name is now familiar. Harriet Tubman, unrecognized in that time and place for her courageous feats, gave only one paragraph to the interviewer:

> I grew up like a neglected weed,—ignorant of liberty, having no experience
> of it. Then I was not happy or contented: every time I saw a white man, I was
> afraid of being carried away. I had two sisters carried away in a chain-gang,—
> one of them left two children. We were always uneasy. Now I've been free, I
> know what a dreadful condition slavery is. I have seen hundreds of escaped
> slaves, but I never saw one who was willing to go back and be a slave. I have
> no opportunity to see my friends in my native land. We would rather stay in
> our native land, if we could be as free there as we are here. I think slavery
> is the next thing to hell. If a person would send another into bondage, he
> would, it appears to me, be bad enough to send him into hell, if he could.[27]

In contrast, Drew's interview with J. (James) C. Brown covered nine pages. The interview contained the story of Brown's life in slavery and in freedom in Virginia, Kentucky, Ohio, and Canada but was remarkable more by what it left out: Brown never mentioned the failed community of Wilberforce and his part in it.

Drew described Dresden, near the site of the BAI, as having about one hundred white residents and seventy Blacks, with about one-third of the people owning land with others involved in a trade. The BAI's three-hundred-acre parcel was bordered on one side by the Sydenham River, and one of the first buildings along the river Drew described was an old abandoned sawmill.[28] This may have been the original sawmill Josiah labored so hard to collect funding to finance and that he built with his own hands and the help of his sons. According to Josiah, after he left for England, the sawmill was leased to an unscrupulous unnamed man who ran it prosperously for a couple of years and then left the country with a load of lumber before paying the mill workers. The disgruntled workers trashed the mill in their anger.[29]

John Scoble took Drew on a tour of the premises of the BAI, where "three or four families support themselves on the Institute farm," but no institute buildings were then in existence.[30] Scoble regaled his visitor with his plans to build a church and two schoolhouses (one for boys and one for girls), a college, and a house for the superintendent. Drew included in his account this report:

> The First Annual Report to the Anti-Slavery Society of Canada, presented March 24, 1852, says of the Educational Institute, "About sixty pupils are attending the school. The Institution is soon to be placed under the management of the British and Foreign Anti-Slavery Society, a change likely to prove favorable to its future success. The property of the Institute has since been conveyed through John Scoble, Esq., by 'lease and release.'"[31]

At this time the children of the area attended segregated government schools. Drew reported that the land of the BAI was fertile, about half cleared, and that the river was navigable and capable of carrying cargo into Lake Huron. He wrote that "Mr. Scoble is ready to assist any enterprise which would be of advantage to the Institute."[32]

One of the people Drew interviewed in Dresden may have been familiar to Josiah. This was William Bradley, formerly known as Abraham Young when he was enslaved by Adam Robb in Maryland. William spoke of how he abhorred slavery and thought every day about those he had left in bondage. He also criticized white people of the country where he was now living for their prejudice toward and mistreatment of the new immigrants, saying, "There are many respectable colored people moving in, but I have not much hope of a better state of things. Public sentiment will move mountains of laws."[33]

Drew visited two other organized settlements near the BAI of formerly enslaved people that can be reasonably compared to the institute: Elgin and the Refugee Home Society. Unlike the BAI, these settlements were not focused on a self-supporting industrial school but instead were organized farming communities with an emphasis on education and self-reliance.

Elgin, named for the then-governor of Canada Lord Elgin, was established by Rev. William King, a white Presbyterian minister born in Ireland. King had lived in Louisiana for a few years and later inherited fifteen slaves from his wife's Louisiana family upon her death. He freed the slaves and brought them to Canada, where he settled alongside them. He formed the Elgin Association in 1849 and raised money through donations from members of the Presbyterian Church and on his own money-raising tours of Canada, the United States, and Great Britain. The association purchased 4,300 acres of land, to which 7,000 additional acres were added by 1853.[34] The Elgin settlement was located in the township of Buxton about forty kilometers south of Dresden. The success of this most prosperous of the settlements was due to careful planning and staging. Streets and lots were laid out, with minimum requirements for the size of houses and the acreage of farms. Emphasis was on education, religion,

Figure 10.4. Henry Bibb. Bentley Historical Library, http://cooks.aadl.org /gallery/sol/henry_bibb.jpg.html.

temperance, and becoming citizens and voting. The settlement had an elected governing body and encouraged individual independence. Annual reports show steady advancement, production, and self-sufficiency. The school, giving a classical education, was of such good quality that many white families sent their children there. Benjamin Drew remarked that "the settlers at Buxton are characterized by a manly, independent air and manner."[35]

The Refugee's Home Society, founded in 1852 near Sandwich (now part of Windsor), was planned in a similar fashion to Elgin but had less success. This was mainly due to a lack of funding, changing rules, and the death of the founder, Henry Bibb (figure 10.4), in 1854. Interviews with inhabitants of the settlement by Benjamin Drew reveal a great deal of dissatisfaction with the Refugee's Home Society and the management of the settlement.[36]

Another tragedy entered Josiah's life when beloved son Isaac died in 1856 at the age of thirty-seven, leaving Josiah bereft and prompting him to escape to New England on a speaking tour to help ease his grief. Both the United States and Canada were fast being crisscrossed by railroads in the 1850s, making travel fast and easy. The Niagara suspension bridge, with the railroad on one level and wagons and pedestrians on the other, was completed in 1855 and allowed for continuous rail travel from Windsor, Ontario, to the Atlantic coast. This bridge made possible a direct connection of the Great Western Railway of Canada with the New York Central Railroad in the United States, which had a connection to Boston. A railroad also ran from New York to Boston to Bangor, Maine, where Josiah gave a talk in May 1856.[37] He was also seen in Massachusetts at the end of that year and undoubtedly visited many more places in New England.[38] "After my successful visit to England," Josiah wrote, "I travelled in Canada, and in Maine, New Hampshire, Vermont, Massachusetts, Connecticut, and Rhode Island. In all these states I was cordially welcomed as a speaker in the pulpits of the Congregationalists, Presbyterians, Methodists, Baptists, and Universalists. I held many meetings, and discussed the subject of slavery in all its bearings on society."[39] Josiah's spreading fame as a model for "Uncle Tom" also may have influenced his popularity on the speaking circuit.

In May 1857 Mary Ann Shadd, based on the testimony of recent immigrants from Springfield, Massachusetts, charged that Josiah Henson had been collecting money from various churches for the benefit of the "refugees of Canada" and accused him of falsely representing himself as an agent of the BAI and "begging for himself."[40]

No legal action seems to have come out of this accusation, but it was about this time that Henson separated himself from Scoble and the BAI. After more than four years of management of the institute, Scoble had done nothing but raze the old buildings. None of his grandiose plans, not even rebuilding the church, had come to fruition. The people in the area looked up to Josiah as their spiritual leader and as their contact with Scoble, who seemed to not want to speak with anyone else in the community, so Josiah was hard-pressed to defend a man whom he was beginning to doubt himself. In the beginning of Scoble's tenure as manager of the BAI, Josiah had believed that the man had the best interest of the community at heart, but as the years progressed he saw that the English gentleman had no real grasp of farming and was more theoretical than practical in his methods.[41] Scoble's apparent inability to make a profit from farming and his lack of progress in reinstating the school concerned Josiah greatly.

In addition, perhaps because of the Panic of 1857 or perhaps because he intended to enter the political arena, Scoble began to call in his outstanding loans that autumn. Josiah had borrowed money from Scoble two times, using eighty acres of his farm as collateral, and so was one of the people asked to pay up.[42] At this point, Josiah says, "The scales fell from my eyes; I saw through the man's motives."[43] Josiah no longer trusted the man he had once revered and realized that the BAI, which he had hoped Scoble could save, was now most likely doomed to failure. Scoble sued Henson for repayment of the loans, but the suit would not be heard until 1863. Henson never mentioned Scoble's name in his autobiographies after this except as a member of the BFASS in London.

During the winter of 1857–1858 Josiah was lonely and still in mourning for his son, and his thoughts turned to his brother John, still enslaved in Maryland. Josiah had tried to persuade his brother to escape on the Underground Railroad by way of a message from a New York friend, William Chaplin, who was helping people escape from that area, but Chaplin reported that John was too afraid to make the attempt.[44] Now Josiah was thinking of another way to free his brother from the bonds of slavery.

11

New Directions

IN THE SPRING OF 1858 JOSIAH HENSON HAD HIGH HOPES. HE HAD LONG DREAMED OF purchasing his brother John's freedom and bringing him to Canada to live with him but never had enough money. After learning how much his fame had spread from his connection to the popular novel *Uncle Tom's Cabin*, Josiah got a new idea on how to raise the necessary funds. He would use this new fame to have a new autobiography published. Two autobiographies were already in print: the 1849 autobiography published by Samuel Eliot and the one published in 1851 in England by Rev. Thomas Binney. But much had happened in Josiah's life since then, and remembered past experiences untold in the previous books could also be added to a new volume. Josiah had already approached two friends to write down, from his dictation, these new additions to this anticipated publication. What he needed now was a publisher to put it all together and print the book. Of course, an endorsement by Harriet Beecher Stowe, author of the famous novel, would help, and perhaps she might recommend a publisher.

First, Josiah needed to go to Boston and locate a friend who could introduce him to Stowe. This must be someone whom she knew well, someone who knew where she lived. Josiah claimed in a later autobiography (1877) that he visited Stowe in Andover, Massachusetts, in 1849.[1] Since Stowe did not reside in Andover until the summer of 1852 and Henson was in England that summer, he could not have met her then.[2] Perhaps he may have been mistaken about the year of the visit. In a letter written late in her life to Rev. W. H. Gilley, Stowe told of a "visit he [Henson] paid her in Andover after the publication of *Uncle Tom's Cabin*" but did not mention a specific date.[3] Since Josiah remained in Canada between the death of his wife in 1852 and that of his son Isaac in 1856, the visit must have taken place after 1856.

Josiah claimed in an 1881 interview that he was accompanied on his visit to Stowe by a "White" man named George Clark.[4] This may have been Lewis Clarke (also known as George Lewis Clark), the model for the character George Harris in *Uncle*

Tom's Cabin who could pass for white. Josiah referred to Lewis Clarke as a friend, saying "he has traveled and lectured with me in the New England States," and also that he knew Clarke's wife, the model for Eliza in the novel, when they lived in Ontario.[5] Josiah may have met Clarke at the June 1853 convention in Amherstburg (as mentioned in chapter 10). Lewis Clarke was well known to Stowe, as he had worked for a relative of hers, and she had interviewed him extensively to create the George Harris character and incidents in her famous novel.

While both Stowe and Henson might have been unclear about the date of their meeting, improvements in transportation made travel much faster and easier than in the 1840s when Josiah Henson was making fundraising tours between Dresden, Canada, and Boston, Massachusetts. The opening of the Niagara suspension bridge in 1855 connected Canada with the United States, and new railroad lines in both countries made connections easy between all of the large cities and many towns and villages in between. Josiah traveled to New England on speaking tours in 1856 and 1857 and was known to have been in Boston in 1858.[6] Andover was just a day's ride by horse or carriage from Boston, so it would have been possible for Josiah to go there on one of his visits to that city. This visit most likely took place in the spring of 1858 when Stowe was at home in Andover writing *The Minister's Wooing*, which would be published in serial form in December 1858 in the *Atlantic Monthly*.[7] If Henson did meet Stowe in the spring of 1858 he may have been rewarded with a letter of introduction to her publisher, John P. Jewett.[8] Whether or not this meeting occurred, Henson did go to Stowe's publisher John P. Jewett of Boston to have his story published, and Stowe did write an introduction to the book, dated April 5, 1858, so either Josiah or her publisher, Jewett, must have contacted her at that time.

The five short paragraphs of Harriet Beecher Stowe's introduction to Henson's autobiography are undoubtedly her writing style, filled as they are with Christian language and references to the Bible. She never mentions the "Uncle Tom" character of her novel but instead compares Josiah to an African man in the Bible: "Africa was represented in the person of Simon the Cyrenean, who came patiently bearing after him the load of the cross; and ever since then poor Africa has been toiling on, bearing the weary cross of contempt and oppression after Jesus." She indicates her familiarity with details of Josiah's story when she says that "one sermon, one offer of salvation by Christ, was sufficient for him, as for the Ethiopian eunuch, to make him at once a believer from the heart and a preacher of Jesus."[9]

Josiah's depiction of his "self-conversion" to Christianity after hearing a sermon by an itinerant preacher in his first autobiography was noted in similar words in Stowe's *A Key to Uncle Tom's Cabin*:

> Henson grew up in a state of heathenism, without any religious instruction,
> till, in a camp-meeting, he first heard of Jesus Christ, and was electrified
> by the great and thrilling news that He had tasted death for every man, the
> bond as well as the free. This story produced an immediate conversion, such

as we read of in the Acts of the Apostles, where the Ethiopian eunuch, from one interview, hearing the story of the cross, at once believes and is baptized. Henson forthwith not only became a Christian, but began to declare the news to those about him.[10]

Stowe also stated in her preface that Henson was trying to raise money to free his brother from bondage.

Josiah did not mention the publisher, John Jewett, in his later autobiographies but instead said, "I consulted some of the Anti-Slavery friends in Boston, particularly Amos Lawrence, Esq., and they agreed to publish the story of my life, as I had suggested to them, that I might be able, from its sale, to raise a sufficient sum of money to buy my brother's freedom."[11] Henson had the habit of omitting from his autobiographies the names of people he disliked.

Josiah's autobiography was published by John Jewett, not Amos Lawrence, and Jewett remembered meeting Josiah in an interview published in *The Manhattan* magazine in 1883. Jewett, not being aware of the 1849 (Boston) or the 1851 (London) autobiographies or trying to avoid any copyright infringement, said, "It is certain that the first edition of 'Father Henson's Life' did not appear until 1858 . . . for I was obliged to write about one-quarter of the book myself." Jewett went on to say,

> "It was necessary for someone to construct the story out of fragmentary hints dropped by the old negro. To get the details of any incident required a tedious cross-examination. The first person who undertook to write 'Henson's Life' was a Unitarian clergyman of Springfield, Mass. [Rev. Francis Tiffany].[12] Father Henson then induced the Rev.—afterward, Bishop—Gilbert Haven, at that time editor of *Zion's Herald* in Boston, to take up the work. Mr. Haven had written another quarter of the book."[13]

Jewett claimed to have tried unsuccessfully to find someone else to finish Henson's autobiography but ended up having to do it himself. He said, "It was not an easy job, for it required not a little patience to make a connected story out of Father Henson's jumbled and incoherent talk." When asked by the interviewer how the three parts of the writing fit together, Jewett replied, "Wonderfully well. No one seemed to perceive that they were by different hands."[14]

John Jewett gave a very revealing description of Henson in that interview, noting that because of his broken bones "he had so little control over his fingers and arms that he could not put a hat on his head. He had to lay the hat on a table and, by a wriggling motion, insert his head into it."[15]

The 1858 edition, *Truth Stranger Than Fiction: Father Henson's Story of his Own Life*, was published in mid-May of that year and had an advanced sale of five thousand copies.[16] It was three times the size of Josiah's first autobiography (1849), which formed the first part of the new one and was unchanged except for stating the full names of people instead of initials and the addition of some dialogue. About one-quarter of the additional material in this edition was due to Josiah's recounting of incidents he had neglected to mention in the first book and about one-quarter of his experiences since the publishing of the first book. The rest was composed of dialogues—perhaps recalled or perhaps made up—and of embellishments by his ghostwriters.

Instead of the usual agreement with a publisher for the writer to receive a percentage of the sales, Josiah seems to have taken his payment in a lump sum and in books. As he said, "I took a package of the books on my back and travelled in the New England States, and succeeded in interesting the people, so that I was enabled to raise the money I required."[17] He thought that his brother's owner would sell him for $400, and Josiah would then need an additional $150 for transportation, which totaled $550.[18]

Josiah was unable to make the trip to Maryland himself, being well known there as a fugitive from enslavement even though his previous owner had passed away in 1850. So, he arranged for a third party to purchase his brother. In Josiah's words, "through the negotiation of Mr. Charles C. Berry, cashier of the City Bank in Boston, Massachusetts, who had friends at the South, I joyfully sent the ransom." The transaction took place and was recorded in the county records on September 8, 1858, when Jane Elizabeth Beall of Montgomery County, Maryland, sold John Henson, age about sixty, to Josiah Henson for $250.[19] Previously, John Henson had been valued at $150 when he came to Jane Beall in 1847 from her grandfather Adam Robb's estate.[20] Based on the inventory of the Robb estate and on the inventory of the Josias McPherson estate in 1805, John Henson's actual age at the time of his freedom was sixty-five. Even at this advanced age, it seems that John was worth $100 more than he had been years earlier.

After John Henson was purchased by his brother, he traveled to Baltimore, then by ship to Boston, where he was greeted by Josiah, who took John to his home in Canada. But John's wife (who may have been deceased) and children remained in the South. According to Josiah, one of John's sons came to visit him after the American Civil War. That son returned in 1872 to take his then seventy-nine-year-old father to his home in Pennsylvania, where he and his family lived and worked on a dairy farm.[21]

While Josiah was in Massachusetts in 1858, he attended several weekly gatherings of Methodist ministers that took place on the second floor of the Methodist bookstore in the Cornhill section of Boston, the same section where the New England Anti-Slavery Society office was sited. The meetings included Rev. Gilbert Haven (figure 11.1), an active abolitionist and later a bishop, and Rev. Edward Thompson Taylor, a well-known unconventional pastor of the Seaman's Bethel Church.[22] Attending a meeting in July of that year was Rev. Henry Bleby, a missionary in Barbados, who was in the city to raise money for his mission. Reverend Bleby, meeting Josiah Henson for the first time, was surprised that this "scion of the negro race is manifestly regarded by those who sat near him as a man and a brother." Bleby describes Josiah in detail as being of medium height and very dark-skinned with a bright smile and a hearty laugh, dressed all in "clerical black" with a white cravat and white beaver hat. Bleby remarked

Figure 11.1. Rev. Gilbert Haven. United Methodist Insight, https://um-insight.net/downloads/1354/download/Haven__Gilbert-2.

that on shaking Josiah's hand he noticed that his arms were crippled so that he could not move them freely.[23]

Bleby was giving a lecture titled "The Results of Emancipation in the British West India Colonies" at churches and antislavery meetings.[24] Josiah was interested in the topic and attended many of Bleby's presentations, accompanying him on his walks home after the meetings and talking about his life experiences. Ten years later Bleby published *The Maimed Fugitive: A True Story* in London, which took the text of the 1858 edition of Josiah's autobiography, changed pronouns from the first person to the third person, and added embellishments and an abundance of fictional material.[25]

One incident in Bleby's book did not appear in any other of Josiah's publications. The reverend took notes on a story told by Josiah at a meeting in a mutual friend's home, where Henson described how he was able to deny a seated member of the Canadian Parliament reelection by transporting opposition voters to the polls because this representative had disparaged "his people." Bleby related this story in dialogue with great gusto and humor, ending with Josiah's revelation that after returning from a few weeks' journey after the election, the Lord had blessed him with great natural increase in his livestock and the addition to his household of four grandchildren.[26] This revelation demonstrates how Josiah was involved in politics and also how he could associate politics and religion.

While Josiah was absent from home in the spring of 1858, a white man who would later become famous organized a historic meeting nearby. John Brown had arrived in

Chatham, Ontario, on April 30 to hold secret meetings to formulate a government for a settlement of freed slaves after a slave uprising he was planning. Twelve whites and thirty-four Blacks attended the meetings, and on May 8, 1858, a constitution for the new republic was approved.[27] John Brown subsequently led a raid on the US armory at Harpers Ferry on October 16, 1859. Several of his men were killed and he, along with some others in his group, were arrested and later tried and hanged. Rev. Gilbert Haven, whom Josiah knew from gatherings in Boston and who had taken his dictation for portions of his 1858 autobiography, wrote a letter to the imprisoned John Brown offering blessings and approval of Brown's actions.[28]

Had Josiah been at home and attended those meetings in Chatham, he surely would have opposed the plan, because he spoke against a similar proposal in August 1858 when he attended the State Convention of Massachusetts Negroes in New Bedford, Massachusetts. William Wells Brown led that meeting, where Charles L. Remond made a motion that a committee be appointed "to prepare an address suggesting to the slaves at the South to create an insurrection." According to the report of the meeting, Josiah Henson opposed the motion, saying he "didn't want to see three or four thousand men hung before their time." Henson wondered how such a large uprising could be coordinated and communicated, adding that the slaves had no weapons with which to fight.[29]

Josiah's opposition to armed conflict was based on his Christian faith and had been evident even while he was still enslaved. He told of opposing another planned insurrection that occurred in "his neighborhood," most likely in Kentucky:

> I could not agree with the leaders, and yet I felt that the evils of slavery
> could not be exaggerated, and that we had a right to our freedom. Little by
> little the light came to my soul, till I was convinced that it was not a feasible
> or Christian plan of procedure; so, I began to raise doubts and queries, to
> discuss the subject, and finally, I had the moral courage to speak my mind
> plainly. I said, "Suppose we should kill one thousand of the white population,
> we should surely lose our own lives, and make the chains of those in bondage
> heavier and more securely riveted. No, let us suffer in God's name, and
> wait His time for Ethiopia to stretch forth her hands and be free." At last I
> prevailed on them to abandon the project.[30]

At the end of 1858, Josiah brought home with him to his farm not only his brother but also a new wife. He had not considered remarrying in the first years after the death of his beloved wife, Charlotte, but out of loneliness he had finally decided four years after her death to find another companion:

> I had travelled extensively, and had made many acquaintances, but I knew
> of but one woman whom I cared to have for a wife. She was a widow, an
> estimable woman, one who had been a faithful teacher in the Sunday

school, and quite a mother in the church to which she belonged. She
had been brought up by a Quaker lady in Baltimore, and had received a
good education in the ordinary branches. Her mother had been a slave,
but was such a superior laundress, that she earned enough to buy her
freedom of her mistress, and then she earned enough to buy her husband's
freedom.[31]

Josiah visited Nancy Gambell several times when visiting Boston before asking for
her hand, and they were married in 1858 in Boston "by our Bishop who was holding a
series of meetings in the city at the time." Nancy was a widow, age forty-two at the time
of their marriage, with three children: Lucinda, age twenty-three; Rebecca, nineteen;
and Peter, age sixteen.[32] It is not known if they all moved to Canada with their mother.

Josiah, age sixty-two, had seven living children at the time, but all had married
and moved out of his house, hence his loneliness. Thomas, age forty, was living in
California; Josiah, age thirty-eight, had a wife named Mary, and they lived in Jackson,
Michigan, where he was a plasterer and farmer; Celia Jane, thirty-one, was married
to a man named Christee, and they lived nearby; Charlotte Matilda, twenty-six, had
married Everett Charles Richey, and they may have moved to Michigan by this time;
Elizabeth, age twenty-four, was married to William Thomas, who was a millwright
operating Josiah's gristmill; Peter, age twenty-two, married Elizabeth Goens and operated his own and his father's farms; and his youngest, Julia Ann, age eighteen, had
recently married Reuben Wheeler, a local young man.[33]

After his marriage to Nancy, Josiah seemed to be doing well, farming with the help
of his son Peter, and preaching. As a Methodist Episcopal elder he covered a district of
three hundred miles and attended many meetings and conferences as well as giving
sermons. He also traveled often to New England to raise money with book sales and
lectures. During the winter of 1858–1859 he was in the United States, according to a
traveling journalist visiting the area looking for him who was disappointed with his
absence.[34] This may have been when Josiah was accepted in Boston into the Freema-
sons. On his return to Canada, he joined Mount Moriah Lodge No. 11 in Dresden, a
Prince Hall Masons affiliate, and is listed as its secretary in 1866.[35]

The American Civil War had a great impact on the Henson family. Josiah's oldest
son, Tom, enlisted in the US Navy from his home in San Francisco, California. Tom
was never heard from again and presumed dead. Josiah's son-in-law William Thomas
enlisted in Detroit in the spring of 1864 when the US Colored Troops were formed,
leaving his wife and children under Josiah's care.[36]

Josiah, wanting to aid in the cause but being too old to enlist, found other ways to
help that got him into some trouble. The recruitment office in Detroit was offering
bounties to men who enlisted in the US Colored Troops, and Josiah encouraged the
young men in his community to join up. After enlisting, the young men had no safe
way to deliver the cash money back to their families unless they had brought a trusted
person with them, so Josiah, experienced in traveling to Detroit, offered his services

to some. It was against the law in Canada to actively recruit men for service in the US Army, so Josiah was careful never to pay anyone to join up. However, being the generous person that he was, he sometimes gave provisions from his farm to needy families who had lost their main source of support when the father joined up.

These dual activities twice embroiled Josiah in court cases. While he was away in Boston, a man by the name of John Alexander, whom Josiah had accompanied to Detroit but who subsequently decided not to join the army, accused Josiah of actively inducing him and others to enlist and paying his family with provisions, a crime for which the penalty was seven years in prison. Josiah's wife telegraphed him telling him to stay away, but he came home anyway and was arrested the next morning by the local constable, William Nellis, a friend of Josiah. One of the two magistrates of the court was also a friend of Josiah, and one was an enemy, so they came to an impasse and passed the case to a higher authority, the county attorney. The attorney deemed that it was one man's word against another, so the judge would have to weigh the truthfulness of Josiah's statement of innocence against the truthfulness of his accuser. Just before the hearing where the two men would testify, Josiah found a man who had known John Alexander before he moved to Dresden and knew that there was a warrant out for the man's arrest for thievery in that district. This man testified before the judge, and Josiah was subsequently released from custody.[37]

Soon after this Josiah was before the court again. This time a man accused him of stealing the money paid to his son and brother-in-law after they had enlisted. Henson had guided the two men, at their request, to the recruiting office in Detroit and returned to the father and brother-in-law with the money. Josiah soon proved that the two men had enlisted of their own free will under false names and then deserted, showing that their word could not be trusted, so the matter was dropped. After this second case, Josiah decided to not be involved with any such activities again.[38]

Between 1861 and 1868 Josiah was involved in several lawsuits that eventually put him in a precarious financial situation. According to court records, in November and December 1855 Josiah Henson borrowed money from John Scoble using eighty acres of his farm as collateral. When Josiah did not repay the money, Scoble sued him in 1861 and was awarded judgment in his favor. Scoble sued Josiah again in a similar case in which Josiah admitted to fraud and complicity to cheat his creditors, adding that therefore the debt was invalid. The court ruled that "a man cannot set up an illegal act of his own in order to avoid his own deed" and awarded judgment to the plaintiff, Scoble, again.[39]

The only lawsuit that Josiah mentioned in his memoirs is one he conducted against John Scoble on behalf of the British-American Institute of Science and Industry (BAI). According to Josiah, he believed that the only way to save the BAI was to take it out of the hands of John Scoble, whom he never actually names but referred to as "the gentleman from London," and give it back to the people. With the "Power of Attorney" granted to him by "a convention of the coloured people of the region," he hired the law firm of Wilson and McKenzie to sue Scoble for "non-fulfillment of trusts and maladministration of the affairs of the school." The lawyers insisted that Josiah "find two substantial men, one coloured and one white, who owned freehold property unencumbered, and were willing to pledge themselves to pay the costs" and agreed to undertake the case on the condition that Josiah kept in the background while the two men should be the ostensible "relators." This strategy was probably because Scoble was suing Josiah in another matter, so Josiah might be considered prejudiced. Josiah found the men as requested, and after arguing the case over a period of seven years, the lawyers offered to give up the case as a nonsuit if Josiah and his friends would pay their expenses. To do this, Josiah had to mortgage most of his farmland and the houses that he owned. He then claimed that "the important case was decided in our favor."[40] There is no record of this litigation in the Court of Chancery, as it was settled out of court.

The result, however, was that Scoble finally agreed to resign and give up the BAI in 1868. The new board of trustees incorporated the BAI, something that Scoble had tried to do for many years. The board then sold the land of the BAI, the money to be spent on a new school within the same district. This became the Wilberforce Educational Institute for Negro and white children in Chatham, currently still operating as a school.[41] The legacy of the BAI to the education of the Black population of Kent County was in this way carried on and is still active.[42]

Before he sued Scoble, Josiah found an ingenious, or perhaps devious, way to protect one of his assets during the lawsuits by turning a permanent structure into a mobile one. A gristmill that he owned and had built was located on the BAI's property, so he moved it to another location so he could sell it.

> My son-in-law [William Thomas] was the miller, and acceded to my proposition, which was that twenty men should be secreted in the mill one Sunday night, and as soon as the hour of midnight had struck, these men should carefully take down the mill and remove every vestige, foundation, engine, and timber, a short distance on to the road, which was the common highway. By ten o'clock on Monday morning the mill had vanished, as if by magic, from its old resting-place, and by noon it was carried off, in ten or twelve teams that were in readiness, to Dresden. It was erected speedily, and it remains there to this day, in splendid working order.[43]

Josiah needed to pay off a debt of $1,300 to clear the mortgage on his farm after the lawsuits.[44] To raise the funds, he began a touring circuit from Pittsburgh to Boston in the spring of 1875, speaking at churches and auditoriums as arranged by his friends. Advertisements for the talks identified him as "The Real Uncle Tom," and he told stories from his own life experiences and would often "sing a real plantation melody" at the end of his talk.[45] To a newspaper correspondent Josiah proudly proclaimed that he had forty-four grandchildren and six great-grandchildren.[46] The traveling and speaking became too much for the eighty-year-old, and Josiah was "stricken with paralysis"

Figure 11.2. Rev. Thomas Hughes (1818–1876), Christ Church, Dresden, Ontario, Canada. Flickr, Don Hughes, https://www.flickr .com/photos/dnh1/7027823963/.

near the end of March.[47] He then left for home, having collected $700 toward the needed sum.[48]

With rest and care Josiah soon recovered, but he still owed $600 to save his farm. Having exhausted the New England circuits and not knowing where to turn next, he sought advice from an old friend, Rev. Thomas Hughes (figure 11.2), secretary of the Colonial Church and School Society and founder of an integrated Anglican church and school in Dresden. Hughes, an Anglican minister and teacher from Stafford-shire, England, had been sent by the society to Canada to open an integrated mission school. He had moved to Dresden with his family in 1859 to accomplish this task, and by the mid-1860s the church and school were flourishing. He was also one of the final trustees of the BAI.[49]

Hughes suggested that Josiah go to England, where he had been so well received before, to raise the needed funds. Very ill at the time (he would pass away in a month), Reverend Hughes dictated a letter of recommendation to his secretary for Josiah to carry with him to England. This letter is quoted here because it was read to the audience at many of Josiah's subsequent talks in England and made quite an impression on the people there:

Dresden, Ontario, Canada, March 10, 1876.—Mr. Josiah Henson being about to proceed to England, has requested me to give him a letter testimonial.

Mr. Henson is so highly respected throughout Western Canada, and also so well known to many influential persons, both in the United States and in England, that he scarcely needs anything of the kind from any individual. I have known Mr. Henson for more than sixteen years, and have great pleasure in bearing my testimony to his sterling Christian character. Mr. Henson's life has been an unusually active and eventful one. For many years he was a slave, and was most cruelly treated; and since his escape to Canada, now more than forty years ago, he has occupied a foremost place in all movements for the advancement of his people. Through his efforts for their good he has, unfortunately, suffered considerable pecuniary loss, and has been compelled in consequence to mortgage his farm. It is with the view of lifting this incumbrance that he has, in his extreme old age, resolved, in response to a cordial invitation given him, to visit England. I heartily commend him and his cause to the British public, and hope that he may have, in every respect, a "prosperous journey by the will of God."—Thos. Hughes, Missionary of the Church of England, Dresden.[50]

Josiah gathered other letters of recommendation from several other friends in Canada and set off for Liverpool with his wife, Nancy, in June 1876 on the Cunard steamer *Marathon*.[51] Thus, he set off on a new adventure and a new stage of his life with high hopes, unaware that while in England he would be tricked once again by a white man (previously by Isaac and Amos Riley and John Scoble).

12

Royalty and Remembrance

LONDON HAD CHANGED IN THE QUARTER CENTURY SINCE JOSIAH HENSON'S LAST VISIT. With the ending of slavery in the United States, the British and Foreign Anti-Slavery Society that had helped Josiah raise money for the British-American Institute of Science and Industry had now shifted its focus to the ending of slavery in East Africa and the Middle East. The Ragged School movement Josiah aided had achieved its goal, and there was now public funding of schools for the poor children. The Crystal Palace that had housed the Great Exhibition of the Works of Industry of All Nations where he had spent so many days had been dismantled and moved from Hyde Park to Sydenham Hill in South London. Prince Albert, organizer of the Great Exhibition, had died, and Queen Victoria was in permanent mourning. Britain was experiencing a golden age of prosperity with the many goods coming from her colonies. There were more factories, more people, and, of course, more traffic.

Josiah Henson brought with him to England testimonials to his good character and trustworthiness from the judge and the sheriff of Kent County, Ontario, and the mayor of Chatham, Ontario, among other individuals, as well as the Colonial and Continental Church Society in London, Ontario. Josiah also carried the praising letter that his friend Rev. Thomas Hughes, missionary of the Church of England in Dresden, had dictated to his secretary just a month before his death.[1] This letter was read at several of Josiah's forthcoming speaking engagements as part of his introduction.

On his arrival in London in July 1876, Josiah, now eighty years old, was sad to find that his good friend from his previous visit, Rev. Thomas Binney, had died three years earlier and that another friend from that visit, George Hitchcock, had also passed away. But Josiah was overjoyed to renew his acquaintance with his former benefactor and host Samuel Morley, who was to become one of Josiah's staunchest supporters. Now as a member of Parliament, Morley held great influence with the public. Another strong supporter was George Sturge, of the Quaker antislavery Sturge family, who had served on the committee set up by the British and Foreign Anti-Slavery Society in 1851 to defend Josiah against the slanderous accusations brought against him in 1851.[2] These wealthy friends most likely provided accommodations for Josiah and his wife, Nancy.

A public appeal for funds to help Josiah dissolve his debts first appeared in London newspapers on August 2, 1876. It advertised that "Mr. S. Morley, M.P. has subscribed 50£, Sir T. F. Buxton, Bart., 30£, and Mr. G. Sturge 50£. Contributions will be received by Messrs. Samuel Morley and George Sturge; at Messrs. Barclay, Bevan, and Co.'s, Lombard Street, London; and by the Rev. J.C. Morgan at the Colonial and Continental Church Society, No. 9, Serjeant's Inn."[3] According to this appeal, Josiah was said to owe £500, which was about the equivalent of 600 Canadian dollars at that time.

Soon after he arrived, Josiah became acquainted with John Lobb, a thirty-seven-year-old journalist and publisher of the *Christian Age*, a Methodist weekly paper.[4] Lobb introduced Josiah to phrenologist Lorenzo Fowler. Phrenology, a pseudoscience that uses bumps and indentations of the skull to determine personality traits and mental ability, gained popularity in the Victorian age, and Fowler was its foremost practitioner in England. Fowler gave a detailed analysis of the bumps on Josiah's head that described certain characteristics inherited from his father, his love for his family, and his "great mental vigor," independence of mind, perseverance, sense of moral obligation and love of truth and much more about his personality. This nine-hundred-word description, along with a portrait of Henson, was published by Lobb in his *Christian Age* weekly and was such a hit that he had to print a third edition of the newspaper.[5]

From this success, Lobb realized that Josiah Henson had exceptional monetary potential. Lobb proposed an arrangement to Josiah: Lobb would become Josiah's publicist and agent, arranging for all his public speaking engagements in England while he was in the country, in exchange for the sole copyright to a new autobiography of Reverend Henson that Lobb would publish.[6] At these talks Lobb would sell the books, and Josiah would accept donations from the audience. Josiah readily agreed to this arrangement, perhaps because from past experience he had come to distrust written contracts and would much prefer cash in hand.[7] Also, in the past he had garnered much more money from his speaking engagements than from the sale of either of his previous autobiographies.

Lobb immediately interviewed Henson on the events of his life since 1858, which he added to the 1858 autobiography and published as *Uncle Tom's Story of His Life: An Autobiography of Rev. Josiah Henson (Mrs. Harriet Beecher Stowe's "Uncle Tom"), from 1789 to 1876.* This edition included the original 1858 preface by Harriet Beecher Stowe (minus the date and the reference to Josiah's brother) and "Introductory Notes" by George Sturge and S. Morley, Esquire, member of Parliament (figure 12.1).

The tour that Lobb arranged, and presumably paid for, was extensive. In a later edition of Josiah's autobiography, Lobb listed ninety-two places in England where "Uncle Tom" gave speeches in just six months: from August 1876 to January 1877. Two of these were attended by more than two thousand people and two by more than

Figure 12.1. Josiah Henson portrait etching with signature. This is an exact copy of the signature from the 1858 autobiography (see Gallery 6.1).New York Public Library sLUqc_kVQVST82FgjY_48Qs(1).

one thousand people, according to Lobb. Others ranged from small congregations to meetings with several hundred attendees. Josiah toured the southern coast of England and made presentations at Portsmouth, Southampton, Ryde, and the Isle of Wight as well as to the officers and crew of HMS *Victory,* famous as the vessel where Adm. Horatio Nelson received his death wound in the Battle of Trafalgar. Honoring his old friends, now deceased, of twenty-five years earlier, Josiah addressed the employees of the drapery factory of George Hitchcock and preached at the Weigh House Chapel of Rev. Thomas Binney. Josiah gave a tribute at the nearby Radnor Street school, a former Ragged School, at the famous chapel of the founder of Methodism, John Wesley. After speaking at the Congregationalist church in Tonbridge, Kent, Josiah, and Nancy were hosted by Samuel Morley at his estate. Josiah's wife accompanied him on these out-of-town trips. The entire list of the speaking engagements can be found at the end of the 1881 edition of Josiah Henson's autobiography published by John Lobb in London, Ontario, Canada. To emphasize Josiah's association with the popular book, Lobb labeled him as "The Real Uncle Tom" in advertisements and introduced him as "Uncle Tom" at the meetings.[8]

An emotional event occurred when Josiah visited the Wesleyan Chapel in Kent. When he could not recall preaching there twenty-five years earlier, "the register was shown him with the date, his text, his own autograph, and that of his son Isaac, now in heaven! The revival of his memory gave him much joy."[9] This encounter with the past touched Josiah's heart deeply.

The talks usually opened with a prayer by a local minister, followed by an introduction of Josiah Henson as "Uncle Tom" by a local dignitary. Josiah would begin by
making humble and self-effacing comments and then talking about his life, inter-
spersing scenes of cruelty with descriptions of humorous incidents. He would always
end by singing a hymn. Singing had always been a part of slave life, easing the pain,
celebrating joyful times, and expressing religious faith.[10] After giving so many talks,
Josiah had honed his public speaking skills and could fill the halls with alternating
applause and laughter. (For examples of his speeches, see appendix C in this volume.)

From "a writer in the *Globe*" in September 1876 came a good description of the
aging Father Henson: "He has a short beard, snowy white, a heavy moustache, a few
shades darker, and eyes wonderfully keen considering his age." The journalist also
remarked that because Henson had been a leading member of his church in Canada,
"it is no wonder that his speech is correct and grammatical, or that he has long since
cultivated the manners of a person familiar with the usages of polite society."[11] Josiah
had actually begun to cultivate those skills in the marketplace of Georgetown in his
youth.

Near the end of his tour in England, Josiah packed the Great Albert Hall in Sheffield, north of London, for a two-part event that began at noon, was interrupted for
dinner, and resumed in the evening. Sheffield boasted that the city raised 186 pounds,
4 shillings, 10 pence, even more than the neighboring city of Nottingham. Showing
amazing resilience, the very next day Josiah was back in London for a grand farewell reception held at the Metropolitan Tabernacle in London on Tuesday, January 31,
1877, which was attended by "nearly 6,000 persons," according to John Lobb.[12] The
tabernacle, one of the largest venues in London at the time, was a Baptist church in
the center of South London, completed in 1861 under the leadership of Rev. Charles
Spurgeon.[13] The notable event was presided over by Lord Shaftesbury, while Reverend
Spurgeon led the opening prayer. Josiah Henson was introduced by Lord Shaftesbury
and spoke for almost an hour, with Mrs. Henson seated by his side. Josiah ended by
singing the "Slave's Parting Hymn," a composition of his own:

> My brethren, fare ye well,
> I do you now tell,
> I'm sorry to leave you,
> I love you so well.
>
> I shortly must go,
> And where I don't know;
> Wherever I'm stationed
> The trumpet I'll blow.
>
> Strange people I'll find,
> I hope they'll prove kind;

Neither places nor faces
Shall alter my mind.

Wherever I'll be
I'll still pray for thee;
And you, my dear brethren,
Do the same for poor me.

There was then a tribute to Lord Shaftesbury and a closing hymn composed for the oc-casion sung by the audience.[14] It was stated that "Mr. Henson's mission to this country had been successful, 1,300£ having been collected for his benefit."[15]

Josiah was impressed by the crowds he attracted, noting that "there were probably 2,000 to 3,000 people outside who could not get in.... They were obliged to open the rear doors at the close of the meeting to let the crowd out, having first conducted me out this way, to avoid the crowds. Often the policemen were obliged to make a passage for us through the crowd, who were so curious to see me; and even after I had entered my cab, and was driven away, some enthusiastic people would run a quarter of a mile after me." He attributed this attention to his association with "Uncle Tom" rather than his "own humble powers of speech."[16]

After being honored at various dinners and religious services in London during the first part of February, Josiah and Nancy accepted the invitation of Rev. J. Davis Bowden to visit him in Edinburgh and give some presentations in Scotland.[17] This was not a part of the agreement with John Lobb, which had ended with the farewell reception and the presentation of the funds raised in the southern part of England. Henson took time at this point in his autobiography to pay tribute to his wife, Nancy, describing her as a "dear faithful soul" and adding that he is "beginning to get a little old, not much, but just a little. I can't run and jump as I used to, and I have to keep pretty steady, and I should not like very well to have to travel about without her by my side."[18]

Shortly after their arrival in Scotland while attending a dinner party in his honor, Josiah was handed a dispatch by a special messenger. Seeing the royal seal on the en-velope, he handed it to his host, Reverend Bowden, to read aloud. It was an invitation from Queen Victoria to call on her at Buckingham Palace the very next day, Friday, March 2, at 2:00 p.m. After speaking to an audience that evening, Josiah, Nancy, and Reverend Bowden took the night train to London.[19] On arriving, they discovered that the queen had moved the date to Monday at Windsor Castle, giving them some time to rest and prepare.[20] Josiah had to cancel his speaking engagements in Scotland for that week but would resume them on his return.[21]

Josiah was nervous about meeting the queen, not knowing what to wear or how to address her or talk to her, so he called on his friend Lord Shaftesbury, who kindly took time to explain to Josiah and his wife that they need not go out and purchase new clothes and should just wear their best clothing. Josiah reported that Shaftesbury also said that "no ceremony would be necessary; that I would only have to conduct myself as a gentleman, and to answer her questions, reserving any remarks of my own until after she had had her say."[22]

So, Josiah and Nancy Henson proceeded to Windsor Castle, he dressed in a black suit with a white tie and white gloves and she in a simple black dress with white lace at the throat and white gloves. They were accompanied by Reverend Bowden and Reverend Long of London.[23] The company was met by the queen's secretary, Sir Thomas Biddolph, who directed the party into a dining room, where they were joined by "some gentlemen of the household" and sat down to a grand feast.[24] After dining, Sir Thomas directed them to the reception hall, Josiah and Reverend Long followed by Reverend Bowden and Nancy Henson. Josiah described the scene: "As we entered the handsome hall, we saw the Queen at the upper end, surrounded by her ladies in waiting and maids of Honor. Her youngest children, the Princess Beatrice and Prince Leopold, were also with her. She was dressed in a rich black silk, the long white crepe veil of her widow's cap falling behind to the edge of her robe."[25]

After remarking on each being surprised at the other's appearance, they talked of Josiah's family and the current situation in Canada. Queen Victoria presented Josiah with a framed full-length portrait of herself in a gold vined frame and said, "Will you kindly accept this from my hands as a token of my respect and esteem, for I have taken the deepest interest in your afflicted people all my life, and now, on seeing you, my feelings are intensified." Nancy Henson was then presented to the queen, and they "exchanged a few pleasant words," after which the Hensons signed the queen's book of visitors and were given a tour of the castle.[26]

Josiah then resumed his speaking tour of Scotland in Edinburgh the next evening with a humorous rendition of his meeting with the queen. He said, "She was neatly dressed; so was I. (Laughter.) She came and made a very polite bow to me; and so did I. (Applause.) She said, she had long read of me, and heard a great deal about me, and was very happy to see me indeed, and I did not say ditto. (Applause.) But I thought so—(renewed laughter)."[27]

Josiah had spoken at several places in Edinburgh and at towns in eastern Scotland and had raised £350 when he was asked to attend a meeting of "leading citizens" in Glasgow on March 19.[28] These gentlemen agreed to set up an account in the Bank of Scotland to receive subscriptions.[29] Donations were gathered from his speaking engagements in the great halls and churches around Glasgow and western Scotland over the next month.

Josiah's speeches in Scotland were a little different than those on the earlier book tour arranged by John Lobb. The most striking difference is that in some of the talks he tried to separate himself from the identification with Uncle Tom. For instance, in his last address in Scotland, in Dumfries, he said, "Now allow me to say that my name is not Tom, and never was Tom, and that I do not want to have any other name inserted in the newspapers for me than my own. My name is Josiah Henson, always was, and always will be. I never change my colours. (Loud laughter.) I would not if I could, and I could not if I would. (Renewed laughter.)"[30]

On Friday, April 20, 1877, during a farewell meeting and presentation at the Glasgow City Hall, Josiah Henson received a check for £750, the combined amount gathered from all of Scotland. The hall was packed with well-wishers, and dignitaries lined the stage. The long night was filled with speeches, prayers, and the singing of hymns. Reverend Bowden, with whom the Hensons had stayed for four weeks, gave a short talk and presented Nancy Henson with a gold watch and chain as a token of her "worth as a Christian lady." The watch was inscribed as follows: "Presented as a token of respect to Mrs. Josiah Henson, along with a testimonial to her husband, in the City Hall, Glasgow, on 20th April 1877."[31]

In his speech, Josiah recalled the generous Scotsman captain who had graciously taken him and his family across Lake Erie to freedom in Canada and provided him with some funds to start a new life. This act of kindness had given him a special feeling of affiliation with Scotland, and he expressed how happy he was to finally get to see the home country of his benefactor. This farewell meeting, with all the speeches and testimonials transcribed along with a list of donors, was printed and published in May, and copies were sent to Queen Victoria and to Lord Shaftesbury. Sir Thomas Biddolph wrote an acceptance letter on behalf of the queen, and Lord Shaftesbury replied with a letter honoring Josiah.[32]

The weary travelers boarded the Cunard steamer *China* sailing from Liverpool on April 26, avoiding the crowds of well-wishers at the dock by boarding early. They arrived in Boston on May 6.[33] Josiah and Nancy traveled immediately to their home, where they were greeted by those of their children and grandchildren who still lived in the area, all happy to see each other after ten months apart.

Along with more than enough money to redeem Josiah Henson's mortgaged farm, they brought home many happy memories, the cheers and applause still ringing in their ears, and grand stories to tell of their adventures. Besides the gold watch and chain presented to her at the farewell ceremony in Scotland, Nancy Henson had been given a gold locket by friends in Scotland and a German music box by Mr. and Mrs. Horniman of London. Josiah also received a gold watch and chain by the Hornimans.

Josiah and Nancy left behind in England many happy memories with all their kind hosts. Of course, Josiah also left a lasting impression on the many people who attended his talks of slave life in the United States and living conditions of the refugees from slavery in Canada. One other sign of Josiah Henson's impact on the people of London can be illustrated by a wax figure of "Uncle Tom" in Josiah's likeness that appeared in an exhibition at Madame Tussaud's wax museum in August 1877 (figure 12.2).[34]

After the departure of Josiah and Nancy Henson from England, John Lobb published many reprints of the 1876 autobiography of Josiah that would reach and inspire many people to come (figure 12.3). Seventy thousand books were sold in just the

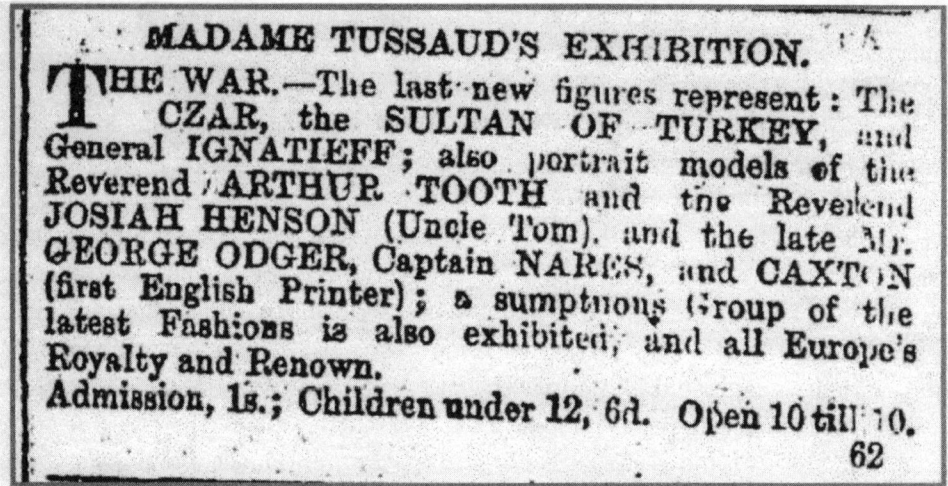

MADAME TUSSAUD'S EXHIBITION.

THE WAR.—The last new figures represent : The CZAR, the SULTAN OF TURKEY, and General IGNATIEFF; also portrait models of the Reverend ARTHUR TOOTH and the Reverend JOSIAH HENSON (Uncle Tom), and the late Mr. GEORGE ODGER, Captain NARES, and CAXTON (first English Printer); a sumptuous Group of the latest Fashions is also exhibited, and all Europe's Royalty and Renown.

Admission, 1s.; Children under 12, 6d. Open 10 till 10.

62

Figure 12.2. Newspaper ad for Madame Tussaud's Wax Museum. *The Hull Packet; and East Riding Times* (Hull, East Yorkshire, England), Friday, August 10, 1877, 1.

first six months of publication.[35] Lobb also published in 1877, just after the Hensons sailed for home, *The Young People's Illustrated Edition of "Uncle Tom's" Story of His Life,* which features an etched portrait of John Lobb and Josiah Henson together, a preface by Lord Shaftesbury, and "Uncle Tom's Address to the Young People of Great Britain." This edition is not a Josiah Henson autobiography but instead is a fictionalized version of his life depicting him as "Uncle Tom." As Lobb in the author's note says, "It will be seen that the book is not merely an abridgment, or a condensation of the larger work, but is, to a great extent, a new book."[36] The text is preceded by eight pages of reviews from various newspapers and individuals. It is written in the third person and includes many embellishments, biblical references, and comments by Lobb about Henson's life and slavery in general, modified for a young reader and to give moral lessons.

At home, Josiah and Nancy spent a comfortable summer, but that winter Josiah said that "a strange, inexpressible longing came over me to see again the home of my boyhood" in Maryland. Nancy wanted to visit her sister in that same state, so in December 1877 they set off, hoping to spend Christmas with Nancy's sister in Baltimore. Unfortunately, they were delayed by bad weather and did not arrive until the day after Christmas, but the sisters were joyful to reunite after so many years.[37] An article in the *Baltimore American* remarked on Josiah's visit and referred to some of his remarkable accomplishments.[38]

Josiah and Nancy remained in Baltimore for a couple of months. While there, Josiah was persuaded to give a talk at the Maryland Land Institute in Baltimore on January 14, 1878.[39] Josiah and Nancy then proceeded to Washington, DC, where in late February and early March Josiah visited old friends in the area and explored the much-changed markets where he used to sell his master's produce.[40] One of the

Figure 12.3. Cover, Swedish edition, 1877. New York Public Library F7a5ycOgT-mXjo7IRMQazA7(1).

friends Josiah visited was Frederick Douglass, whom he had hosted in his home in 1854. Douglass provided him with an introductory letter to the secretary of President Rutherford B. Hayes (figure 12.4).[41] Consequently, the Hensons paid a visit to President and Mrs. Hayes at the White House, where Josiah had a conversation with the president while Lucy Hayes gave Nancy a tour of the presidential mansion.[42]

They then took a carriage up the Frederick Road toward Rockville, Maryland, to visit the place where Josiah had been enslaved many years before. He knew that his former master, Isaac Riley, had died but expected that perhaps Riley's much younger wife might still be there. Josiah envisioned the farm and houses as they were when he last saw them:

> I still pictured to myself the great fertile plantation, with its throngs of busy laborers sowing the seed, tilling the ground, and reaping the valuable harvests as of yore. I saw the "great house," well furnished and sheltering a happy, luxurious, and idle family; I saw the out-door kitchen, where the colored cook and her young maids prepared and carried the dinners into the house; I saw the barns and storehouses bursting with plenty; the great cellars filled with casks of cider, apple-brandy, and fruit; and plainer than all, I saw

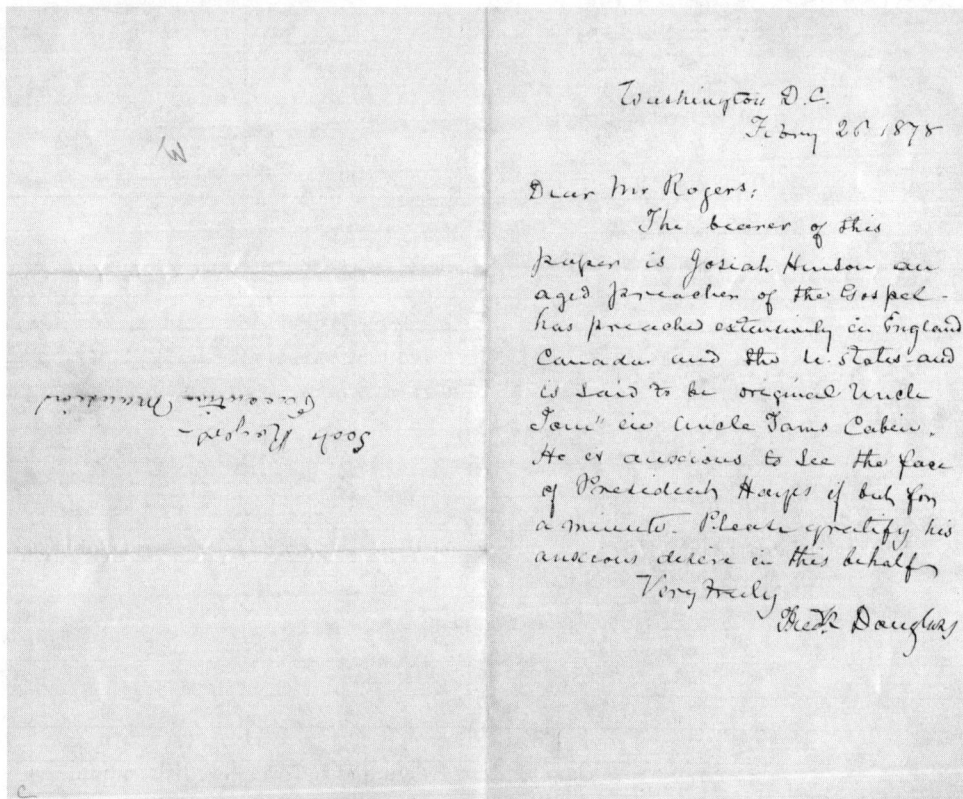

Figure 12.4. Letter of introduction from Frederick Douglass for Josiah Henson to President Rutherford B. Hayes, addressed to his secretary Mr. Rogers, February 26, 1878. Douglass to WKR, February 26, 1878, Rutherford B. Hayes Presidential Library, Freemont, Ohio, Frederick Douglass, MISC MSS

the little village of huts called the niggers' quarters, which used to be so full of life, and alas! so full of sorrow.[43]

What Josiah saw when they drove up was quite different. The fields were over-grown, the orchard trees were dead, and the fences and outbuildings were gone. He was not disappointed, however, in his plan to see his former mistress. Matilda Riley, now old and ailing, was propped up in bed in what used to be the parlor. She did not recognize Josiah at first in his fine clothes but remembered him well after feeling his broken arms. Josiah reported that she said, "Why Si, you are a gentleman!" to which he replied, "I always was, madam." Mrs. Riley complained of being poor now with only her daughter and granddaughters to help. In a newspaper interview in 1883 after Josiah's death, Matilda claimed that "Uncle Si" still owed her $500 that he had borrowed from her husband to purchase his freedom (the amount owed was actually $100).[44] Josiah was able to help her in another way by answering her questions about her deceased husband's military record and his commander in the War of 1812 so she could apply for an army pension. He then asked to be shown where his mother was buried, the main object of his visit. He was taken to the burial ground for the Riley slaves and knelt to pray at the overgrown unmarked mound that was the final resting place of his beloved mother.[45]

In April on the way back to Canada, the Hensons stopped in Philadelphia, where Josiah gave a talk at the Union African Methodist Episcopal Church, which was filled to overflowing, and "among the audience were to be seen many white people seated among the brethren of a darker color."[46] While he was in that city he gave an interview to a correspondent for the *Philadelphia Record* in which he changed some of the facts and words of conversations in his published autobiographies, perhaps due to an aging mind.[47]

After returning home, Josiah visited some of his children now living in the United States. On June 13, 1878, he was on the Steamer *Hiawatha* from Sarnia, Canada, to Michigan when he was interviewed by a correspondent for the *Star-Tribune* in which he named some individuals in his life who resembled characters in *Uncle Tom's Cabin*, but when asked how Mrs. Stowe had come to know his story, he said that she had read his first autobiography and added "that's where she got the idea for it." They then spoke of his visit to Queen Victoria.[48]

In October 1878 Josiah was to give a series of lectures in Michigan, but the poor attendance at Kalamazoo and Battle Creek caused his manager to cancel the remaining talks.[49] Josiah went on to visit family and friends living in that state. On October 14, 1878, he enjoyed a special treat when a group of newspapermen paid for a box at Whitney's Opera House in Detroit, where he saw a production of *Uncle Tom's Cabin* by the Gotthold and Rial Company. After the performance the manager introduced Josiah to the audience.[50] It is not recorded what Josiah thought of the play or if he made any connections from it to his own life. Josiah may not have read the novel or had it read to him, since he never actually quotes from it in his speeches. The book is 469 pages long. People of that era, not having radio or television or internet for entertainment, liked their books as well as their speeches and operas long.

The final edition of Josiah's life history, *"Truth Is Stranger Than Fiction": An Autobiography of the Rev. Josiah Henson (Mrs. Harriet Beecher Stowe's "Uncle Tom"), from 1789 to 1879*, was published for him by friends in Boston in 1879 so that "from its proceeds he can carry out his last pet plan of building for the 3,000 colored people of Dresden, a substantial brick church, where they may worship God in the years to come."[51] This volume included the chapters added by John Lobb in his 1876 edition bringing Josiah's life up to the summer of 1876 as well as the list of speaking engagements from the *Christian Age*, but it omitted John Lobb's "A Lost Continent" in the appendix. Instead, in the appendix of the 1879 edition was "The Exodus," an essay by Josiah's old friend Bishop Gilbert Haven (figure 12.5).

In addition, this 1879 edition was the first volume, other than Lobb's fictionalized *Young People's Edition*, to have illustrations. It included the preface by Harriet Beecher Stowe from the 1858 edition and added "Introductory Notes" by the American poet

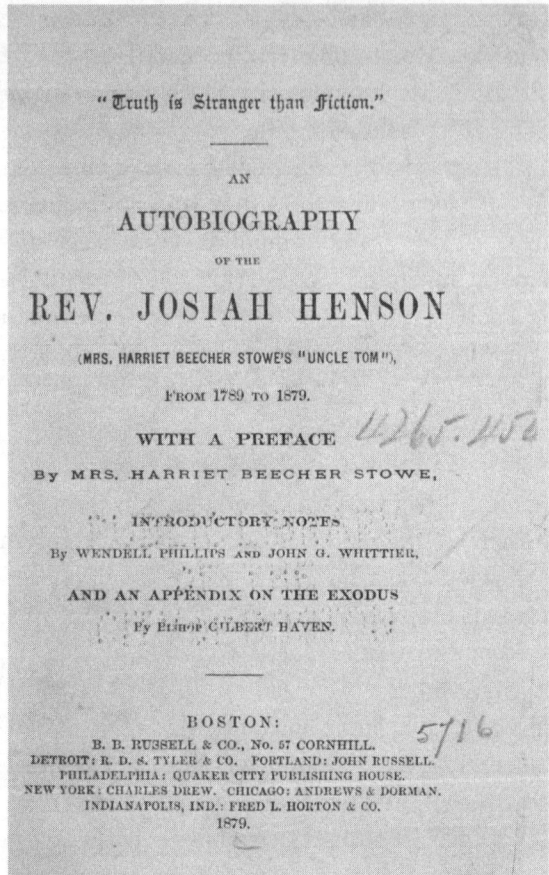

"Truth is Stranger than Fiction."

AN

AUTOBIOGRAPHY

OF THE

REV. JOSIAH HENSON

(MRS. HARRIET BEECHER STOWE'S "UNCLE TOM"),

FROM 1789 TO 1879.

WITH A PREFACE

By MRS. HARRIET BEECHER STOWE,

INTRODUCTORY NOTES

By WENDELL PHILLIPS AND JOHN G. WHITTIER,

AND AN APPENDIX ON THE EXODUS

By Bishop GILBERT HAVEN.

BOSTON:
B. B. RUSSELL & CO., No. 57 CORNHILL.
DETROIT: R. D. S. TYLER & CO.   PORTLAND: JOHN RUSSELL.
PHILADELPHIA: QUAKER CITY PUBLISHING HOUSE.
NEW YORK: CHARLES DREW.   CHICAGO: ANDREWS & DORMAN.
INDIANAPOLIS, IND.: FRED L. HORTON & CO.
1879.

Figure 12.5. Front of the 1879 autobiography. Internet Archive, https://archive.org/details/auto biographyofroohens/mode/2up.

and abolitionist John Greenleaf Whittier and by Wendell Phillips, the well-known activist for the emancipation of slaves and the rights of women. The publisher's preface described how the life of Josiah Henson influenced Mrs. Stowe in creating the character of the fictional Uncle Tom.[52]

Most notably, the additions to Josiah's life story in this volume included his personal description of his meeting with Queen Victoria, which is not in any other edition, and his report of his visit to President Hayes and to his old home in Maryland. One important omission is the paragraph at the end of the last chapter of the British 1876 edition (page 209) where he grants the copyright of his 1876 autobiography to Lobb.

John Lobb traveled to Canada in 1881 and usurped this 1879 edition, supposing that he had the right from Josiah's signing over of the copyright to his 1876 edition published in England. There are very few copies of this 1879 edition to be found today, and the one in the Boston Public Library is missing the pages describing Henson and his wife visiting Queen Victoria, which does not mention John Lobb.

Lobb's reprint of Josiah's 1879 autobiography, titled *An Autobiography of Rev. Josiah Henson ("Uncle Tom")*, was published in London, Ontario, in 1881. At the bottom of

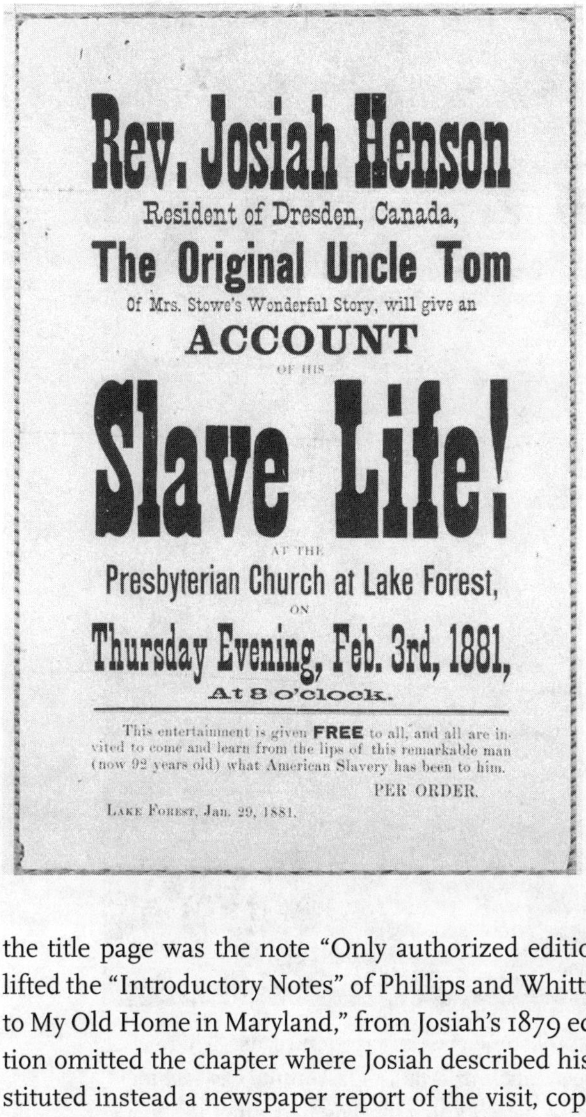

Figure 12.6. "Josiah Henson Speaking Engagement," February 3, 1881, Schomburg Center for Research in Black Culture, Photographs and Prints Division, New York Public Library, New York Public Library Digital Collections, 2024. https://digitalcollections .nypl.org/items/510d47db-bbfe -a3d9-e040-e00a18064a99.

the title page was the note "Only authorized edition, and copyright."[53] This reprint lifted the "Introductory Notes" of Phillips and Whittier as well as chapter 33, "My Visit to My Old Home in Maryland," from Josiah's 1879 edition without citation. Lobb's edition omitted the chapter where Josiah described his visit to Queen Victoria and substituted instead a newspaper report of the visit, copied from a press release by Lobb, since it is identical in several newspapers on the same day. This account mentioned Lobb's name more times than Henson's, and Lobb even went so far as to say that "as incorrect accounts have appeared, we give the following extract from the *Times*, for the accuracy of which we can vouch."[54] In the appendix Lobb wrote a new "Conclusion," resurrected his "Sketch of Mrs. H. Beecher Stowe," and usurped the essay "Exodus" by Bishop Gilbert Haven from Josiah's 1879 edition. To the list of Josiah's speaking engagements in England from the 1876 edition, Lobb added in this version a description of the farewell meeting in London, Josiah's talks in Scotland, and a copy of a newspaper article about Josiah's last public appearance in Dumfries, Scotland.

Josiah stayed close to home in the last years of his life, with a few articles about him popping up in newspapers from time to time. In the fall of 1881 (the same time that John Lobb was in Canada), there was a false report of Josiah's death that spread

Figure 12.7. Josiah Henson tombstone. The inscription reads: "There is a land of pure delight where saints immortal reign. Infinite day excludes the night and pleasures banish pain. I know that my Redeemer liveth. Henson" Dresden, Ontario, Canada. Photo by author.

for a few weeks until finally corrected. How that rumor began is unknown. Josiah retained his humor to the end. In an interview in June 1882 when Josiah said that his master had treated him well and the interviewer said, "You are a fool for running away," he replied, "Well, my friend, that place is still vacant. You can have it."[55] In the last year of his life as Josiah's mind deteriorated, he increasingly identified himself as the fictional Uncle Tom in Stowe's novel. In early 1881 he gave a speech at the Presbyterian church at Lake Forest (figure 12.6). In 1882 in a speech at the Park Street Baptist Church in Hamilton, Ohio, he rambled on for two and a half hours, assuring his audience repeatedly that he was the real Uncle Tom until he had to be led from the platform.[56]

Figure 12.8. Portrait of Josiah Henson in later years, 1876. Wikimedia Commons, https://commons.wikimedia.org/wiki/Category:Josiah_Henson.

Josiah Henson died from paralysis (stroke) on May 5, 1883, in Dresden, Ontario.[57] His age, always taken from his autobiographies, is listed as ninety-three, but he was actually eighty-seven years old at his death. His obituary appeared in more than two dozen newspapers, some with just a notice and some with a whole column dedicated to him. At his funeral in Dresden "fifty wagons followed his hearse to the graveside, a negro band from nearby Chatham played, nine negro preachers prayed."[58]

In his will Josiah bequeathed to his daughter Julia Wheeler two and a half acres from his farm. His son Peter received Josiah's gold watch and chain and half of the proceeds of the sale of his Hambletonian stallion. Nancy Henson was bequeathed the household furniture, one cow, one horse, and a buggy and harness. From the sale of the estate, Nancy received three-sevenths, son Peter received two-sevenths, and daughter Mrs. Celia Kersey received two-sevenths. Daughters Mrs. Charlotte Clay and Mrs. Elizabeth Thomas each received $200, and $100 each was bequeathed to sons Josiah; grandsons Thomas Henson, James Clay, Charles Henson, and William Henson; and Matilda Titus. The British Episcopal Methodist Church of Dresden also received $100.[59]

Josiah Henson's final resting place, marked by a marble obelisk bearing a Mason square and compass symbol, lies across from the cemetery of the British-American Institute of Science and Industry near Dresden, Ontario, Canada (figure 12.7). Nancy died in 1888 in Kent County, Ontario, but her gravesite is unknown.[60] The last-known portrait of Josiah Henson was taken in 1876 (figure 12.8).

EPILOGUE

Legacy

Josiah Henson's story describes not just the life journey of one man but also reveals the mechanism and long-term effects of racism: how human beings can keep other human beings enslaved and continually subjugated and manipulated even after they are free.

Josiah Henson was intelligent, adaptable, and clever. He was a pious Christian who loved his family more than anything and had a kind heart. He was courageous, outspoken, and self-confident. He had the respect of his community and was looked on as a leader. But he was enslaved and had a Black skin, so none of these assets impressed the white world. Josiah was denied education and the ability to read, and that limited his ability to maneuver in the white man's world. In enslavement and in freedom he was manipulated by people who thought it was their right to manipulate him because of the color of his skin. They took advantage of his Christian piety, his love of his family, his kind, and his leadership, and his lack of education and knowledge of the world to use him to their own advantage.

They thought they could do this because they had been taught since childhood that Black people were inferior to white people in intelligence and self-discipline, were closer to savages than to civilized man, and were born this way and could never change. So, Black people needed to be guided and taken care of like children. This was ingrained in white society, both North and South, and was reinforced by laws, taught in schools, and even preached from the pulpit.

That slavery was confined to the South did not mean that these ideas were confined to the South. The pervasiveness of the erroneous idea of white superiority in the Northern states can be seen in the refusal of the antislavery societies to aid the people they had freed from enslavement, indicating that they were interested only in emancipating enslaved people, not in promoting their individual welfare after they were free. They were abhorrent of slavery, usually for religious reasons, but for the most part were unwilling to accept Black people as equals. The segregation of Blacks and the racist attitudes of many white people in the free country of Canada portends the Jim Crow laws that prevailed in the United States after emancipation.

This in-depth study of the life of Josiah Henson brings to light not only new information about his life and character but also new reflections on the many different relationships between enslaved people and their enslavers and of the development of racism in America, Canada, and England.

Josiah's ability to negotiate with his enslavers (even if not on an equal basis), his skill at tricking his master, and the freedoms granted to him while still in bondage demonstrate that those who were enslaved sometimes had some control over their lives. On the other hand, his observation of his enslaved friends languishing on death-camp plantations, his seeing enslaved families split apart forever, and his almost being sold himself away from his wife and children show the utter cruelty and heartlessness of many enslavers and the callousness of the institution itself.

The association later in life of Josiah with the fictional character Uncle Tom helps to explain his rise and fall from fame. Readers of Harriet Beecher Stowe's novel in the North at first embraced the story of a Black enslaved man who, through his strong Christian faith, martyred himself to save two escaping women from capture. Some people even placed the novel as one of the impetuses to the American Civil War.

But after the slaves were emancipated, the meaning of the story and the attributes of the main character were changed by not just the adjustment of society to a new social structure but also the manipulation of people's minds through the media. Plays and minstrel shows that originated in the South depicted "Uncle Tom" as an ignorant Black person overeager to win the approval of whites by obsequious and overly subservient behavior, willingly cooperating with and assisting them. This caricature, emphasized by ads and products, was used to promote the idea of white superiority and became permanently associated with the name "Uncle Tom." In this way Uncle Tom was turned from a hero into a fool, and the name became derogatory.

The "romantic racism" of Harriet Beecher Stowe and indeed of most of the white people of the eighteenth and nineteenth centuries, Northerners and Southerners alike, began to fade and be replaced in many minds by a pseudoscientific approach to racism that would develop into the eugenics movement of the early twentieth century.

Before he was catapulted to fame by his association with Uncle Tom of the novel, Josiah Henson was already a leader and a person of influence in his community, a minister and a spiritual guide. He had traveled extensively throughout Canada, New England, and England giving speeches to large crowds and attending abolitionist and religious meetings. He was a participant in the Underground Railroad network and had led many people to freedom. He knew and had the respect of important people in all three countries.

Josiah Henson was a complex man who was full of contradictions, both heroic and human, pious and devious, altruistic and self-interested, humble and self-righteous. His ability to adapt and learn from every experience led him to positions of higher and higher authority in the various cultures in which he found himself. Because he was a man with faults as well as good intentions, his struggle and his rise resonate with many and gives us hope.

Besides teaching about the man Josiah Henson, his story reveals much about the cultures he lived in, the people he knew, and the institutions with which he was involved, including the abolitionist societies. His story can also teach us much about the institution of slavery in America and the struggle of African Americans after reaching freedom to find autonomy and authority within their new world.

We can see through Josiah's experiences and his travels a veritable "pilgrim's progress," advancing from enslavement to freedom, from innocence to worldly wisdom, and from helplessness to helper as he found his real inner strength of spirit. Touching in his travels upon important power centers of the world—Boston, London, and Washington, DC—led him to a greater knowledge of various cultures, ways of conducting business, and religious practices. His meeting with famous people of his time demonstrates his incredible rise from a field slave to a person of prominence, from the powerless to the powerful.

Josiah's travels take us through time as he goes from using only his feet to travel to traveling on trains and steamships, going from taking sixty days to travel seven hundred miles from Maryland to Kentucky to taking only sixteen days to travel the four thousand miles from London to Dresden, Ontario, demonstrating the industrialization and progress of the world of the second half of the nineteenth century.

Josiah's travels also demonstrate how he was able to adapt to the different cultures of the places where he lived and learn new skills. As a small boy in Southern Maryland, he experienced the culture of large plantations with many enslaved people where punishment was the means of control. He was fortunate as a child to have a kind owner there who treated him almost like a son. Here he learned that white people were not always the enemy.

In Rockville, Maryland, Josiah was on a small farm with few enslaved people and a variety of produce. The rules were different here, and instead of harsh punishment, enslavers for the most part used rewards and the denial of privileges to control the people they owned. Here Josiah learned that he could trick and manipulate his enslaver, who may have had his own agenda. Here Josiah was introduced to the life of the city by being his owner's marketman in Georgetown and Washington, DC. The market was Josiah's school for learning the art of selling and how to behave like a gentleman. In taking his owner's slaves to Kentucky, Josiah learned how to adapt to life on the road, skills that would help him escape to Canada with his family and later lead others on the road to freedom.

The frontier country of Kentucky presented new challenges where the farms were still being cleared and were very large and far apart. But Josiah learned to adapt and remain an asset to his enslavers. Because of his knowledge of math and his skill at selling, Josiah would ride from farm to farm counting the seeds in the spring and the harvest in the fall, keeping an eye on the productivity of the enslaved workers. He would then accompany the produce to the shipping dock for sale. From selling retail he went to selling wholesale. In Kentucky he also discovered that he had a talent for oration and that this talent could bring him income, money he used to purchase his freedom. The respect and goodwill he received from white people in Ohio and Pennsylvania on his trip back to Maryland to purchase his freedom gave him a taste of what it would be like to be free, boosted his self-confidence, and hardened his resolve to achieve freedom for his wife and children as well as for himself.

Even on his almost fatal trip to New Orleans, he learned the most useful skill of how to steer a flatboat downriver. On his escape to Canada, he became acquainted with people who would later aid him in making connections with the Underground Railroad when he was aiding others to escape. He also broadened his knowledge of people and cultures when he and his family were taken in by a tribe of Indigenous people.

Josiah arrived in Canada a different man than the one who had toiled in the fields of Isaac Riley in Maryland. Josiah's leadership qualities, first honed in the slave community of his youth, now came to full fruition. Always quick to adapt, Josiah had gained much knowledge and self-confidence in his journey from enslavement to freedom. His good heart and Christian ideals led him to focus on his fellow refugees from enslavement and help them find a good life in this new country and newfound freedom. His courage and dedication to freedom led him to help others break the chains of bondage. His devout Christianity, goodwill, and powers of oration made him a respected leader in his community. His talent with numbers and his salesmanship were a great advantage in raising money for his cause.

On the other hand, Josiah's trusting nature led him into entanglements with men who wanted to take advantage of him. Discord among the abolitionists and dissatisfaction among those who had achieved freedom but were unsure how to handle it, being used by unscrupulous men both white and Black, drove him into poverty and disillusionment.

On his final trip to England, Josiah demonstrated that he had learned how to give a good speech, interjecting humor in personal stories, and even though he was again cheated by a white man he had trusted, he gained enough funds with the help of friends to ensure a comfortable retirement for himself and his wife and leave an adequate inheritance for his children.

The story of Josiah Henson's life still has relevance today, inspiring hope and perseverance to the oppressed. Slavery still exists in many forms around the world, including things not usually equated with the chattel slavery of America's past such as wage slavery and incarceration slavery. I hope that this delving deep to tell the entire and the factual story, to the best of my ability, of this remarkable man will add to the lessons he has to give us all and make his struggles and his achievements more relevant in our own time.

There are two museums dedicated to Josiah Henson, one in Ontario, Canada, and the other in Montgomery County, Maryland. The Josiah Henson Museum and Park in Maryland opened in September 2021 on the site of the farm where Josiah grew up enslaved and includes the original house of his enslaver. The museum is managed by Montgomery Parks. The museum in Canada, managed by the Ontario Heritage Trust, has been in existence for many more years, but in July 2022 the name was changed from Uncle Tom's Cabin Historic Site to the Josiah Henson Museum of African-Canadian History.

Appendix A

Josiah Henson Timeline

1796, June	Born in Charles County, Maryland, on farm of Francis Newman
1797, May	Enslaver Josias H. McPherson first appears in Rockville, MD
1798	Francis Newman purchases La Grange, Port Tobacco, Maryland (may have lived there earlier)
1800	Owner J. H. McPherson in Rockville tax assessment with no slaves or family
1801/1802	Father beaten and sold by Francis Newman
1802–1804	Owner J. H. McPherson in Rockville tax assessment with all of his slaves but no family
1805	Owner J. H. McPherson dies before April
1805, April	Inventory of deceased owner shows Josiah to be age nine and brother John to be age twelve
1805, after April	Josiah is sold to Adam Robb along with brother John, age twelve to thirteen
1805–1806	Josiah is acquired by Isaac Riley, who had purchased Josiah's mother
1808	Josiah is beaten by Riley for having a spelling book
1813	Josiah finds religion
1814, August	Burning of Washington, DC, during the War of 1812
1815	Josiah is beaten and maimed by Brice Letton
1816 or 1817	Josiah becomes the marketman for Riley
1818	Josiah marries Charlotte Stevenson, whom he met at religious meetings
1818, December 10	Owner Isaac Riley marries Matilda Middleton, and her young brother Francis comes to live with them
1818	Son Thomas Henson is born

1819	Son Isaac Henson is born
1825, February	Josiah leads twelve of Isaac Riley's slaves out of Maryland toward Kentucky
1825, April	Josiah and his charges reach the Amos Riley farm in Daviess County, Kentucky
1828, September	Josiah sets out alone from Kentucky for Maryland via Cincinnati
1828, Christmas	Josiah reaches Isaac Riley's farm in Maryland (Josiah's mother had died)
1829, March 9	Josiah purchases his freedom in Montgomery County, Maryland, and returns to Kentucky by May
1830	Josiah is taken to New Orleans to be sold (embarks late May)
1830, July 10	Josiah returns from New Orleans (the trip took twelve days, so he left New Orleans on June 28)
1830, mid-September	Josiah escapes with Charlotte and four children (Isaac, Tom, Celia Jane, and Josiah)
1830, October 28	Josiah and his family reach Canada, Fort Erie
1830–1833	Josiah works near St. Catharines, Ontario, on farm of Mr. Hibbard, and son Tom attends school
1832	Josiah makes his first trip back to Kentucky to lead a group of slaves to freedom from Bourbon County, Kentucky
1833, November	Josiah makes a second trip back to Kentucky to lead members of the Lightfoot family to freedom (the Leonid meteor shower occurs on November 12–13, 1833)
1833–1834	Josiah works near St. Catharines, Ontario, for Mr. Riseley, and forms a resettlement group
1835–1841	Josiah works with a group on government land in Colchester, Essex County, Upper Canada
1837, December	In the Upper Canada Rebellion, Josiah is involved in the capture of the grounded rebel ship *Anne*
1838, June	Hiram Wilson and Josiah call a convention in London, Upper Canada, for the establishment of a manual labor school
1841	Upper Canada becomes Canada West
1842	Josiah moves his family to a farm near the British-American Institute
1842, December	The British-American Institute is established on-site
1846–1850	Josiah travels in Massachusetts and other New England states on speaking tours to raise funds for the British-American Institute
1849	Samuel Eliot publishes Josiah's first autobiography to aid the British-American Institute
1850, September	The Fugitive Slave Act becomes law

1850, November 11	Josiah joins with Henry Bibb to call a meeting in Sandwich, Canada West, to form an association to aid fugitive slaves
1850, November 27	Josiah travels to England with son Isaac
1851, January–May	Josiah gives speeches at various churches in and near London
1851, March	Enemies in Canada publish a tract accusing Josiah of misrepresenting himself as an agent of the British-American Institute
1851, April	The British and Foreign Anti-Slavery Society in London creates a committee to oversee the funds raised by Josiah and appoints John Scoble to go to Canada to investigate the situation
1851, May	Josiah exhibits polished black walnut boards produced at the British American Institute sawmill at the World Exhibition at the Crystal Palace in London (May 1—October 15)
1851, August	Josiah returns to Canada with John Scoble to answer accusations of fraud
1851, September 11–12	Josiah attends the North American Convention in Toronto, Canada, with Scoble
1851, end of September	Josiah makes a second trip to England to finish the exhibition and continue his speaking engagements. Rev. Thomas Binney publishes Josiah's second autobiography.
1852, March 20	*Uncle Tom's Cabin* is published as a book
1852, September 4–20	Josiah returns to Canada from London because his wife is dying (son Josiah remains in England)
1853, March	*The Key to Uncle Tom's Cabin* is published, and Josiah Henson's name becomes associated with the central character "Uncle Tom"
1853, June	Josiah attends and is elected president of the General Convention for the Improvement of the Colored Inhabitants of Canada that is held in Amherstburg and is a continuation of the November 1850 meeting
1853, July 14	Son Isaac Henson returns to Boston from England
1854, August	Frederick Douglass visits Dresden and stays with Josiah
1855	A railroad and pedestrian bridge over Niagara River connects Canada and New York and Boston
1856	Son Isaac Henson dies
1858, April	Josiah may have met Harriet Beecher Stowe at Andover
1858, May	John Brown convenes a Constitutional Convention in Chatham, Canada West, near Josiah's home while Josiah is in Boston
1858	Josiah marries Nancy Gambell
1858, May	Josiah meets John Jewett, who publishes Josiah's third autobiography

1858, July	Josiah meets Rev. Henry Bleby at a meeting of Methodist ministers in Boston that Rev. Gilbert Haven also attends
1858, August	Josiah attends the State Convention of Massachusetts Negroes in New Bedford, Massachusetts, and prevents members from planning an insurrection
1858, September 8	Josiah purchases the freedom of his older brother John Henson
1858–1859	Josiah is in Boston and while there joins the Freemasons
1861–1865	American Civil War. Son Thomas Henson enlists in the US Navy
1863	Josiah is accused of recruiting Canadians for the US Army and is acquitted
1864	Josiah is accused of stealing bounty money and is acquitted
1867	Canada West becomes Ontario
1867	The British-American Institute closes (the land sold in 1868, and the school moves to Chatham)
1876, August–1877, April	Josiah travels to England (his third such trip) with wife Nancy
1876, October	John Lobb publishes the fourth autobiography of Josiah Henson
1877, March 5	Josiah meets Queen Victoria
1878, March	Josiah visits President Rutherford B. Hayes and goes to his old home in Maryland with wife Nancy
1879	Josiah's fifth autobiography is published by friends in Boston
1883, May 5	Josiah dies in Dresden at age eighty-eight
1983	Josiah Henson becomes the first person of African descent to be featured on a Canadian stamp
1999	The Canadian government erects a plaque designating Josiah Henson as a Canadian of National Historical Significance. The plaque stands in the Henson family cemetery near Dresden.
2021, September	The Josiah Henson Museum and Park opens in Bethesda, Maryland
2022, July	Uncle Tom's Cabin Historic Site is renamed the Josiah Henson Museum of African-Canadian History and Culture in Ontario, Canada

Gallery 1.1. A typical nineteenth-century port city market. Washington Market, New York City, 1868. New York City Public Library, The Miriam and Ira D. Wallach Division of Art, Prints and Photographs: Picture Collection.

Gallery 1.2. 1865 Georgetown Market building today. Photo by author.

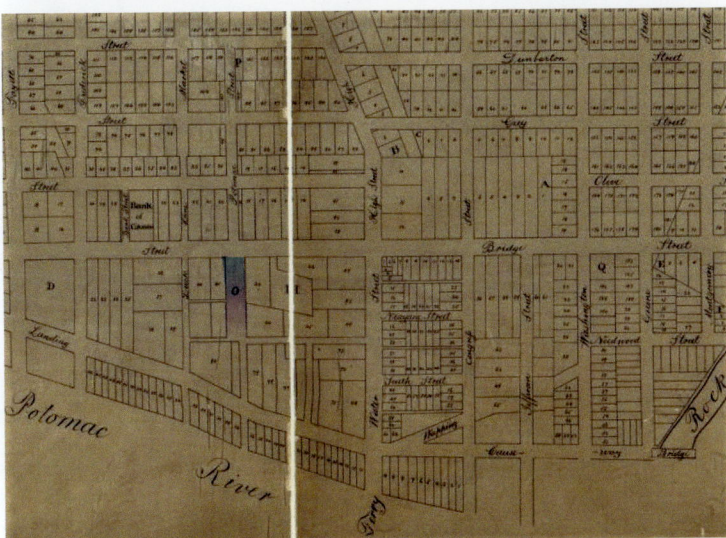

Gallery 1.3. 1814 map of Georgetown with the site of the Georgetown Market at "O." Francis Fenwick, Hugh T. Taggart, and District of Columbia, Office of the Surveyor. https://www.loc.gov/item/88693289/

Gallery 2.1. Traveling by flatboat at night. Wood engraving by Alfred R. Waud, 1855–1890. Wikimedia, https://en.wikipedia.org/wiki/Flatboat.

Gallery 2.2. New Orleans. William James Bennett, "New Orleans, Taken from the Opposite Side a Short Distance above the Middle, or Picayune, Ferry," 1841, aquatint print. New York Public Library, The Miriam and Ira D. Wallach Division of Art, Prints and Photographs: Print Collection. Universal Unique Identifier (UUID): cb8b8630-c5ed-012f-1ece-58d385a7bc34.

Gallery 3.1. Hull's Trail column marker. Location: County Road 106 three miles west of Kenton, Ohio. One of several markers erected along the trail by the Fort McArthur Chapter of the Daughters of the Revolution, 1912, from columns of the old Kenton Courthouse to commemorate the one hundredth anniversary of the War of 1812. Photo by Dale K. Benington, 2008, The Historical Marker Database, https://www.hmdb.org/m.asp?m=18416.

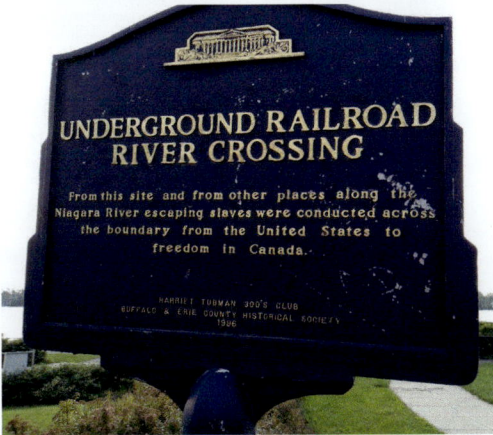

Gallery 3.2. "Underground Railroad River Crossing. From this site and from other places along the Niagara River escaping slaves were conducted across the boundary from the United States to freedom in Canada." Erected by the Harriet Tubman 300's Club, Buffalo & Erie County Historical Society, 1996. Broderick Park, Buffalo, New York.

Gallery 3.3. Niagara River crossing to Canada at the ferry landing, Broderick Park, Buffalo. Photo by author.

Gallery 4.1. Josiah's benefactor, transcriber and publisher Samuel Atkins Eliot by Gilbert Stuart, ca. 1808. Wikimedia Commons, https://commons.wikimedia.org/wiki/Category:Samuel_Atkins_Eliot_(politician).

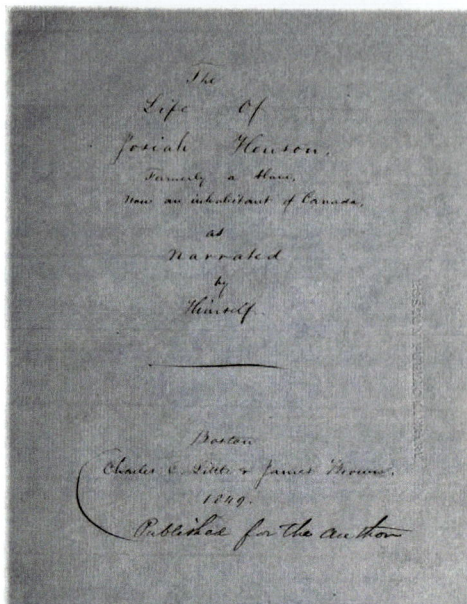

Gallery 4.2. Front of the original handwritten transcript of Josiah Henson's 1849 autobiography. Boston Public Library, Internet Archives, https://archive.org/details/lifeof josiahhens00hens_0/page/n1/mode/2up.

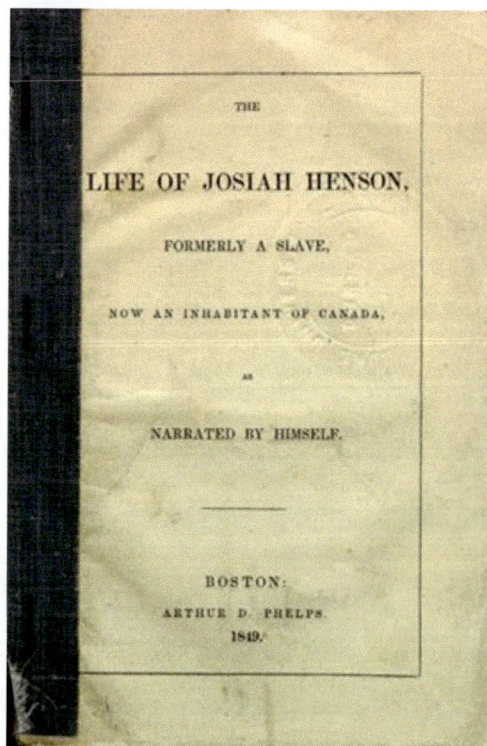

Gallery 4.3. Front of the 1849 published autobiography. Documenting the American South, https://docsouth.unc.edu/neh /chronautobio.html.

Gallery 5.1. Crystal Palace from the northeast during the Great Exhibition of 1851. Dickenson's Comprehensive Pictures from the Great Exhibition, 1854.

Gallery 5.2. The Anti-Slavery Convention of 1840, by Benjamin Robert Haydon. Robert Haydon presiding, John Scoble seated front center. National Portrait Gallery, London. For a full list of people depicted, see "The Anti-Slavery Society Convention, 1840," National Portrait Gallery, https://www.npg.org.uk/collections /search/portrait/mw00028/The-Anti-Slavery-Society-Convention-1840.

Gallery 6.1. Early portrait of Josiah Henson that appeared in his 1858 autobiography. Schomburg Center for Research in Black Culture, Manuscripts, Archives and Rare Books Division, New York Public Library. "Josiah Henson," New York Public Library Digital Collections, https://digitalcollections.nypl.org/items/510d47da-74d7-a3d9-e040-e00a18064a99.

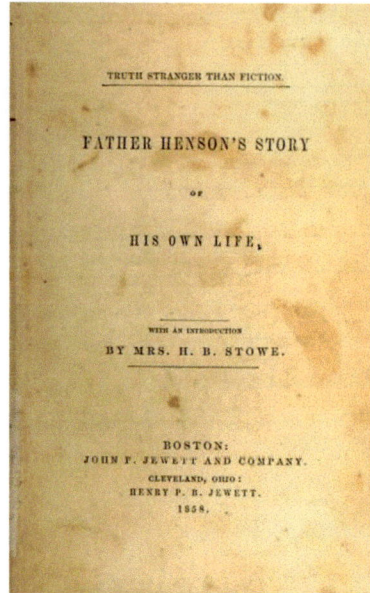

Gallery 6.2. Title page, Josiah Henson's 1858 autobiography. Documenting the American South, https://docsouth.unc.edu/neh/chronautobio.html.

Gallery 6.3. Niagara Suspension Bridge, by Charles Parsons. The bridge, completed in 1855, was designed by civil engineer John Augustus Roebling. Wikimedia Commons, https://en.wikipedia.org/wiki/Niagara_Falls_Suspension_Bridge.

Gallery 7.1. Josiah and Nancy Henson, 1876. Schomburg Center for Research in Black Culture, Jean Blackwell Hutson Research and Reference Division, New York Public Library. "Rev. Josiah Henson and Wife," New York Public Library Digital Collections, https://digitalcollections.nypl.org/items/510d47dd-e468-a3d9-e040-e00a18064a99.

Gallery 7.2. Last photograph of Josiah Henson, Scotland, 1877, by John Moffat, 125 Princess Street, Edinburgh. Library of Congress, Prints and Photographs Division, LOT 15158-1, no. 119.

Gallery 7.3. Josiah Henson and publisher John Lobb carte de visite, 1876. Bradshaw & Godart, successors to the London School of Photography, 103, Newgate Street, E.C., London, Library of Congress, William H. Gladstone Collection, https://www.loc.gov/pictures/item/2010647932/.

Gallery 7.4. Framed portrait of Queen Victoria given to Josiah Henson by the queen. Courtesy of the Chatham-Kent Museum, Chatham, Ontario, Canada.

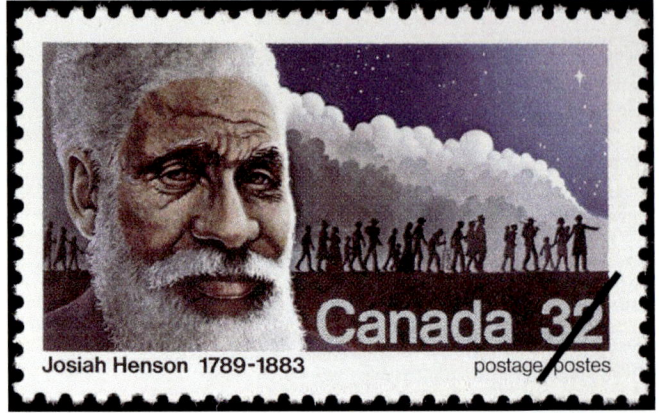

Gallery 8.1. Josiah Henson Canadian postage stamp https://postagestampguide .com/canada/stamps/16260 /josiah-henson-1789-1883 -1983-canada-postage-stamp.

Gallery 8.2. Josiah Henson Museum of African Canadian History, Dresden, Ontario, Canada. https://www.heritage trust.on.ca/properties/josiah-henson -museum.

Gallery 8.3. Josiah Henson Museum and Park in Montgomery County, Maryland. https://montgomery parks.org/parks-and-trails/josiah-henson-park/.

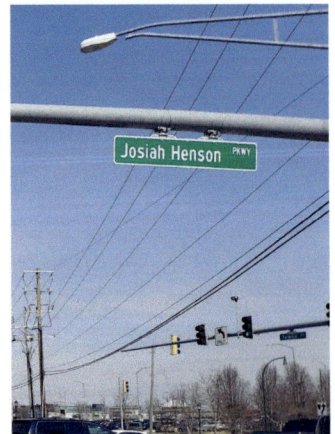

Gallery 8.4. A major road in downtown Rockville, Maryland, was renamed Josiah Henson Parkway. Photo by Keir Soderberg.

Appendix B

Josiah Henson's Family

Josiah Henson m. 1818 Charlotte Stevenson[1]
- Thomas, b. ca. 1818. Went to California ca. 1850, not heard from again
- Isaac, b. ca. 1819.[2] Educated in England, became Wesleyan minister. Died in 1856, age thirty-seven
- Celia Jane, b. 1827. m. (1) ___ Christee, m. (2) Elisha Kersey, December 8, 1859[3]
- Josiah, b. 1828.[4] Immigrated to Jackson, Michigan, where he worked as a plasterer and a shoemaker
  o m. (1) Mary
    - Frank, b. 1864[5]
  o m. (2) Charlotte Showls[6]
    - Howard Henson, b. 1871 (occupation, janitor), m. March 29, 1921, Roxanna Brown, b. 1885 in Ann Arbor, Michigan[7]
- Charlotte Matilda, b. 1832. m. (1) Everett Charles Richey,[8] m. (2) ___ Clay[9]
- Elizabeth, b. 1834. m. William Thomas, millwright[10]
- Peter, b. 1836.[11] Farmer in Dresden, m. Elizabeth Goens (daughter of Eli and Susan Goens), b. 1844, September 7, 1866, in Kent, Ontario, Canada[12]
- Julia Ann, b. February 18, 1840, d. May 22, 1913. m. Reuben Wheeler[13]

Eudora, daughter of Peter, b. 1868. m. June 27, 1886, Raymond Royal Bradley in Dresden, Ontario[14]

m. 1856 Nancy Gambell, b. ca. 1816–1819 (d. November 1888, age sixty-nine, in Kent, Ontario, Canada)[15]
   Three children from first marriage: Lucinda, John, Rebecca

Appendix C

Josiah Henson's Speeches

Josiah Henson's Speech at Albert Hall in Sheffield, United Kingdom, January 29, 1877, as Reported in the *Sheffield and Rotherham Independent*

"Uncle Tom" at the Albert Hall: The Story of His Life

Yesterday, at the Albert Hall, the Rev. Josiah Henson, popularly known as "Uncle Tom," told the story of his 42 years' slave life in America, with an account of his escape into Canada.[1] The first meeting was held at twelve o'clock [the meeting was held in two parts, afternoon and evening], and notwithstanding the hour and the inclemency of the weather, the hall was filled in every part. Persons began to assemble as early as half past ten, and very shortly after the doors were open, the galleries and back seats were filled, and the issue of tickets was stopped. There was then a run on the tickets for the better places, and by twelve o'clock there were sufficient persons present to fill the hall. The crowding at the back was relieved by the throwing open of the orchestra and front seats. The Rev. Canon Blakeney presided, and the Rev. Josiah Henson was accompanied by the Rev. R. Stainton, Mr. Hardy, Mr. Hovey, Mr. Peach, of Nottingham, and other gentlemen. There were a great many clergymen and ministers present. The Rev. R. Stainton offered prayer.

The CHAIRMAN, who was received with loud cheers, said he believed a certain amount of incredulity existed abroad as to the genuineness of the character assumed by their venerable friend, the Rev. Josiah Henson. A very great number of people in Sheffield had asked him very seriously, "Is he really the 'Uncle Tom' of Mrs. Beecher Stowe's book, entitled, 'Uncle Tom's Cabin?'" He had replied, "Yes, I believe he is, so far as his history, as related by himself to Mrs. Stowe, was the means of supplying her with most of the facts." In that way he helped her in her noble and grand efforts to free the poor slave. Mr. Henson had received letters of commendation from some of the most eminent men in America and men of high standing in this country, who had received him in the most kind and Christian manner. That noble man, the Earl of Shaftesbury—(cheers)—would preside at Mr. Henson's farewell meeting. So much about "Uncle Tom." The question was, what was the Rev. Josiah Henson doing now? He is a minister of the Gospel of the blessed Jesus—(hear, hear)—and doing everything in his power to elevate his people socially, religiously, and morally. (Cheers) He held in his hand a letter of commendation from the Rev. Thomas Hughes, secretary and missionary of the Colonial and Continental Church Society in Canada. It was dated Dresden, Ontario, Canada, March 10, 1876, and he said:—

"Mr. Josiah Henson being about to proceed to England has requested me to give him a letter testimonial. Mr. Henson is so highly respected throughout Western Canada, and also so well known to many influential persons both in the United States and England, that he scarcely needs any of the kind from any individual. I have known Mr. Henson for more than 16 years, and have great pleasure in bearing my testimony to his sterling Christian character. Mr. Henson's life has been an unusually active and eventful one. For many years he was a slave, and was most cruelly treated. And since his escape to Canada, now more than 40 years ago, he has occupied a foremost place in all movements for the advancement of his people. Through his efforts for their good, he has unfortunately suffered considerable pecuniary loss, and been compelled, in consequence, to mortgage his farm. It is with the view of lifting this incumbrance that he has in his extreme old age, resolved, in response to a cordial invitation given him, to visit England. I heartily commend him and his cause to the British public, and hope that he may have in every respect 'A prosperous journey by the will of God.'" He thought, therefore, they might now listen with pleasure, interest, and profit to their venerable friend, whom he had pleasure in introducing to the meeting. (Cheers.)

The Rev. JOSIAH HENSON, who was received with loud cheers, said: I feel thankful for the honour that seems to be conferred on me at this moment. Considering the inclemency of the weather, and this being Monday and rather an unusual hour for an assembly—to think that this congregation of people have favoured me with their presence from some cause, I am not able to say what, is a wonderful thing. I suppose it arises from the announcement that I have been a slave; and last, though not least, that I am a black man. (Laughter). Well, so much of that expectation I suppose has been realized. I have been an abject slave; and I suppose you are all satisfied that I am a black man. (Loud laughter.)

I am not able at this moment to find language sufficient to express my deep sense of gratitude to God and to his people for the kind, warm, hearty reception which has been extended to me since I have been in England. (Hear, hear.) It is more than I am able to express. I think, however, I can sum it up in a word or two:—"It is marvelous in our eyes, but it is the Lord." (Cheers.) I attribute it all to the goodness of God, which has been conferred upon me in every trial and conflict of life.

It has been announced that I would give the details of my 42 years' slave life, allow me to say that it would be almost impossible for me to do that at one or two, or even a dozen meetings. If I had physical strength and mental ability, I could talk, I suppose, while I live and then not reach the end. (Laughter and cheers.) It has been assumed that the book that Mrs. Stowe wrote was a fabrication, a falsehood—that there was no truth in it—that nothing of the kind ever occurred. She was challenged to present a key to it; and as an author I suppose she felt herself bound to do that for the general information of the people. In that key Mrs. Stowe tells you who was the hero of the book; and if you will get that key you will find from pages 37 to 57 what Mrs. Stowe says about me. (Laughter.)

In alluding to my life I must be as brief as I can for I am not so strong as I was 50 years ago. Look at the people crowding in that gallery (pointing to the upper gallery). They look like angels! I don't know whether they are. (Laughter.) You all look as if you were Christians, and I hope you are. (Hear, hear.) If you are not you ought to be. It is the joy of my heart, the glory of my expectations, that Christ has pardoned my sins; and I hope he will pardon the sins of all my enemies, and that I shall meet them in heaven.

My name is Josiah Henson. My parents had not the honour of naming me; I was named by my master, and my parents had to submit to it. My master was a young man, a physician; and as I was the first little negro born on his place he gave me his name, Josiah; the Hensons being relatives of his. He was rather proud of me, and said I would be a fine fellow, and I don't think he was much mistaken. (Laughter and cheers.) He used to pat me on the head like ladies pat their little dogs. (Renewed laughter.) He said when I was born that my head was so peculiar that it was in two parts, and had to be tied together with a napkin. (Great laughter.)

One day when in the old cabin I heard a row, and on going out I saw some men dragging along a poor old fellow whose hands were tied behind him. On getting nearer I saw it was my father they were pulling along! They took him to where there was a sign post, and suspended by his arms until his toes just touched the ground. A man then pulled his clothes from his back; took a cowhide and began to beat him, every blow making the flesh to fly and the blood to run. (Sensation.) I have never been able to restrain my feelings when I have thought of that scene. (Hear, hear.) When the man commenced you might have heard my father's screams two miles off; but he grew weaker and could only groan. They gave him what they called a "hundred lashes," and then the man went to him and said, "Will you ever do the like of that again?" My father replied, "She was my wife!" and that was all they could make him say. The man pushed his ear against the post, took a tack, and drove through it, and then cut it off, leaving his ear on the post. (Sensation.) they took him to gaol, and he was sold away into Alabama, and I have never seen him since. (Renewed sensation.)

That was a red letter day in my history; for the events of it burnt themselves into my very soul. When I grew old I inquired what was the crime my father had committed. Francis Newman who owned my father and Josiah Macpherson who owned my mother had adjoining farms, and one day my father heard my mother screaming. He ran and saw a man brutally assaulting my mother. He forgot there was no law to protect his manhood, but leaping over the fence he sprang like a tiger on my mother's assailant, threw him to the ground, and trampled on him as though he were a dog. (Loud cheers.) For that crime he was punished as I have told you, and I have never seen him since. If my father had died at the stake, with his ear cut off and blood streaming from his shoulders, I should have thought he died one of the most honourable deaths that ever man died in the world. (Loud cheers.) A man who would not risk or lose his life for his wife is not worthy to have a wife. (Cheers.)

Now the young gentleman who owned me and my mother, and who was never known to hurt a slave in his life[,] used to get a little "muddled," or "fuddled," or "a brick in his head," or a "little top heavy in the upper story," as people would say. (Laughter.) One night, when returning home, he was thrown from his horse and killed; and eighteen months later my mother and her family were put upon the block to be sold one by one. My brothers and sisters were sold, and I have never seen but one of them since. I, as the youngest, was put up last, and my mother, whose heart had been wrung with agony, went to the man who had bought her, fell on her knees, and said "Oh, master, buy my babe! All the rest have gone; let me have my babe." He kicked her away, and asked her how she dared to take such a liberty with him. (Sensation.)

It was said that a negro had no soul; but I believe, taking all things into consideration, that a negro is as good as any other man. (Cheers.) The master who bought me was a bad man; I'll say no more of him than that. I'll set him down at that, and let him go. (Cheers.) His name was Adam Robb, and he was a Scotchman—(great laughter)—and when an Irishman, or an Englishman, or a Scotchman gets into a bad way he is no better than any one else. (Laughter and cheers.) My master took me home to his own farm and put me in with the rest of the negroes. I now compare my condition at that time to a little pig among [a] lot of overgrown hogs. (Laughter.) I was soon taken ill, and grew so weak that I could not crawl across the cabin to get a drop of water. My master, thinking I should die, sold me a bargain to the man who had bought my mother, and under her tender care I recovered.

One Sunday morning, when my mother had combed my hair—and as it was only combed once a week it was rather hard work—(laughter and cheers)—she asked me to go and ask my master to let me go to meeting. I refused, not because I did not want to go to meeting, but because I did not want to go to my master. As I have said, he was a bad man—one of those long-nosed, blue-eyed fellows, you know. (Great laughter and cheers.) I afterwards went to him, and when he had tantalized me a long time he said I might go to meeting. I went, and heard that which led me to resolve to become a Christian, and before I reached him that night I had given my heart to God. (Cheers.) As I went along I leaped and skipped and praised God. I suffered for it afterwards. One day when I was praying in the stable my master came and said "What you doing there?" I said, "I was praying." "Who are you praying to?" he asked. "Praying to the Lord," I answered, "to save my soul." "You think you got a soul?" "Yes, sir," I said. He answered, "You have got no more soul than a dog. Let me catch you praying; I'll pray you." I got up and he walked off grumbling like a bear with a sore head. (Laughter.) I said to myself, "Well, if I have got no soul, I know religion makes my body happier." (Loud laughter and cheers.)

If I had no anticipation of one day being in a more delightful world than I am to-day; if I had no hope of being happier than I am in this hall, I would still devote my time and talents to the service of God for what I enjoy to-day. (Cheers.) When I think that a few years ago I was a slave, dragging the chains of oppression, and that now I am here in this society, I cannot but praise God. (Cheers.) I lived with that old master until he was convinced that there was a reality in religion. (Cheers.) I convinced him by being faithful to God and faithful to him. (Cheers.) I believe that the abolition of slavery in America has benefitted the master as much as the slave; that both are more likely to obtain the salvation of their souls. (Cheers.)

Master had on his farm some fifteen or twenty women, and they had to go into the fields to work just like the men. At times some of them would be ill, and not able to do their share of work, and then master would beat them with raw hide until their backs were raw. I used to run away and hide, for I could not endure the sight. I could not help them, but I adopted another plan. I was a smart fellow, and could do as much work as any two or three other men, so I used to select a row between the rows of these poor women, and now help one a bit and now another and so helped them to keep up with their work. (Cheers.)

When those poor creatures returned to their cabin at night there was nothing for them to eat but a little bread and herring, although there was plenty on the plantation that was going to waste. I had to feed the horses—and a horse is not like a man, he does not swallow everything he gets into his mouth. (Laughter.) Some of the corn would drop, and the chickens would pick it up. Now and then, one would get hurt, and to put it out of its misery I used to wring its neck. I would then strip off its jacket, get some potatoes, and make a big potful of chicken soup and potatoes. (Laughter.) In the dead of the night I would go round and give the soup to these poor women, and then stand on guard while they eat it. (Laughter and cheers.) I think in doing that I did right; because I never was suspected and I never was detected. (Roars of laughter and cheers.)

I would quite as soon the old man should have known it if he would have discussed the subject with me. (Laughter.) But he was such an old calf-headed fellow he would not look upon it in the proper light, so it was best he should know nothing about it. (Laughter.) If he had seen me he would have said—"What! caught you stealing chickens have I?" I should have said, "No, sir. I have not stolen anything." "What, did you not cook some chickens last night?" he would have asked. "Yes, sir." "Where did you get them?" "Out of the barnyard, sir." "You stole them, then?" "No, sir." I should have answered, "Because the law of the United States says that no slave can steal anything from his master. (Laughter.) Neither can he prosecute his slave for stealing anything from himself, because he and all that he is his master's." (Laughter.) I would have discussed the matter upon another ground, and I think a very philosophical one, although perhaps he would not have agreed with me. I took a piece of property from one side of the house and invested it in another piece of property on the other side of the house, marking that piece of property as more valuable. (Laughter and cheers.) Master got the benefit of it by their increased labour. I got more work out of them than any other overseer, and by and by he turned off all the other overseer, and I was promoted to be the biggest duck in the pie. (Laughter and cheers.)

The venerable gentleman, who had been speaking nearly an hour and a half, and had been listened to with the most rapt attention, said he must conclude his story in the evening, and after thanked them for the cordial reception they had given to him, resumed his seat amidst loud cheers.

Mr. HOVEY said he thought the meeting ought not to separate without passing a resolution something like this, "That this meeting expresses its gratification that slavery no longer exists in the United States of America; and hope the time it not far distant when it shall be swept from the face of the earth." (Cheers.) They were all assured that slavery degraded alike the master and the slave. England paid a large sum of money to free the slaves in her dominions. America had paid infinitely more than we paid, in the terrible civil war that raged there. What they purchased was well worth all that was paid—(cheers)—and he hoped the time would soon come when slavery would no longer exist on the earth. (Cheers.)

The Rev. R. STAINTON seconded the motion, and it was carried with loud cheers.

The CHAIRMAN pronounced the benediction, and the meeting concluded.

THE EVENING MEETING

The hall was crowded again in the evening to hear the conclusion of the story. The people began to assemble at an early hour, and, in a very short time, all the galleries and back seats were crowded. The balconies and front seats filled more slowly, but, when the time arrived for the commencement of the proceedings, the hall was filled. In the unavoidable absence of Dr. Webster, the American Vice-Consul, through indisposition, the Rev. R. Stainton was voted to the chair, and, after opening the meeting with singing and prayer, he gave a brief summary of the morning's address for the information of those who were unable to be present. In explaining the circumstances which had brought Mr. Henson to England again, he said that the gentleman who was appointed the treasurer of his institution frittered away the money, and to prevent all the property being wasted he commenced a law suit against him, which lasted seven years. Mr. Henson beat him at last, but he had to mortgage his farm to do it. (Cheers.) He was invited to return to England to raise money to free his place from debt, and he had done so, Mr. S. Morley, M.P., and Mr. Sturge being his trustees. (Cheers.)

Of all the meetings which Mr. Henson had attended up and down the country, those in Sheffield had been the most loyal, enthusiastic, practical, and responsive. (Cheers.) When he went back to London on Tuesday, and attended his last meeting in England, in Mr. Spurgeon's tabernacle, he would tell them how well Sheffield had behaved towards him. (Cheers.) Before leaving England her Majesty had requested an audience with their hero, and then it was his intention to present her with a copy of the narrative of his life. (Cheers.) He hoped God would bless him in his later days and take him home to his family in peace. (Cheers.)

The Rev. JOSIAH HENSON was then asked to address the meeting, and was received with loud cheers. He said:—

I do not know hardly how to express my deep sense of gratitude for the reception you have extended to me to-night. As I have been sitting here and looking at the faces of the people, I have thought within myself I hope I shall meet you all in heaven. (Cheers.) While I am able to remember anything, I shall remember the liberality and the hospitality that I have received since I came into your town. (Cheers.) God bless you all; for I should not wonder if some of you don't need it. (Laughter.) In my remarks this morning I stopped at a pot of soup with some chickens in it—a very pleasant place. (Laughter and cheers.) The chickens were often missed, and the misses used to come looking about, and ask me if I had seen anything of them. I used to say, "May be there has been a fox round here mam." (Laughter.) If she had seen the fox she would have seen it was a black one. (Renewed laughter.)

Although my master was a bad man, I did my duty by him, as I wanted to gain his confidence and earn a dollar to put in my pocket. He got involved in a law suit arising out of a good stiff family quarrel; lost his case, and one day he came and told me that all his negroes would have to be sent to Montgomery Court-house to be sold. He asked me to run away, take the other negroes with me, and go to his brother's in Kentucky, about 300 miles away. I did not want to be sold, so I gave him my word that I would go and deliver up his people to his brother.

There was myself, my wife, and two children, and eighteen others. He directed me what route to take, and we started. Several times on the road people wanted me to sell the horse and wagon, and all of us escape, but I had pledged my word before God that I would go, and that was enough for me. (Cheers.) I kept my word, and delivered up myself and the other negroes to my master's brother. He promised to come to us in two years, but he did not come. He had married a lady who if she had not a mind to do a thing would not do it, and nobody could make her. (Laughter.) He would have come, but she would not accompany him, and he had to knock under. (Laughter.) In the year 1828 he sent out an agent to sell all his slaves except me and my wife and children; we were to stop and work for his brother.

Two years later he sent a man to take me down to New Orleans to be sold. When I stood on board the boat, and saw my wife and children weeping on the shore, and thinking we should never meet again, then, for the first time since I became converted, I lost the image of God in my heart. There were three men on board the boat, and I resolved the first opportunity I had I would kill them. One night I was left on watch, and taking an axe I sent to where they were sleeping, raised it, and was about to kill the first when I seemed to hear a voice—"What! You do murder, and you a Christian? Have you not heard that no murderer hath eternal life abiding in him?" I replied, "No, Lord, I would not do murder for all the world," and I crept away and wept bitterly. (Cheers.) We reached New Orleans, and on the day I was to be sold my young master was taken ill, and he begged me to return with him home, and not to let him die there and be buried on the river side. You may be sure I was glad to do that—(cheers and laughter)—and I returned with him, and great was the joy when I met my wife and children again.

In a little while I began to lay my plans to run away; but I could not get my wife to agree with me. "Well," I said, "if you won't go you must stay, but I am going to go"—(laughter and cheers)—and when she found I was going to take the children with me she said, "Well, I shall have to try to go to." (Laughter.) On a Saturday night I put my two youngest children into a knapsack, and slung them on my back; the two eldest were able to walk, and with my wife we were ferried across the river. We took to the woods and travelled 600 miles before we struck Lake Erie. (Cheers.) We suffered much from hunger and thirst, but the hope of freedom sustained us. (Cheers.) One day when my children had been crying for water I left them and started in search of it. I found a well, but I had nothing in which to carry water. I first thought of saturating my shirt in water, and taking it and wringing it out in their mouths. I hit upon a better plan. I washed out my shoes and carried them full of water and they drank of it. (Laughter and cheers.)

We passed tribes of Indians and they helped us and gave us food to eat. We reached Lake Erie, and there saw a vessel being laden with grain. I left my wife and children in the woods and went down to where the men were at work. The captain was a Scotchman and he set me to work, and when he found out that I wanted to go to Canada he offered to take me. (Cheers.) I told him I should like to go if I could get ready. (Laughter.) Said he, "What have you to get ready?" I told him I should like to take my wife and children. "How long will it take you to move down?" said he. "Not long," I replied. (Laughter.) He sent three men to help me to bring down my wife and children, and when she saw us coming she thought I had been detected, and they fled into the woods. I asked the men to stop a little bit while I sent and got my wife tame. (Laughter.) I went to her and told her all, and we went on board the vessel, and he took me down to Buffalo, and then we dropped down to within a short distance of the Canadian shore. He paid the ferry-man to take us across; gave me a dollar; put his hand on my head, and told me to be a "good fellow"! (Cheers.) I have tried to be good; and the Lord has abundantly blessed me. (Cheers.)

He then gave an interesting account of his interview with the Archbishop of Canterbury, and told how his Grace slipped a £50 note into his hand when leaving—(cheers)—and concluded by singing a slave song and a farewell hymn. (Cheers.)

The CHAIRMAN moved a vote of thanks to Mr. Henson for his interesting story.—This was seconded by Mr. PEACH, under whose care Mr. Henson had come to Sheffield.—The motion was carried with loud cheers, and the meeting closed.

Description of Josiah Henson's Farewell Address at the Tabernacle in London on January 30, 1877

"UNCLE TOM" IN LONDON

"Uncle Tom," the popular hero of Mrs. Beecher Stow's celebrated story, took his farewell of the metropolitan public on Tuesday night, at a meeting held in Mr. Spurgeon's tabernacle.[2] The Rev. Josiah Henson—such is the ministerial name of the famous negro character—has been on a visit to London engaged in raising funds on behalf of the religious and charitable institution in Canada, of which he is the head.

The Earl of Shaftesbury presided; and when his lordship appeared on the spacious pulpit, closely followed by Uncle Tom, there were hearty and genial bursts of cheering. Uncle Tom himself met with a reception in full keeping with the interest he commands in Mrs. Stowe's tale of his slave career. Though in his 88th year he looks hale and vigorous. His hair, including beard and moustache, is decidedly grey, and his features bear the marks of toil and time. He is tall and stoutly built. The countenance in its first aspect is rather heavy than vivacious; but as he spoke it soon became apparent that he has the mercurial temperament and the latent elasticity and fun of the negro race. Mrs. Henson sat near him. Uncle Tom has 44 grandchildren, 8 great grand-children, and 10 children now living. A gentleman on the platform bespoke indulgence for Mr. Henson, observing that his arms were both broken nearly 70 years ago through the cruelties of "Legree," whose real name was Bryce Litton, and that in consequence he had been unable since to raise his hands to his head.

The Rev. J. Henson then proceeded to address the meeting on his 42 years' slave life. He began by describing vividly his recollection of a terrible flogging inflicted, while he was himself a little boy, on his own father, because he forcibly resisted a white man whom he found assaulting his wife, appealing to the meeting whether anyone worthy of having a wife would not have done the same. Such scenes were, he observed, imprinted on his memory with red ink—that is, with blood. He saw blood run down his father's clothes that day; and he was afterwards taken away to gaol, and he had never seen him since.

He next dwelt on the scattering of all the rest of the family, as well as of the other slaves on the estate, by an auction, in consequence of the owner's sudden death, and gave some touching incidents connected with it, one of these being that a mother having entreated a man who had bought her to buy her baby as well, he kicked her away. After telling of his own restoration to his own mother in consequence of an illness which led his master to part with him to a slaveowner named Riley, on whose estate she lived, in order that she might nurse and rear him, he entered into some interesting details of negro life, including a humorous sketch of the tantalising behavior of his master when he asked him at his mother's instigation to let him go and hear Mr. M'Kenny preach, describing the master as "one of those long-nosed, blue-eyed fellows." Consent was, he said, at last given, and though he dared not enter the chapel, because that would have "desecrated" it, he heard what led to his conversion and to his beginning to lead a Christian life.

Coming to the story of his escape, he said he simply ran away. (Laughter.) While he was preparing for it he saw poor women who were ill cruelly beaten because they did not do sufficient work, and to save one or two of them from such treatment he did part of the task allotted to them, and even worked in the night. He also confessed that he used some of his mistress's chickens to make chicken soup for those poor women in the night, it not being stealing to do that under the laws of the United States.

After this he gave a narrative of his being sent to New Orleans for sale, and the temptation which came upon him on his way in a boat to kill with an axe three white men who had charge of him, and said that he was about to do it when he was stopped by something appearing to say to him, "What! you a Christian, and commit murder!" Among those who went with him was a son of Riley, whose life he had helped to save during a dreadful fever, and with that man he returned home after his unexpected recovery.

He then related the familiar facts connected with his escape, his wanderings with his wife and children for several hundred miles in the bush, and the difficulties which he had in procuring sufficient food to live upon. At last, he said, he reached Lake Erie, where he found a Scotch captain, who spoke English so badly that he could hardly understand him—(laughter)—the result being that he was landed with his wife and children in Buffalo.

The address lasted about half an hour, and was kept interesting to the end through a capital style of narration, set off by telling dramatic action. In conclusion, Uncle Tom sang alone, in accordance with the programme for the evening, the "Slave's Parting Hymn," beginning, "My brethren, fare ye well," after which the audience sang a hymn of corresponding character, called "Parting words."

Josiah Henson's Account of Meeting Queen Victoria, Given in Edinburgh on March 6, 1877

"UNCLE TOM" AND THE QUEEN

On Tuesday night the Rev. Josiah Henson ("Uncle Tom") addressed a meeting in the London-road United Presbyterian Church, Edinburgh, and referred to his interview with the Queen.[3]

He said that when he saw the Queen she met him very gracefully, and they might rely upon it that he endeavoured to meet her as gracefully. (Laughter.) He continued—she was neatly dressed; so was I. (Laughter.) She came and made a very polite bow to me; and so did I. (Applause.) She said, she had long read of me, and heard a great deal about me, and was very happy to see me indeed, and I did not say ditto. (Applause.) But I thought so—(renewed laughter)—and I said this, that I had had for a long time a great desire to see her Majesty in person, that I might have the honour of presenting to her Majesty my private thanks for the honour which she had conferred upon herself by granting us slaves an asylum from the hands of cruel oppressors, that whenever a slave struck the soil of Great Britain he was a man and a free man. (Applause.)

At every sentence she would make a polite bow and so would I. (Applause.) And I told her how our petitions had been ascending to God in prayer and thankfulness for the privileges which she had given us in Canada from the armed hand of the oppressor. (Applause.) I said that we would be always an honour to the Crown, and the greatest blessing we could confer upon her Majesty would be to hope that all her subjects should behave themselves. (Applause.)

The Queen then turned round to one of her ladies in attendance and got something, and walked back to me and asked me if I would have this as a token from her. It was a beautiful—what do you call it?—(applause)—portrait. Here it is. (Mr. Henson here exhibited the portrait amid loud applause.) I was not (he proceeded to say) very nervous for I had just got one of the finest dinners I ever had—(applause)—and I must say that both I and Mr. Bowden enjoyed it very much. (Applause.) There were three or four men bowing around us, and I thought I had got to a very fine place, as indeed I had. (Applause.)

The Queen then sent for my better-half and Mr. Bowden, and when they came up I found that he had found out the knack of bowing and scraping as well as myself—(applause)—and so we kept up bowing and becking to our fill. (Applause.)

Josiah Henson's Acceptance Speech after Receiving a Testimonial with a Gift of a Gold Watch and Chain from the People of Scotland at the Farewell Reception Given for Him and His Wife in Glasgow at City Hall on April 20, 1877

Mr. Chairman, ladies and gentlemen, and Christian friends, I have the honour of standing before you in all probability for the last time in this life.[4] I do not know, Sir, in the present state of my health, that I shall be able to make those satisfactory remarks which this audience ought to have. My bodily health is so impaired that I am scarcely able to stand, but I am thankful to be permitted to be here, and I hope to be able to present the deepest affections of my heart for the warm reception I have received since I had the honour of putting my foot in Scotland. (Applause.) It has far exceeded my expectations; and allow me to say that what has been done has been a spontaneous, a voluntary effort. I had no thought of spending more than a fortnight in Scotland, but the manner in which I have been treated has been so far beyond anything I could have expected that I have been induced to prolong my stay. Now, Sir, I don't know that I could do anything more than tender an expression of thanksgiving to you and to all my friends that have so kindly taken me by the hand, and presented me with a token of respect such as I never before had presented to me in my life. (Applause.) I can scarcely control my own feelings at this moment. I thank God that I have been permitted, through all the toils and conflicts of life, to have the honour of standing before a British audience —(applause)—whose minds and hearts are right upon what we in America call "the goose question."[5] (Laughter.) That is one of the greatest questions in America. If there is anything done good and noble, they call it "a grand thing upon the goose question." (Laughter and applause.) This is a goose question indeed. (Renewed laughter.)

I look back from whence I came, and see by the eyes of my mind what you cannot see with your eyes, because you have not been there, and feel in my heart what you cannot feel, and I hope never will feel, and no one can feel it but the man who has had the iron through his own soul. (Applause.) A few years ago I was dragging the chains of oppression and groaning beneath the bondsman's burden, with not an eye to pity nor an arm to deliver, and could not tell which way the thing would turn, but I looked steadfastly to God, and depended upon His word —at least as well as I understood it —(Applause)—and now these dark clouds have all been dispersed and blown asunder, and I have the honour to-night of standing upon British soil, among British people, with British feelings, and a love of liberty. (Loud applause.)

I wanted, Sir, when speaking to my friend, Mr. Bowden—I wanted to come to Scotland before I left for Canada, because I had a reason for it. It was not for money—I did not know I was going to get any. (Laughter.) I did not think much about it; but I wanted to put my foot in Scotland, for when I was, as it were, between heaven and earth, and exposed to death, dragging through the wilderness with my dear little woman and four little children—when I had got to the extreme point and could get no farther, having reached the waters of Lake Erie, I knew not what to do. I hid my wife and children in the wood, in the prairie bushes, and went out and exposed my life, because I could not do better. I lay in the woods and groaned till the groans of my wife and children, who were starving with hunger, aroused my heart. I said—"Lord, I cannot bear this; for if I lie here I must die. I can only die, and I am bound to try and save my wife and children."

I went out, not knowing where I was going or what I should meet; but, as the Lord would have it, something was prepared for me, as something was prepared for Jonah. It was not a whale. (Laughter.) Well, what was it? It was a man with a heart in him as big as a great fat ox. (Laughter.) And he was not only a man but a Scotchman. (Applause.) I don't say this because I am among Scotch people now. I have written this some thirty-seven years ago, and you will find it in the history of my life written then; so I am not making a speculation of it now. And I don't need to do that to have your affectionate sympathies and prayers, because I have got them already, and shall remember your kindness in all time coming, when I get home to my land where I expect to live and die.

This man, a Scotchman, in the hour of trial, stepped forward, took me by the hand, brought myself and family on board his vessel, and took us to Buffalo city. He asked me what I had to live on. I told him—"Three threepenny bits"—that is, about 18 cents in American coin. "Is that all you have got?" "Yes; every cent." "What are you going to do?" "I will give you all I have got." "Well," he said, "never mind. You see those trees across the river there?" "Yes, Sir." "Well," says he, "you are not a man till you get there; but when you get there you stand a man."

"That good man helped me and my wife and children. He stood on the deck above me." "I am a poor man myself," he said, "and have a wife and four or five children. I sail this boat; I am hired to do it, and am but a servant. If I had anything worth while I would give you something to help you to buy some bread. I will pay your ferry over. Here is one dollar. Go away, then," he said, and, putting his hand on my head, added, "be a good fellow—won't you?" I told him I would. (Applause.) I have nothing to brag about my goodness; but I promised him; and I promised the Lord before, that while I lived I would be a good man what whatever took place—if I starved—I would be a good man. I made up that in my mind ever since the Lord converted my soul; and I hope I am a good man now, and that I shall live and die a good man—a straightforward man.

I went to work in Canada. I toiled with my hands during the week for a livelihood and preached on the Sabbath for a living. (Laughter) I suppose you call a livelihood a living—(laughter)—but I toiled with my hands to make a living, and preached to live hereafter. (Applause.) I may tell you a few things about how I got on. I used to walk from twelve to fifteen miles on Sabbath on my feet, and preached twice and sometimes three times a day the best way I could. I could not read, but then I could sing and talk a little, and kneel down and pray with them, and would teach them to be honest, and upright, and frugal, and to serve God, and by and by they would be better. I preached "repentance toward God and faith toward our Lord Jesus Christ."

I happened to say that to Archbishop Sumner in my interview with him when I visited London in 1851, and he said it was very good preaching. I used to go almost naked. I went barefooted every day during the week, and on Saturday night got a pair of shoes tied with string, had them blackened up a little, wrapped them in a cloth, and took them with me on Sabbath. I walked barefooted till I got in sight of the place where I was going to try to hold forth, when I put the shoes on. (Applause.) I put them on when I came in sight of the houses or cabins, because God commands respect, and I think a minister ought to command respect (hear, hear)—and be as good a looking man as any of the rest. (Laughter and applause.)

I preached as well as I could; if they gave me something to eat, I took it, and if they had nothing to give, I went home without it. (Renewed laughter and applause.) Frequently I was asked to stay all night, having nine or ten miles to go, but I would beg to be excused. "You had better stop," they would say; "you are tired, and it will be ten or eleven before you get home." Well, I would think the matter over, and would have been glad enough to have stayed, for I was tired, but I found I could not do so without dis-honouring the cause of Christ. My wife had fixed on my shirt collar—(laughter)—and put a white rag round my neck to make me look something like a minister. I would have been glad to have stayed, but if I had done so I would have been obliged to take off my coat, and how would I have been! (Laughter.) Sooner than I would dis-honour the Lord that way, and let the people know I was so poor as not to have a shirt on, I would walk home, and get there at ten or eleven, and go to work next morning.

Hymn Composed by Josiah Henson and Sung by Him at the End of His Speech at the Farewell Meeting in London on January 30, 1877, as Recorded by John Lobb

"Slaves' Parting Hymn"

My brethren, fare ye well,
I do you now tell,
I'm sorry to leave you,
I love you so well.

I shortly must go,
And where I don't know;
Wherever I'm stationed
The trumpet I'll blow.

Strange people I'll find;
I hope they'll prove kind;
Neither places nor faces
Shall alter my mind.

Wherever I'll be,
I'll still pray for thee;
And you, my dear brethren,
Do the same for poor me.[6]

Josiah Henson's Address at a Meeting in Mechanics' Hall, Dumfries, Scotland

Mr. Henson had made up his mind to make his recent appearance in Glasgow be his last public appearance in Scotland; but a committee of gentlemen had been formed in Dumfries to endeavour to persuade him to pay a visit, and plied by the pertinacious importunity of Mr. John Johnstone, merchant, he at last consented.[7]

Mr. Henson addressed a monster meeting in the Mechanics' Hall, Dumfries. Every part of the hall was crowded, platform, aisles, and doorways; and numbers of people had come in from Annan, Kirkeudbright, and other places nearer and more remote, the audience including several of the county families. On Mr. Henson entering the hall, he was received with great cheering. Mrs. Henson was also on the platform. The chair was taken by Dr. Gilchrist, of the Crichton Royal Institution; and among those present were—Mr. Maxwell, of Munches, Mr. Starke, of Troqueer Holme, Mr. Starke, Jr., and Mrs. Starke, Mrs. Davies, Mrs. S. Adamson, Rev. John Paton, Rev. Marshall N. Goold, Rev. John D. M'Kinnon, Rev. G. Rae, Rev. W. Graham, Rev. R. M'Kenna, Rev. J. Strachan, Rev. J. Duff, Rev. W. Tiplady, Rev. T. Bowman, Rev. L. M'Pherson, Rev. Mr. Simpson (Crichton Institution), Mr. Boyd, Kinder House, Mr. Walter Grierson, Chapelmount, Mr. W. Gregan, St. Christopher's, Mr. J. B. Milligan, Mr. James Rodger, Mr. John Johnstone, merchant, Mr. Johnston, Bank of Scotland, Mr. M'Neillie, of Castlehill, Provost Gillies, Mr. R. B. Carruthers, Mr. M'Dowall, Mr. J. Ewing, Mr. J. Clarke, Mr. Scott, Mr. W. F. Johnstone, Mr. Allan, ironmonger, &c.

Mr. HENSON, who was loudly cheered, in the opening part of his address, said:

There has been so much said and written about me, so much read about me, and so many things thought about me, that I did not know that I could do better than come and let you see me. (Laughter and applause.) It has been spread abroad that "'Uncle Tom' is coming," and that is what has brought you here. Now allow me to say that my name is not Tom, and never was Tom, and that I do not want to have any other name inserted in the newspapers for me than my own. My name is Josiah Henson, always was, and always will be. I never change my colours. (Loud laughter.) I would not if I could, and I could not if I would. (Renewed laughter.) Well, inquiry in the minds of some has led to a deal of inquiry on the part of others. You have read and heard some persons say that, "'Uncle Tom' was dead, and how can he be here? It is an imposition that is being practised on us." Some people in this town have said so. Very well, I do not blame you for saying that. I do not think you are to blame. A great many have come to me in this country and asked me if I was not dead. (Laughter.) Says I, "Dead?" Says he, "Yes. I heard you were dead, and read you were." "Well," says I, "I heard so too, but I never believed it yet. (Laughter.) I thought in all probability I would have found it out as soon as anybody else." (Laughter.) Well, now, to remove this difficulty, if it exist in your minds. As a matter of course, it is not a very pleasant thing to me to hear that I am traversing the country and practising an imposition upon the people. No, it is not pleasant; and the only way I have to meet it is to say that when people have this doubt upon their minds it shows me they ain't well read, or have forgotten what they have read, if they have ever read at all. (Laughter.) They have forgotten that Mrs. Stowe's "Uncle Tom's Cabin" is a novel; and it must have seemed a glorious finish to that novel that she should kill her hero—a glorious finish. Now you get the Key to "Uncle Tom's Cabin"—you can buy it for about sixpence, fifteen or sixteen cents—and you commence and read it. I see that gentleman along there setting it down. That is all right. (Laughter.) I see you. (Laughter.) Well, you commence at the 34th chapter and read up to the 57th chapter of the "Key to Uncle Tom's Cabin," and I think you will there see me. (Laughter and applause.) You remember that when this novel of Mrs. Stowe came out, it shook the foundations of this world. It shook Americans almost out of their shoes, and out of their shirts. (Laughter.) It left some of them on the sandbar barefooted and scratching their heads, without knowing where to go, or what to do or say. However, they came to the conclusion to say that the whole thing was a fabrication, a falsehood, and a lie; and they accused her of writing it, and they demanded of her a clue or key to the novel she had written, the exposure she had made, and the libel she had fixed on the United States. And so, as she was in duty bound to give something, she, I think in 1853, brought out the "Key," between you and she, and in that she spoke of me, and in that way set the negro free. (Laughter and applause.) I am not a Robert Burns—(laughter)—but that is a fact. (Applause.) You will find in that "Key" of me the position which I held in relation to her work. They said there were never any such things perpetrated on the negroes; never any negroes so afflicted, and that the book was a libel on the people of the United States; and when she took to this "Key," she told them where they would find a man called Josiah Henson. She gave me a great name, and said I was a venerable fellow, in which she was not much mistaken, for I was an old man, to be found in Canada West, labouring there as a minister of the gospel of Jesus Christ, preaching to the fugitive slaves, encouraging the cause of education, and building up the poor afflicted race of negroes. (Applause.) Josiah Henson, then, is my name. I am not responsible for anything written in Mrs. Stowe's novel, but only for what she wrote about me. You can find that wherever I have been I have never changed my predilections of colours—(laughter)—for mine is a good substantial, fast colour—(laughter and cheers)—one of the best in the world, and the ladies all love it, for they like to dress in black. (Laughter.) I have nothing but the truth, the whole truth, and my manhood; and they who don't like that may let me alone. I am not ashamed to show my face, and never did anything that I am ashamed of. Do you suppose that such men as Samuel Crossley, Samuel Morley, George Sturge, the Earl of Shaftesbury, Earl Gray,

Baptist Noel, and others who have honoured me with their friendship and given me their pulpits, would be deceived by me, or that I, by falsifying one of the highest principles in this world, would practise an imposition on my friends? Never! never! (Cheers.) Too much of a man for that, even though I am a black man.

Mr. Henson then proceeded to tell the story of his life. He concluded by thanking them for their patient hearing, and by singing the slave hymn of parting, the audience taking the chorus, "Glory, glory, hallelujah, freedom reigns to-day!" a hymn, which after Lincoln's proclamation received new words, "John Brown," and a quicker time, for the negroes were then made happy from their heads to their heels—he bounding and beaming as he rendered a stave of the joyous strain, the immense audience cheering him to the echo.

Notes

Introduction

1. *Dumfries and Galloway Standard*, Wednesday, April 25, 1877.
2. *The Weekly Standard and Express* (Blackburn, Lancashire, England), Saturday. September 9, 1876, 6; *The Nottinghamshire Guardian* (Nottingham, Nottinghamshire, England), Friday, December 15, 1876, 3; *Sheffield and Rotherham Independent* (Sheffield, South Yorkshire, England), Tuesday, January 30, 1877, 6; *Sheffield and Rotherham Independent* (Sheffield, South Yorkshire, England), Thursday, February 1, 1877, 7; *Sheffield and Rotherham Independent* (Sheffield, South Yorkshire, England), Saturday, February 3, 1877, 11; *The Graphic: An Illustrated Weekly Newspaper* (London, Greater London, England), Saturday, February 3, 1877, 9; *Belfast News-Letter* (Belfast, Antrim, Northern Ireland), Thursday, February 8, 1877, 4; *The Leeds Mercury* (Leeds, West Yorkshire, England), Saturday, February 3, 1877, 11; and *St. Louis Globe-Democrat* (St. Louis, Missouri), Sunday, March 11, 1877, 3.
3. Harriet Beecher Stowe, *A Key to Uncle Tom's Cabin, Presenting the Original Facts and Documents upon Which the Story Is Founded Together with Corroborative Statements Verifying the Truth of the Work* (Boston: John P. Jewett & Co., 1853); republished by Applewood Books, Bedford, MA) 23–30.
4. *New York Times*, Saturday, August 5, 1882, 2.
5. Susanna Ashton, "A Genuine Article: Harriet Beecher Stowe and John Andrew Jackson," Commonplace, commonplace.online/article/genuine-article/; and Joan D. Hedrick, *Harriet Beecher Stowe: A Life* (New York: Oxford University Press, 1994), 206. Josiah Henson was in Boston at this time embarking on a voyage to England with his son.
6. David S. Reynolds, *Mightier Than the Sword: Uncle Tom's Cabin and the Battle for America* (New York: Norton, New York, 2011), 107–8.
7. Hedrick, *Harriet Beecher Stowe*, 221.
8. "Uncle Tom," *Star Tribune* (Minneapolis), June 6, 1877, 1.
9. *New York Sun*, August 7, 1882, 2, col. 6; *New York Times*, August 5, 1882, 2; *Atchison Daily Patriot* (Atchison, KS), August 11, 1882, 1; *The Sedgewick Pantograph* (Sedgewick, KS), September 9, 1882), 4; and *Chicago Star Tribune*, July 9, 1877), 4.
10. Harriet Beecher Stowe, *Uncle Tom's Cabin*, edited by Elizabeth Ammons (New York: Norton, 1994), 359.
11. Stowe, *Uncle Tom's Cabin*, 344.
12. Josiah Henson, *The Life of Josiah Henson, Formerly a Slave, Now an Inhabitant of Canada, as Narrated by Himself* (Boston: Arthur D. Phelps, 1849), 42–43, https://docsouth.unc.edu/neh henson49/henson49.html.
13. Stowe, *Uncle Tom's Cabin*, 358.

14. Henson, *The Life of Josiah Henson, Formerly a Slave, Now an Inhabitant of Canada*, 36.

15. Harriet Beecher Stowe, "The Story of Uncle Tom's Cabin," *Old South Leaflets*, no. 82, https://www.bartonccc.edu/library.

16. Josiah Henson, *"Truth Is Stranger Than Fiction": An Autobiography of the Rev. Josiah Henson (Mrs. Harriet Beecher Stowe's "Uncle Tom"), from 1789 to 1879, with a Preface by Mrs. Harriet Beecher Stowe, Introductory Notes by Wendell Phillips, and John G. Whittier, and an Appendix on The Exodus by Bishop Gilbert Haven* (Boston: B. B. Russell & Co., 1879), 303–4.

17. Hedrick, *Harriet Beecher Stowe*, 193–94.

18. William H. Pease and Jane Pease, *Black Utopia: Negro Communal Experiments in America* (Madison: State Historical Society of Wisconsin, 1963), 178n19; Josiah Henson, *Truth Stranger Than Fiction: Father Henson's Story of His Own Life* (Boston: John P. Jewett Company, 1858), 176–77.

19. "Was He the Real Uncle Tom?," *The Semi-Weekly New Era* (Lancaster, PA), Saturday, August 8, 1896, 7, reprinted from *Connecticut Times* (New Hartford, CT).

20. Charles Edward Stowe and Lyman Beecher, "How Mrs. Stowe Wrote *Uncle Tom's Cabin*," *McClure's Magazine* 36 (November 1910–April 1911), 605–21, http://hathitrust.org/access_use #pd-google.

21. *New England Farmer* (Boston, MA), May 29, 1858, 2.

22. Samuel Eliot's "Advertisement" at the front of Henson, *The Life of Josiah Henson, Formerly a Slave, Now an Inhabitant of Canada*.

23. Blassingame, *Slave Testimony*, xxxiii.

24. Many of these narratives are available online at "North American Slave Narratives," University of North Carolina, https://www.docsouth.unc.edu/neh/.

25. Blassingame, ed., *Slave Testimony: Two Centuries of Letters, Speeches, Interviews, and Autobiographies* (Baton Rouge: Louisiana State University Press, 1977), xviii.

26. Henson, *The Life of Josiah Henson, Formerly a Slave, Now an Inhabitant of Canada*, prologue. This is the truest depiction of Henson's life, although only up to 1849, and is the core, word for word, of all the subsequent publications.

27. "The Life of Josiah Henson, Formerly a Slave, Now an Inhabitant of Canada," 1849, Internet Archive, https://archive.org/details/lifeofjosiahhenso0hens_0/page/n1/mode/2up. According to a note by Eliot on the first page, this manuscript was originally destined to be published by Little, Brown & Co.

28. Josiah Henson, *The Life of Josiah Henson, Formerly a Slave, as Narrated by Himself, with a Preface by T. Binney, London* (London: Charles Gilpin, Bishopsgate Without, 1851), 118.

29. Henson, *Truth Stranger Than Fiction*, vii.

30. Henry Bleby, *Josiah, the Maimed Fugitive: A True Tale* (London: Printed by William Nichols, 1878), 2–7; and Herbert Aptheker, ed., "A Public Discussion of Insurrection, 1858," in *A Documentary History of the Negro People in the United States*, vol. 1 (New York: Citadel Press, 1961), 406–8.

31. Josiah Henson, *Uncle Tom's Story of His Life: An Autobiography of the Rev. Josiah Henson (Mrs. Stowe's "Uncle Tom," from 1789 to 1876, with a Preface by Mrs. Harriet Beecher Stowe, and Introductory Note by George Sturge and S. Morley, Esq, M.P.)*, edited by John Lobb (London: Christian Age, 1876), 157.

32. It is unlikely that Henson would have met Jewett otherwise, and the fact that the publication that resulted had an introduction by Stowe, advertised as part of the title of the book, indicates that Stowe and Jewett were in communication about Josiah Henson. Henson made a habit of getting letters of introduction from well-known people he knew to present to people he was visiting.

33. Derek Strahan, "Unitarian Church, Springfield, Mass.," Lost New England, https//lostnewengland.com/2018/12/unitarian-church-springfield-mass/. There were few Unitarian

churches at that time, and this was the only one in Springfield. Rev. Francis Tiffany was pastor there from 1852 to 1864, when he left to accept a position in Ohio.

34. Rev. Gilbert Haven was one of the ministers attending the meetings in Boston in 1858 with Henson and was the editor of a leading Methodist newspaper in New England. Bleby, *Josiah, the Maimed Fugitive,* 3.

35. "Uncle Tom's Cabin," *The Manhattan,* 28–29. Since Henson purchased his brother in December 1858 for $250, it may be inferred that he accepted a lump sum offer from Jewett rather than a percentage of sales.

36. Henson, *Truth Stranger Than Fiction,* 6.

37. Henson, 23.

38. Henson, *Uncle Tom's Story of His Life,* 209.

39. John Lobb, ed., *An Autobiography of the Rev. Josiah Henson ("Uncle Tom") from 1789 to 1881* (London, Ontario: Shuyler, Smith & Co., 1881), 200, 228–36.

40. Henson, *Truth Stranger Than Fiction,* vii.

41. Lobb, 158.

42. Hedrick, *Harriet Beecher Stowe,* 221.

43. Lobb, *An Autobiography of the Rev. Josiah Henson ("Uncle Tom") from 1789 to 1881,* 205.

44. Henson, *Uncle Tom's Story of His Life,* 209.

45. Henson, *"Truth Is Stranger Than Fiction,"* 333.

46. Henson, viii, xi.

47. *Owensboro Messenger & Examiner* (Owensboro, KY), Wednesday, September 10, 1884, 1, col. 2.

48. Charles T. Davis and Henry Louis Gates Jr., *The Slave's Narrative* (New York: Oxford University Press, 1985), 26–28.

49. Bleby, *Josiah, the Maimed Fugitive,* 7–8.

50. Uncle Tom's Cabin," *The Manhattan,* 28–29.

51. The three portraits are in the frontispieces of the autobiographies. The photograph is of Henson seated and his publisher John Lobb standing on a carte de visite from a photograph by the London School of Photography in the Paul Fredker collection, the Library of Nineteenth Century Photography, http://themissingchapter.co.uk/portfolio_page/josiah-henson-and -john-lobb-london-1877/. An etching of this photograph is at the front of the Young People's edition of Henson's autobiography, *Uncle Tom's Story of His Life.* The other two photographs are in the collection of the Uncle Tom's Cabin Historic Site, Ontario, Canada.

52. "Uncle Tom's Cabin," *The Manhattan,* 28–29.

53. M. R. Delany to Frederick Douglass, *Frederick Douglass' Paper* (Pittsburgh), April 29, 1853, 3 col. 3, https://utc.iath.virginia.edu/africam/afar030t.html.

54. Mary Ann Shadd, "Remittances," *The Provincial Freeman and Weekly Advertiser,* Saturday, May 2, 1857, 142, col. 1.

55. Henson, *Uncle Tom's Story of His Life,* 201.

56. Henson, *Truth Stranger Than Fiction,* 13.

57. Sister Mary Ellen Doyle, "Josiah Henson's Narrative: Before and After," *Negro American Literature Forum* 8, no. 1 (Spring 1974): 176–82.

58. Robin W. Winks, *The Blacks in Canada: A History,* 2nd ed. (Montreal: McGill-Queen's University Press, 1997), 184.

Chapter 1. Born Enslaved

1. This lack of knowledge of being a slave is noted in a number of slave narratives, among them that of Frederick Douglass. Frederick Douglass, *The Life and Times of Frederick Douglass, Written by Himself* (New York: Macmillan, 1962), 27.

2. Robert J. Brugger, *Maryland, a Middle Temperament, 1634–1980* (Baltimore: Johns Hopkins University Press, 1990), 5–9.

3. Brugger, *Maryland, a Middle Temperament*, 23.

4. Ira Berlin, *Many Thousands Gone: The First Two Centuries of Slavery in North America* (Cambridge, MA: Belknap Press of Harvard University Press, 1998), 17.

5. "Mathias de Sousa," Maryland State Archives, https://msa.maryland.gov/megafile/msa/speccol/sc3500/sc3520/002800/002810/html/2810bio.html.

6. Brugger, *Maryland, a Middle Temperament*, 43.

7. Berlin, *Many Thousands Gone*, 40.

8. Berlin, 8.

9. The definition of "plantation" as growing a single crop and having fifty or more slaves and of a "farm" as growing multiple crops and having fewer slaves will be the definitions used throughout this book.

10. Berlin, *Many Thousands Gone*, 124–25.

11. The Mason-Dixon Line is the boundary dividing Maryland from Delaware and Pennsylvania that was surveyed by Charles Mason and Jeremiah Dixon between 1763 and 1767.

12. The abolition of enslavement in the Northern states was the beginning of the abolition movement, the first national success of which was the passage of the Slave Trade Act of 1794, which put severe restrictions on the importation of slaves from outside the United States, and the second national success was the Slave Trade Act of 1807, promoted by Thomas Jefferson, which prohibited the importation of slaves.

13. Berlin, *Many Thousands Gone*, 264.

14. Berlin, 271.

15. Berlin, 279.

16. Berlin, 272–73.

17. Josiah Henson, *The Life of Josiah Henson, Formerly a Slave, Now an Inhabitant of Canada, as Narrated by Himself* (Boston: Arthur D. Phelps, 1849), 1.

18. Henson, *The Life of Josiah Henson, Formerly a Slave, Now an Inhabitant of Canada*, 3.

19. Margaret Brown Klapthor and Paul Dennis Brown, *The History of Charles County, Maryland, Written in Its Tercentenary Year of 1958* (La Plata, MD: Charles County Tercentenary, 1958), 9–10.

20. Brugger, *Maryland, a Middle Temperament*, 781.

21. Kim R. Kihl, *Port Tobacco* (Baltimore: Maclay and Associates, 1982), 19.

22. Henson, *The Life of Josiah Henson, Formerly a Slave, Now an Inhabitant of Canada*, 1.

23. Maryland State Archives, microfilm, M1168_12-2112.

24. Maryland State Archives, Charles County Land Records, 1796, IB2 17–18, IB2 133–135, IB 2/456–458.

25. Rebecca J. Webster, Alex J. Flick, Julia A. King, and Scott Strickland, *In Search of Josiah Henson's Birthplace: Archaeological Investigations at La Grange Near Port Tobacco, Maryland* (St. Mary's City: St. Mary's College of Maryland, 2017), 16.

26. US Census 1800, Charles County, Maryland, Port Tobacco Parish, p. 88, line 10.

27. "Francis Newman," A Newman Family Tree, http://www.newman-family-tree.net/Francis-Newman.html; and Webster et al., *In Search of Josiah Henson's Birthplace*, 18.

28. Henry Wright Newman, *Charles County Gentry* (Baltimore: Genealogical Publishing Co., 1971), 235.

29. Klapthor and Brown, *The History of Charles County*, 11–13. Josias Fendall was part of a revolt led by the former governor William Stone in 1659. Order was restored in the colonies, as in England, after Charles II became king in 1660. This confusion in the colonies was due to Oliver Cromwell, a Puritan, taking over the British rule from 1653 until his sudden death in September 1658. There ensued a period of chaos until Charles II was restored to the throne

in 1660. Cromwell was very anti-Catholic and precipitated a brief anti-Catholic movement in Maryland.

30. "Alexander McPherson of Pomfret, Charles County, Maryland," Southern Maryland History Room, College of Southern Maryland, Harry Wright Newman Collection.

31. "Alexander McPherson of Pomfret, Charles County, Maryland"; and "McPherson's Purchase," CH 347, MAGI 0903472505, National Register of Historic Places Inventory Nomination Form.

32. Alexander McPherson of Pomfret, Item 8, p. 7.

33. Orphans Court Proceedings 1799–1803, Charles County, MD, CT, 87: "sum of six pounds current money in full for my part of a legacy left to the heirs of my father Henry McPherson . . . 19 Dec 1798," signed by J. H. McPherson. The legacy included other children of Henry McPherson as well as granddaughter Margaret McPherson, who was most likely the daughter of John McPherson because she never married and died in 1803 so could have been the companion of her grandmother.

34. Henry McPherson, "Early Colonial Settlers of Southern Maryland and Virginia's Northern Neck," https://www.colonial-settlers-md-va.us.

35. Charles County Will Book A1-10, 1788–1791, p. 381.

36. Will of Dorothy Marlow, Prince George's County, Maryland, Liber T#1, folio 608, Dorothy Marlow, widow of Samuel Middleton Marlow 09/05/1805, "Elizabeth Beall McPherson, niece (daughter of brother Samuel Hanson), to have the sum of 30 pounds current money and the sum to be deducted from the claim of her deceased husband's estate."

37. Charles County Orphans Court Proceedings 1803–1806, February term 1805, p. 250, children placed under the guardianship of Elizabeth McPherson.

38. "Josias H. McPherson," Charles County Probate Records, Inventories 1802–1808, conducted on April 9, 1805, Maryland State Archives CR 39593-2.

39. Bryan Prince, *A Shadow on the Household: One Enslaved Family's Incredible Struggle for Freedom* (Toronto: McClellan & Stewart, 2009), 36.

40. A third evidence of Josiah being younger than he claimed in his autobiographies is in his manumission record, dated March 9, 1829, where he is described as being "about thirty years of age."

41. Douglass, *The Life and Times of Frederick Douglass, Written by Himself*, 27.

42. "Death of Uncle Tom," *Sacramento Daily Record-Union*, July 21, 1883, 6, https://chroniclingamerica.loc.gov/lccn/sn82014381/1883-07-21/ed-1/seq-6/. The date of his birth quoted by an anonymous interviewer of Josiah Henson is "June 15, 1787."

43. "Josias H. McPherson," Charles County Probate Records, Inventories 1802–1808.

44. *Maryland Gazette*, September 17, 1789, referenced in *Maryland Historical Magazine* 40 (1945): 271.

45. Webster et al., *In Search of Josiah Henson's Birthplace*, 105.

46. Josiah Henson, *Truth Stranger Than Fiction, Father Henson's Story of His Own Life, with an Introduction by Mrs. H. B. Stowe* (Boston: John P. Jewett, 1858), 2–7.

47. Henson, *The Life of Josiah Henson, Formerly a Slave, Now an Inhabitant of Canada*, 2.

48. US Army, Register of Enlistments, 1798–1914, Original data: National Archives microfilm M233, 81 rolls; Records of the Adjutant General's Office, 1780–1917, Record Group 94; National Archives, Washington, DC, accessed through ancestry.com; and "Captain Francis Newman," A Newman Family Tree, http://www.newman-family-tree.net/francis-newman.html.

49. Charles County Inventories, 1791–1797, February term 1797, p. 419.

50. Montgomery County, Maryland Land Records, Liber G, folio 496–497.

51. Archives of Maryland, Proceedings of the House of Delegates, 1799, Vol. 98, p. 18.

52. US Census 1800, Maryland, Montgomery County, District 3 (Rockville), 152A, line 10.

53. *A Certification of the Personal Property in Sugarloaf & Linganore Hundreds, Being the 3rd District*, John Linthicum, 1798; *Montgomery County Tax Assessments, Changes 1802*; and *Montgomery County Tax Assessments, 1804* (Montgomery County Historical Society library, tax assessment file).

54. Montgomery County Land Records abstracts, Liber L, folio 11; *Laws of Maryland*, Chapter LXXVI, passed Dec. 31, 1801, L JG, #4, p. 148; and Eleanor V. Cook, "A New Look at Early Rockville and Its People," *Montgomery County Story* 44, no. 1 (February 2001): 169.

55. "I Hereby Certify . . . ," *Washington Federalist*, June 13, 1803, 2.

56. Edgefield County, SC, Deed Book 12, 301–3.

57. Henson, *Truth Stranger Than Fiction*, 8; and Brugger, *Maryland, a Middle Temperament*.

58. The name "Josias," which seems to have come from his mother's side of the family, is associated with the old Douay-Rheims Bible (now known as the Catholic Bible), where in the book of Kings a king is named Josias, but in the new King James version of the Bible the same king is named Josiah. However, the naming of children as Josias or Josiah could indicate either a religious affiliation or a family tradition.

59. Berlin, *Many Thousands Gone*, 95–96.

60. In the original documents different spellings were used for Josiah Henson's nickname, including "Si," "Siah," and "Sye."

61. Henson, *Truth Stranger Than Fiction*, 8.

62. Montgomery County tax assessments, March 1804, Montgomery County Historical Society; and "Josias H. McPherson," Charles County Orphan's Court Proceedings, 1803–1806, 219–20.

Chapter 2. Growing Up Enslaved

1. Charles County Orphan's Court Proceedings, 1803–1806, February term 1805, 219–20.

2. Charles County Register of Wills, Inventories 1801–1808, AL 12, 196–199, location 01/08/10/013, MdHr No. 7293, MSA citation C681-13.

3. Charles County Orphan's Court Proceedings, 1803–1806, April term 1805, 245.

4. The only states that had laws against the separation of children under age ten from their mother were Louisiana, Alabama, Mississippi, and Georgia, but except for Louisiana, these laws were to protect the owner from creditors, not from compassion for the enslaved family. Frederick Bancroft, *Slave Trading in the Old South* (Columbia: University of South Carolina, 1996), 197–99.

5. Modern psychology supports these conclusions. See also atrocities committed in the slave uprisings such as Nat Turner's Rebellion.

6. Bancroft, *Slave Trading in the Old South*, xxxvi.

7. Josiah Henson, *The Life of Josiah Henson, Formerly a Slave, Now an Inhabitant of Canada, as Narrated by Himself* (Boston: Arthur D. Phelps, 1849), 3.

8. Lewis Clarke, who was a friend of Josiah's before his first autobiography was published, describes just such a scene in his own autobiography of a mother whose seven children were sold to different slaveholders before her eyes until she fainted from the anguish of parting. Lewis Clarke, *Narrative of the Sufferings of Lewis Clarke, during a Captivity of More Than Twenty-Five Years, among the Algerines of Kentucky, One of the So Called Christian States of America: Dictated by Himself* (Boston; David H. Ela, printer, 1845), 71.

9. Josiah Henson, *Truth Stranger Than Fiction: Father Henson's Story of His Own Life* (Boston: John P. Jewett and Company, 1858), 13.

10. Henson, 14.

11. Mayvis Fitzsimmons, "Uncle Tom in Montgomery County," *Montgomery County Story* 18, no. 1 (February 1975): 4.

12. Bryan Prince, *A Shadow on the Household: One Enslaved Family's Incredible Struggle for Freedom* (Toronto: McClellan & Stewart, 2009), 27–36.

13. Montgomery County, Maryland Land Records, Liber G, folio 496–97.

14. US Census 1800, Maryland, Montgomery County, District 3 (Rockville), 152A, line 10.

15. Bryan Prince, *A Shadow on the Household: One Enslaved Family's Incredible Struggle for Freedom* (Toronto, Ontario: McClellan & Stewart, 2009), 17–19.

16. Ray Eldon Hiebert and Richard K. McMaster, *A Grateful Remembrance: The Story of Montgomery County, Maryland* (Rockville, MD: Montgomery County Government and the Montgomery County Historical Society, 1976), 115–21.

17. Barbara Jean Fields, *Slavery and Freedom on the Middle Ground: Maryland during the Nineteenth Century* (New Haven, CT: Yale University Press, 1985), 11.

18. Hiebert and McMaster, *A Grateful Remembrance*, 152.

19. Fields, *Slavery and Freedom on the Middle Ground*, 24.

20. Eileen S. McGuckian, *Rockville: Portrait of a City* (Franklin, TN: Hillsboro, 2001), 29.

21. Jean B. Russo, "The Early Towns of Montgomery County, 1747–1831," *Montgomery County Story* 34, no. 2 (May 1991): 153–56.

22. McGuckian, *Rockville*, 28–34.

23. When the turnpike, now Rockville Pike (Route 355), was completed in the 1840s it was made straighter, and some former portions, such as the long curve of the current Old Georgetown Road, were bypassed. This can be seen by comparison of pre-1805 and newer maps.

24. "Riley/Bolton House," National Register of Historic Places, Registration M:30-5, 12.

25. Stephen Stec, "Riley v. Worthington: Joseph Willson's Feuding Family of Early Montgomery County," *Montgomery County Story* 60, no. 1 (Winter 2017): 8–9.

26. The house is in the Josiah Henson Museum and Park, 11420 Old Georgetown Rd., North Bethesda, MD, https://www.montgomeryparks.org/parks-and-trails/josiah-henson-park/.

27. Mutual Fire Insurance Company policy #1684, taken out April 11, 1856, by Matilda Riley (Montgomery County Historical Society file). The "no interior access" is from an interview of Frances Mace Hansbrough by Joey Lampl of Montgomery Planning conducted in 2006 (Montgomery County Parks files).

28. The Riley House/Josiah Henson Site, Historic Structures Report for John Milner Associates, Inc., June 2008, Executive Summary, iii.

29. Henson, *The Life of Josiah Henson, Formerly a Slave, Now an Inhabitant of Canada*, 41.

30. US Census 1800, Maryland, Montgomery, District 1, 161A; 1820, Maryland, Montgomery, District 3, 557.

31. National Archives and Records Administration, Index to the Compiled Military Service Records for the Volunteer Soldiers Who Served during the War of 1812, M602, 234 rolls; and War of 1812 Pension application files. Both accessed via Ancestry.com.

32. Henson, *Truth Stranger Than Fiction*, 22, 24.

33. Henson, 18.

34. Henson, 43–44.

35. Mark Walston, "A Survey of Slave Housing in Montgomery County," *Montgomery County Story* 27, no. 3 (August 1984), 113–15, 119–21, 126.

36. Henson, *The Life of Josiah Henson, Formerly a Slave, Now an Inhabitant of Canada* 6.

37. Henson, 6.

38. Henson, *Truth Stranger Than Fiction*, 19–20.

39. Robert J. Brugger, *Maryland, a Middle Temperament, 1634–1980* (Baltimore: Johns Hopkins University Press, 1990), 235–36.

40. Henson, *The Life of Josiah Henson, Formerly a Slave, Now an Inhabitant of Canada*, 13.

41. John W. Blassingame, *The Slave Community: Plantation Life in the Antebellum South*, revised and enlarged ed. (New York: Oxford University Press, 1979), 132–33; Brugger, *Maryland, a Middle Temperament*, 243; and Ira Berlin, Marc Favreau, and Steven F. Miller, *Remembering Slavery: African Americans Talk about Their Personal Experiences of Slavery and Emancipation* (New York: New Press, 1998), 192.

42. This was not an unusual reaction and is noted in many slave narratives. See, for instance, Maron Wilson Starling, *The Slave Narrative: Its Place in History* (Washington, DC: Howard University Press, 1988), 84–94.

43. Edward E. Baptist, *The Half Has Never Been Told: Slavery and the Making of American Capitalism* (New York: Basic Books, 2014), 33.

44. Blassingame, *The Slave Community*, 249–57, 315–17.

45. Blassingame, 292.

46. The land in this area was only partially cultivated, leaving large wooded areas to provide firewood and building material. Pigs were allowed to roam wild in the woods so they could feed themselves.

47. John Vlatch, *In Back of the Big House: The Architecture of Plantation Slavery* (Chapel Hill: University of North Carolina Press, 1993), ix. Vlatch writes that after the American Civil War, freed slaves wanted to return to the plantations where they worked because they felt that since they had worked the land and raised the crops, it belonged to them. Berlin, Favreau, and Miller, *Remembering Slavery*, 73.

48. Henson, *Truth Stranger Than Fiction*, 23–24.

49. William L. Anderson, *Slavery and Class in the American South: A Generation of Testimony, 1840–1865* (New York: Oxford University Press, 2019), 67.

50. This was a common excuse for taking animals from the farm to feed themselves. Berlin, Favreau, and Miller, *Remembering Slavery*, 192–93.

51. Henson, *The Life of Josiah Henson, Formerly a Slave, Now an Inhabitant of Canada*, 9.

52. John Hope Franklin and Loren Schweninger, *Runaway Slaves: Rebels on the Plantation* (New York: Oxford University Press, 1999), 236.

53. Anderson, *Slavery and Class in the American South*, 7.

Chapter 3. Maimed and Adapting

1. Josiah Henson, *The Life of Josiah Henson, Formerly a Slave, Now an Inhabitant of Canada, as Narrated by Himself* (Boston: Arthur D. Phelps, 1849), 14–15. The name of the overseer as Brice Letton is revealed in the 1858 autobiography. The surname is variously spelled as Litton, Lutton, Lyton, and Letton. The latter is the one in most of the public records pertaining to Brice, so it is the one used here.

2. The Letton/Litton family of Rockville, compiled by Anne Cissel (Montgomery County Historical Society library files, Rockville).

3. The Letton/Litton family of Rockville, compiled by Anne Cissel.

4. Henson, *The Life of Josiah Henson, Formerly a Slave, Now an Inhabitant of Canada*, 14.

5. Henson, 17–18.

6. Henson, 17–18.

7. "Uncle Tom's Cabin," *The Manhattan: An Illustrated Literary Magazine for the People* 1, no. 1 (1881): 28–31. Accessed on the Internet Archive; original at Harvard University.

8. Josiah Henson, *Truth Stranger Than Fiction: Father Henson's Story of His Own Life* (Boston: John P. Jewett and Company, 1858), 40.

9. Henson, *The Life of Josiah Henson, Formerly a Slave, Now an Inhabitant of Canada*, 7–8.

10. Many medical studies have indicated that the psychological effects of a major physical

trauma follow this pattern: shock, confusion, anger, anxiety and fear, and sadness. This can be followed by either resilience and adaptation or despondency.

11. Henson, *Truth Stranger Than Fiction*, 38.

12. Henson, 40.

13. John W. Blassingame, *The Slave Community: Plantation Life in the Antebellum South*, revised and enlarged ed. (New York: Oxford University Press, 1979), 239.

14. Henson, *Truth Stranger Than Fiction*, 43–44.

15. Josiah Henson, *Uncle Tom's Story of His Life: An Autobiography of the Rev. Josiah Henson (Mrs. Stowe's "Uncle Tom," from 1789 to 1876, with a Preface by Mrs. Harriet Beecher Stowe, and Introductory Note by George Sturge and S. Morley, Esq, M.P,* edited by John Lobb (London: Christian Age, 1876), 187.

16. Henson, *Truth Stranger Than Fiction*, 43.

17. Henson, *The Life of Josiah Henson, Formerly a Slave, Now an Inhabitant of Canada*, 20.

18. Eleanor M. V. Cook, "Georgetown: Jewel of Montgomery County—Part I," *Montgomery County Story* 41, no. 4 (November 1998): 52.

19. Cook, "Georgetown," 74.

20. Kathleen M. Lesko, Valerie Babb, and Carroll R. Gibbs, *Black Georgetown Remembered: A History of Its Black Community from the Founding of "The Town of George" in 1751 to the Present* (Washington, DC: Georgetown University Press, 1991).

21. Lesko, Babb, and Gibbs, *Black Georgetown Remembered*, 74.

22. National Register of Historic Places Inventory, "Georgetown Market," 71.5.11.0005, April 1971.

23. David Mould and Missy Loewe, *Remembering Georgetown: A History of the Lost Port City* (Charleston, SC: American Chronicles, The History Press, 2009), 51.

24. George J. Olszewski, *A History of the Old Georgetown Market, Georgetown, D.C.* (Washington, DC: US Department of the Interior, National Park Service, Washington Service Center, 1966), 7.

25. Richard P. Jackson, *The Chronicles of Georgetown from 1751 to 1878* (Washington, DC: R. O. Polkinhorn, Printer, 1878), 102.

26. James H. Johnston, *From Slave Ship to Harvard: Yarrow Marmout and the History of an African American Family* (New York: Fordham University Press, 2012), 104.

27. Johnston, *From Slave Ship to Harvard*, 63–111; and James H. Johnston, "Yarrow Marmout," *Montgomery County Story* 47, no. 2 (May 2004): 13–23.

28. Olszewski, *A History of the Old Georgetown Market*, 7.

29. Helen Tangires, "Contested Space: Life and Death in the Center Market, *Washington History* 7, no. 1 (Spring–Summer 1995): 46–67, https://www.jstor.org/stable/40073136.

30. Helen Tangires, "Public Markets and the City: A Historical Prospective," Sixth International Public Market Conference, October 29, 2005, https://www.pps.org/article /6thmktstangiers.

31. Henson, *Truth Stranger Than Fiction*, 197.

32. Henson, *Uncle Tom's Story of His Life*, 188.

33. Henson, *Truth Stranger Than Fiction*, 44–45.

34. Henry Bleby, *The Maimed Fugitive: A True Story* (London: William Nichols, 1878), 8; and Interview with Amos Riley [Jr.], *Owensboro Messenger & Examiner*, September 10, 1884, 1.

35. Henson, *Truth Stranger Than Fiction*, 43.

36. Henson, 196–97.

37. Nina Honemond Clarke, *History of the Nineteenth-Century Black Churches in Maryland and Washington, D.C.* (New York: Vantage Press, 1983), 174.

38. Ira Berlin, *Many Thousands Gone: The First Two Centuries of Slavery in North America* (Cambridge, MA: Belknap Press of Harvard University Press, 1998), 172–273.

39. Robert J. Brugger, *Maryland, a Middle Temperament, 1634–1980* (Baltimore: Johns Hopkins University Press, 1990), 244; and Ray Eldon Hiebert and Richard K. McMaster, *A Grateful Remembrance* (Rockville, MD: Montgomery County Government, 1976), 154–55.

40. In the 1849 autobiography Henson says that he met her at "the chapel I attended," but in subsequent autobiographies he says "the religious meetings that I attended." In both instances he was probably referring to these clandestine religious meetings, often held in outbuildings on farms.

41. Charles County Orphans Court Proceedings 1803–1806, February term 1805, 250. The children were placed under guardianship of their mother, Elizabeth McPherson. Henry Thomas McPherson is listed as being age seventeen in 1806, which would make his birth date 1789.

42. The Riley House/Josiah Henson Site, Historic Structures Report, Appendix I: Riley Family Bible, Family Record Pages: J, Riley Family Tree.

43. Maryland Records of Wills Records 1629–1999, Montgomery County, Accounts, Inventories, Wills 1816–1817, accessed through https://familysearch.org.

44. Henson, *Truth Stranger Than Fiction*, 43.

45. The Riley House/Josiah Henson Site, Historic Structures Report, Context, 12.

46. Henson, *Truth Stranger Than Fiction*, 43.

47. US States Census, Election District 3, Montgomery County, Maryland, 1810 and 1820.

48. "Crew Lists of Vessels Arriving at Boston, Massachusetts, 1917–1943," National Archives and Records Administration, Washington, DC, Microfilm Serial T938, Microfilm Roll M277_44, on board the ship *Calcutta* from London to Boston arriving July 14, 1853, lists his age as thirty-four and birth date as 1819.

49. Blassingame, *The Slave Community*, 151.

50. Henson, *Truth Stranger Than Fiction*, 30.

51. Henson, 41.

Chapter 4. Journey to Kentucky

1. Josiah Henson, *The Life of Josiah Henson, Formerly a Slave, Now an Inhabitant of Canada, as Narrated by Himself* (Boston: Arthur D. Phelps, 1849), 21.

2. Josiah Henson, *Truth Stranger Than Fiction: Father Henson's Story of His Own Life* (Boston: John P. Jewett and Company, 1858), 46–47.

3. Hugh Riley will, Montgomery County probate records, L E f 333, L 2 f 82.

4. Anne W. Cissel, "The Families of a Derwood Farm through Two Centuries," *Montgomery County Story* 27, no. 2 (May 1984): 5–6.

5. Cissel, "The Families of a Derwood Farm through Two Centuries," 6.

6. Jamie Ferguson Kuhns, *Sharp Flashes of Lighting Come from Black Clouds* (Silver Spring: Maryland-National Capital Park and Planning Commission, 2018), 66.

7. John Milner Associates, Inc., "The Riley House/Josiah Henson Site: Historic Structures Report," June 2008, Historical Context, 4.

8. An account of the stealing of a whole plantation of slaves is described in the novel *The Entailed Hat* by George Alfred Townsend, published in 1884, based on true accounts of the kidnappings by the gang of the infamous Patty Cannon.

9. Henson, *Truth Stranger Than Fiction*, 47.

10. Even though Henson says in his 1858 autobiography *Truth Stranger Than Fiction* that "there were eighteen negroes, besides my wife, two children, and myself," the tax and census

records in both Kentucky and Maryland indicate there were actually eight slaves plus Henson and his family, totaling twelve. According to the US census for Montgomery County, Maryland, 1820, Isaac Riley owned twelve slaves. According to the Daviess County tax record, the number of slaves owned by Amos Riley in 1825 was twenty-one and in 1826 had grown to thirty-four, an addition of thirteen people (one of these could have been a new birth). This number is also more logical for fitting into the small oar-propelled boat in which they all traveled down the Ohio River.

11. Henson never mentions his mother's name in any of his autobiographies, but the fact that a woman named Celia, age fifty, was listed in the death inventory of Josias McPherson along with Josiah and his older brother John, combined with the claim in Henson's autobiographies that he was the first enslaved person born under the ownership of McPherson, would indicate that her name was Celia.

12. Henson, *The Life of Josiah Henson, Formerly a Slave, Now an Inhabitant of Canada,* 31.

13. Josiah Henson's wife, Charlotte, would give birth to eight children who lived to adulthood. They were born about two years apart except between 1820 and 1827 (see appendix B in this volume). So, it is logical to think that she may have lost a child or had a miscarriage on the trip to Kentucky.

14. Henson, *The Life of Josiah Henson, Formerly a Slave, Now an Inhabitant of Canada,* 23.

15. Alexander Ross, *Recollections and Experiences of an Abolitionist* (Toronto: Rowsell and Hutchison, 1875), 9. In his memoir Alexander Ross (1832–1897) describes how, disguised as an ornithologist, he gave long, detailed instructions to those wanting to escape, covering hundreds of miles of landmarks and changes of direction that were memorized and repeated back to him. These directions helped an untold number of freedom seekers reach Canada from the slave states.

16. Henson, *Truth Stranger Than Fiction,* 49.

17. "Long Bridge," Wikipedia, https://en.wikipedia.org/wiki/Long_Bridge_(Potomac_River)#History.

18. Winifred Gallagher, *How the Post Office Created America* (New York: Penguin Random House, 2016), 53.

19. The National Road, the first road to be financed with taxpayers' money, began with an appropriation of money by Congress in 1805 to lay a road from Cumberland to Wheeling, crossing the several mountain ranges that had been impeding commerce between east and west and extending the road from Baltimore to Cumberland that had been built by merchants. This section was completed in 1818. Eventually the road would extend all the way to the Mississippi River, with the various states that it crossed contributing to the cost. Norris F. Schneider, *The National Road, Main Street of America* (Columbus: Ohio Historical Society, 1975), 3–7.

20. Since they reached the Riley plantation in Kentucky in mid-April and the trip down the Ohio River took ten to twelve days, they must have reached Wheeling about April 1.

21. Josiah Henson, *Uncle Tom's Story of His Life: An Autobiography of the Rev. Josiah Henson (Mrs. Stowe's "Uncle Tom," from 1789 to 1876, with a Preface by Mrs. Harriet Beecher Stowe, and Introductory Note by George Sturge and S. Morley, Esq, M.P.,* edited by John Lobb (London: Christian Age, 1876), 41. See also appendix B in this volume.

22. Stephen Stec, "Riley v. Worthington: Joseph Willson's Feuding Family of Early Montgomery County," *Montgomery County Story* 60, no. 1 (Winter 2017): 5–15.

23. Schneider, *The National Road,* 7.

24. "Coffle" was a common term in the nineteenth-century South. The Oxford English dictionary defines the term as "a line of animals or slaves fastened or driven along together; from mid-18th century Arabic 'qafila,' caravan."

25. Henson, *Truth Stranger Than Fiction,* 50.

26. A yawl today is a two-masted sailboat, but in this case it would have been a six-oar row-boat. Josiah Henson, *Truth Stranger Than Fiction*, 50–51.

27. Charles Henry Ambler, *A History of Transportation in the Ohio Valley* (Glendale, CA: Arthur H. Clark Co., 1932), 38–43.

28. Ambler, *A History of Transportation in the Ohio Valley*, 20–22.

29. Wheeling, West Virginia, is at mile 91 (measuring from Pittsburgh), and Owensboro, Kentucky, is at mile 752. "Ohio River Nautical Chart," Fishermap, https://usa.fishermap.org /depth-map/ohio-river/.

30. Henson, *Truth Stranger Than Fiction*, 52.

31. Henson, 52–53.

32. Ohio County Deed Book D, 170–72.

33. "Explore Daviess County," ExploreKYHistory, https://explorekyhistory.ky.gov/tours /show/44.

34. The name was shortened to Owensboro in 1893. "Owensboro-Daviess County History," Visit Owensboro, https://visitowensboro.com/explore-owensboro/history/?olink=%2F%3Fs %3D1893%26rform%3D0&otitle=Search+Results&rform=0.

35. Ivan E. McDonough, PhD. "Slavery in Kentucky 1792 to 1865," Internet Archive, https:// archive.org/details/slaveryinkentuck01mcdo, 3.

36. Richard Campanella, *Lincoln in New Orleans: The 1828–1831 Flatboat Voyages and Their Place in History* (Lafayette: University of Louisiana at Lafayette Press, 2010), 14–18.

37. "Kentucky Slave Law Summary and Record," using primary sources of Digests of the Statute Laws of Kentucky, attached to the family chart of Richard Griffin (1855–1926) by Charles Griffin Jr., http://trees.ancestry.com/tree/9376172/person/-741608835, accessed June 2010.

38. Henson, *Truth Stranger Than Fiction*, 48. In an equity suit of August 24, 1825, in Mont-gomery County, Maryland, granting named slaves of Isaac Riley to Arnold T. Winsor, Josiah Henson and his family are not named: John Milner Associates, Inc., "The Riley House/Josiah Henson Site," 12n15.

39. Daviess County Tax Records, 1824–1830, Daviess County Public Library, Owensboro, Kentucky, microfilm. Josiah's claim in his 1849 autobiography *The Life of Josiah Henson, For-merly a Slave, Now an Inhabitant of Canada* (25) that there were eighty to one hundred enslaved people working the farms of Amos Riley may have been due to one farm being indistinguish-able from another, to the fact that Riley was renting more slaves for the spring plowing and planting, or that Henson was exaggerating.

40. *History of Daviess County, Kentucky* (Chicago: Interstate Publishing Co., 1883), 52, 850, http://archive.org/details/cu31924028845787.

41. *An Illustrated Historical Atlas Map, Daviess County, KY, Yelvington Precinct, No. 3* (Leo McDonough & Co., 1876).

42. US Census 1810, Jefferson County, Kentucky.

43. Paper by unknown in the "Uncle Tom's Cabin" file, Kentucky Room, Daviess County Public Library, Owensboro, KY, listing Daviess County Deed Books, A, B, C, D, E, F, G and tax assessment record for 1825 as references.

44. Henson, *The Life of Josiah Henson, Formerly a Slave, Now an Inhabitant of Canada*, 25.

45. The original pass was found among the papers of Camden Riley that were purchased at auction by the Owensboro Museum of Science and History in 2013. The author has viewed and copied the pass.

46. Rev. L. M. Hagood, MD, *The Colored Man in the Methodist Episcopal Church* (Cincinnati: Cranston & Stowe; New York: Hunt & Eaton, 1890), 29.

47. Hagood, *The Colored Man in the Methodist Episcopal Church*, 35–46.

48. There are many examples in the slave narratives of unschooled African Americans, enslaved and free, memorizing Bible verses and preaching with passion. Ira Berlin, Marc

Favreau, and Steven K. Miller, eds., *Remembering Slavery: African Americans Talk about Their Experiences of Slavery and Emancipation* (New York: New Press, 1998), 55, 125, 191–92.

49. Fergus M. Bordewich, *Bound for Canaan: The Underground Railroad and the War for the Soul of America* (New York: HarperCollins, 2005), 97.

50. Henson, *Truth Stranger Than Fiction*, 57.

51. Henson, 58.

52. Henson, *The Life of Josiah Henson*, Formerly a Slave, Now an Inhabitant of Canada, 28.

Chapter 5. The Cost of Freedom

1. Josiah Henson, *The Life of Josiah Henson, Formerly a Slave, Now an Inhabitant of Canada, as Narrated by Himself* (Boston: Arthur D. Phelps, 1849), 24.

2. Henson, *The Life of Josiah Henson, Formerly a Slave, Now an Inhabitant of Canada*, 28–29.

3. William Erastus Arnold, *A History of Methodism in Kentucky*, vol. 2, *From 1820 to 1846* (Wilmore, KY: First Fruits Press, 1936; first printed by Herald Press, Louisville, KY, 1936), 134.

4. US Census 1830, Ohio, Miami County, Piqua; and Wilbur H. Siebert, *The Underground Railroad from Slavery to Freedom* (New York: Macmillan, 1898), 95.

5. Siebert, *The Underground Railroad from Slavery to Freedom*, 94–95.

6. Josiah Henson, *Truth Stranger Than Fiction: Father Henson's Story of His Own Life* (Boston: John P. Jewett, 1858), 63.

7. Ancel H. Bassett, *A Concise History of the Methodist Protestant Church from Its Origins* (Pittsburgh, PA: Press of Charles A. Scott, 1877), 84–85.

8. Henson, *Truth Stranger Than Fiction*, 64.

9. Bassett, *A Concise History of the Methodist Protestant Church*, 60.

10. Henson, *Truth Stranger Than Fiction*, 65.

11. Henson, *The Life of Josiah Henson, Formerly a Slave, Now an Inhabitant of Canada*, 30.

12. Henson, 67–70.

13. Josiah Henson, *Uncle Tom's Story of His Life: An Autobiography of the Rev. Josiah Henson (Mrs. Stowe's "Uncle Tom," from 1789 to 1876, with a Preface by Mrs. Harriet Beecher Stowe, and Introductory Note by George Sturge and S. Morley, Esq, M.P.*, edited by John Lobb (London: Christian Age, 1876), 194–95.

14. Henson, *The Life of Josiah Henson, Formerly a Slave, Now an Inhabitant of Canada*, 33. The amount is not noted in the record of the sale at the county courthouse or in the manumission paper carried by Josiah Henson.

15. Montgomery County Land Records, L:BS2, F167.

16. Newspaper clipping, copy of original document (unknown Flint, Michigan, newspaper, February 9, 1923), files of Peerless Rockville, Rockville, MD.

17. Henson, *The Life of Josiah Henson, Formerly a Slave, Now an Inhabitant of Canada*, 34.

18. Henson, 34.

19. Henson, 35–36.

20. *Owensboro Messenger & Examiner* (Owensboro, KY), Wednesday, September 10, 1884, 1, col. 2.

21. The term "uppity negro" was used in the South to refer to Black persons who talked back to a white person on equal or superior terms.

22. In his memoirs Josiah lists Amos Riley Jr.'s age as twenty-one when they set off on the voyage to New Orleans, but he was actually just shy of twenty years of age when they embarked in April or May 1830, as the date of his birth was June 10, 1810. Robert Shean Riley, *The Colonial Riley Families of the Tidewater Frontier*, vol. 1, *History of Several Riley Families of Maryland and Virginia* (Utica, KY: McDowell Publications, 1999), 410.

23. Henson, *The Life of Josiah Henson, Formerly a Slave, Now an Inhabitant of Canada*, 38–39.

24. "A Pictorial History of the Mississippi Steamboating Era," Steamboat Times, https:// steamboattimes.com/flatboats.html, accessed November 22, 2020.

25. "A Pictorial History of the Mississippi Steamboating Era."

26. Richard Campanella, *Lincoln in New Orleans: The 1828–1831 Flatboat Voyages and Their Place in History* (Lafayette: University of Louisiana at Lafayette Press, 2010), 36–39; and *An Illustrated Historical Atlas Map, Daviess County, KY, Yelvington Precinct, No. 3* (Leo McDonough & Co., 1876).

27. Henson, *The Life of Josiah Henson, Formerly a Slave, Now an Inhabitant of Canada*, 45–47. If they arrived home by steamboat on about July 10, as noted by Josiah, then they must have left New Orleans on about June 27, and seeing that most flatboaters would not have spent more than two weeks in New Orleans, then they had arrived in New Orleans in mid-June.

28. Campanella, *Lincoln in New Orleans*, 51; and Montgomery County Land Records, I BS2, F167.

29. "At 20:00:00 UT Saturday 01 May 1830 the Moon's Phase Was Waxing Gibbous (69.18% Full)," Moonpage, https://www.moonpage.com/lunarindx.html?go=T&auto_dst=T&totphase= WAXING+GIBBOUS+%2878.98%25+full%29&m=5&d=1&y=1830&hour=20&min=0&sec=0.

30. Campanella, *Lincoln in New Orleans*, 61–62; and Zadok Cramer, *The Navigator, or The Traders' Useful Guide to Navigating the Monongahela, Allegheny, Ohio and Mississippi Rivers* (Pittsburgh: Cramer and Spear, 1818), 127.

31. Henson, *The Life of Josiah Henson, Formerly a Slave, Now an Inhabitant of Canada*, 40.

32. Campanella, *Lincoln in New Orleans*, 75–76.

33. Campanella, 65.

34. *Owensboro Messenger & Examiner* (Owensboro, KY), Wednesday, September 10, 1884, 1, col. 2. A white beaver hat is noted later in Josiah's life by two different witnesses as being a singular feature of his wardrobe.

35. Henson, *The Life of Josiah Henson, Formerly a Slave, Now an Inhabitant of Canada*, 41.

36. Henson, 39.

37. Henson, 42–43.

38. This is the incident that drew the attention of Harriet Beecher Stowe as she was trying to find a real enslaved person who had such a strong Christian faith that he would sacrifice his own life as a model for her fictional character, Uncle Tom, as she was coming to the conclusion of her novel, *Uncle Tom's Cabin*.

39. Campanella, *Lincoln in New Orleans*, 117.

40. Campanella, 88, 118.

41. Henson, *The Life of Josiah Henson, Formerly a Slave, Now an Inhabitant of Canada*, 45.

42. John Hope Franklin and Loren Schweninger, *Runaway Slaves: Rebels on the Plantation* (New York: Oxford University Press, 1999), 272–73.

43. Solomon Northup, *Twelve Years a Slave* (Mint Editions, 2020; original published 1853), chap. 6.

44. Campanella, *Lincoln in New Orleans*, 281.

45. Josiah Henson, *The Life of Josiah Henson, Formerly a Slave, Now an Inhabitant of Canada*, 46

46. *Owensboro Messenger & Examiner* (Owensboro, KY), Wednesday, September 10, 1884, 1, col. 2–3.

47. Henson, *The Life of Josiah Henson, Formerly a Slave, Now an Inhabitant of Canada*, 47–48.

Chapter 6. Escape

1. John Hope Franklin and Loren Schweninger, *Runaway Slaves: Rebels on the Plantation* (New York: Oxford University Press, 1999), 116–17.

2. According to Robert Brugger, the first actual railroad with steam-powered locomotives in the United States was completed from Baltimore to Frederick, Maryland (about fifty miles), in 1831. This marked the beginning of a "railroad mania" that infected all the states. This first railroad reached the Ohio River on Christmas Eve 1852, joining the steam power of the rails with the steam power of the river. See Robert J. Brugger, *Maryland, a Middle Temperament, 1634–1980* (Baltimore: Johns Hopkins University Press, 1990), 216.

3. Tom Calarco, *People of the Underground Railroad: A Biographical Dictionary* (Westport, CT: Greenwood, 2008), 72.

4. Newport, Indiana, is now named Fountain City.

5. Larry Gara, *The Liberty Line: The Legend of the Underground* Railroad (Lexington: University Press of Kentucky, 1996), 79–81.

6. Keith P. Griffler, *Front Line of Freedom: African Americans and the Forging of the Underground Railroad in the Ohio Valley* (Lexington: University Press of Kentucky, 2004), 65–67; and Gara, *The Liberty Line*, 79, 94.

7. As the cities grew, the river traffic between Cincinnati and Louisville also grew, with many boats both large and small, and by the 1830s those propelled by steam-driven wheels were fast replacing the old pole-driven up-current vessels. See Charles Henry Ambler, *A History of Transportation in the Ohio Valley* (Glendale, CA: Arthur H. Clark, 1932), 44–49, 196–97.

8. Josiah Henson, *The Life of Josiah Henson, Formerly a Slave, Now an Inhabitant of Canada, as Narrated by Himself* (Boston: Arthur D. Phelps, 1849), 49.

9. Henson, *The Life of Josiah Henson, Formerly a Slave, Now an Inhabitant of Canada*, 48–49.

10. Jane: "Ontario County Marriage Registers, 1858–1869," database with images, *Family Search* (https://familysearch.org), Jane Christee, born 1827, Father Josiah Henson and mother Charlotte Henson, marries Elisha Kersey in December 1859, in Kent, Ontario, Canada. Josiah Henson, age forty-two, listed in the 1870 US Census, Adrian Michigan, Ward 3, Lewanee.

11. Henson, *The Life of Josiah Henson, Formerly a Slave, Now an Inhabitant of Canada*, 49–50.

12. Josiah Henson, *Truth Stranger Than Fiction: Father Henson's Story of His Own Life* (Boston: John P. Jewett and Company, 1858), 108.

13. Henson, *Truth Stranger Than Fiction*, 107. Author Bryon Gysin used this phrase for the title of his biography of Henson, *To Master—A Long Good Night: The Story of Uncle Tom, a Historical Narrative* (New York: Creative Age, 1946).

14. Henson, *The Life of Josiah Henson, Formerly a Slave, Now an Inhabitant of Canada*, 50.

15. "At 20:00:00 UT Thursday 16 September 1830 the moon was NEW," Moonpage, https://www.moonpage.com/lunarindx.html?go=T&auto_dst=T&totphase=WAXING+CRESCENT+(0.78%25+full)&m=9&d=16&y=1830&hour=20&min=0&sec=0.

16. Henson, *Truth Stranger Than Fiction*, 108.

17. "Narrative of Arnold Gragston," National Humanities Center, http://nationalhumanitiescenter.org/pds/maai/community/text7/gragstonwpanarrative.pdf; and Ira Berlin, Marc Favreau, and Steven F. Miller, *Remembering Slavery: African Americans Talk about Their Personal Experiences of Slavery and Emancipation* (New York: New Press, 1998), 64–70. It was Gragston who revealed that the code word used to verify his passengers was "menare," an Italian word that is part of the phrase "to lead the sheep to pasture" and is now the title of a foundation dedicated to research on the Underground Railroad, The Menare Center (https://www.menare.org).

18. Josiah Henson, *Uncle Tom's Story of His Life: An Autobiography of the Rev. Josiah Henson (Mrs. Stowe's "Uncle Tom," from 1789 to 1876, with a Preface by Mrs. Harriet Beecher Stowe, and Introductory Note by George Sturge and S. Morley, Esq, M.P.)*, edited by John Lobb (London: Christian Age, 1876), 83.

19. "Lick Creek African American Settlement," US Department of Agriculture, August

2022, https://www.fs.usda.gov/Internet/FSE_DOCUMENTS/stelprdb5303625.pdf; and La-Roche, Cheryl Janifer, *Free Black Communities and the Underground Railroad: The Geography of Resistance* (Hartford, University of Illinois Press, 2014), 57–70.

20. Henson, *The Life of Josiah Henson, Formerly a Slave, Now an Inhabitant of Canada*, 51; and Henson, *Truth Stranger Than Fiction*, 111. There is a difference in the facts presented in the two autobiographies. In the 1849 version (*The Life of Josiah Henson*), the man in the first house approached said, "No, they had nothing for black fellows." In the 1858 version (*Truth Stranger Than Fiction*) the man in the first house approached said ,"No, he had nothing for niggers!" In the first version, in the second house approached was "a man who wanted to see how little he could give me for my quarter of a dollar." This man is eliminated in the second version and replaced by a woman who gave him a good deal of venison and bread and refused to take any money. Josiah, no doubt, visited many houses asking for food during this journey and chose which representative encounters to put in his memoir.

21. The "Miami River" that Henson spoke of fording in his 1858 autobiography (*Truth Stranger Than Fiction*, 154) was the Little Miami River, since it is seven miles east of central Cincinnati as indicated, and he was leading a party from Maysville, Kentucky, which is east of Cincinnati.

22. See the reference to Elijah Anderson in Calarco, *People of the Underground Railroad*, 5; and "Henry Ward Beecher: American Minister," Britannica, https://www.britannica.com/biography/Henry-Ward-Beecher.

23. Henson, *Truth Stranger Than Fiction*, 113.

24. Henson, *The Life of Josiah Henson, Formerly a Slave, Now an Inhabitant of Canada*, 51.

25. "Population History of Cincinnati from 1810–1990," Boston University Arts & Sciences. https://physics.bu.edu/~redner/projects/population/cities/cincinnati.html.

26. Henson, *Truth Stranger Than Fiction*, 64.

27. Richard C. Wade, "The Negro in Cincinnati, 1800–1830," *Journal of Negro History* 39, no. 1 (January 1954): 44.

28. Wade, "The Negro in Cincinnati, 1800–1830," 52–57.

29. Wade, 47.

30. Henson, *Truth Stranger Than Fiction*, 114.

31. Henson, *The Life of Josiah Henson, Formerly a Slave, Now an Inhabitant of Canada*, 52.

32. Wilbur Siebert, *The Underground Railroad from Slavery to Freedom* (New York: Macmillan, 1898), 39.

33. General Hull's army reached Detroit on July 5, 1812. The Battle of Detroit on August 15 resulted in a disastrous defeat for the Americans. Hull was court-martialed and sentenced to death, but President James Madison commuted his sentence to dismissal from the army in recognition of his honorable service in the American Revolution.

34. Gen. Robert P. Kennedy, "Hull's Trace or Trail," *Ohio Archeological and Historical Publications*, vol. 24, Ohio Archaeological and Historical Society (Columbus, OH: Fred J. Heer, 1925), 583–90.

35. According to the historic marker at the site, the fort consisted of a half-acre timber stockade enclosing huts and was constructed under the command of Col. Duncan McArthur. Sixteen soldiers are buried there.

36. The author followed Hull's Trail by car from Findley to Kenton. The trail is marked by state gold on green (or brown) metal historic markers and at three points by six-foot-tall stone columns erected in 1912 by the Daughters of the American Revolution. For the location of the markers and columns, along with photos, see "Hull's Trace #1957," Waymarking, https://waymarking.com/waymarks/wm25QW_Hulls_Trace_1957.

37. Henson, *The Life of Josiah Henson, Formerly a Slave, Now an Inhabitant of Canada*, 52.

38. Henson, 52.

39. "History of Cincinnati," Wikipedia, https://en.wikipedia.org/wiki/History_of_Cin cinnati; and "Wyandotte," Oklahoma History Center, https://www.okhistory.org/publica tions/enc/entry.php?entry=WY001.

40. Henson *The Life of Josiah Henson, Formerly a Slave, Now an Inhabitant of Canada*, 55.

41. "Sandusky, Ohio," Wikipedia, https://en.wikipedia.org/wiki/Sandusky,_Ohio.

42. Henson, *Truth Stranger Than Fiction*, 121.

43. Henson, 122.

44. Siebert, *The Underground Railroad from Slavery to Freedom*, 83, 183.

45. Siebert, 146–49. See also the map facing page 113, available at "Underground Railroad Routes of New York State Map," Ohio Memory, https://ohiomemory.org/digital/collection /siebert/id/14896.

46. If they left on September 18, spent two weeks on the two hundred miles to Cincinnati, ten days in the city, another two weeks on the two hundred miles to Sandusky and then two days on the boat, and arrived in Canada on October 28, it would add up to forty days, which is a very biblical number. Josiah never mentions this number or the significance in any of his autobiographies, so perhaps the family left Kentucky on a different date, September 17 or 19, since he is very positive about the date of the arrival in Canada.

47. Henson, *The Life of Josiah Henson, Formerly a Slave, Now an Inhabitant of Canada*, 56. The name of the ferryman as "Green" appears in the 1858 (*Truth Stranger Than Fiction*) auto biography and subsequent autobiographies, but the name "Captain Burnham" only appears in the 1849 autobiography (*The Life of Josiah Henson*). The reason for that may have been to pro tect the captain from prosecution, as the 1850 Fugitive Slave Act had been passed since the first book was published, and the good captain may still have been aiding freedom seekers in 1858. Henson, *Truth Stranger Than Fiction*, 126; and Henson, *The Life of Josiah Henson, Formerly a Slave, Now an Inhabitant of Canada*, 58.

48. Don J. Wood, "Sandusky, Ohio Shipping Personnel," Rutherford B. Hayes Presidential Center Library, LH-291, https://www.rbhayes.org/collection-items/local-history-collections /sandusky-ohio-shipping-personnel/.

49. Henson, *Truth Stranger Than Fiction*, 126. This conversation was not in the 1849 ver sion of Henson's memoirs (*The Life of Josiah Henson*) but is important, as he refers to his promise later in his narrative and speeches.

Chapter 7. Freedom in Canada

1. The Dominion of Canada was formed in 1867, uniting several provinces into one country.

2. Robin W. Winks, *The Blacks in Canada: A History*, 2nd ed. (Montreal: McGill-Queen's University Press, 1997), 2–6.

3. Winks, *The Blacks in Canada*, 5–6.

4. In 1841 Upper Canada was separated from Lower Canada (Quebec) and became known as Canada West. In 1867 when the new constitution was adopted, creating the country of Canada, Canada West became Ontario. The naming of the provinces as Upper and Lower was based on the St. Lawrence and Niagara Rivers, which flow north and separate Canada from the United States.

5. Winks, *The Blacks in Canada*, 24–28.

6. Winks, 96–99, 110.

7. Bryan Prince, "The Illusion of Safety: Attempts to Extradite Fugitive Slaves from Canada,"

in *A Fluid Frontier: Slavery, Resistance and the Underground Railroad in the Detroit River Borderland*, edited by Karolyn Smardz Frost and Veta Smith Tucker (Detroit: Wayne State University Press, 2016), 68.

8. William H. Pease and Jane H. Pease, *Black Utopia: Negro Communal Experiments in America* (Madison: State Historical Society of Wisconsin, 1963), 8.

9. Pease and Pease, *Black Utopia*, 4.

10. Josiah Henson, *The Life of Josiah Henson, Formerly a Slave, Now an Inhabitant of Canada, as Narrated by Himself* (Boston, Arthur D. Phelps, 1849), 59–60. No Hibbard is listed in the 1831 Canadian census for that area, although there is an Andrew Hibbard and a David Hibbard listed in the township of Bröme in Shefford County south of Toronto, but since this is about sixty miles north of Fort Erie, this is probably not the Hibbard family Josiah speaks of.

11. Henson, *The Life of Josiah Henson, Formerly a Slave, Now an Inhabitant of Canada*, 60.

12. Henson, 61.

13. Salem Chapel BME Church Harriet Tubman Underground Railroad National Historic Sites, http://www.salemchapelbmechurch.ca/index.html. It is noted here that the Canadian AME Church split off from the American Conference in 1856 and formed its own conference, the British Methodist Episcopal Church, reportedly because of the stigma on the United States created by the 1850 Fugitive Slave Act.

14. Henson, *The Life of Josiah Henson, Formerly a Slave, Now an Inhabitant of Canada*, 61.

15. Henson, 62.

16. Henson, 63. Although in his autobiographies Josiah only talks about his oldest son, Tom, going to school, the chapter subheading in the 1858 autobiography says "Boys Go to School." See Josiah Henson, *Truth Stranger Than Fiction: Father Henson's Story of His Own Life* (Boston: John P. Jewett and Company, 1858), 128. Isaac later attends a seminary in England, so Isaac must have had some formal schooling.

17. Henson, *The Life of Josiah Henson, Formerly a Slave, Now an Inhabitant of Canada*, 63.

18. Josiah Henson, *"Truth Is Stranger Than Fiction": An Autobiography of the Rev. Josiah Henson from 1789 to 1879* (Boston: B. B. Russell & Co., 1879), 267–68.

19. Henson, *"Truth Is Stranger Than Fiction,"* 65.

20. Henson, 65.

21. As will be seen in later chapters of this book, Josiah had friends read the letters he received in the mail and write answers he dictated.

22. Henson, 66.

23. Henson, *Truth Stranger Than Fiction*, 144–45.

24. "Our History," St Paul's Anglican Church, https://www.stpaulsfe.com/about/our-history.

25. Henson, *Truth Stranger Than Fiction*, 145.

26. Josiah's second trip to Kentucky, one year after this one, is dated to be in the fall of 1833 because he noted the historical celestial event of November 13, 1833, the Leonid meteor shower.

27. Henson, *Truth Stranger Than Fiction*, 146.

28. Henson, 147.

29. As explained later, the number of people Josiah escorted to Canada from Bourbon County may actually have been sixteen rather than thirty. Josiah always left on escapes to Canada on a Saturday night because, as he explains, Sunday was a day off for the enslaved people, and they were allowed to visit friends and family on other plantations, so their absence would not be missed until Monday, giving them a full day of travel before discovery of their escape.

30. Maysville has an Underground Railroad museum, the National Underground Railroad Museum, https://nurm.org, visited by the author. About ten miles downstream from Maysville a modern road, Ripley Road, leads straight to the Ohio River directly across from Ripley, Ohio. This is most likely the landing where boats were launched taking freedom seekers to Ripley.

31. Larry Gara, *The Liberty Line: The Legend of the Underground Railroad* (Lexington: University Press of Kentucky, 1996), 174.

32. Tom Calarco, *People of the Underground Railroad: A Biographical Dictionary* (Westport, CT: Greenwood, 2008), 224–50; and Wilbur H. Siebert, *The Underground Railroad from Slavery to Freedom* (New York: Macmillan, 1898), 108–9.

33. Siebert, *The Underground Railroad from Slavery to Freedom*, 111.

34. Calarco, *People of the Underground Railroad*, 65–75.

35. Siebert, *The Underground Railroad from Slavery to Freedom*, 76.

36. Henson, *Truth Stranger Than Fiction*, 148–49.

37. For first-person accounts of the historical 1833 Leonid meteor shower, see "Meteor Shower of 1833," Joseph Smith Foundation, https://josephsmithfoundation.org/meteor-shower-of-1833.

38. Henson, *Truth Stranger Than Fiction*, 150–52.

39. Henson, 153–58.

40. US Census 1830, Mason County, Kentucky, Family Search, https://www.familysearch.org/ark:/61903/3:1:33SQ-GYY1-PBJ?i=8&cc=1803958&personaUrl=%2Fark%3A%2F61903%2F1%3A1%3AXHP1-Z9R.

41. "African American Slave Owners in Kentucky," Notable Kentucky African Americans Database, University of Kentucky Library, https://nkaa.uky.edu/nkaa/items/show/2080.

42. Henson, *Truth Stranger Than Fiction*, 163.

43. Henson, *The Life of Josiah Henson, Formerly a Slave, Now an Inhabitant of Canada*, 70.

44. Henson, 67.

45. Henson, 67–68.

46. Irene Moore Davis, "Canadian Black Settlements in the Detroit River Region," in *A Fluid Frontier*, edited by Karolyn Smardz Frost and Veta Smith Tucker, 88.

47. Henson, *Truth Stranger Than Fiction*, 69.

48. Winks, *The Blacks in Canada*, 151.

49. Davis, "Canadian Black Settlements in the Detroit River Region," 84.

50. Josiah Henson, *Uncle Tom's Story of His Life: An Autobiography of the Rev. Josiah Henson (Mrs. Stowe's "Uncle Tom," from 1789 to 1876, with a Preface by Mrs. Harriet Beecher Stowe, and Introductory Note by George Sturge and S. Morley, Esq, M.P.)*, edited by John Lobb (London: Christian Age, 1876), 176.

51. The author could find no Josiah Henson (born 1785–1796) on muster roles of "All Canada, British Army, and Canadian Militia Muster Rolls and Pay Lists," 1831–1841, accessed on https://www.ancestry.ca, on March 9, 2021.

52. Henson, *Truth Stranger Than Fiction*, 167.

53. Henson *The Life of Josiah Henson, Formerly a Slave, Now an Inhabitant of Canada*, 73.

Chapter 8. A New Dream

1. Josiah Henson, *The Life of Josiah Henson, Formerly a Slave, Now an Inhabitant of Canada, as Narrated by Himself* (Boston: Arthur D. Phelps, 1849), 72.

2. Henson, *The Life of Josiah Henson, Formerly a Slave, Now an Inhabitant of Canada*, 75.

3. William H. Pease and Jane Pease, *Black Utopia: Negro Communal Experiments in America* (Madison: State Historical Society of Wisconsin, 1963), 10; and Henson, *The Life of Josiah Henson*, 74.

4. Amoaba Gooden, "Establishing Communities," in *Unsettling the Great White North: Black Canadian History*, edited by Michele A. Johnson and Funké Aladejebi (Toronto: University of Toronto Press, 2022), 194.

5. Deidre McCorkindale, "Black Education: The Complexity of Segregation in Kent County's Nineteenth-Century Schools," in U*nsettling The Great White North*, 335.

6. Joan D. Hedrick, *Harriet Beecher Stowe: A Life* (New York: Oxford University Press, !1994), 103.

7. William H. Pease and Jane Pease, *Bound with Them in Chains: A Biographical History of the Antislavery Movement* (Westport, CT: Greenwood, 1972), 117–18.

8. Pease and Pease, *Bound with Them in Chains*, 121.

9. Pease and Pease, 116.

10. Milton H. Sernett, *Abolition's Axe: Beriah Green, Oneida Institute, and the Black Freedom Struggle* (New York: Syracuse University Press, 1986), 33.

11. Deidre McCorkindale, "Black Education," in *Unsettling the Great White North*, 319.

12. Henson, *The Life of Josiah Henson, Formerly a Slave, Now an Inhabitant of Canada*, 73–74.

13. "James Canning Fuller and Lydia Fuller House," Preservation Association of Central New York, https://pacny.net/freedom_trail/Fuller.htm.

14. Pease and Pease, *Black Utopia*, 64.

15. Pease and Pease, 176n2.

16. Henson, *The Life of Josiah Henson, Formerly a Slave, Now an Inhabitant of Canada*, 74.

17. Pease and Pease, *Black Utopia*, 64.

18. Josiah Henson, *The Life of Josiah Henson, Formerly a Slave, as Narrated by Himself, with a Preface by T. Binney, London* (London: Charles Gilpin, Bishopsgate Without, 1851), 116.

19. Pease and Pease, *Black Utopia*, 64; and Pease and Pease, *Bound with Them in Chains*, 124.

20. Henson, *The Life of Josiah Henson, Formerly a Slave, as Narrated by Himself*, 74–75.

21. *The Voice of the Fugitive*, July 15, 1852, 2, col. 4.

22. Deidre McCorkindale, "Black Education," in *Unsettling the Great White North*, 343.

23. Marie Carter, "Reimagining the Dawn Settlement," in *The Promised Land, History and Historiography of the Black Experience in Chatham-Kent's Settlements and Beyond*, edited by Boulou Ebanda De B'Beri, Nina Reid-Maroney, and Handel Kashope Wright, epilogue by Afua Cooper (Toronto: University of Toronto Press, 2014), Kindle.

24. Carter, *"Reimagining the Dawn Settlement."*

25. Carter, *"Reimagining the Dawn Settlement."*

26. Daniel Francis and Clayton Ma, "Dresden," The Canadian Encyclopedia, https://www.thecanadianencyclopedia.ca/en/article/dresden; and "Dresden, Ontario," Wikipedia, https://en.wikipedia.org/wiki/Dresden,_Ontario.

27. The region known as Upper Canada became Canada West in 1841 and in 1867 was renamed Ontario.

28. David Brion Davis, "Slavery and Anti-Slavery in History Now: National Expansion and Reform, 1815–1860," The Gilder Lehrman Institute of American History, https://www.gilderlehrman.org/history-now/slavery-and-anti-slavery.

29. Pease and Pease, *Black Utopia*, 13.

30. In 1834 a mob smashed up Lewis Tappan's house in New York and burned his furnishings. In 1835 Garrison was almost lynched by a Boston mob. Davis, "Slavery and Anti-Slavery in History Now."

31. Pease and Pease, *Bound with Them*, 11.

32. Davis, "Slavery and Anti-Slavery in History Now."

33. Pease and Pease, *Bound with Them*, 13–14.

34. Pease and Pease, 13–14.

35. Pease and Pease, 28–33, 56.

36. Douglas H. Maynard, "The World's Anti-Slavery Convention of 1840," *Journal of American History* 47, no. 3 (December 1960): 452, https://doi.org/10.2307/1888877.

37. Davis, "Slavery and Anti-Slavery in History Now."

38. Pease and Pease, *Bound to Them*, 15–17.

39. Pease and Pease, 124–25.

40. Pease and Pease, *Black Utopia*, 65. The sawmill and gristmill were probably in the same building, as it was the custom to use the water-powered mill for grinding wheat and corn in the harvest and saw wood in the early spring, directing the power to the saw blades instead of the grinding stones.

41. Henson, *The Life of Josiah Henson, Formerly a Slave, as Narrated by Himself*, 117.

42. Benjamin Drew, *A North Side View of Slavery: The Refugee, or the Narratives of Fugitive Slaves in Canada; Related by Themselves, with an Account of the History and Condition of the Colored Population of Upper Canada* (Boston: John P. Jewett & Company, 1856), 30–31.

43. "The British American Institute in Dawn, Canada West, London, September 30th, 1843," published tract, "The Letters of Hiram Wilson," Huron University College, https://hiramwilson.wordpress.com/category/1843/.

44. *Green-Mountain Freeman* (Montpelier, VT), January 24, 1845, 3.

45. *New York Tribune*, November 22, 1844, 2.

46. Samuel Longfellow, ed., *Life of Henry Wadsworth Longfellow, with Extracts from His Journals and Correspondence*, vol. 2 (Boston: Ticknor and Company, 1886), 47–48.

47. "Hiram Wilson to Hamilton Hill, February 26, 1845," The Letters of Hiram Wilson, https://hiramwilson.wordpress.com/category/1845/.

48. William F. Cheek and Aimee Lee Cheek, *John Mercer Langston and the Fight for Black Freedom, 1829–65* (Champaign: University of Illinois Press, 1996), 119–20.

49. Robin Winks, *The Blacks in Canada: A History*, 2nd ed. (Montreal: McGill University Press, 1997), 199–200.

50. Convention of the Colored Population (Drummondville, Quebec, Canada, 1847), "Report of the Convention of the Colored Population, Held at Drummondville, Aug, 1847," 14. Colored Conventions Project Digital Records, https://omeka.coloredconventions.org/items/show/451.

51. Convention of the Colored Population, 11.

52. Convention of the Colored Population, 15.

53. "James Canning Fuller and Lydia Fuller House," Preservation Association of Central New York, https://pacny.net/freedom_trail/Fuller.htm.

54. Winks, *The Blacks in Canada*, 200.

55. Winks, 67.

56. Josiah Henson, *Truth Stranger Than Fiction: Father Henson's Story of His Own Life* (Boston: John P. Jewett and Company, 1858), 174–75.

57. "Amos Lawrence," Wikipedia, https://en.wikipedia.org/wiki/Amos_Lawrence.

58. "Samuel Atkins Eliot," Wikipedia, https://en.wikipedia.org/wiki/Samuel_Atkins_Eliot_(politician).

59. "Henry Ingersoll Bowditch," Wikipedia, https://en.wikipedia.org/wiki/Henry_Ingersoll_Bowditch.

60. Pease and Pease, *Black Utopia*, 75.

61. Pease and Pease, 75; and Henson, *Truth Stranger Than Fiction*, 175.

62. "Welland Canal," Wikipedia, https://en.wikipedia.org/wiki/Welland_Canal.

63. Henson, *Truth Stranger Than Fiction*, 176–77.

64. Winks, *The Blacks in Canada*, 183.

65. Henson, *The Life of Josiah Henson, Formerly a Slave, as Narrated by Himself*, frontispiece. The original manuscript is in the rare documents section of the Boston Public Library, and a digital copy can be found at the Internet Archives, https://archive.org/details/lifeofjosiahhensoohens_0/page/n1/mode/2up.

66. "Was He the Real Uncle Tom?," *The Semi-Weekly New Era* (Lancaster, PA), Saturday, August 8, 1896, 7, reprinted from *Connecticut Times* (New Hartford, CT).

67. Josiah Henson, *Uncle Tom's Story from 1789 to 1876* (London: John Lobb, Christian Age Office), 209.

68. Charles T. Davis and Henry Louis Gates Jr., *The Slave's Narrative* (New York: Oxford University Press, 1985), 26–28.

69. *Voice of the Fugitive*, January 1, 1851, col. 1.

70. Karolyn Smardz Frost and Veta Smith Tucker, *A Fluid Frontier: Slavery, Resistance and the Underground Railroad in the Detroit River Borderland* (Detroit: Wayne State University Press, 2016), 143–45.

71. Frost and Tucker, *A Fluid Frontier*, 217; and Sylvia D. Hamilton, "Stories from the Little Black School House," in *Unsettling the Great White North: Black Canadian History*, edited by Michele A. Johnson and Funké Aladejebi (Toronto: University of Toronto Press), 314.

72. Winks, *The Blacks in Canada*, 200; and Pease and Pease, *Black Utopia*, 68.

73. Ontario Black History Society, https://blackhistorysociety.ca.

74. Frost and Tucker, *A Fluid Frontier*, 124–25.

75. Even though he was described as a blacksmith originally, BAI trustee Peter Smith, born 1827, was from a milling family living in Haldiman County, Canada West. His grandfather had built the first sawmill in Fort Erie, and two of his uncles had patents for mill equipment. "Re: Smith Family in Ontario," Genealogy.com, https://www.genealogy.com/forum/surnames/topics/smith/58641/.

76. William Lloyd Garrison letter, February 14, 1851, *The Liberator* 30, no. 10, Friday, March 7, 1851, 2.

77. "Samuel Atkins Eliot," *The Liberator* 30, no. 10 (March 7, 1851),, cols. 2–3.

78. "Samuel Atkins Eliot"; and Pease and Pease, *Black Utopia*, 75.

79. *The Voice of the Fugitive*, June 1, 1851, 3, col. 4.

80. *Boston Evening Transcript* (Boston, MA), November 27, 1850, 2.

Chapter 9. England

1. William Lloyd Garrison letter, February 14, 1851, *The Liberator* 30, no. 10 (Friday, March 7, 1851): 2; M. R. Delany to Frederick Douglass, *Frederick Douglass' Paper* (Pittsburgh), April 29, 1853; and "Uncle Tom," Martin Delany Letter (2) (April 29 1853), University of Virginia, *Frederick Douglass' Papers*, exhibit, https://utc.iath.virginia.edu/africam/afar03ot.html.

2. Evidence shows that he took Josiah Jr. with him in early 1851, his son Isaac in late 1851, and his wife Nancy in 1876 on trips to England.

3. Josiah Henson, *Truth Stranger Than Fiction: Father Henson's Story of His Own Life* (Boston: John P. Jewett and Company, 1858), 180.

4. Robin W. Winks, *The Blacks of Canada: A History*, 2nd ed. (Montreal: McGill-Queen's University Press, 1997), 180, 201.

5. Robert E. Saunders, "Robinson, Sir John Beverley," Dictionary of Canadian Biography, http://www.biographi.ca/en/bio/robinson_john_beverley_9E.html.

6. Peter Baskerville, "MacNab, Sir Allan Napier," Encyclopedia of Canadian Biography, http://www.biographi.ca/en/bio/macnab_allan_napier_9E.html.

7. R. Alan Douglas, "Prince, John," Dictionary of Canadian Biography, http://www.biographi.ca/en/bio/prince_john_9E.html.

8. Jeff Hoyt, ed., "1809–1930: History of Hospitals in Michigan," April 19, 2018, Senior Living, https://www.seniorliving.org/history/1809-1930-history-hospitals-michigan.

9. "Shubael Conant of Detroit Michigan," *Shubael Conant, of Detroit*, a paper prepared by William Shubael Conant, 1944, https://leemwithey.webflow.io/shubael-conant.

10. "Wilkins, Ross," House Divided: The Civil War Research Engine at Dickinson College, http://hd.housedivided.dickinson.edu/node/44611.

11. "Charles Sumner: A Featured Biography," US Senate, https://www.senate.gov/senators/FeaturedBios/Featured_Bio_Sumner.htm.

12. Henson, *Truth Stranger Than Fiction*, 101.

13. "Thomas Binney," Wikipedia, https://en.wikipedia.org/wiki/Thomas_Binney.

14. "Dictionary of National Biography, 1885–1900, Gurney/Samuel," https://en.wikisource.org/wiki/Dictionary_of_National_Biography,_1885-1900/Gurney,_Samuel.

15. "Henry Brougham, 1st Baron Brougham and Vaux," Wikipedia, https://en.wikipedia.org/wiki/Henry_Brougham,_1st_Baron_Brougham_and_Vaux.

16. "Abbott Lawrence," Wikipedia, https://en.wikipedia.org/wiki/Abbott_Lawrence; and Henson, *Truth Stranger Than Fiction*, 181.

17. Josiah Henson, *The Life of Josiah Henson, Formerly a Slave, as Narrated by Himself, with Preface by T. Binney, London (Third Thousand Printing)* (London: Charles Gilpin, Bishopsgate Without, 1851), iii.

18. "Roaf, John," Dictionary of Canadian Biography, http://biographi.ca/en/bio/roaf_john_9E.html.

19. Henson, *The Life of Josiah Henson, Formerly a Slave, as Narrated by Himself*, iv–v.

20. Wikipedia entries for "William Brock (pastor)," Wikipedia, https://en.wikipedia.org/wiki/William_Brock_(pastor); "Earl of Gainsborough," Wikipedia, https://en.wikipedia.org/wiki/Earl_of_Gainsborough; "William Chalmers Burns," Wikipedia, https://en.wikipedia.org/wiki/William_Chalmers_Burns; and James Sherman (minister), Wikipedia, https://en.wikipedia.org/wiki/James_Sherman_(minister). Henson in his 1858 autobiography *Truth Stranger Than Fiction* also mentions George Smith, but Bishop George Smith was in Hong Kong at that time.

21. Abstract of James Heartfield, *The British and Foreign Anti-Slavery Society, 1838–1956: A History* (2017), Cambridge University Press, https://www.cambridge.org/core/journals/journal-of-british-studies/article/james-heartfield-the-british-and-foreign-antislavery-society-18381956-a-history-oxford-oxford-university-press-2016-pp-xii-486-6500-cloth/2A8DA4653E1C8EB5DAE42FAB3A191934.

22. *The Voice of the Fugitive* (Sandwich, Canada West), June 1, 1851, 3, col. 1. This newspaper, published and edited by escaped slave Henry Bibb beginning in January 1851, was the first newspaper representing the escaped slave population of Canada West.

23. *The Voice of the Fugitive*, June 1, 1851, 3, col. 1, and 4, col. 1.

24. Bryan Prince, *A Shadow on the Household: One Enslaved Family's Incredible Struggle for Freedom* (Toronto, Ontario: McClellan and Stewart, 2009), 58.

25. Prince, *A Shadow on the Household*, 47–51, 198–205.

26. "The Great Exhibition 1851," Historic UK, https://www.historic-uk.com/HistoryUK/HistoryofEngland/Great-Exhibition-of-1851/; and "The Great Exhibition of 1851," Random History by Gretchen Stringer-Robinson, https://gretchenstringerrobinson.wordpress.com/2020/07/10/the-great-exhibition-of-1851/.

27. Henson, *Truth Stranger Than Fiction*, 189.

28. Henson, 188–90.

29. Henson, 191. It is estimated that over six million people visited the Great Exhibition.

30. *Catalogue of the Great Exhibition of the Works of Industry of All Nations* (London: Spicer Brothers, Wholesale Stationers; W. Clowes and Sons, Printers, 1851), 963, no. 79; *Montreal Gazette* (Montreal, CA), November 1, 1851, 2; and Henson, *Truth Stranger Than Fiction*, 192–93.

31. Henson, *Truth Stranger Than Fiction*, 196. Although this meeting was never recorded in the archbishop's diary, it is quite possible that it took place, as Samuel Gurney was a man of great influence and the archbishop a man of great curiosity.

32. John Kevin Anthony Farrell, "The History of the Negro Community in Chatham, Ontario, 1887–1865," (PhD dissertation, University of Ottawa, 1955), 153–64.

33. "Transcription: AHN Newman's Letter to Douglass," New Research on Old Connections: William Newman and the Black Abolitionist Movement, accessed May 24, 2021, https://williampnewman.wordpress .com/

34. The quote from the sheriff was a testament that there had been no arrests of Negroes in his jurisdiction for criminal offenses in fifteen years, published in *The Voice of the Fugitive* 1, no. 1 (Sandwich, Canada West), January 1, 1851, 1, col. 1.

35. *The Liberator* (Boston, MA), April 11, 1851, 4.

36. Henson, *Truth Stranger Than Fiction*, 183.

37. Winks, *Blacks in Canada*, 201.

38. Prince, *A Shadow in the Household*, 77.

39. *Voice of the Fugitive* 1, no. 1, August 27, 1851, p. 1, col. 1; *Voice of the Fugitive* 1, no. 20, September 24, 1851, p. 1, col. 1; *Voice of the Fugitive* 1, no. 20, November 5, 1851, p. 1. col. 1; and *Voice of the Fugitive* 2, no. 20, October 7, 1852, p. 1, col. 1.

40. "Scoble, John," Dictionary of Canadian Biography, http://www.biographi.ca/en/bio /scoble_john_9E.html.

41. "Uncle Tom," Martin Delany Letter (2) (April 29, 1853).

42. "North American Convention," *Voice of the Fugitive* (Sandwich, Canada West), Wednesday, September 21, 1851, 2, col. 2.

43. Winks, *Blacks in Canada*, 201.

44. This is near today's King's Cross station.

45. *The Morning Chronicle* (London, UK), May 15, 1852, 1.

46. Henson, *Truth Stranger Than Fiction*, 194.

47. Henson, 199.

48. Henson, 200–201. The prayer, said or sung, is a variation on a Methodist grace, with the first two lines always being the same but the last three varied according to denomination or custom.

49. Henson, 202.

50. Henson, *The Life of Josiah Henson, Formerly a Slave, as Narrated by Himself,* 95–118.

51. Henson, *Truth Stranger Than Fiction*, 203–4.

52. Josiah claims that the name of the steamer was *Canada*, but the Liverpool port records show no ship by that name. Josiah may have been mistaken about the name, perhaps confusing it with his destination or with another ship on which he had voyaged.

53. The Boston and New York Central Railroad began operation in 1852, and the New York Central Railroad, merging several smaller companies, was established in May 1853. "New York Central Railroad," Wikipedia, https://en.wikipedia.org/wiki/New_York_Central_Railroad.

54. "The First Suspension Bridge: Niagara Falls, New York–Niagara Falls, Ontario," Niagara Falls Info, https://www.niagarafallsinfo.com/niagara-falls-history/niagara-falls-municipal -history/historic-bridges-in-niagara/the-first-suspension-bridge/.

55. The Great Western Railroad (later Railway) began construction in 1849 and was completed from Niagara Falls to Windsor, Canada, by January 1854, passing through Hamilton and London with a stop between London and Windsor at Chatham. It had probably not been completed that far in September 1852 but may have gotten him part of the way. "Great Western Railway," The Canadian Encyclopedia, https://www.thecanadianencyclopedia.ca/en/article /great-western-railway.

56. Henson, *Truth Stranger Than Fiction*, 208.

57. Henson, 208. The hymn was written by William Hiley Bathurst, an Anglican minister, but was a popular hymn in Methodist hymnals. "The Christian's Parting Hour," Hymnary.org, https://hymnary.org/text/how_sweet_the_hour_of_closing_day.

58. Boston passenger and crew lists, 1820–1943, London to Boston on ship *Calcutta* arrived

July 14, 1853, Ancestry, https://www.ancestry.com/search/categories/img_passlists/?name=_Henson&birth=_usa_2&arrival=1853-7-14&arrival_x=0-0-0&name_x=_ps.

59. "Ontario, County Marriage Registers, 1858–1869," database with images, Family Search, https://www.familysearch.org/ark:/61903/1:1:Q2CB-C17Z.

60. US Census 1870, Adrian Ward 3, Lenawee, Michigan, mistakenly has Josiah Jr.'s birthplace as Virginia instead of Kentucky.

61. 1861 Census of Canada, 105, line 28.

62. Adrienne Shadd, *The Journey from Tollgate to Parkway: African Canadians in Hamilton* (Toronto: Dundurn Press, 2010), 294.

63. "Peter Henson," Find a Grave, https://www.findagrave.com/memorial/74924015/peter-henson.

64. Julia Ann Henson Wheeler, Obituary, United States, GenealogyBank Historical Newspaper Obituaries, 1815–2011, https://www.familysearch.org/ark:/61903/1:1:Q597-GGTK.

65. The names of the grandchildren are in a "working draft" of the Henson family tree in Jamie Ferguson Kuhns, *Sharp Flashes of Lightning Come from Black Clouds* (Silver Spring, MD: Maryland–National Capital Park and Planning Commission, 2018), 136–37. It should be noted that some of the information in this family tree is incorrect and it is not evidenced by citations.

66. Josiah married Charlotte circa 1818 when he was twenty-two, but there is no record of her age at that time, so it may be assumed that she was between sixteen and twenty-five. Her last child was born in 1840, and it was unusual for a woman to bear children at that time after age forty-five.

67. Josiah Henson, *The Life of Josiah Henson, Formerly a Slave, Now an Inhabitant of Canada, as Narrated by Himself* (Boston: Arthur D. Phelps, 1849), 19; and Josiah Henson, *Uncle Tom's Story of His Life: An Autobiography of the Rev. Josiah Henson (Mrs. Stowe's "Uncle Tom," from 1789 to 1876, with a Preface by Mrs. Harriet Beecher Stowe, and Introductory Note by George Sturge and S. Morley, Esq, M.P.)*, edited by John Lobb (London: Christian Age, 1876), 43.

68. "Uncle Tom," Martin Delany Letter (2) (April 29, 1853).

Chapter 10. Discord at Home

1. Josiah Henson, *"Truth Is Stranger Than Fiction": An Autobiography of the Rev. Josiah Henson (Mrs. Harriet Beecher Stowe's "Uncle Tom")* (Boston: B. B. Russell & Co., 1879), 230.

2. Marie Carter, "Reimagining the Dawn Settlement," in *The Promised Land: Historiography of the Black Experience in Chatham-Kent's Settlements and Beyond*, edited by Boulou Ebanda de b'Beri, Nina Reid-Maroney, and Handel K. Wright (Toronto: University of Toronto Press, 2014), Kindle edition.

3. *Voice of the Fugitive* (Sandwich, Canada West), July 15, 1852, 3, col. 1.

4. Elwood H. Jones, "Scoble, John," Dictionary of Canadian Biography, http://www.biographi.ca/en/bio/scoble_john_9E.html.

5. Estlin to Chapman, Boston Public Library, manuscript collection, Ms.A.9.2. v.26.

6. Mitchell to Chapman, Boston Public Library, manuscript collection, Ms.A.9.2. v.26.

7. "Scoble, John," Dictionary of Canadian Biography, http://www.biographi.ca/en/bio/scoble_john_9E.html.

8. Robin W. Winks, *Blacks in Canada: A History*, 2nd ed. (Montreal: McGill-Queen's University Press, 1997), 155, 158, 161.

9. Benjamin Drew, *A North-Side View of Slavery* (Boston: John Jewett and Co., 1856), 245–46.

10. William H. Pease and Jane Pease, *Black Utopia: Negro Communal Experiments in America* (Madison: State Historical Society of Wisconsin, 1963), 46–55.

11. "Scoble, John."

12. *The Liberator* (Boston, MA), November 7, 1851, 2.

13. *Minutes and Proceedings of the General Convention for the Improvement of the Colored Inhabitants of Canada, Held by Adjournments in Amhrstburg [sic], C.W., June 16th and 17th, 1853* (Windsor, Ontario: Bibb & Holly, 1853), 8–10, https://digital.library.cornell.edu/catalog/may853719.

14. *Minutes and Proceeding of the General Convention for the Improvement of the Colored Inhabitants of Canada*, 21st Resolved, 10.

15. Josiah Henson, *Uncle Tom's Story of His Life: An Autobiography of the Rev. Josiah Henson (Mrs. Stowe's "Uncle Tom," from 1789 to 1876, with a Preface by Mrs. Harriet Beecher Stowe, and Introductory Note by George Sturge and S. Morley, Esq, M.P.)*, edited by John Lobb (London: Christian Age, 1876), 158.

16. National Archive and Records Administration, Washington, DC, Boston Passenger and Crew Lists, 1820–1943, accessed through Ancestry.com, February 2011; and Henson, *Uncle Tom's Story of His Life*, 198.

17. *Frederick Douglass' Paper* (Rochester, NY), August 11, 1854, 2, cols. 4–5.

18. *Frederick Douglass' Paper*, August 11, 1854, 2, cols. 4–5.

19. "The Power and Proximity: Frederick Douglass and His Transitional Relations with British Canada, 1847–1861," The Free Library, https://www.thefreelibrary.com/The+Power+of+Proximity%3a+Frederick+Douglass+and+His+Transnational...-a0654815590.

20. The paper was announced in 1853 with editor and publisher Samuel Ringgold Ward in Windsor, Canada West, but he soon left for England, so Shadd took over in March 1854 in Toronto and then moved the press to Chatham in 1855. Winks, *Blacks in Canada*, 394–95.

21. "William Newman," Union Baptist Church, https://www.union-baptist.net/about-us/our-history/pastors/william-newman/.

22. A Descendent of the African Race, "Correspondence," *The Provincial Freeman* (Toronto, Canada West), August 26, 1854, 2, cols. 4–6.

23. "The Dawn Institute," *The Provincial Freeman* (Chatham, Canada West), April 7, 1855, 2, col. 5.

24. J. C. Brown, "The Dawn Institute," *The Provincial Freeman* (Chatham, Canada West), April 7, 1855, 22, col. 3; and J. C. Brown, "Dawn Institute," *The Provincial Freeman* (Chatham, Canada West: May 12, 1855), 38, col. 5.

25. "The Chatham Meeting and Dawn," *The Provincial Freeman* (Chatham, Canada West), August 29, 1855, 2, col. 3–4; "Man about Town," Correspondence, *The Provincial Freeman*, August 29, 1855, 2, col. 5–6.

26. M. A. Shadd, "Correspondence, No. 1, The Dawn Convention," *The Provincial Freeman*, (Chatham, Canada West), September 22, 1855, 2, col. 5–6.

27. Drew, *A North-Side View of Slavery*, 30.

28. Drew, 309–10.

29. Josiah Henson, *"Truth Is Stranger Than Fiction,"* 243.

30. Drew, *A North-Side View of Slavery*, 310.

31. Drew, 311.

32. Drew, 312.

33. Drew, 313.

34. Pease and Pease, *Black Utopia*, 89–93.

35. Drew, *A North-Side View of Slavery*, 297.

36. Drew, 323.

37. *Bangor Daily Whig and Courier* (Bangor, ME), May 15, 1856, 2.

38. "Exposed at Last," *The Provincial Freeman* (Chatham, Canada West), May 2, 1857, 2, col. 1.

39. Henson, *Uncle Tom's Story of His Life*, 156.

40. "Exposed at Last," 2, col. 1.

41. Henson, *Uncle Tom's Story of His Life*, 167.

42. In his autobiographies Josiah Henson claims that Scoble borrowed money from him, but Chancery Court records show that it was the other way around.

43. Henson, *Uncle Tom's Story of His Life*, 169.

44. Henson, 152–53.

Chapter 11. New Directions

1. Josiah Henson, *Uncle Tom's Story of His Life: An Autobiography of the Rev. Josiah Henson (Mrs. Stowe's "Uncle Tom," from 1789 to 1876, with a Preface by Mrs. Harriet Beecher Stowe, and Introductory Note by George Sturge and S. Morley, Esq, M.P.),* edited by John Lobb (London: Christian Age, 1876).

2. Joan D. Hendrick, *Harriet Beecher Stowe: A Life* (New York: Oxford University Press, 1994), 221; and John Lobb, ed., *An Autobiography of the Rev. Josiah Henson ("Uncle Tom") from 1789 to 1881* (London, Ontario: Shuyler, Smith & Co., 1881), 147.

3. Lyman Beecher, *Saints, Sinners and Beechers* (Indianapolis: Bobbs-Merrill, 1934), 181.

4. Josiah Henson, *"Truth Is Stranger Than Fiction": An Autobiography of the Rev. Josiah Henson (Mrs. Harriet Beecher Stowe's "Uncle Tom")* (Boston: B. B. Russell & Co., 1879), 220; and *Boston Post*, Saturday, June 4, 1881, 6.

5. Harriet Beecher Stowe, *A Key to Uncle Tom's Cabin* (Bedford, MA: Applewood Books, 1998), 19–29; and "George Lewis Clark Obituary," *Lexington Herald* (Lexington, KY), December 17, 1897, 1.

6. *Bangor Daily Whig and Courier* (Bangor, ME), May 15, 1856; *The Provincial Freeman* (Chatham, Canada West), May 2, 1857, 2, col. 1.

7. Harriet Beecher Stowe's introduction to Josiah Henson's 1858 autobiography is dated April 5, 1858. Joan D. Hedrick, *Harriet Beecher Stowe: A Life* (New York: Oxford University Press, 1994), 279, 287.

8. It is unlikely that Henson would have met Jewett otherwise, and the fact that the publication that resulted had an introduction by Stowe, advertised as part of the title of the book, indicates that Stowe and Jewett were in communication about Josiah Henson. Henson made a habit of getting letters of introduction from well-known people he knew to present to people he was visiting.

9. Josiah Henson, *Truth Stranger Than Fiction: Father Henson's Story of His Own Life* (Boston: John P. Jewett and Company, 1858), iii.

10. Harriet Beecher Stowe, *A Key to Uncle Tom's Cabin* (Bedford, MA: Applewood Books, 1998), 42.

11. Henson, *Uncle Tom's Story of His Life*, 154.

12. Rev. Francis Tiffany served as the pastor of the Unitarian church in Springfield, MA, from 1852 until 1864. Derek Strahan, "Unitarian Church, Springfield, Mass," December 4, 2018, Lost New England, https://lostnewengland.com/2018/12/unitarian-church-springfield-mass/.

13. "Uncle Tom's Cabin," *The Manhattan: An Illustrated Literary Magazine for the People* 1, no. 1 (1882): 28–31. Gilbert Haven was a strong abolitionist and a believer in the equality of the races, giving aid to the freed men and the fugitives in New England. He was made a bishop after the American Civil War and pastored in Georgia. He knew John Brown and wrote a letter to him when Brown was incarcerated in Virginia after his arrest at Harpers Ferry.

14. "Uncle Tom's Cabin," 29.

15. "Uncle Tom's Cabin," 28.

16. Charles T. Davis and Henry Louis Gates Jr., *The Slave's Narrative* (New York: Oxford University Press, 1985).

17. Henson, *Uncle Tom's Story of His Life*, 154. Harriet Beecher Stowe had an arrangement with the same publisher to receive 10 percent of the sales, which made her a rich woman. See Hedrick, *Harriet Beecher Stowe*, 223.

18. Henson, *Uncle Tom's Story of His Life*, 154.

19. Montgomery County, Maryland, Land Records, JGH #7, f121.

20. Bryan Prince, *A Shadow on the Household: One Enslaved Family's Incredible Struggle for Freedom* (Toronto, Ontario: McClelland & Stewart, 2009), 36.

21. Henson, *Uncle Tom's Story of His Life*, 154–55. The 1871 Canada census shows John Henson living with Josiah Henson in Ontario, Canada, so he must have left after that year. Josiah claims that the Pennsylvania dairy farm was owned by John's previous owner, but this cannot be true, as Jane Beall lived and died in Rockville, Maryland, so it may have been John's son's former owner, as John's wife and children may have been owned by a different person than the person who owned him.

22. Henry Bleby, *Josiah: The Maimed Fugitive* (London: Printed by William Nichols, 1878), 2–7.

23. Bleby, *Josiah*, 7–8.

24. "Speech of Rev. Henry Bleby, missionary from Barbados, on the results of emancipation in the British West Indies colonies, 1858," delivered at the celebration of the Massachusetts Anti-Slavery Society, held at Island Grove, Abington, July 31, 1858, National Library of Jamaica, digital library of the Caribbean, https://ufdc.ufl.edu/CA01099989/00001.

25. Bleby, *Josiah*.

26. Bleby, 183–86.

27. "At the Chatham Convention in Ontario, John Brown Sets Up His Provisional Constitution," House Divided: The Civil War Research Engine at Dickinson College, https://hd /housedivided.dickinson.edu/node/29341.

28. Gilbert Haven Collection, United Methodist Church archives, https://www.umnews .org/en/news/methodist-history-mixed-on-abolitionism.

29. Herbert Aptheker, ed., "A Public Discussion of Insurrection, 1858," in *A Documentary History of the Negro People in the United States*, vol. I (New York: Citadel Press, 1961), 406–8.

30. Henson, *Uncle Tom's Story of His Life*, 193–94.

31. Henson, 197–98.

32. Massachusetts State Census 1855, Boston, Suffolk. US Federal Census 1850, Boston, Ward 6, Massachusetts. The latter also lists John Gambell, age twelve, but he is not listed in the 1855 census, and Josiah refers to his new wife having only one son, so John may have died. The spelling of "Gambell" is the same in both censuses, so that is the spelling used here, although there are other spellings of the name elsewhere.

33. For complete family information with citations, see appendix B in this volume.

34. *The Liberator* (Boston, MA), December 24, 1858, 3.

35. Excerpt from Wallace McLeod, "Grand Historian Report," *2003 Proceedings*, Grand Lodge of Canada in the Province of Ontario, 115. See also "Josiah Henson (1789–1883)," Ontario Masons, https://glcpovadocumentvalet.blob.core.windows.net/communication/2003 %20Josiah%20Henson_a93b766a-8abc-828c-cd63-22dc3ad12cbd.pdf?sv=2023-11-03&se= 2024-08-05T16%3A40%3A07Z&sr=b&sp=r&sig=sriczXvpShq5al8taK9b8f%2Fos2pqbPZl %2Bp970Y7DoEk%3D; Charles E. Holmes, *Masonic Light,* January 1950, Montreal, where he asks his readers to submit a photo. "Josiah Henson," Freemasonry, https://freemasonry.bcy.ca /biography/henson_j/henson_j.html, notes that "the lodge is cited online on the Waller Lodge, Texas website [http://www.mastermason.com/WallerLodge/oddsends.htm] as 'Mount Moriah Lodge No. 4.'"

36. Henson, *Uncle Tom's Story of His Life*, 177.

37. Henson, 177–83.

38. Henson, 184–86.

39. William H. Pease and Jane Pease, *Black Utopia: Negro Communal Experiments in America* (Madison: State Historical Society of Wisconsin, 1963), 81.

40. Henson, *Uncle Tom's Story of His Life*, 170.

41. Robin W. Winks, *The Blacks in Canada*, 2nd ed. (Montreal: McGill-Queens University Press, 1997), 201.

42. Deirdre McCorkindale, "Black Education: The Complexity of Segregation in Kent County's Nineteenth-Century Schools," in *Unsettling the Great White North: Black Canadian History*, edited by Michele A. Johnson and Funke Aladejebi (Toronto: University of Toronto Press, 2022), 349.

43. Henson, *Uncle Tom's Story of His Life*, 175.

44. "Josiah Henson," *The Pittsburgh Daily Commercial* (Pittsburgh, PA), March 22, 1875, 2; and "Josiah Henson," *The Cincinnati Daily Star* (Cincinnati, OH), April 9, 1875, 4.

45. "The Original Uncle Tom," *Boston Post*, March 23, 1875, 1; and "The Original Uncle Tom," *Boston Globe*, March 23, 1875, 1.

46. "The Original Uncle Tom," *Vermont Farmer* (Newport, VT), June 23, 1876, 2.

47. "Illness of 'Uncle Tom,'" *Wisconsin State Journal* (Madison, WI), March 27, 1875, 1; and "Josiah Henson," *The St. Albans Advertiser* (Saint Albans, VT), March 26, 1875.

48. "Josiah Henson," *The Cincinnati Daily Star* (Cincinnati, OH), April 9, 1875, 4.

49. The biography and diary of Rev. Thomas Hughes (1818–1876) are housed at Huron University College in London, Ontario, as a part of the "Promised Land Project." See "The Biography of Rev. Thomas Hughes," https://www.uwo.ca/huron/promisedland/hughes/hughesbio.html.

50. Henson, *Uncle Tom's Story of His Life*, 203.

51. "Movement of Cunard Steamers," *Boston Globe*, June 29, 1876, 8.

Chapter 12. Royalty and Remembrance

1. Josiah Henson, *Uncle Tom's Story of His Life: An Autobiography of the Rev. Josiah Henson (Mrs. Stowe's "Uncle Tom," from 1789 to 1876, with a Preface by Mrs. Harriet Beecher Stowe, and Introductory Note by George Sturge and S. Morley, Esq, M.P.)*, edited by John Lobb (London: Christian Age, 1876), 202–3.

2. See chapter 9.

3. "Mr. Josiah Henson," *Daily News* (London, UK), August 2, 1876, 3; and "An Appeal is being circulated in behalf of Mr. Josiah Henson . . . ," *The Examiner* (London, UK), August 19, 1876), 23.

4. "John Lobb," London Wiki, https://london.wikia.org/wiki/John_Lobb.

5. Henson, *Uncle Tom's Story of His Life*, 206–8.

6. Henson, 209.

7. The main legal document leading to Josiah's distrust was his manumission paper and the promissory note referenced in chapter 5, but it has also been established that Josiah could not read script (see chapter 8) and so was unable to read legal contracts that were mostly written in script at that time.

8. John Lobb, ed., *An Autobiography of the Rev. Josiah Henson ("Uncle Tom") from 1789 to 1881, with a Preface by Mrs. Harriet Beecher Stowe, and Introductory Notes by George Sturge, S. Morley, Esq., MP, Wendell Phillips, and John Greenleaf Whittier* (London, Ontario: Shuyler, Smith & Co., 1881), 228–36. This is a reprint of Josiah Henson's 1879 autobiography with the substitution of Lobb's own words for chapter 32, "My Visit to Windsor Castle."

9. Lobb, *An Autobiography of the Rev. Josiah Henson*, 232.

10. Ira Berlin, Marc Favreau, and Steven Miller, eds., *Remembering Slavery: African Americans Talk about Their Personal Experiences of Slavery and Emancipation* (New York: New Press, 1998), 184–85.

11. "'Uncle Tom's Life-Story,'" *The Weekly Standard and Express* (Blackburn, Lancashire, UK), September 9, 1876, 6.

12. John Lobb, *An Autobiography of the Rev. Josiah Henson*, 236.

13. "Metropolitan Tabernacle," Wikipedia, https://en.wikipedia.org/wiki/Metropolitan_Tabernacle#/map/0.

14. Lobb, *An Autobiography of Josiah Henson*, 237–38.

15. "The Rev. Josiah Henson (Mrs. Stowe's Uncle Tom)," *The Graphic: An Illustrated Weekly Newspaper* (London, UK), February 3, 1877, 9.

16. Josiah Henson, *"Truth Is Stranger Than Fiction": An Autobiography of the Rev. Josiah Henson (Mrs. Harriet Beecher Stowe's "Uncle Tom"), from 1789 to 1879, with a Preface by Mrs. Harriet Beecher Stowe, Introductory Notes by Wendell Phillips, and John G. Whittier, and an Appendix on The Exodus by Bishop Gilbert Haven* (Boston: B. B. Russell & Co., 1879), 302–3.

17. *Report of Farewell Meeting and Presentation in the City Hall, Glasgow, Friday, April 20, 1877* (Glasgow: George Gallie and Son, 1877), 6. Rev. J. Davis Bowden is named in this document as the main host of Josiah and Nancy Henson and is mentioned several times. The fact that he is named Rev. Boardman in Henson's 1879 autobiography *Truth Is Stranger Than Fiction* must be a mistake in transcription or with Henson's memory.

18. Henson, *Truth Is Stranger Than Fiction*, 305.

19. Henson, 306.

20. Henson, 306–7.

21. "Her Majesty and 'Uncle Tom,'" *The Leeds Mercury* (Leeds, West Yorkshire, UK), Saturday, March 3, 1877, 15.

22. Henson, *Truth Is Stranger Than Fiction*, 307.

23. Henson, 308.

24. Henson, 308–9.

25. Henson, 309.

26. Henson, 310–12.

27. "'Uncle Tom' in Glasgow," *Glasgow Herald* (Glasgow, Scotland), Tuesday, March 20, 1877, 4. For the full speech, see appendix C in this volume.

28. "'Uncle Tom' in Glasgow."

29. Lobb, *An Autobiography of the Rev. Josiah Henson*, 238.

30. *Dumfries And Galloway Standard*, Wednesday, April 25, 1877. For the full speech, see appendix C in this volume.

31. *Report of Farewell Meeting and Presentation in the City Hall, Glasgow, Friday, April 20, 1877* (Glasgow: George Gallie & S, 99 Buchanan Street, 1877), 10–14; and *Glasgow Herald* (Glasgow, Glasgow, Scotland), Monday, May 21, 1877, 4.

32. *Report of Farewell Meeting and Presentation in the City Hall, Glasgow, Friday, April 20, 1877*.

33. "'Uncle Tom,'" *Manchester Weekly Times and Examiner* (Manchester, UK), Saturday, April 28, 1877, 7; and "The Cunard Steamer China," *Boston Globe*, Monday, May 7, 1877, 6.

34. "The Hero of Mrs. Harriet Beecher Stowe's Tale ...," *The Hull Packet and East Riding Times* (Hull, East Yorkshire, UK), Friday, August 10, 1877, 1.

35. John Lobb, *The Young People's Illustrated Edition of "Uncle Tom's" Story of His Life (from 1789 to 1877)* (London: Christian Age Office, 1877), 8.

36. Lobb, *The Young People's Illustrated Edition of "Uncle Tom's" Story of His Life*, 7.

37. Henson, *Truth Is Stranger Than Fiction*, 315.

38. "The Real Uncle Tom Still Living" (from the Baltimore American), *Fall River Daily Herald* (Fall River, MA), January 30, 1878, 3.

39. "Hear Him! See Him, He Is Still Living," *Baltimore Sun* (Baltimore, MD), Friday, January 11, 1878, 2; and "'Uncle Tom' Still Living," *The News Journal* (Wilmington, DE), Monday, January 14, 1878, 4.

40. Henson, *Truth Is Stranger Than Fiction*, 316.

41. Frederick Douglass, letter to Secretary Rogers, Executive Mansion, February 26, 1878, The Rutherford B. Hayes Presidential Library & Museums, Spiegel Grove, Freemont, Ohio. Original viewed on-site September 16, 2021.

42. Henson, *Truth Is Stranger Than Fiction*, 317.

43. Henson, 317.

44. Fergus M. Bordewich, *Bound for Canaan: The Underground Railroad and the War for the Soul of America* (New York: HarperCollins, 2005), 101.

45. Josiah Henson, *Truth Is Stranger Than Fiction*, 318–24.

46. "Uncle Tom," *The Saint Paul Globe* (Saint Paul, MN), April 2, 1878, 3.

47. "Uncle Tom," *Valley Spirit* (Chambersburg, PA), June 5, 1878, 1.

48. "'Uncle Tom': A Talk with Mrs. Stowe's Hero," *Star Tribune* (Minneapolis, MN), July 15, 1878, 3.

49. "Rev. Josiah Henson, the Original 'Uncle Tom,'" *Detroit Free Press* (Detroit, MI), Sunday, October 20, 1878, 1.

50. "Mrs. H. B. Stowe's Hero," *Valley Falls Register* (Valley Falls, KS), Friday, June 15, 1883, 1.

51. Henson, *Truth Is Stranger Than Fiction*, xi.

52. Henson, xii.

53. John Lobb, *An Autobiography of Josiah Henson*, title page. It is interesting to note that copies of the 1879 edition *Truth Is Stranger Than Fiction* are extremely rare, indicating that perhaps some of them were confiscated. Also, the copy in the Boston Public Library has the pages of Josiah's description of meeting Queen Victoria torn out.

54. Lobb, *An Autobiography of Josiah Henson*, 210.

55. "The Original of Mrs. Stowe's 'Uncle Tom,'" *Chicago Tribune*, Saturday, June 10, 1882, 3.

56. Robin W. Winks, *The Autobiography of the Reverend Josiah Henson* (Reading, MA: Addison-Wesley, 1969), xxix.

57. *The Bury and Norwich Post* (Bury, Suffolk, UK), Tuesday, June 5, 1883, 2.

58. Winks, *An Autobiography of Josiah Henson*, xxix.

59. "Last Will and Testament of Josiah Henson," Henson-Nevels Family, https://henson nevelsfamily.com/2012/08/15/last-will-and-testament-of-josiah-henson/.

60. Canadian Death Records, 1869–1936.

Appendix B. Josiah Henson's Family

1. Michigan Death Records 1867–1950, #217, Flint, Michigan, Julia Ann Henson Wheeler, colored, widow.

2. Boston Passenger and Crew Lists, 1820–1943, London to Boston on ship *Calcutta*, arrived July 14, 1853.

3. "Ontario, County Marriage Registers, 1858–1869," database with images, Family Search, https://www.familysearch.org/search/collection/2568642.

4. 1870 US Census, Adrian Ward 3, Lenawee, Michigan [mistakenly has his birthplace as Virginia instead of Kentucky].

5. 1870 US Census, Adrian Ward 3, Lenawee, Michigan.

6. Michigan Marriage Records 1867–1952, Washtenaw County, for quarter ending April 1, 1921.

7. Michigan Marriage Records 1867–1952, Washtenaw County, for quarter ending April 1, 1921.

8. Michigan Death Records 1867–1950, #217.

9. "Last Will and Testament of Josiah Henson," August 15, 2012, Henson-Nevels Family, https://hensonnevelsfamily.com/2012/08/15/last-will-and-testament-of-josiah-henson/.

10. Adrienne Shadd, *The Journey from Tollgate to Parkway: African Canadians in Hamilton* (Toronto: Dundurn Press, 2010), 294.

11. "Peter G? HENSON, 1836–1891," Henson Burial Ground Cemetery, CanadaGenWeb's Cemetery Project, https://cemetery.canadagenweb.org/person-search-details/?wpda_search_column_ID=960656.

12. Ontario, Canada, Marriages, 1801–1926, Family Search, https://www.familysearch.org/ark:/61903/1:1:Q2CB-C17Z.

13. 1861 Census of Canada, 105, line 28.

14. Ontario, Canada, Marriages, 1801–1926, Family Search, https://www.familysearch.org/ark:/61903/1:1:Q2CB-C17Z.

15. Canadian Death Records, 1869–1936, Family Search, https://www.familysearch.org/search/discovery/results?q.givenName=Nancy&q.surname=Henson&q.anyPlace=Ontario&q.birthLikeDate.from=1819.

Appendix C. Josiah Henson's Speeches

1. This account is taken from the *Sheffield and Rotherham Independent* (Sheffield, South Yorkshire, England), Tuesday, January 30, 1877, page 6, https://www.newspapers.com/image/410220092.

2. This account is taken from the *Western Mail* (Cardiff, South Glamorgan, Wales), Thursday, February 1, 1877, page 7, https://www.newspapers.com/image/393976489.

3. This account is taken from the *Cheshire Observer* (Chester, Cheshire, England), Saturday, March 10, 1877, page 2, https://www.newspapers.com/image/395471528.

4. This account is taken from "The Rev. Josiah Henson, 'Uncle Tom,' in Scotland," Report of Farewell Meeting and Presentation in the City Hall, Glasgow, Friday, April 20, 1877 (Glasgow: George Gallie & S, 99 Buchanan Street, 1877), 10–14.

5. Before the American Civil War, there was much disagreement about slavery and abolition in the Northern states, especially in the border states. If you did not know whether a person or anyone within hearing was for or against slavery, you would refer to it as "the goose question."

6. This account is taken from John Lobb, ed., *An Autobiography of the Rev. Josiah Henson ("Uncle Tom") from 1789 to 1881* (London, Ontario: Shuyler, Smith & Co., 1881), 236–37.

7. This account is taken from the *Dumfries and Galloway Standard*, Wednesday, April 25, 1877.

Bibliography

Archives and Collections

Boston Public Library, Special Collections, Boston, MA. https://bpl.bibliocommons.com/v2 /record/S75C4604790.

Documenting the American South, University of North Carolina, https://docsouth.unc.edu.

The Internet Archive, https://archive.org.

National Register of Historic Places, https://www.nps.gov/subjects/nationalregister/database -research.htm.

New York Public Library, Schomburg Center for Research in Black Culture. Manuscripts, Archives, and Rare Books Division. Digital Collections. https://digitalcollections.nypl.org.

Manuscript Collections

Anti-Slavery Collection. Boston Public Library.

Chronicling America. Library of Congress. https://chroniclingamerica.loc.gov.

Harry Wright Newman Collection. Southern Maryland History Room, College of Southern Maryland.

Haven, Gilbert Collection. United Methodist Church Archives, https://catalog.gcah.org /publicdata/gcah5250.pdf, https://archive.org/details/gilberthavenmethoooograv.

Hiram Wilson, Letters of. Huron University College, Canada.

Hiram Wilson, Papers. Oberlin College Library, Oberlin, OH.

North American Slave Narratives. Documenting the American South.

Ohio History Connection. https://ohiomemory.org/digital/collection.

Paul Fredker Collection. Library of Nineteenth Century Photography, http://www.19thcentury photos.com/?nav=about.

Rutherford B. Hayes Papers. Presidential Library & Museums. Spiegel Grove, Freemont, OH.

Samuel May Anti-Slavery Collection. Cornell University, Ithaca, NY.

Schomburg Center for Research in Black Culture. Manuscripts, Archives, and Rare Books Division. New York Public Library, Digital Collections. https://digitalcollections.nypl.org.

Thomas Hughes Diary Project. Huron University College, Canada.

Historical Publications

Ambler, Charles Henry. *A History of Transportation in the Ohio Valley*. Glendale, CA: Arthur H. Clark Co., 1932.

Aptheker, Herbert, ed. "A Public Discussion of Insurrection, 1858." In *A Documentary History of the Negro People in the United States*, vol. I. New York: Citadel Press, 1961.

Bassett, Ancel H. *A Concise History of the Methodist Protestant Church from Its Origins*. Pittsburgh: Press of Charles A. Scott, 1877.

Bleby, Henry. *Josiah, the Maimed Fugitive: A True Tale*. London: William Nichols, 1878. Documenting the American South.

Clarke, Lewis. *Narrative of the Sufferings of Lewis Clarke, during a Captivity of More Than Twenty-Five Years, among the Algerines of Kentucky, One of the So Called Christian States of America: Dictated by Himself*. Boston: David H. Ela, printer, 1845.

Drew, Benjamin. *A North-Side View of Slavery. The Refugee: or the Narratives of Fugitive Slaves in Canada. Related by Themselves, with an Account of the History and Condition of the Colored Population of Upper Canada*. Boston: John P. Jewett, 1856.

Hagood, Rev. L. M., MD. *The Colored Man in the Methodist Episcopal Church*. Cincinnati: Cranston & Stowe; New York: Hunt & Eaton, 1890.

Henson, Josiah. *The Life of Josiah Henson, Formerly a Slave, Now an Inhabitant of Canada, as Narrated by Himself*. Boston: Arthur D. Phelps, 1849. Documenting the American South.

Henson, Josiah. *The Life of Josiah Henson, Formerly a Slave, as Narrated by Himself, with a Preface by T. Binney, London*. London: Charles Gilpin, Bishopsgate Without, 1851.

————— *"Truth Is Stranger Than Fiction": An Autobiography of the Rev. Josiah Henson (Mrs. Harriet Beecher Stowe's "Uncle Tom")*. Boston: B. B. Russell & Co., 1879. Internet Archive, https://archive.org, and New York Public Library, Schomburg Center for Research in Black Culture, Manuscripts, Archives, and Rare Books Division. Digital Collections. https://digitalcollections.nypl.org/items/510d47df-9555-a3d9-e040-e00a18064a99.

————— *Truth Stranger Than Fiction: Father Henson's Story of His Own Life*. Boston: John P. Jewett and Company, 1858. Documenting the American South, University of North Carolina. https://docsouth.unc.edu.

—————. *Uncle Tom's Story of His Life: An Autobiography of the Rev. Josiah Henson (Mrs. Stowe's "Uncle Tom," from 1789 to 1876, with a Preface by Mrs. Harriet Beecher Stowe, and Introductory Note by George Sturge and S. Morley, Esq, M.P.)*. Edited by John Lobb. London: Christian Age, 1876.

Jackson, Richard P. *The Chronicles of Georgetown from 1751 to 1878*. Washington, DC: R. O. Polkinhorn, Printer, 1878.

Lobb, John, ed. *An Autobiography of the Rev. Josiah Henson ("Uncle Tom") from 1789 to 1881*. London, Ontario: Shuyler, Smith & Co., 1881. Documenting the American South.

The Young People's Illustrated Edition of "Uncle Tom's" Story of His Life (from 1789 to 1877). London: Christian Age, 1877.

Northup, Solomon. *Twelve Years a Slave* (Mint Editions, 2020; original published 1853), chap. 6.

Ross, Alexander. *Recollections and Experiences of an Abolitionist*. Toronto: Rowsell and Hutchison, 1875.

Siebert, Wilbur H. *The Underground Railroad from Slavery to Freedom*. New York: Macmillan, 1898.

Still, William, *The Underground Rail Road: A Record of Facts, Authentic Narratives, Letters, &c*. New York: Porter & Coates, 1872. The Internet Archive.

Stowe, Harriet Beecher. *A Key to Uncle Tom's Cabin*. Bedford, MA: Applewood Books, 1998. Originally published in 1853 by John P. Jewett & Co. of Boston.

———. "The Story of Uncle Tom's Cabin." *Old South Leaflets*, no. 82. https://www.barton ccc.edu/library.

———, *Uncle Tom's Cabin; or, Life among the Lowly*. Boston: John P. Jewett & Company, 1852; Norton Critical Edition, Elizabeth Ammons, ed., New York: Norton, 1994.

Modern Publications

Andrews, William L. *Slavery and Class in the American South: A Generation of Slave Narrative Testimony, 1840–1865*. New York: Oxford University Press, 2019.

Arnold, William Erastus. *A History of Methodism in Kentucky*, vol. 2, *From 1820 to 1846*. Wilmore, KY: First Fruits Press, 1936. First printed by Herald Press, Louisville, KY, 1936.

Bancroft, Frederic. *Slave Trading in the Old South*. Columbia: University of South Carolina Press, 1996.

Baptist, Edward E. *The Half Has Never Been Told: Slavery and the Making of American Capitalism*. New York: Basic Books, 2014.

Bates, Marlene Strawser, and F. Edward Wright. *Early Charles County Maryland Settlers, 1658–1745*. Westminster, MD: Heritage Books, 2006.

Beecher, Lyman. *Saints, Sinners and Beechers*. Indianapolis: Bobbs-Merrill, 1934.

Berlin, Ira. *Many Thousands Gone: The First Two Centuries of Slavery in North America*. Cambridge, MA: Belknap Press of Harvard University Press, 1998.

Berlin, Ira, Marc Favreau, and Steven E. Miller, eds. *Remembering Slavery: African Americans Talk about Their Personal Experiences of Slavery and Emancipation*. New York: New Press, 1998.

Blassingame, John W. *The Slave Community: Plantation Life in the Antebellum South*. Revised and enlarged ed. New York: Oxford University Press, 1979.

Blassingame, John W., ed. *Slave Testimony: Two Centuries of Letters, Speeches, Interviews, and Autobiographies*. Baton Rouge: Louisiana State University Press, 1977.

Bordewich, Fergus M. *Bound for Canaan: The Underground Railroad and the War for the Soul of America*. New York: HarperCollins, 2005.

Brugger, Robert J. *Maryland, a Middle Temperament, 1634–1980*. Baltimore: Johns Hopkins University Press, 1990.

Calarco, Tom. *People of the Underground Railroad: A Biographical Dictionary*. Westport, CT: Greenwood, 2008.

Campanella, Richard. *Lincoln in New Orleans: The 1828–1831 Flatboat Voyages and Their Place in History*. Lafayette: University of Louisiana at Lafayette Press, 2010.

Carter, Marie. "Reimagining the Dawn Settlement." In *The Promised Land: Historiography of the Black Experience in Chatham-Kent's Settlements and Beyond*, edited by Boulou Ebanda de b'Beri, Nina Reid-Maroney, and Handel K. Wright (Toronto: University of Toronto Press, 2014), Kindle edition.

Cheek, William F., and Aimee Lee Cheek. *John Mercer Langston and the Fight for Black Freedom, 1829–65*. Champaign: University of Illinois Press, 1996.

Cissel, Anne W. "The Families of a Derwood Farm through Two Centuries." *Montgomery County Story* 27, no. 2 (May 1984): 5–6. Rockville, MD: Montgomery County Historical Society.

Clarke, Nina Honemond. *History of the Nineteenth-Century Black Churches in Maryland and Washington, D.C.* New York: Vantage Press, 1983.

Cohen, Anthony. *The Underground Railroad in Montgomery County, Maryland: A History and Driving Guide*. Rockville, MD: Montgomery County Historical Society, 1994.

Cook, Eleanor M. V. "Georgetown: Jewel of Montgomery County—Part I." *Montgomery County Story* 41, no. 4 (November 1998): 49–60. Rockville, MD: Montgomery County Historical Society.

Davis, Charles T., and Henry Louis Gates Jr. *The Slave's Narrative*. New York: Oxford University Press, 1985.

De B'beri, Boulou Ebanda, Nina Reid-Maroney, and Handel Kashope Wright, eds. *The Promised Land: History and Historiography of the Black Experience in Chatham-Kent's Settlements and Beyond*. Epilogue by Afua Cooper. Toronto: University of Toronto Press, 2014.

Farrell, John Kevin Anthony. "The History of the Negro Community in Chatham: Ontario, 1787–1865." PhD dissertation, University of Ottawa, 1955.

Fields, Barbara Jean, *Slavery and Freedom on the Middle Ground: Maryland during the Nineteenth Century*. New Haven, CT: Yale University Press, 1985.

Fitzsimons, Mavis. "Uncle Tom in Montgomery County." *Montgomery County Story* 18, no. 1 (February 1975). Montgomery County Historical Society, Rockville, MD. https://mchdr .montgomeryhistory.org/xmlui/handle/20.500.12366/97.

"Francis Newman, 1759–1818." Newman Family website. A Newman Family Tree. http://www .newman-family-tree.net/Francis-Newman.html.

Franklin, John Hope, and Loren Schweninger. *Runaway Slaves: Rebels on the Plantation*. New York: Oxford University Press, 1999.

Frost, Karolyn Smardz, and Veta Smith Tucker, eds. *A Fluid Frontier: Slavery, Resistance, and the Underground Railroad in the Detroit River Borderland*. Detroit: Wayne State University Press, 2016.

Gallagher, Winifred. *How the Post Office Created America*. New York: Penguin Random House, 2016.

Gara, Larry. *The Liberty Line: The Legend of the Underground Railroad*. Lexington: University Press of Kentucky, 1996.

Griffler, Keith P. *Front Line of Freedom: African Americans and the Forging of the Underground Railroad in the Ohio Valley*. Lexington: University Press of Kentucky, 2004.

Gysin, Bryon. *To Master—A Long Good Night: The Story of Uncle Tom, a Historical Narrative*. New York: Creative Age Press, 1946.

Harrold, Stanley. *Subversives: Antislavery Community in Washington, D.C., 1828–1865*. Baton Rouge: Louisiana State University, 2003.

Hedrick, Joan D. *Harriet Beecher Stowe: A Life*. New York: Oxford University Press, 1994.

Hiebert, Ray Eldon, and Richard K. McMaster. *A Grateful Remembrance: The Story of Montgomery County, Maryland*. Rockville, MD: Montgomery County Government and the Montgomery County Historical Society, 1976.

Johnson, Michele A., and Funke Aladejebi, eds. *Unsettling the Great White North: Black Canadian History*. Toronto: University of Toronto Press, 2022.

Johnston, James H. *From Slave Ship to Harvard: Yarrow Marmout and the History of an African American Family*. New York: Fordham University Press, 2012.

Kennedy, Gen. Robert P. *Ohio Archeological and Historical Publications*, vol. 24. Columbus, OH: Fred J. Heer, 1925. Ohio Archaeological and Historical Society.

Kihl, Kim R. *Port Tobacco*. Baltimore: Maclay and Associates, 1982.

Klapthor, Margaret Brown, and Paul Dennis Brown. *The History of Charles County, Maryland, Written in Its Tercentenary Year of 1958*. La Plata, MD: Charles County Tercentenary, 1958.

Kuhns, Jamie Ferguson. *Sharp Flashes of Lightening Come from Black Clouds: The Life of Josiah Henson*. Silver Spring, MD: Maryland National-Capital Park and Planning Commission, 2018.

"La Grange." National Register of Historic Places. Reference number 76000990. https:// npgallery.nps.gov/NRHP/AssetDetail/8ae8cc16-359f-46fe-b775-2671771a8467.

LaRoche, Cheryl Janifer. *The Geography of Resistance*. Urbana: University of Illinois Press, 2014.

———. *Resistance to Slavery in Maryland: Strategies for Freedom*. National Underground Railroad Network to Freedom, prepared for the Organization of American Historians under cooperative agreement with Northeast Region, National Park Service, US Department of Interior, 2007.

Larson, Kate Clifford. *Bound for the Promised Land: Harriet Tubman, Portrait of an American Hero*. New York: Random House, 2004.

Lesko, Kathleen M., Valerie Babb, and Carroll R. Gibbs. *Black Georgetown Remembered: A History of Its Black Community from the Founding of "The Town of George" in 1751 to the Present*. Washington, DC: Georgetown University Press, 1991.

Longfellow, Samuel, ed. *Life of Henry Wadsworth Longfellow, with Extracts from His Journals and Correspondence*, vol. 2. Boston: Ticknor and Company, 1886.

McGuckian, Eileen S. *Rockville: Portrait of a City*. Franklin, TN: Hillsboro, 2001.

McPherson, Henry. "Early Colonial Settlers of Southern Maryland and Virginia's Northern Neck." https:www.colonial-settlers-md-va.us.

"McPherson's Purchase." National Register of Historic Places. Reference number 85000019. https://npgallery.nps.gov/NRHP/GetAsset/34d5c56f-e78f-4364-ac63-02aef4ef01ee/thumbxlarge.

Mould, David, and Missy Loewe. *Remembering Georgetown: A History of the Lost Port City*. Charleston, SC: American Chronicles, the History Press, 2009.

Newman, Henry Wright. *Charles County Gentry*. Baltimore: Genealogical Publishing, 1971.

Olszewski, George J. *A History of the Old Georgetown Market, Georgetown, D.C.* Washington, DC: US Department of the Interior, National Park Service, Washington Service Center, 1966.

Pease, Jane H., and William H. Pease. *Bound with Them in Chains: A Biographical History of the Antislavery Movement*. Westport, CT: Greenwood, 1972.

———. *They Who Would Be Free: Blacks' Search for Freedom, 1830–1861*. New York: Atheneum, 1974.

Pease, William H., and Jane Pease. *Black Utopia: Negro Communal Experiments in America*. Madison: State Historical Society of Wisconsin, 1963.

Prince, Bryan. *My Brother's Keeper: African Canadians and the American Civil War*. Toronto, Ontario: Dundurn, 2015.

———. *A Shadow on the Household: One Enslaved Family's Incredible Struggle for Freedom*. Toronto, Ontario: McClellan & Stewart, 2009.

Reynolds, David S. *Mightier Than the Sword: Uncle Tom's Cabin and the Battle for America*. New York: Norton, 2011.

Ricks, Mary Kay. *Escape on the Pearl: The Heroic Bid for Freedom on the Underground Railroad*. New York: HarperCollins, 2007.

"Riley/Bolton House." National Register of Historic Places. Maryland Historic Trust, property M: 30-6. https://apps.mht.maryland.gov/medusa/PDF/Montgomery/M;%2030-6.pdf.

Robinson, Gwendolyn, and John W. Robinson. *Seek the Truth: A Story of Chatham's Black Community*. Chatham, Ontario: Self-published, 2005.

Russo, Jean B. "The Early Towns of Montgomery County, 1747–1831." *Montgomery County Story* 34, no. 2 (May 1991): 153–56. Rockville, MD: The Montgomery County Historical Society.

Schneider, Norris F. *The National Road: Main Street of America*. Columbus: Ohio Historical Society, 1975.

Sernett, Milton H. *Abolition's Axe: Beriah Green, Oneida Institute, and the Black Freedom Struggle*. New York: Syracuse University Press, 1986.

Shadd, Adrienne. *The Journey from Tollgate to Parkway: African Canadians in Hamilton*. Toronto, Ontario: Dundurn Press, 2010.

Starling, Marion Wilson. *The Slave Narrative: Its Place in American History*. 2nd ed. Washington, DC: Howard University Press, 1988.

Stec, Stephen. "Riley v. Worthington: Joseph Willson's Feuding Family of Early Montgomery County." *Montgomery County Story* 60, no. 1 (Winter 2017): 8–9. Rockville, MD: Montgomery County Historical Society.

Stowe, Charles Edward. *Life of Harriet Beecher Stowe Compiled from Her Letters and Journals*. Honolulu: University Press of the Pacific, 2004. Reprinted from the 1890 edition.

Switaka, William J. *Underground Railroad in Delaware, Maryland, and West Virginia*. Mechanicsburg, PA: Stackpole Books, 2004.

Tangires, Helen. "Contested Space: Life and Death in the Center Market." *Washington History* 7, no. 1 (Spring–Summer 1995): 46–67. Historical Society of Washington, DC. 17:02 UTC. https://www.jstor.org/stable/40073136.

———. "Public Markets and the City: A Historical Prospective." Project for Public Spaces, October 29, 2005. https://www.pps.org/article/6thinktstangires.

Ullman, Victor. *Look to the North Star: A Life of William King*. Toronto, Ontario: Umbrella Press, 1969.

Vlatch, John. *In Back of the Big House: The Architecture of Plantation Slavery*. Chapel Hill: University of North Carolina Press, 1993.

Wade, Richard C. "The Negro in Cincinnati, 1800–1830." *Journal of Negro History* 39, no. 1 (January 1954): 43–57.

Walston, Mark. "A Survey of Slave Housing in Montgomery County." *Montgomery County Story* 27, no. 3 (May 1984). Montgomery County Historical Society, Rockville, MD. https://mchdr.montgomeryhistory.org/xmlui/handle/20.500.12366/1/browse?type=dateissued&value=1984-08.

Webster, Rebecca J., Alex J. Flick, Julia A. King, and Scott Strickland. *In Search of Josiah Henson's Birthplace: Archaeological Investigations at La Grange Near Port Tobacco, Maryland*. St. Mary's City: St. Mary's College of Maryland, 2017. Report prepared for L. Gordon Croft, Mr. and Mrs. Kevin Wilson, and the Charles County Branch NAACP.

Winks, Robin W. *The Blacks in Canada: A History*. 2nd ed. Montreal: McGill-Queen's University Press, 1997.

Winks, Robin W., ed. *An Autobiography of the Reverend Josiah Henson*. Reading, MA: Addison-Wesley, 1969.

Index

Page numbers in italics refer to figures and maps. Gallery illustrations indicated by "g."

About the Author

A passionate seeker of truth about the past, Susan Cooke Soderberg has been active for more than forty years writing, lecturing, testifying, and leading tours of historic sites to bring history to the public in ways they can understand. While working as a public historian with the Maryland–National Capital Park and Planning Commission, she created the Underground Railroad Experience Trail, trained docents to interpret the trail as well as a cabin that had housed enslaved people, wrote historic markers and interpretive panels, designed exhibits, and successfully nominated two sites and a trail to the Underground Railroad National Network to Freedom. Soderberg has written several books on state and local history as well as numerous scholarly articles and was a researcher and consultant for the Emmy Award–winning documentary *Life in a War Zone: Montgomery County in the Civil War*, produced by Heritage Montgomery.